MW00823889

20
1-32897

INVENTING THE AMERICAN GUITAR

INVENTING ★★★ ★
THE AMERICAN
GUITAR

★ ★ ★ ★ ★ ★

THE PRE–CIVIL WAR INNOVATIONS OF
C. F. MARTIN AND HIS CONTEMPORARIES

Edited by

ROBERT SHAW and PETER SZEGO

Essays by

DAVID GANSZ, RICHARD JOHNSTON, DAVID LAPLANTE,

ARIAN SHEETS, and JAMES WESTBROOK

Hal Leonard Books
An Imprint of Hal Leonard Corporation

Copyright © 2013 by Peter Szego

All rights reserved. No part of this book may be reproduced in any form, without written permission,
except by a newspaper or magazine reviewer who wishes to quote brief passages in connection with a review.

Published in 2013 by Hal Leonard Books
An Imprint of Hal Leonard Corporation
7777 West Bluemound Road
Milwaukee, WI 53213

Trade Book Division Editorial Offices
33 Plymouth St., Montclair, NJ 07042

Printed in China through Colorcraft Ltd., Hong Kong

Book design by Steve J. Hill

Library of Congress Cataloging-in-Publication Data is available upon request.

ISBN 978-1-4584-0576-0

www.halleonardbooks.com

To Jim Bollman and Roddy Moore—
ingenious scholars, inspired collectors, and good friends

CONTENTS

★ ★ ★

FOREWORD

Christian Friedrich Martin was one of eight million Germans who emigrated to the United States between 1820 and World War I. Martin came to New York, a major center of industry, finance, and entertainment, to pursue success. Looking for freedom from the restrictive economic model of his native Germany's guild system, Martin realized that there was a growing market for musical instruments in New York. The city also offered him a global trade network that made it easy for him to obtain raw materials, to import musical items for resale, and to ship finished guitars around the globe. Yet, the cultural landscape of the city was far different from what residents and visitors experienced even a generation or two after Martin. Although New York already had a bustling music scene, many of the city's most venerable music institutions and venues would not be established for some time. The New York Philharmonic, the nation's oldest symphony orchestra, was founded in 1842, three years after Martin moved to Pennsylvania. The Metropolitan Opera was not organized until 1880, Carnegie Hall would not open until 1891, and Juilliard would not begin educating young musicians until 1905. C. F. Martin arrived even before Henry Steinway, the music manufacturer perhaps most closely associated with the City, who came to New York City from Braunschweig, Germany, in 1850 to build pianos.

When Martin arrived, the city was in the midst of an economic boom that was the result of the opening of the Erie Canal in 1825. Although New York had been the largest city in the United States since the first census was taken in 1790, its growth accelerated tremendously in the early nineteenth century, topping one hundred thousand residents in 1810 and doubling to more than two hundred thousand inhabitants by 1830. Although the area of the city was confined to the southern tip of the island of Manhattan, with most of the island consisting of estates and farmland, the population would grow to more than half a million citizens by 1850.

As a German immigrant, Martin used his connections within the German community to establish himself in New York. The population of German immigrants and German-Americans was already more than 24,000 in 1840. That population exploded over the next two decades; by 1855, New York City boasted the third largest population of German-speakers in the world, behind only Berlin and Vienna. When the Martin family relocated to Nazareth, Pennsylvania, they again chose a place with a large German population that made the transition easier.

Martin opened his music store and lived in the same building at 196 Hudson Street, in an area of New York City that is now known as Tribeca, near the entrance of the present day Holland Tunnel. During Martin's time in New York, this was a growing residential and commercial neighborhood built on land that had been farmland owned by Trinity Church. The 1830s, when Martin was establishing his business, were tumultuous times in New York. In July of 1834, the city erupted in anti-abolitionist riots, and the nearby Laight Street Presbyterian Church and the home of its pastor Samuel Hanon Cox were targeted

and vandalized during several days of rioting. The church was a mere two blocks from the Martin shop. In December 1835, the Great Fire of New York City destroyed seventeen city blocks, and perhaps as many as 700 buildings. As a result, many New Yorkers looked to move their homes and businesses farther uptown, and many flocked to the area around Martin's workshop. Then, in May 1837, a financial panic hit, throwing the city and the nation into a years-long recession that contributed to the Martin family's decision to leave New York.

However, New York City remained an integral part of the Martin story even after the family moved to Pennsylvania. The city remained the most important market for Martin instruments, and it was necessary to maintain the business connections he built while living in the city. New York was so important for Martin that the city name continued to be stamped on his guitars long after his death.

C. F. Martin was similar to many other immigrants who came to New York City in the nineteenth century, embodying many of the ideals of the time. He was a highly skilled immigrant who sought a freer economic system; an entrepreneur who tried several business models; a successful businessman who built a manufacturing company; and an innovative craftsman who combined his own knowledge with ideas that he encountered in the United States. This book focuses on new research that pieces together the story of Martin's guitar-building influences and innovations. This history begins in New York, where he encountered an international variety of instruments brought into his shop for repair or resale and establishes that Martin invented a guitar that is significantly different from instruments that were being built in Europe. His path really did lead to a uniquely American form of the instrument.

JAYSON KERR DOBNEY

Associate Curator
Department of Musical Instruments
The Metropolitan Museum of Art

PREFACE

This book is the first to attempt to describe in detail the early history of American guitar design. It tells the story of how a European instrument was transformed into a guitar with all of the design and construction features—except size—that would define the iconic American flat-top guitar. This transformation happened within a mere twenty years, a remarkably brief period.

The person who dominates this history is C. F. Martin Sr., America's first major guitar maker and the founder of the Martin Guitar Company, which continues to produce outstanding flat-top guitars today. We were able to draw upon the extraordinarily comprehensive Martin Archives of business records and correspondence, which extends as far back as the senior Martin's arrival in America in 1833. However, there is a dearth of detailed descriptions of the earliest guitars within the archives and other contemporary accounts. In addition, virtually no Martin documents have survived from 1840 to 1850, a critical decade in this history. In the absence of historic documentation, we have created a plausible chronology of design innovation leading to the invention of the American guitar by locating, identifying, and studying a variety of early guitars produced by C. F. Martin Sr. and his contemporaries and allowing the instruments to yield their stories.

This book would not have been possible without Philip Gura's pioneering *C. F. Martin and His Guitars 1796–1873*, published in 2003. Gura's book, the first in-depth biography of C. F. Martin Sr., also offered a history of the guitar prior to its production in the United States and a detailed study of the antebellum guitar trade in America. However, since Gura's book focused primarily on biography, trade, and cultural history, we realized that there was an opportunity to delve more deeply into the creative process that Martin went through and the chronological development of the design and construction of his guitars. As C. F. Martin & Co. archivist Dick Boak observed, we envisioned the "other half of Gura's book," relying on his insightful biography of Martin and trade history as a springboard to focus on the guitars themselves.

After reading Gura's book, Philadelphia musical instrument dealer (and Martin expert) Fred Oster and I decided to create a database of all the high-grade pre–Civil War Martin guitars that we could locate in publications and in private and museum collections. We quickly realized that the same examples of prime antebellum instruments had been pictured in multiple publications. While there was a large quantity of lower-grade "trade" guitars, our initial database included less than thirty discrete examples of Martin's best work.

To better understand Martin's early guitar design and production, we decided to gather as many of his early guitars as possible and to invite a small group of Martin experts—collectors, dealers, restorers, and scholars—to inspect and document these instruments, with the goal of placing them in chronological order and explaining how and why this order made sense. Fred Oster's Vintage Instruments and the Martin Guitar Company hosted the first Early Martin Guitar Conference in Philadelphia and

Nazareth in May 2008. Fred and I were joined by seven other Martin scholars: Dick Boak, Jim Baggett of Mass Street Music, Matt Umanov and Tom Crandell of Matt Umanov Guitars, Richard Johnston of Gryphon Stringed Instruments, Ashborn scholar David Gansz, and guitar maker and Spanish guitar scholar David LaPlante. We limited our focus to the period between 1833, when Martin arrived in New York, and 1867, when he formed a partnership with his son and nephew and formally established C. F. Martin & Co. The latter date was especially propitious, because, upon forming the partnership, Martin changed his stamped brand from "C. F. Martin–New York" to "C. F. Martin & Co.–New York." This gave us a cutoff date for identifying all of Martin's earliest guitars, since those with the earlier stamped brand likely preceded the partnership. In addition, by 1867, Martin had completed his period of creative design and development and had standardized the styles and sizes of his guitars. We put together a study collection of twenty significant early Martin guitars, by far the largest such collection amassed to date. Additional guitars in the study collection included instruments by Martin's contemporaries Louis Schmidt, George Maul, Henry Schatz, and James Ashborn, and early nineteenth century Austrian and Spanish guitars similar to instruments that we assumed had influenced the design and development of Martin's work.

At the beginning of the conference, we arranged the guitars in hypothetical chronological order, and, over two long days of inspecting, measuring, documenting, and discussing the significant design and construction details of each guitar, we periodically rearranged them as we arrived at new insights about the chronology.

The conference yielded two broad insights:

- The development of Martin's guitars from the Austro-German tradition to the fully developed "modern" American X-braced guitar was much more compressed than we initially assumed. The transformation took less than two decades.

- The chronology of structural and design changes in Martin's guitars was anything but a straight line. Like any craftsman operating in the everyday world of commerce, Martin mixed and matched features in response to customer requests, market demand, and availability of materials. Changes in design and construction happened in fits and starts, not in a few transformative instruments.

By the end of the conference, it was clear to us all that a large body of information about the historical development of guitar design could be gleaned from an in-depth study of the instruments themselves. This book is the result.

Several months after the first Early Martin Guitar Conference, I brought independent researcher Greig Hutton on board as project researcher and introduced him to Dick Boak, who generously gave him full access to Martin's archives. While the editors and authors take full responsibility for the book's narrative, Hutton's research and documentation of Martin's pre-partnership history and his extensive databases provided a substantial amount of the raw material on which this book is based.

In October 2009, we held the second Early Martin Guitar Conference. Participants in the first conference were joined by Greig Hutton; Arian Sheets, who serves as curator of stringed instruments at the National Music Museum; collector, builder, and restorer Marc Silber of Marc Silber Music; luthier Steve Kovacik; and Richard Brunkus, an American furniture and decorative arts restorer.

In addition to a presentation by each of the contributors to this book, which introduced the content that would evolve into their essay(s), we conducted a second round of inspection, measurement, and discussion surrounding the study collection amassed for this conference, which had more than doubled in size from the first conference, now totaling approximately forty antebellum Martin guitars. After the second conference, we set out in earnest to produce this book.

This project has yielded a more substantial understanding of the early history of the American guitar that would have been impossible to achieve without the ongoing collaboration of the contributors. While each had a unique area of knowledge, many of the insights that resulted in this book emerged out of a continuous dialogue through two conferences, ongoing correspondence, and nonstop sharing of material, discoveries, and insights.

For the first time, we also provide for the American reader the context in which Martin developed his craft in the very active luthiery trade in Markneukirchen, his homeland in Saxony, and the innovative workshop of the Stauffers in Vienna. We also present important new research by David LaPlante on the significance of early Spanish guitars from Cadiz on the early development of C. F. Martin's guitars, and by David Gansz on guitar and banjo maker James Ashborn in Connecticut and the cultural impact of the Spanish guitar in the United States before 1850. We are especially grateful to Richard Johnston, who combined his decades of Martin scholarship, the data generated by Hutton, and the emerging insights of the other contributors to produce the heart of this book: the story of C. F. Martin's unique contribution to the invention of the American guitar.

We strongly encourage the reader to study Philip Gura's book and to look upon ours as "Gura Volume II," an update and expansion of his work. We have chosen not to repeat much of the content of Gura's work, and we revisit specific material that he covered only if our research has yielded significant new information or led to new insights.

Through the recent discovery and study of several extant guitars by Henry Schatz, we have been better able to understand the intertwined relationship between C. F. Martin and his younger colleague, who emigrated from Markneukirchen to America and established his guitar trade in 1830, three years before Martin's arrival.

We include several guitars by Louis Schmidt and George Maul, former Martin colleagues who set up their own shop and were among the very few luthiers discovered to date who produced guitars during Martin's early years, but we have not uncovered any information about the luthiers themselves beyond that presented by Gura. We have therefore looked at the guitars themselves to determine what we could learn about Schmidt and Maul.

Although William Tilton registered his first patent for a guitar improvement in 1854, and his first guitars were produced at around the same time, he is not included in this book because his career began at the end of Martin's period of innovation. In addition, we are unaware of further research into Tilton beyond Gura's substantial presentation on him in *C. F. Martin and His Guitars.*

By design, the organization and content of this book are addressed to the general reader. We have chosen a narrative approach that serves our objective of tracing the chronological steps Martin and his contemporaries took to transform guitar design and construction and create a uniquely American guitar.

We have left to future scholars the challenge of taking a synoptic approach to the same material, which will likely be of even greater appeal to knowledgeable guitar collectors, scholars, players, and other members of the focused guitar community.

Since scholarship on the creation of the American guitar is ongoing, we see our work as an "interim report" on where research currently stands. We hope that we inspire scholars to continue to uncover material that leads to new insights and understanding of this early history of the American guitar.

PETER SZEGO

Legend

- ▬ C. F. Martin Austro-German Style guitars
- ▬ C. F. Martin Spanish-Style guitars
- ▬ C. F. Martin American-Style guitars
- ▬ James Ashborn guitar production

- ● Important Austro-German guitar precedents
- ● Important Spanish guitar precedents
- ● C. F. Martin, events related to
- ● James Ashborn, events related to
- ● Contemporary historic events

● 1822 Stauffer introduces "Legnani model" guitar

● 1803 Johann Georg Stauffer sets up shop in Vienna

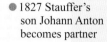
● 1827 Stauffer's son Johann Anton becomes partner

● 1796 C. F. Martin born

● 1813 Stauffer invents in-line machine tuners

● 1825 C. F. Martin marries Otillia Kuhle in Vienna

| 1790 | 1796 | 1800 | 1805 | 1810 | 1815 | 1820 | 1825 | 1830 |

● 1792 Juan Pagés in Cadiz builds fan-braced, six course Spanish guitars

●1816 James Ashborn born

1829 Asa Hopkins incorporates woodwind factory in Fluteville, CT ●
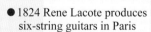

● 1803 Augustin Caro, Granada, produces fan-braced guitar with six single strings

● 1819 Louis Panormo makes guitars in "Spanish Style" in London

● 1804–06 Lewis & Clark Expedition

● 1824 Rene Lacote produces six-string guitars in Paris

● 1793 Eli Whitney invents cotton gin

● 1825 Erie Canal opens

● 1806 Eli Terry clocks: first mass production with interchangeable parts, Windsor, CT

● 1815 Napoleon defeated at Waterloo

● 1833 Martin arrives in NYC from Bremen

● 1850 John Coupa dies—C. F. Martin Jr. moves temporarily to 325 Broadway

● 1834 Martin opens shop at 196 Hudson St

● 1835 Partnership with Schatz   ● 1843 Earliest extant Martin X-braced guitar

● 1837 Martin moves to 212 Fulton St.

● 1839 Martin sells inventory to Ludecus & Wolter and purchases property in Cherry Hill, PA

● 1867 Martin forms partnership with son and nephew

● 1840 John Coupa exclusive NY agent for Martin at 385 Broadway

● c.1834
Profile 5

● c.1835
Profile 6

● c.1838
Profile 11

● c.1839
Profile 15

● c.1841
Profile 20

● c.1842
Profile 23

● c.1843
Profile 26

● c.1855
Profile 43

● c.1860
Profile 38

C. F. MARTIN

| 1835 | 1840 | 1845 | 1850 | 1855 | 1860 | 1865 | 1870 |

JAMES ASHBORN

● 1864 Ashborn stops factory guitar production

● c.1845
Profile 29

● c.1852
Profile 31

● c.1856
Profile 30

● c.1863
Profile 32

● 1847 Wm Hall & Son and Firth Pond & Co founded

● 1865 Civil War ends

● 1842 Ashborn in charge of Firth & Hall guitar production, Fluteville

● 1860 Abraham Lincoln elected President and South Carolina secedes from Union

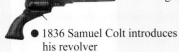

● 1836 Samuel Colt introduces his revolver

● 1856 Antonio De Torres builds "La Leona" in Seville

● 1844 A. T. Stewart builds the first department store in New York

● 1837 Financial Panic

● 1858 First transatlantic cable laid

● 1837 Samuel F. B. Morse invents the telegraph

● 1850 California becomes a state

● 1859 Charles Darwin's *Origin of Species* published

PART I AUSTRO-GERMAN STYLE

CHAPTER 1

JOHANN GEORG STAUFFER AND THE VIENNESE GUITAR

JAMES WESTBROOK

Johann Georg Stauffer's origins, his life as a luthier, and the school of guitar making his work and inventiveness engendered all nestle within the rich and complex cultural context of Viennese musical life during the Classical period. By the time of Stauffer's birth, on January 26, 1778, Vienna was the musical heart of Europe. Both chronologically and stylistically, Stauffer's working life embraces the Biedermeier period, during which the ponderous decorative excesses of the Rococo—in music, art, architecture, furniture, and fashion alike—gave way to the simple, elegant forms and lines of classicism. It was a time of great intellectual innovation, and Vienna was replete with musical geniuses, including Joseph Haydn, Wolfgang Amadeus Mozart, Ludwig van Beethoven, and Franz Schubert. Mozart died when Stauffer was thirteen, and Haydn, when he was thirty-one. Beethoven and Schubert were his contemporaries. Johann Strauss the elder was born and died during Stauffer's lifetime, and the rise of Viennese popular music was well underway.

As in other great German-speaking cultural centers, such as Leipzig and Nuremberg, Viennese instrument making was highly developed and organized. The guild system was particularly powerful in Vienna, where guild regulations controlled the right to work, the price one could charge, and whom one could train. Stauffer received his training in the workshop of the premier "Geigenmacher"—violin maker—of the time, Franz Geissenhof, who, in turn, was the foremost pupil of the last of the older generation of "Lauten-und-Geigenmacher"—lute and violin makers—Matthias Thir.[1] At this time, the august tradition of the Germanic lute and violin making was giving way to new influences coming north from Italy. The violin-making style of the Austrian luthier Jakob Stainer (c. 1617–1683), which had a singular influence in all of Europe during the Baroque era, was being replaced by the designs of Stradivari and Guarneri.

The German baroque lutes and guitars of Sellas, Hieber, Tieffenbrucker, Schelle, Hoffman, and Widhalm had already been abandoned by composers and musicians, and their place taken by the newly developed six-string guitars of Fabricatore and Vinaccia of Naples and the Guadagnini family of Turin.[2] These had been brought north by touring Italian virtuoso guitarists such as Mauro Giuliani, Ferdinando Carulli, Niccolò Paganini, and Luigi Legnani. These profound generational changes swept all of Europe but were nowhere more embraced than in Vienna.

Early published Viennese guitar music includes Leopold Neuhauser (1801) and Bartolomeo

Figure 1-1. The title page of Bortolazzi's method for six-string guitar, published in Vienna c. 1805. Although it was published in Vienna, it was written in both German and Italian, perhaps because many Italian musicians were living in that city.

Figure 1-2. Giuliani's decorative 1809 Gennaro Fabricatore guitar. Notice the bridge moustachios, which are similar to those adopted by Stauffer, and the flat profile of the sides compared to the arched profile later used by Stauffer.

Bortolazzi's (c. 1805) methods for six-string guitar.[3] However, it is not known what their guitars were like or where the instrument makers' influences came from. By the beginning of the nineteenth century, important guitarist/composers living in Vienna included Giuliani, Legnani, and Anton Diabelli, who later set up Vienna's most famous music publishing company.[4] Giuliani moved from Naples to Vienna in 1806, and the Italian-made guitars he played (one of his surviving guitars being an 1809 Gennaro Fabricatore) profoundly influenced Viennese guitar makers.[5] His Studio par la Chitarra, an influential 1812 work for guitar students that includes studies for the right and left hands, ornaments, and short pieces, offers considerable insight into Giuliani's technique and why he probably continued to choose Italian-made guitars.

The newly emerging middle class took joy in newfound intellectual and cultural pursuits. Craftsmen began inventing and patenting their ideas. A tremendous sense of competition arose in all the crafts and trades, and Stauffer was one of the foremost proponents of this new approach. Together with Johann Ertl and his own son and successor, Johann Anton Stauffer, Georg Stauffer registered a series of patents

Figure 1-3. The Italian guitar virtuoso Mauro Giuliani's magnificent travelling guitar case, which must have signified his importance within the Viennese music community.

Figure 1-4. *Below,* an early Johann Georg Stauffer guitar, c. 1816. Notice the Fabricatore-style moustachios.

Figure 1-5. *Far right,* Stauffer's new six-a-side mechanical tuners. The brass back plate covers the mechanism, while the holes offer easy access for lubrication.

JOHANN GEORG STAUFFER'S ACTIVITY AS A GUITARMAKER

Stauffer's first guitar model was very well received in Vienna. While he took credit, the guitar was actually a careful copy of the style of six-string guitar produced by Giovanni Battista Fabricatore of Naples. Fabricatore's model was taken up by other Italian makers, including Carlo Bergonzi, Guiseppe Sciale, and Antonio Vinaccia. It is little wonder, then, that it quickly reached Vienna and was instantly adopted, first by Stauffer, and soon thereafter by other Viennese makers, many of whom, like Franz Feilnreiter, carefully copied Stauffer.

This instrument remained the standard in Vienna until almost 1820 and served to establish Georg Stauffer as the premier guitar maker of the time. The principal features of this first model are:

a. A string length of more or less 625 millimetres.
b. A figure-8-shaped peghead with six rear–mounted pegs.
c. An enlarged body with a narrower waist than earlier baroque designs, although not as deep in the sides.
d. A fretboard at the same level as the belly, the upper part set into the belly, with twelve frets before joining the body and outlined with multiple black and white wood purflings.
e. A low bridge with pins anchoring the strings. The low bridge allowed the little finger of the right hand to rest on the belly.
f. A simple system of laterally oriented soundboard and back bars.
g. A back and sides of maple, a black-stained pearwood neck and pegs, and a fingerboard and bridge of fruitwood.
h. A lightly varnished or sealed pine belly about 1.8–2.3 mm thick with ornate black wood appliqué foliage moustachios below the bridge.

Between 1800 and 1818, Stauffer also became a for design improvements for guitar, violin, cello, double-guitar, bowed guitar (arpeggione), and piano.

"bürgerliche Lauten und Geigenmacher," took over the workshop of the recently deceased Ignaz Christian Bartl, applied unsuccessfully for the long vacant position of "Hof Geigenmacher" (the equivalent of royal patronage as bestowed in England), registered a patent for a double guitar, and moved his premises three times.[6] In addition, he appears to have been involved in developments in pianoforte design, which were many and varied at that time. Stauffer's workshop produced a range of instruments, including violins, violas, cellos, double basses, arpeggiones, mandolins, and guitars, both six-stringed and multi–stringed. Stauffer also was the first luthier to use in-line machine tuners. J. G. Thielemann patented the first mechanical guitar tuners in 1806. In 1813, Stauffer relocated the guitar's tuning keys from "above and below," i.e. three on each side of the head, to all on one side.

Probably in 1822, Stauffer first met the virtuoso Italian guitarist and instrument maker Luigi Rinaldo Legnani (1790–1877), who lived in Vienna in 1822

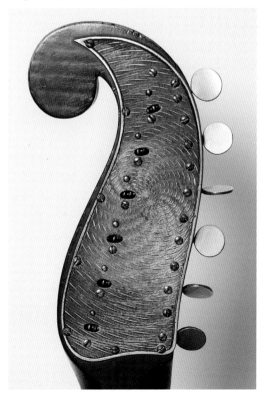

and 1823. Legnani was a mighty influence, both on Stauffer and on his contemporary performers on the guitar; Paganini considered him the premier guitarist of his age. He brought with him an unusual combination of virtuosic capacity as a performer and composer and profound working knowledge of guitar and violin making. After retiring from the concert stage in 1850, he turned to luthiery, an activity he had practiced during an 1833 stay in Vienna.

Also in 1822, Stauffer, together with fellow luthier Johann Ertl, registered a patent for improvements in the manufacture of guitars,[7] which consisted of:

a. The raising and separation of the fingerboard from the soundboard of the guitar and the extension of the guitar's upper range to twenty-one, twenty-two, or twenty-three frets.

b. A screw mechanism set into the heel of the neck that permitted instant, clock–key adjustment of the action.

c. The use of an amalgam of brass, copper, silver, and arsenic for the frets, to avoid corrosion and lessen fret wear in comparison to the brass, silver, or ivory frets in use by other makers at the time.

d A new, single-sided, machine-adjustable tuning system, mounted on a decoratively engraved brass plate. This innovative single unit replaced the individual wooden pegs that had been used by virtually all previous luthiers.

The guitar described above is the famous "Legnani Model" (Profile 1), which carried the label:

Nach dem Modell
Des Luigi Legnani
Johann Georg Stauffer
Anno18__Wien No. 480

The label usually carried a red wax seal with the double-headed Austrian eagle.

In modern terms, Legnani endorsed the new guitar but probably had neither direct influence on the model nor input into its design. Instead, Stauffer intended the guitar as a tribute to the renowned virtuoso and used his name to promote and add prestige to the model's radical design innovations.

Once this new guitar became available in Vienna, the whole of the guitar-making industry—and there were many makers—almost immediately changed to copy and interpret the radically new design. Three sizes of the instrument evolved, the largest with a string length of 610 mm or less; a middle size with a string length of 580–590 mm, which afforded great playability; and the smallest, the terz with a string length of 530–563 mm.

Figure 1-6. The function of Stauffer's adjustable neck was facilitated by the space created by the fingerboard floating above the soundboard.

Figure 1-7. The red wax seal found on many of Stauffer's paper labels. The central motif shows the Habsburgian double eagle.

Almost every aspect of the design was different from preceding guitars. The fretboard usually carried either twenty or twenty-two frets. The neck could be detached from the body, and the fretboard stood well above the belly, angled toward the low, wide pin-mounted bridge. The body outline was broader and shorter than previous models, accentuating the waist, and the back was relatively thick, often four-five mm, being heavily barred and bent into a complex arch by the bars and the shaped sides, which were some twenty mm deeper at the center of the bout than at either end.

The barring was similar to the earlier model, but a little stouter. It retained the angled cut-off bar

Figure 1-8. A Stauffer Company guitar with an array of accessories, including a clock key to adjust the neck, a Viennese string tin with spare gut strings, a capo, and pitch pipes with the chromatic notes written in the Germanic form: A–B–H–C–C#–D–D#–E–F–F#–G–G#. The music is a duet by Küffner for guitar and guitar with capo on third fret, or terz guitar.

in front of the bridge, which tightened the treble side of the soundboard and loosened the bass. The adjustable neck allowed immediate adjustment of the action, with the guitar under tension and without affecting the tuning. The basis for this body design and barring can be seen in the much larger, but similarly conceived, design of Gaetano Guadagnini of Turin.

Later guitars by Stauffer took on a shorter scale-length, commonly under 600 mm, while the average by other luthiers was around 630 mm. The more common, longer scale length of course extended the instrument's range of notes, thus allowing composers such as Legnani to write music like his Caprice no. 5 Op. 20, which starts on a high D played at the twenty-second fret. The idea of extending the upper register without the difficult task of playing over the body of the guitar was resolved by the terz guitar, which was tuned a minor third higher that a regular guitar. The

terz's brighter sound was deemed more suitable for ensemble playing, but it was considered a professional instrument and was used to play soloist's parts. Perhaps the earliest reference to published music for terz guitar is by the Viennese composer Leonard de Call in 1807.

Giuliani wrote many works that specified the use of terz guitar instead of asking guitarists to place a capo on the third fret. In an 1824 letter, he wrote: "This last piece, Op. 36...is newly written so that it can be played with a full orchestra—not with the old guitar, but arranged for the modern terz-guitar."[8] Many Viennese-made terz guitars have body measurements similar to that of a standard guitar, with just a shorter string length (in the vicinity of 530–560 mm). However, one guitar by Ries with the terz string length of 546 mm has a total length of just 815 mm (compared to a Viennese average of around 900 mm).

By 1830, all the Viennese makers were offering this style of guitar in many levels of refinement, from simple and inexpensive instruments with the neck fixed, through to the fully "optioned" model with neck adjustment, machine head, and silver alloy frets. The guitars of Stauffer and his contemporaries were enormously popular throughout Europe, and there are even trade notices in Sweden announcing the arrival of a shipment of Stauffer's Legnani-model guitars in the 1830s. C. F. Martin and his colleague Heinrich Schatz, brought the concept of this instrument to the United States when they emigrated from Germany.

This period of Georg Stauffer's working life also saw his increased involvement in the making of bowed instruments. He followed the fashionable style of his own master, Geissenhoff, and copied the pattern of Stradivari, but was also stylistically very much of the new school, rather taken with attempts to improve the violin, especially those patented in 1818 by the French luthier Francis Chanot. Chanot and others sought to adapt and improve Stradivari's experiments with "cornerless" violins that eliminated the traditional notched, C-bout form of the instrument's waist in favor of a gently curved, rounded body similar to a guitar. Stauffer himself copied Chanot's violin-family designs, which attempted to adapt some aspects of guitar design to the violin, including attaching the strings to a plate in the belly rather than to a tailpiece.

Stauffer's capacity for creative adaptation was perhaps best displayed in his taking Chanot's principles for cello design and employing them to create a hybrid "bowed guitar," also called guitar–cello and guitar d'amour, and best known today by Schubert's name for it, "arpeggione." This instrument, which first appeared in 1823, was the size of a bass viol and

Figure 1-9. Print of woman playing a guitar with a violin-shaped body, one of many early nineteenth century attempts to combine design concepts from the two instruments.

was fitted with six strings in guitar tuning. Stauffer's arpeggione carried twenty-five fixed frets on the fingerboard, had a bent and strutted back much like a viol, a carved belly, and was set up like a cello, intended to be bowed. The arpeggione was guaranteed a part in musical history when, in November 1824, Franz Schubert, who also owned and is said to have frequently composed on a Stauffer Legnani-model guitar, produced his Sonata for Arpeggione and Piano, D. 821. The first performance of the sonata was given by Vincenz Schuster in Vienna at the end of the same year, and Schuster subsequently published a tutor for the instrument.[9]

The arpeggione was widely discussed in musical circles, and it appears that a number of other works were adapted for it at the time. However, like so many of Stauffer's inventions and patents, it did not enter into mainstream musical usage, despite the wide interest it generated. Quite a few similar instruments were built by various European makers until the 1870s, and surviving examples can be found in a number of public musical instrument collections in Europe and the United States.

Stauffer's experiments produced a number of other instruments, including guitars with double backs and double necks; cellos with adjustable necks; the aforementioned cornerless violins; guitars and violins with internal stiffening rods between the upper and lower blocks; four-stringed, flat-backed mandolins; and various tuning and action modifications for pianos. Details survive of at least eight different patents that Stauffer held during his working life, and it is said that the costs of these, plus the time given to his inventions, ultimately contributed to his ruin. Of all his innovative work, only the Legnani-model guitar achieved a high degree of success; it provided the standard design elements to which most Austrian and German makers adhered until well into the twentieth century, as well as a basis for the development of the guitar in the United States.

The last decade of Georg Stauffer's life saw the maturation and independence of numerous makers who trained with him. His son, Johann Anton Stauffer (approx. 1805–1851), established his own premises in 1833, but he continued to work with his father in Vienna and Kaschau for periods in the 1830s and '40s. His guitars were also highly sought after and copied, to the point that the label in his instruments asserted: "Since many instruments not built by the above named [Joh. Anton Stauffer] are falsely labelled with his name, so is the authenticity of this, and any other instrument by the abovementioned, verified through the personal signature of Carl Gerold.'"

Indeed, at this time, the guitar making seems to have been left largely to Johann Anton, while his father concentrated more on the violin family. Georg Stauffer's fortunes seem to have begun to falter in the mid 1830s, and the periods spent living and working with his son in the 1840s may hint at a waning of his activity and success. Such was Stauffer's preoccupation with invention, design, and patent registration that, despite being the most famous and highly remunerated Viennese luthier of his time, he was finally declared bankrupt. In 1845, at sixty-seven years of age, he entered an establishment for the poor, the aged care house of St Marx in Vienna, with his wife, where he died on January 24, 1853, just before his seventy-fifth birthday.

THE TONAL CONCEPT OF STAUFFER'S GUITARS

The tonal concept and barring system used by Stauffer never dramatically changed during his career and appeared in only two forms. He controlled a small, thin

Figure 1-10. Violin by Johann Georg Stauffer, Vienna, December 1826. Experimental model, in original condition. Because one is so used to seeing violin upper bouts more narrow than the lower, Stauffer's equalized upper bout appears wider than it actually is, an optical illusion.

soundboard with a series of lateral braces. The earlier form included an extra bar between the bridge and the tail block of the guitar, but this is hardly seen in the later version as employed on the Legnani model. This barring was used exclusively in Austrian and German guitars until the mid–twentieth century, except where makers deliberately copied the American-style guitar.

STRINGING AND TENSION

Stauffer and his contemporaries used gut and silk strings for their guitars. A common configuration was three plain gut strings for the trebles and three metal over spun silk core strings for the basses.

STAUFFER'S CONTEMPORARIES AND IMITATORS

Stauffer's design concepts remained the norm for the rest of the nineteenth century but were modified to produce more volume and carry more tension as the century progressed. Foremost among Georg Stauffer's contemporaries was the aforementioned Johann Anton Ertl, with whom Stauffer held the patent for the Legnani-model guitar. Indeed, there was very little straying outside the established models of Stauffer, especially the Legnani model, and the Viennese guitar-making tradition is remarkably uniform from about 1825 onward.

In North America, the German and Austrian makers and players were largely centered in New York City and eastern Pennsylvania and included Christian Friedrich Martin and Heinrich Schatz. It is on the East Coast of the United States that the seeds were sown for what would later become the steel-string guitar.

C. F. MARTIN AND J. G. STAUFFER

Although little is known about his company's day-to-day business, Stauffer's was clearly a large and prolific operation. Serial numbers on extant Stauffer guitars indicate the firm had produced nearly 5,000 guitars by the late 1840s.[10] As did other master luthiers of his time, Stauffer trained apprentices in his way of making and in accordance with the local guild system.

Many of Stauffer's Viennese trainees went on to become famed makers in their own right. Prochart's list of J. G. and J. A. Stauffer's trainees (J. A. having trained with his father) includes Johann Bucher, Andreas Jeremias, Anton Mitteis, Friedrich Schenk, Johann Gottfried Scherzer, and Friedrich Philip Wolf.[11] However, curiously, there is no mention of Martin, Schatz, or other early nineteenth-century Markneukirchen makers who may have worked in Vienna.

The fact that no direct documentation has surfaced to date that Martin and Schatz worked directly with Stauffer may be due to a propensity for Viennese makers to list only their own countrymen. However, there is no doubt that both Martin and Schatz fully

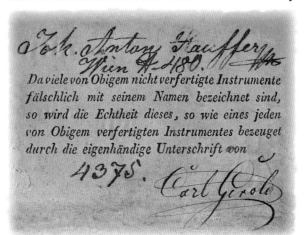

Figure 1-11. The signature of Carl Gerold on the paper label inside a Johann Anton Stauffer guitar, verifying its authenticity.

integrated Stauffer's innovative Legnani design features into their guitars, so stating, on their labels, that they were "pupils of the celebrated Stauffer" was an effective way to underscore this connection.

Stauffer may also have influenced Martin in another, more subtle way. One extant c. 1810 Stauffer is stamped on the back of the body "STAUFFER/WIENN."[12] While it was common practice for violinmakers to mark their instruments in this way, it is seldom seen on early guitars. As it is suggested that Martin was in Vienna at this time, this concept may have stuck in his mind after moving to New York, where he employed a similar stamp on the top back of his guitars, near the heel.

Figure 1-12. *View of Vienna from the Belvedere.* Bernardo Bellotto il Canaletto. 1759-60 Oil on canvas. 53.1 x 83.9 inches (135 x 213 cm). Vienna was a hotbed of musical innovation during the Classical period. Stauffer, the city's premier nineteenth-century guitar maker, had an enormous impact on the evolution of the guitar, both in Europe and the United States.

Figure 1-13 *Oposite page, Masqued ball in the Redoutensaal on occasion of the Congress of Vienna with performance of Beethoven's Seventh Symphony and his composition "Wellington's victory in the battle of Vittoria."* Color print from an engraving by Carl Schuetz, c.1815. Vienna was the musical capital of Europe in the Classical period, the home of such musical giants as Haydn, Mozart, Beethoven, and Schubert.

STAUFFER'S IMPACT IN THE UNITED STATES

C. F. Martin's first American-built guitars were remarkably similar to Stauffer's Legnani model, but within a few years, a number of decisive changes appeared in his instruments. He changed from the Viennese tradition of maple back and sides to Brazilian rosewood and employed a different body shape, taking as his model the Spanish instruments of the Cadiz and Malaga makers, including the Pagés and Benedid families and Antonio de Lorca.

One of the few extant guitars by Martin & Schatz (c. 1835–1837, Profile 7) no longer employs the lateral soundboard braces of the Viennese school but has three fan bars on the belly. In terms of Spanish guitars of the 1830s, the use of only three fan struts was, by this time, somewhat outdated. Many already had five or seven fan struts by this time, and Louis Panormo of London had applied seven fan struts to his Spanish models by 1827. Martin continued to use three or five fan struts until the early 1840s, when he first began to use an X-braced pattern on some models. This single modification provided the bracing pattern that would permit the development of the acoustic steel-string guitar and which remains the standard today.

Many of the salient features of the later American guitar were already present in Stauffer's Legnani–style instruments. The narrow neck, the pin bridge, and the use of machine heads are all elements that passed from the sphere of European classical guitar technology of the early nineteenth-century directly to form the foundation for the modern American guitar. To these elements, Martin added the Spanish-style body geometry, introduced in the later 1830s. This basic pattern was repeatedly enlarged to create various later Martin guitar models, culminating in the now famous "Dreadnought," which was first commissioned by the Ditson company in 1916. The set of components is then completed with the development of the X- or cross–bracing system of the mid 1840s, and this strutting pattern proved sufficiently robust and resonant to eventually evolve into the American steel-stringed guitar.

The fertile ground of early nineteenth-century guitar virtuosity and the demands it placed on instruments (and thus makers) produced a unique period of evolution in the instrument. And, although his influence waned as luthiers such as Martin and Torres pushed farther, Johann Georg Stauffer's early innovations were eventually incorporated into many of the structural elements that are currently taken for granted in classical, jazz, and popular guitars ★

Ansicht des K.K. Redouten Saales
während eines Masquen-Balles.

The fingerboard is raised—separated from the soundboard and extended for higher range—as on bowed instruments and, more recently, on archtop guitars.

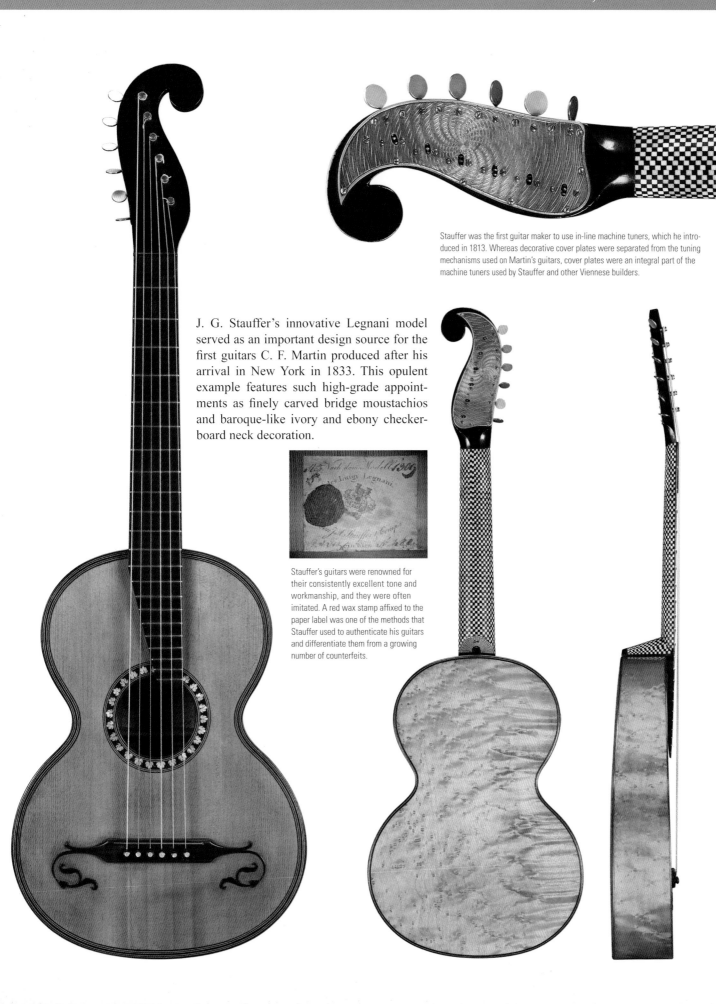

Stauffer was the first guitar maker to use in-line machine tuners, which he introduced in 1813. Whereas decorative cover plates were separated from the tuning mechanisms used on Martin's guitars, cover plates were an integral part of the machine tuners used by Stauffer and other Viennese builders.

J. G. Stauffer's innovative Legnani model served as an important design source for the first guitars C. F. Martin produced after his arrival in New York in 1833. This opulent example features such high-grade appointments as finely carved bridge moustachios and baroque-like ivory and ebony checkerboard neck decoration.

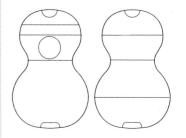

Stauffer's guitars were renowned for their consistently excellent tone and workmanship, and they were often imitated. A red wax stamp affixed to the paper label was one of the methods that Stauffer used to authenticate his guitars and differentiate them from a growing number of counterfeits.

SERIAL NUMBER 1309

DIMENSIONS

TOTAL LENGTH	34"	864 MM
BODY LENGTH	15.5"	394 MM

WIDTH

UPPER BOUT	9"	229 MM
WAIST	6.63"	168 MM
LOWER BOUT	11.5"	291 MM

DEPTH

NECK	2.5"	64 MM
WAIST	3"	76 MM
END	3.25"	83 MM

NUT WIDTH	1.69"	43 MM
SCALE	22"	559 MM
SOUNDHOLE	3.19"	81 MM

BRACING CONFIGURATION

RELATIVE SIZE

42" (1067 MM)

36" (914 MM)

30" (762 MM)

18" (457 MM)

13

This guitar has an unusual abundance of pearl decoration with a pearl quatrefoil on the end of each tuning peg, each bridge pin, and even on the endpin. The Legnani feature of a fingerboard clear of the face of the guitar is clearly evident in this photo.

C. F. Martin claimed that he worked in J. G. Stauffer's workshop in Vienna, and, while no documentary proof of this assertion has been discovered to date, Martin's earliest guitars suggest an intimate knowledge of Stauffer's work, especially his patented Legnani model. Martin incorporated two significant features found in this early example of the Legnani model—a fingerboard clear of the guitar top and a key-operated mechanical adjustment of the angle of the neck. This guitar has another strong visual component that Martin featured in his "Renaissance" models—the sides of the guitar have a reverse curve so that they join the heel and neck obliquely, as in viols, rather than perpendicularly, as in most guitars.

SERIAL NUMBER 2350

DIMENSIONS

TOTAL LENGTH	35.56"	903 MM
BODY LENGTH	17"	432 MM

WIDTH

UPPER BOUT	9.31"	237 MM
WAIST	6.63"	168 MM
LOWER BOUT	11.75"	298 MM

DEPTH

NECK	2.75"	70 MM
WAIST	3.06"	78 MM
END	3.31"	84 MM

NUT WIDTH	1.75"	44 MM
SCALE	23.81"	605 MM
SOUNDHOLE	3.19"	81 MM

Stauffer and his luthier colleague Johann Ertl received a privilege or patent for the adjustable neck feature of their Legnani model in 1822.

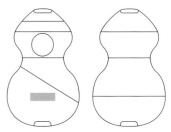

The involvement of the Italian virtuoso Luigi Legnani in the design of this model is referenced on the label, which states, "After the Model of Luigi Legnani."

BRACING CONFIGURATION

RELATIVE SIZE

42" (1067 MM)

36" (914 MM)

30" (762 MM)

18" (457 MM)

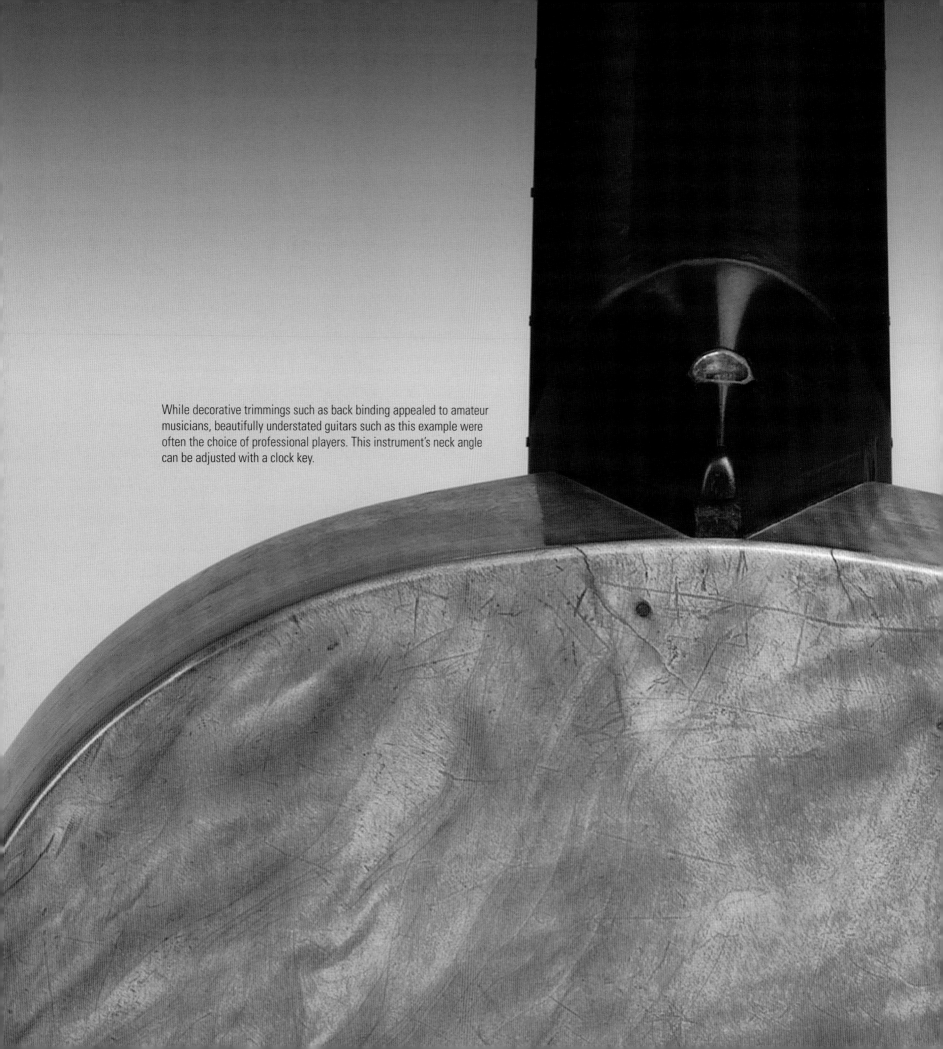

While decorative trimmings such as back binding appealed to amateur musicians, beautifully understated guitars such as this example were often the choice of professional players. This instrument's neck angle can be adjusted with a clock key.

Johann Georg Stauffer's son Anton collaborated with his father in the 1830s and '40s. While Stauffer's guitars were simple in form, they were musically unrivalled by any other contemporary Viennese maker. With its shorter scale length and brighter sound, the terz guitar was used by professionals in ensembles as a solo insturment. Because the bodies of terz guitars were proportionately smaller, the majority were fitted with lighter wooden tuning pegs rather than heavier mechanical tuners.'

SERIAL NUMBER 3347

DIMENSIONS

TOTAL LENGTH	33.13"	842 MM
BODY LENGTH	15.56"	395 MM

WIDTH

UPPER BOUT	9.13"	232 MM
WAIST	6.69"	170 MM
LOWER BOUT	11.31"	287 MM

DEPTH

NECK	2.44"	62 MM
WAIST	2.88"	73 MM
END	2.94"	75 MM

NUT WIDTH	1.69"	42 MM
SCALE	22.13"	562 MM
SOUNDHOLE	3.06"	78 MM

BRACING CONFIGURATION

RELATIVE SIZE

42" (1067 MM)

36" (914 MM)

30" (762 MM)

18" (457 MM)

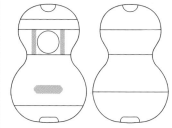

17

CHAPTER 2

C. F. Martin's Homeland and The Vogtland Trade

Arian Sheets

Christian Friedrich Martin Sr.'s early guitar making is most clearly associated with Viennese-style guitars, with their slim-waisted bodies, adjustable necks, and asymmetrical, lobed heads with one-sided machine tuners. It would be easy to assume that the Viennese influence was pervasive in the southern German-speaking regions of central Europe and that Martin simply chose to go to the region's most prestigious musical center to further his career. While both of those statements are true, the fuller picture of guitar making in the region is wonderfully multifaceted, not least because of its unique commercial culture. Despite its small population and secluded location, the area in which Martin was raised was not just any rural backwater. The region is still known as the Vogtland, a term derived from its medieval governance, a cultural identity distinct from the Saxon state in which it is predominantly located. By the late eighteenth century, the area was already well known as one of the most significant centers of European musical instrument production. At the time of Martin's birth in 1796, his hometown, Markneukirchen (called Neukirchen until 1858), was one of the largest of a cluster of municipalities on the Saxon-Bohemian border for which the export of musical instruments was a primary economic activity.

ORIGINS

The first solid evidence for musical instrument production in the region is the marriage registry of Melchior Lorentz in 1631 in Graslitz, on the Bohemian side of the border. Social upheavals caused by fallout from the Thirty Years War resulted in the migration of Protestant musical instrument makers out of Bohemia into Saxony, where they could freely practice their religion. The violin makers, or *Geigenmacher*, who settled in Markneukirchen, founded their guild in 1677, and the profession was often continued by many generations of the same families through apprenticeship.[1] The Vogtland was well suited to find prosperity in manufacturing. The area had poor, rocky soil and a hilly terrain, but rich natural resources in the local woods and the metals mined in the nearby *Erzgebirge*, or Ore Mountains.[2] Due to the isolated geography of the region, professional distributors, of both local and non-local origin, played an important role in transporting goods to larger cities and ports. With the rise of developed trade, there was also awareness of customer demand for a broader range of products, and gradually, through the eighteenth century, the skills for woodwind and brass instruments were established in the area. A hallmark of the region's commercial methodology was adaptability and market consciousness. If there was a market for a particular music product, the Vogtland trade would find a way to satisfy it, as long as it was economically viable to transport over their hills and valleys to the wider world.

THE ROLE OF DISTRIBUTORS AND FORMAL STRUCTURE IN THE EARLY TRADE

The rise of the professional distributor, or *Händler,* was an early, and necessary, occurrence for the Vogtland instrument trade. In order for the industry to grow and

Figure 2-1. Lithograph town view of Neukirchen (later renamed Markneukirchen) before an 1840 fire destroyed much of the town center.

support the addition of younger family members to the instrument-making profession, it was necessary to have an organized, efficient, and competitive system of export. The 1677 articles of the Markneukirchen violin-makers' guild, or *Geigenmacher-Innung*, indicated an advanced awareness of the operations of dealers, and the dangers they presented. Specific mention was made of intense dealer competition driving down prices, non-guild members selling shoddy violins within jurisdiction of the guild, and dealers not paying for wares.[3] Heinrich Götz was the first professional dealer in Markneukirchen whose identity is recorded. He was described in the quarterly business tax list in 1681 as "a violin dealer, who does his business across the country." Elias Pfretzschner was named as the first official guild-sanctioned dealer in 1712, suggesting that the guild desired more structure in its relationship with salesmen. The lines between makers and distributors blurred as certain family members handled different aspects of the trade, including instrument making, string making, and sales. In an area where skills and commercial enterprise

was spreading rapidly, the violin-makers' guild saw the need to exert more control over their segment of the industry, a task that became increasingly unwieldy by the turn of the nineteenth century. By the 1820s, members of the Klemm, Gütter, and Paulus families of Markneukirchen had established musical instrument businesses in the United States, presumably offering wares produced by their associates in the old country. The increased production and dispersal of influence would provide grave threats to the guilds, which chose to fight certain aspects affecting their members, ultimately without success.

THE GUILDS, INSTRUMENT MAKERS, AND FURNITURE MAKERS

The construction of musical instruments, like many other skilled professions in Europe, was regulated by guilds. The guilds formalized the training process for young makers, established standards, and governed business practices. Guild members held exclusive legal right to produce certain finished products, which protected their investment in the training process.

In Markneukirchen, the violin-makers' guild established its authority over not only bowed but also plucked stringed instruments. Young apprentices trained with a master for four years, then undertook a *Wanderschaft*, a two-year period of travel and work as journeymen to perfect their craft. Journeymen were then eligible to apply for promotion to the designation of master upon the successful completion of tests and payment of fees. The skills required for a prospective guild member were covered in several practical tests, described in the Guild Articles, or *Innungsprivilegium*, in 1677:

> *He shall complete three master pieces within*
> *three weeks as follows:*
> *1.) A discant Geige [treble fiddle (violin)] with*
> *beautiful wood, the neck perfectly set, the finger-*
> *board tessellated [inlaid with geometrical purfling*
> *decoration], the back and front also cleanly inlaid*
> *with three-piece*
> *2.) A Zitter [cittern] made from beautiful wood*
> *and pure of register*
> *3.) A Viola di Gambe [viola da gamba] with*
> *bridge and six strings, without fault*
> *And all three pieces should be of a gold color*
> *without spots*

Figure 2-2. *Die Sister oder die teutsche Guitare* (The sister [cittern] or German guitar), as illustrated in a 1799 issue of the periodical *Journal des Luxus und der Moden (Journal of Luxury and Fashion)*, Weimar.

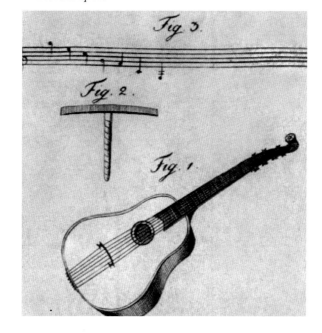

The guild in neighboring Klingenthal listed similar requirements in 1723, also to be fulfilled within three weeks:

> *1.) A Violin oder discant Geige [violin or treble*
> *fiddle] made from beautiful wood and well inlaid*
> *2.) A proficient and well-formed Laute [lute]*
> *3.) A proficient and good-sounding Viol di Gamba*
> *[viola da gamba]*
> *4.) A proficient Davids Harffe [David's harp]*

Clearly, the violin-makers' guilds claimed a variety of stringed instruments, though the period in which the guild articles were written dictated the types of instruments specifically mentioned. As musical fashion changed, however, this left a loophole open that resulted in conflict about the manufacture of instruments whose arrival in the region postdated the writing of the guild articles. Three complaints were lodged by the violin-maker's guild against furniture builders, or *Tischlermacher*, who were producing the newly popular gut-strung guitar. The furniture builders were already engaged to build instrument cases, and some expanded their enterprises to build guitars to go within those cases.

The first action was taken in 1806, with subsequent updates. The complaint to the *Gewerbe-Landesdirektion Sachsen*, the regional Saxon state business directorate, names Carl Friedrich Jacob and Carl Gottlob Wild, but specifically singles out C. F. Martin's father, Johann Georg Martin, who was also a piano maker,[4] as a primary offender. The argument used by the furniture makers was that the guitar was not a violin-family instrument; therefore, its production was free from restriction. An addendum to this document, of unknown date, indicated that Heinrich Schatz, also described as a furniture maker, agreed with the violin-makers' guild that the production of guitars fell under their authority, but since his two years and five months in Vienna, during which time he only built guitars, could qualify as his journeyman's *Wanderschaft*, he requested that he be allowed to take the master examination (by producing a masterpiece) based on that experience, in spite of the lack of a formal Markneukirchen-based violin-making apprenticeship, and offered to pay all associated fees required to obtain legal recognition as a master. No response was recorded to this request. Another addendum to this complaint cited the November 20, 1828 ruling in Klingenthal that guitars were the exclusive purview of the violin makers, and therefore not permitted of carpenters, and states that such precedents are often recognized by other jurisdictions. The ruling was based on the understanding that the *Zitter*, or cittern, was named as part of the masterpieces, and that the name was synonymous with the guitar, and hence the guild was certainly offered protection. Furthermore, the analogy is given that if the violin makers were suddenly to produce coffins or commodes, the furniture builders would certainly take action against them for that blatant trespass.

While these issues were ongoing, another complaint was filed in 1826, with the King of Saxony, Friedrich August. Again, Carl Friedrich Jacob, Carl Gottlob Wild, and Johann Georg Martin were named, but the offenses of these individuals were escalated to include the training of apprentices in guitar building. The guild attributed a crash in guitar prices to the expanded production of these makers and their apprentices. The guild officials imply greed on the part of the furniture makers, who were able to continue their own furniture building while gutting the guitar market.

The action stated that the guitar was the favorite instrument of the time, and, in what was intended as a veiled insult, it was by far the most popular, unlike the other articles in the furniture-makers' profession. Instances were mentioned, but not substantiated, of furniture makers leaving certain areas and establishing competing business outside their home areas, perhaps an oblique and not particularly accurate reference to Heinrich Schatz and Christian Friedrich Martin, who are not mentioned by name. A list was provided of instruments the guild felt were covered in their market protections:

That guitars would be exclusive purview of the guild's profession needed no extensive discussion. [The production of] violins would be the principal objective of the profession. The other varieties claimed are basses, cellos, guitars, mandolins, zithers [or citterns], lutes, and all remaining musical instruments that bring forth sound through strings. [Guild members] would have also produced these instruments forever and from time immemorial.

The final complaint, initiated in 1831, was even shriller in tone. Citing 150 years of guild history, the guild claimed exclusive right to produce all musical instruments incorporating strings and a resonant body, specifically listing basses, cellos, zithers, lutes, mandolins, guitars, and harps. Jacob, then deceased, Wild, and J. G. Martin were once again listed as offenders. The names of three apprentices also were given, and August Paulus and Heinrich Schatz were described as formerly being among them. Another fellow named Seifert, actively apprenticing in 1831, was snidely mentioned as the offspring of farmers from the tiny village of Wohlhausen, hence not even a Markneukirchen resident. The letter describes seven other carpenters building guitars, but does not name them. The violin makers claimed ninety-two of their own guild members, plus one hundred and six members of the Klingenthal violin-makers' guild, two hours distant, and hence indicated that additional competition in the production of guitars was adversely impacting their ability to provide for their families. Furthermore, the threat posed by several furniture makers leaving the area with guitar-making skills acquired locally was cited, a rehash of the complaint in the previous document which may refer to Schatz's and C. F. Martin's work in Vienna.

The violin-makers' masterpiece requirement was listed, with the updated substitution of a guitar for a cittern. Note that no change is made to the requirement for the viola da gamba, which was obsolete by the 1820s, while the German-style cittern continued to maintain use in folk music:

The learning of our profession follows the outline of our most nobly confirmed Guild Articles, and is associated with very great expense. Following these articles, the artisan must produce a very difficult master piece, which includes
1.) a treble violin with beautiful wood, the neck perfectly inserted, the fingerboard tessellated [inlaid with geometrical purfling decoration], the top and back cleanly inlaid with three-piece purfling
2.) a guitar of beautiful wood and pure of register,
3.) a viola da gamba with belly and six strings, without flaw.

The violin makers also claimed that paying higher taxes than the furniture makers put them at a further disdvantage. The case against the Klingenthal cabinet makers was again mentioned as a precedent, and the problem that as Klingenthal was only a village with one master carpenter, the situation was actually much worse in Markneukirchen with ten master carpenters to siphon off revenue from guitar building,

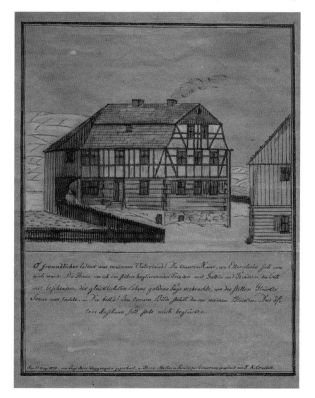

Figure 2-3. Drawing by Friedrich August Crasselt of the Martin family home, dated August 27, 1833.

in addition to what the violin makers considered ample revenue from case making. The authors of the text, Carl Willhelm Glier, Carl Wilhelm Gläsel, and Adam Friedrich Rossbach, ended their appeal with further mention of the starvation of violin-makers' families due to the intrusion of the outsiders upon their livelihoods.

The increasing desperation and virulence of these documents does not speak to a dominant position on the part of the violin-makers' guild. The disputes had been ongoing for decades, without any effective protective relief from the local authorities. The times were changing, and the violin makers were very unhappy about the impact on their livelihoods. The situation was spiraling out of their control. Indeed, the ruling from the local business authority, the Gewerbe-Landesdirektion Sachsen, issued on July 9, 1832, was in favor of the furniture makers, because the guitar was not listed by name in original violin-makers' guild articles.[5]

One of the main reasons Christian Friedrich Martin emigrated to the United States was to escape the restrictive policies of the local guild system.

On September 9, 1833, Martin gathered his family and followed Heinrich Schatz to New York. F.A. Crasselt, a family friend and local historian, presented them with this drawing of their home in Markneukirchen, which bears the inscription: "Oh, friendly symbol of my fatherland! This dear house, where I was wrapped in my parents love. The house, where I spent the luckiest of life's golden days with my beloved wife and children, which God gave me as a gift, where the quiet luck's sun was shining upon us. It is you! In a faithful picture you are standing in my eyes. To look at you often, should always make me happy."

EARLY GERMAN GUITARS

It is well documented that the manufacture of plucked instruments was a required skill of violin makers in Markneukirchen. However, what exactly constituted a guitar was a matter of some question in both Europe and the United States. There had long

Figure 2-4. *Left,* lute-shaped English guitar by John Friedrich Hintz, London, 1761. Hintz was a Moravian furniture and instrument builder who spent part of his career in the American Moravian community before moving to London. Wire-strung instruments in a variety of forms, including lute, pear, teardrop, and festooned shapes, were made in German-speaking lands in the seventeenth and eighteenth centuries and were an important part of Moravian musical practices, both in Germany and in America.

Center, Cittern, Vogtland, eighteenth century. This type of cittern was included in the original guild masterpiece requirements in Markneukirchen and Klingenthal. Confusion over the exact name of various plucked stringed instruments, as well as the increasing tendency to call wire-strung instruments guitars in the eighteenth century led to conflict over which craftsmen were permitted to manufacture such instruments under the Markneukirchen and Klingenthal guild systems. This example is relatively simple in construction and features many similarities with Renaissance forms of the instrument, such as the teardrop-shaped body, offset neck shape, and pierced soundhole. An instrument like this one would have been affordable to a person of modest means.

Right, Guitare allemande, or German guitar, by Gérard Deleplanque, Lille, France, 1777. The pear-shaped form of cittern became fashionable in eighteenth-century France and was specifically associated with a German origin.

been uncertainty and confusion about the exact meaning of certain terms used to describe musical instruments, both from a modern and historical perspective. Spellings, instrument forms, tunings, and usage could vary dramatically in different regions, in concurrent times. Terms such as cittern, gittern, zister, cister, cistre, sister, guitar, gitarre, guitarra, chittara, guittar, guitare, and even variants of the term zither, have designated plucked, fretted stringed instruments with necks in the seventeenth through nineteenth centuries in Europe and America. International trade meant that foreign terms may have been used in a variety of languages and that new instruments were created and assigned fashionable nationalities in the eighteenth century as part of musical trends. One such instrument was the guitare allemande of France, an instrument related to the English guitar, but which derived its pear-shaped body from certain German citterns. The English guitar, in turn, was also predominantly manufactured in its early years by Germans and Moravians

who emigrated to England.[6] The strong association between wire-strung instruments and musicians and makers of German ancestry was likely due to the continuous use of wire-strung, cittern-type instruments in German-speaking lands since the Renaissance, in both folk and art music. Whereas the cittern had declined in use in Italy, France, England, and the Netherlands, modified forms of the instrument continued to appear in German illustrations and literature.

The gut-strung guitar had been more traditionally associated with France, Spain, and Italy since the seventeenth century, and eighteenth- and early nineteenth- century references to these types of instruments were often qualified with one of those three nationalities, to distinguish them from the default, a wire-strung instrument. Confusion over what constituted a guitar absolutely played a role in the guild disputes, as it was certainly not possible that the guitars made "since time immemorial" by violin guild members were of the variety with six gut strings.

Figure 2-5. *Above left,* guitar by Johann Gottlieb Knößing, Leipzig, 1807. This guitar shows interesting features distinctive to early Saxon guitars, before the wider influence of Stauffer's models. Note the violin-style side-mounted pegs, the high soundhole placement, and the simple but graphically dramatic inlay. The fan-type inlay at the bottom of the soundboard can be found on guitars made in Markneukirchen into the twentieth century.

Above right, guitar by Johann G. Thielemann, Berlin, 1808. Thielemann constructed large volumes of musical instruments for mass distribution at a time when Markneukirchen was also expanding into foreign markets and power was shifting to the distribution businesses that had the expertise and scale to compete effectively. Thielemann's guitar was an extremely high-quality product, with a neatly finished interior, simple veneered rosette, and ivory frets. The festooned headstock, minimally curved waist, and curled bridge moustaches were holdovers from earlier baroque-style guitars. The guitar bears the serial number 324 and a manufacturer's label, which were very rare in guitars of the period but more common in factory-made pianos, of which Thielemann was also a purveyor.

Awareness in Saxony of alternate forms of plucked instruments with similar names is in evidence by the 1790s. The composer Johann Georg Albrechtsberger, in his *Thorough Guide to Composition*, Leipzig, 1790, wrote: "The cittern (guitar) is of three forms: the German, the Welsh [probably meaning English], and the Spanish. Each is treated differently. Of no importance."[7] Several gut-strung guitars (of six double courses or single strings) made in Upper Saxony in the 1790s, including Dresden and Jena, are documented or extant. These instruments exhibit body styles more typical of the baroque period than the later Stauffer model, with narrow upper and lower bouts and a waist with less pronounced curvature than later instruments.

Before the 1820s, the six-string guitars manufactured in the German states, including Upper Saxony and Berlin, tended to exhibit a wide variety of eccentric models and features, before the more standardized Viennese and Italian models gained influence. Variations in peghead forms, including side-mounted pegs akin to those of a violin, festooned outlines, and simple figure-eight shapes are all represented. Occasionally, wildly alternate body forms, such as shield-shaped "Wappenguittare" were produced. Simple marquetry or veneer rosettes, are notable, as is varied soundhole placement, sometimes well into the upper bout.

CHANGES IN THE MARKET

The popularity of the guitar and its increasd production in Markneukirchen were well noted in the violin-makers' and furniture-builders' guild disputes. However, another factor that emerged in the 1820s accelerated problems for guild control of instrument production, such that the complaints against individuals like Johann Georg Martin were feeble attempts to close the floodgates of mass production. For decades, the export market, particularly to areas of growing wealth like the United States, was expanding dramatically. Mass production of musical instruments, including guitars and pianos in facilities such as the one operated by Johann Thielemann in Berlin, was well established. Moreover, the world's first musical instrument distributor catalog was published by Israel Kämpffens Söhne around 1830, with a second edition following roughly five years later. The Kämpffens firm, founded in the late eighteenth century as string distributors, had established branches in Frankfurt, Leipzig, and Moscow. Both of their catalogs listed guitars, some of which exhibited local traits as well as Viennese, Italian, and Spanish features.

With the rise of powerful distributors and predetermined catalog models, standardization and price competition became increasingly important. The distributors established a need for consistent features and quality, and they purchased the models made to

Figure 2-6. *Right,* illustrations of guitar-making tools and components from Gustav Adolph Wettengel's 1828 manual on instrument making, Plates XI and XIII. Wettengel was a violin maker in Markneukirchen, and his book, which was republished in 1869, was the major printed source for the techniques practiced in the region. Note details of a slotted headstock in Plate XIII, which are similar to the headstock on one of C. F. Martin's earliest guitars (Profile 6).

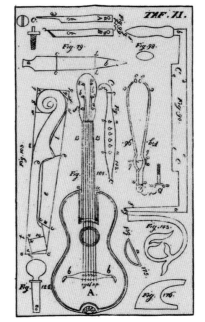

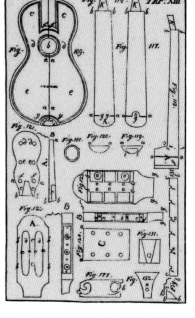

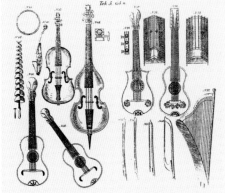

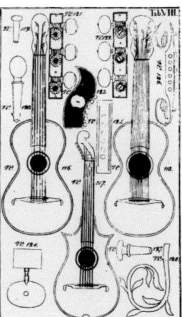

Figure 2-7. *Far left*, the Israel Kämpffens Söhne catalog, published c. 1830–1833, is the first musical instrument catalog produced by a Vogtland distributor. Notice the variety of guitars offered, including a 12-string "Spanish" model.

Figure 2-8. *Center,* guitar built in Markneukirchen, second half of the nineteenth century. As the offerings of Markneukirchen distributors expanded, copies of important makers guitar models became more common. This is a French-style guitar, copied with a Lacote-model bridge. The rosette is mother-of-pearl and abalone set into black paste.

Figure 2-9. *Left,* this later version of the Israel Kämpffens Söhne catalog, published c. 1835, shows some minor modifications from the previous edition, including single-sided tuners. Tuners and instrument parts are also offered for sale separately.

Figure 2-10. *Right*, guitar, Markneukirchen, mid-nineteenth century. This guitar is a copy of an 1840s Martin & Coupa, with the center stripe extending into the separate heal cap, just as Martin imitated the Spanish style while using German construction techniques. The engraved tuner is similar to those imported by Martin from Markneukirchen.

Below center, detail of the Markneukirchen guitar showing its imitation of the delicate neck heel profile of a Martin & Coupa.

Below bottom, neck heel view showing showing separate ebony heel cap into which the back stripe continues. Note also the same material of the back stripe inlaid along the center line of the ribs.

their specifications in bulk. The distributors would source their goods with the provider best able to meet their needs at the lowest cost, and individual pride of craftsmanship and signature models would be of little value to them. The instruments they bought were not permitted to bear any maker's mark. It was probably no coincidence that the violin-makers' guild lashed out at the furniture makers when control of the market was shifting away from them. Note that the complaints made by the guild officials included the quantity of production by the unauthorized guitar makers; increased production at lower cost and with less training was ideally suited to merchants who wished to compete in an international market with inexpensive, standardized wares.

While we may never know all the reasons that Schatz and Martin chose to leave Markneukirchen, it is extremely likely that harassment by the guilds was only one factor. The guilds clearly could do nothing to stop the furniture makers from building guitars, and there were other excellent business reasons to leave the area besides the legal nuisance the violin makers created. The market in the United States was one of the most coveted in the world. The country was growing rapidly, and increased wealth among the middle classes had expanded the market for professionally made musical instruments.

By moving overseas, Martin and Schatz could sell directly to their customers, cutting out expensive middlemen in the form of distributors, transport and customs agents, and retailers. Whatever they chose not to produce themselves, they could source from their contacts back in Markneukirchen and sell at a profit. Indeed, Martin's early business records show much activity with the old country, and he carried many types of instruments that he did not make himself, including a few cheaper guitars in 1836. Also, the rapid expansion of production and falling prices for finished products, a problem blamed by the violin-makers' guild on the furniture makers, was just as likely caused by the distributors, whose rising influence was rapidly eroding the guilds' power The final blow was dealt by the new Saxon *Gerwerbegesetz*, or Trade Act, designed to modernize commerce, which took effect on January 1, 1862, for all crafts, establishing *Gewerbefreiheit,* or freedom of trade. This law eliminated any legal right the guilds had to regulate production of goods, paving the way for mass production without impediment. Markneukirchen was already a very unfriendly environment for any instrument maker who wished to craft a high-quality product using his own models and do so with a prospect of growth and advancement for his own business. Schatz and Martin, through their work with the famous and innovative Viennese maker Stauffer, had already tasted the success that could come through establishing one's own name and reputation in a thriving, cosmopolitan market. The idea of selling cheap guitars by the dozen to wholesalers who took the lion's share of the profit and dictated their terms, was likely to be extremely distasteful to the likes of Schatz and Martin. Surviving Martin

guitars from the 1830s consistently show an excellence of craftsmanship and a creativity of design that was not consistent with the vast majority of Vogtland products of the later nineteenth century. Indeed, while Martin adapted features from a variety of schools to create his own models, much of the workmanship in the homeland increasingly focused on slavishly copying the innovations of others, including Martin himself, possibly as early as the 1840s. The profusion of fake Markneukirchen-made Martins available at the end of the nineteenth century speaks to the wisdom of leaving the area to build a business free of hostile influences, both legal and commercial. Had Christian Friedrich Martin remained in Markneukirchen, it is very likely that his descendants would have been making, at starvation wages, the very same types of cheap, ill cured, and sometimes fraudulent guitars that were being imported to the United States by the thousands from the 1870s through the 1890s. ★

Figure 2-11. Guitar, Markneukirchen, second half of the nineteenth century. This guitar has a Spanish outline as filtered through Martin, but also has the typically Vogtland decorative features of an abalone and paste rosette, fan-shaped soundboard inlay, and floral fingerboard inlay constructed from pearl and nickel-silver wire.

CHAPTER 3

C. F. MARTIN IN NEW YORK, 1833–1839

RICHARD JOHNSTON

Figure 3-1. *Opposite page, Young Woman Playing a Guitar.* George Peter Alexander Healy. Oil on canvas. Signed and dated "G P A Healy 1834" on the lower right hand side. 36 x 26 inches. George Peter Alexander Healy (1813–1894) was one of America's most popular and prolific nineteenth-century portrait artists. In 1834, Healy, already established as a successful portrait painter, left the United States for Europe, where he resided for the next sixteen years. The guitar is stylistically close to the earliest extant Martin guitar (Profile 5), which also was produced in 1834, and it is depicted as being in pristine, new condition.

On September 8, 1833, Christian Friedrich Martin boarded the ship *Columbus* in Bremen, a seaport city in what was then northern Saxony, and set sail for New York, arriving two months later. He was then thirty-seven, and his wife, eight-year-old son, and infant daughter traveled with him. Severe limitations that the local violin-maker's guild had attempted to impose on non-guild members building guitars in Martin's hometown of Markneukirchen have been well documented, but the restrictive nature of the entire musical instrument trade in the Vogtland was probably what compelled him to seek a freer business climate in the New World.[1] The fact that Martin's father, also a guitar maker, had died less than eighteen months earlier suggests that he saw no future in taking over his father's business.[2] Instead, Martin was encouraged to make the dramatic move to New York by his younger compatriot and future partner, Henrich Schatz, who had emigrated to the United States in 1830.[3]

There is little surviving documentation of the time Martin spent in Vienna, but there is no doubt that he was there for several years and that he worked in Johann Stauffer's workshop before joining harp-maker Karl Kuhle, his future father-in-law, in 1825 or earlier.[4] Martin must have built guitars upon returning to Markneukirchen in 1828, with his wife Otillia and young son C. F. Martin Jr., but those guitars were probably not marked, for none with his name on them has survived. That Martin was already building guitars on a commercial level is indicated by the fact that eighteen-year-old Louis Schmidt, a craftsman who would work for Martin in New York, was also on the manifest of the *Columbus*. Since Schmidt, who received room and board in the Martin household as part of his salary, went on to become a successful New York guitar maker in his own right just a few years later, it is reasonable to assume that he was already Martin's apprentice when they sailed together from Saxony.[5]

The real story of C. F. Martin and Martin guitars begins with his arrival in New York, and the surviving records in the Martin Archives of his early business in the city are remarkably complete.[6] These sources make it obvious that Martin was not merely a crafts-man, with only his wits and manual skills to sustain him and his family. Instead, he arrived in the New World an experienced and well-connected entrepreneur who sought to make the most of his Vogtland sources in establishing a wholesale and retail music business that included guitar making, a goal that he achieved quite quickly. His homeland offered a wide network of craftsmen and suppliers of musical goods without direct access to a healthy and growing market. New York was quite the opposite, and Martin saw, and seized, the opportunity open to someone who could bridge that gap.

Although the six-string guitar had already gained considerable popularity in America by the early 1830s, there is no surviving evidence of North American guitar makers who were active before Martin's arrival in 1833. English guitars were being produced, especially in Moravian communities, but these were cittern-like instruments, usually with ten steel strings

See page 35 for
Profile 4
Scherr Patented
Harp Guitar,
c. 1834–1838

See page 15 for
Profile 2
Johann Georg
Stauffer, c. 1830

See page 37 for
Profile 5
C. F. Martin,
c. 1834

See page 39 for
Profile 6
C. F. Martin,
c. 1834–1835

played with a plectrum, and, both in tone and overall shape, they had little in common with the guitars Martin was producing within a few months of his arrival in New York. Unfortunately, no photos of New World guitarists from this period have been discovered, and so there is no record of what they were playing. Even the earliest daguerreotypes, from more than a decade later, almost always show musicians holding guitars that are obviously of European manufacture, usually instruments of far lower quality than the Martin-built guitars illustrated in this book.[7]

There was, however, one patent granted in 1831 for a guitar innovation, the earliest patent in the United States for a plucked instrument,[8] to Emilius Nicolai Scherr, who had arrived in America from Copenhagen at the age of twenty-eight on October 17, 1822.[9] First listed in the Philadelphia directory in 1825 as a pianoforte and organ maker, Scherr built a successful manufactory in Philadelphia producing keyboard instruments.

Scherr's patented Harp-Guitar bears no resemblance to later harp guitars, whose name came from the use of additional, unfretted strings. (See Profile 4). Instead, his innovation was a six-string guitar with an extended body, which, according to Scherr's patent, "created an instrument of an overall length of four feet ten inches, about one and a half feet longer than conventional guitars at the time." The lower end of the elongated body rested on the floor in a fashion similar to a harp (thus the name Harp-Guitar). This precluded the need for the musician to lean the guitar on an upper leg or against the body, which, according to Scherr, muffled the sound. In addition, the left hand was free from the need to support the weight of the neck. As the patent stated: "In reality, the improvement is, that the Harp-Guitar is played resting on the ground." Scherr entered the Harp-Guitar in at least one trade fair in 1832, and, on June 14, 1833—four months before C. F. Martin's arrival in New York—the *New York Evening Post* announced an upcoming program at Niblo's Garden featuring a Scherr Harp-Guitar.

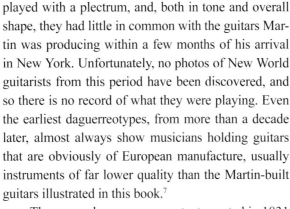

Soirree Musical
Mr. Vincent Schmid, member of the Conservatories of Paris and Vienna, and Mr. Edw. Fehrman.[10] The solos by Mr. V. Schmidt, will be performed on the Harp Guitar, a new invention by Mr. E. Scherr, of Philadelphia, adding infinitely to the tone of this favorite instrument.

Of the eight extant Scherr Harp-Guitars, the three earliest examples are decorated in the Federal style, similar to that found on contemporary high-style furniture and keyboard instrument cases. The later five examples, including that shown in Profile 4, are in the decorative style of Austro-German guitars, with an ebonized neck, cone-shaped heel, and scroll headstock with in-line machine tuners, as well as a spruce top, figured maple sides and back, and herringbone marquetry around the perimeter of the top. We cannot be certain whether the Scherr Harp-Guitar shown here was constructed before or after Martin landed in New York. Nevertheless, this instrument exemplifies the Austro-German style of construction, decoration, and quality of workmanship that Scherr would have had the opportunity to absorb during his apprenticeship in Germany.[11]

C. F. Martin wasted little time getting down to business once in New York. He opened his first shop, at 196 Hudson Street, less than six months after landing, and since he recorded a guitar sale a few weeks later, he was probably building guitars in an earlier rented or shared location before that date. The first sale with a description was for a "No 40 with box to Atwell," almost certainly a reference to Joseph Atwill, who opened a music store on Broadway in 1834 and would become one of Martin's earliest, and largest, New York accounts over the next few years[12] (the "No 40" was the retail price, for which Martin was paid $27). By November of 1834, Martin had made and sold at least another two-dozen guitars, probably with the help of Louis Schmidt. Besides Schmidt, there was another employee who lived in the Martin household, Jacob Hartman, charged with handling business

affairs and the wide range of sales, both wholesale and retail, from the 196 Hudson Street address. Since all correspondence to Martin or his wife during this period was addressed to 196 Hudson, and expenses for no other location appear in the records until years later, it is safe to assume that the Martin family, plus Schmidt and Hartman, lived upstairs, while the business occupied the ground floor.

During the mid 1830s, both the design and construction of Martin's guitars show the strong influence of the workshop of Johann Georg Stauffer, and his son Johann Anton, in Vienna. Not many of these earliest Martins have survived, however; fewer than fifteen Martin guitars that are entirely in the Austro-German style developed by Stauffer have been identified. Virtually all of these Austro-German style Martins have paper labels affixed to the inside of the back, where they can be viewed through the soundhole. Within a relatively brief period, from 1834 through 1840, Martin used eight different paper label designs, which Martin researcher Greig Hutton has placed in their most likely chronological order. This—along with other construction and decorative features—has enabled these early, labeled guitars to be roughly dated.[13] (See page 57 for Martin paper labels.)

The guitar shown in Profile 5 is the only known example with the earliest label design and is believed to be the oldest Martin guitar to have surfaced to date.[14] Entirely in the tradition of Stauffer's Legnani Model, (Profiles 1 and 2) it has a small body with a curved back and upper and lower bouts of almost equal dimensions. Other features identified with the earlier Stauffer-influenced guitars include:

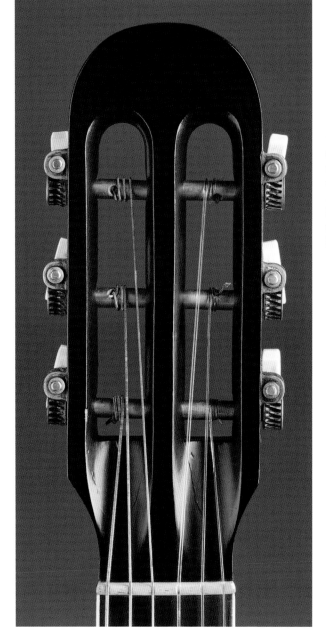

Figure 3-2. *Above left to right,* details of earliest extant guitar by C. F. Martin, c.1834 (Profile 5). Key for adjusting neck angle; label; bridge; rosette.

Figure 3-3. *Left,* headstock, C. F. Martin c. 1834-1835. (See Profile 6). Recent research in the Martin Archives indicates that even from his earliest days in New York, Martin offered both slotted headstocks, like this one, and the more commonly found curved Stauffer-style headstock with tuners all on one side.

Figure 3-4. *Above top*, label, C. F. Martin, c. 1834-1835. (See Profile 6.) Note that by the time this label was printed, Martin had anglicized his name from Friedrich to Frederick.

Figure 3-5. *Above*, label, Martin & Schatz, c. 1835–1837. (See Profile 7.)

See page 41 for Profile 7 Martin and Schatz, c. 1835–1837

- A screw mechanism set into the heel of the neck that permits instant adjustment of the neck angle with a key.
- A fingerboard separate from, and raised above, the soundboard of the guitar to allow adjustment of the entire neck and twenty-one-fret fingerboard as a unit, increasing the guitar's playable range.
- Single-sided machine tuners, which Martin imported from Europe and identified in his journals as "Vienna machines," "Vienna screw," or "one side screw."

The scroll-shaped headstock and the single-piece pin bridge of simple moustache outline are likewise similar to features found on Stauffer's guitars. Martin called this bridge design "steg mit herzchen"—literally, "bridge with little hearts."

The rosette consists of a series of pearl trefoils embedded in black mastic, a common pattern and technique used on Martin's earliest instruments. Like Stauffer's guitars and other very early examples by Martin, this guitar has three lateral braces supporting both the top and the laminated back. The most striking visual feature of this guitar, seen only from the back, is the pattern of alternating ivory and ebony stripes that extends the entire length of the neck, a unique decorative feature for Martin, but one that could be found on Viennese guitars contemporary to Stauffer and on earlier guitars by Fabricatore and other Italian guitarmakers.

Until recently, there was wide agreement that all of Martin's earliest guitars featured the Stauffer-like scroll headstock and "Vienna machines" tuners, but more careful reading of the ledgers and correspondence from this period indicates that a slotted headstock with mechanical tuners on both sides was sometimes requested. The rest of this guitar (Profile 6), including its internal construction, is virtually identical to the example shown in Profile 5, but the label shows that Martin had decided to state his earlier Viennese training with Stauffer where it couldn't be missed. This heavy emphasis on his connection to Stauffer, missing from the earlier label, suggests that Martin had perhaps found a need to establish credibility to bolster sales of what were, even then, quite expensive instruments. However, both the overall shape of the headstock and the subtly curved inner surfaces of the slots are more indicative of the influence that Vogtland guitars, perhaps including those made by Martin's own father, had on his work.

Henry Schatz appears only rarely in Martin's ledgers covering 1834, but, by 1835, he and Martin had formed a partnership and the paper label, shown in the instrument in Profile 7, announces that both Martin and Schatz were "From VIENNA, pupils of the celebrated STAUFFER." There is no surviving record of the terms of this partnership, but considering the long and close connection between Martin and his younger compatriot, perhaps none was needed.

It is not clear that Schatz ever lived in New York, as has been previously assumed, but by 1836, he had purchased land in Millgrove, Pennsylvania.[15] In that year, there are entries in Martin's journals regarding shipments from Schatz of four or more guitars and cases at a time, but sometimes such instruments would be incomplete, suggesting that Martin, or perhaps Schmidt, would finish what Schatz had begun. Schatz often received guitar-making supplies and other goods in trade for his work.[16] Shipments from T. F. Merz in Markneukirchen, Martin's primary supplier of wholesale European goods during this period, were addressed to "Martin & Schatz," indicating that their partnership was recognized among both the American and Vogtland instrument-making communities.

One of Martin's first dealers outside New York City, J. G. Miller in Philadelphia, was shipped several guitars in early March of 1835, and two weeks later, Miller was advertising "Martin & Schatz Guitars" in that city's *National Gazette*. There is no way of knowing if the guitar shown in Profile 7, another example of Martin's New World version of Stauffer's Legnani model, was sold in Philadelphia or New York. However, since its Martin & Schatz label was used for only a short period of time, from 1835 to 1836 or 1837, this guitar is probably a good example of the type of "fashionable instruments" Miller was inviting potential customers to "call and examine for themselves" in early 1835.

Continued on page 42

Figure 3-6. Emilius N. Scherr's patent harp guitar. Lithograph by Charles Fenderich, Philadelphia, Pennsylvania. Undated.

Of the eight extant examples of Scherr's patented instrument, the later five are so similar in details and quality of workmanship to the early guitars of Martin and Schatz, both of whom were in nearby Nazareth, that it is not unreasonable to speculate whether either guitar maker may have been contracted to aid in their construction.

This unusual-looking instrument is another example of the high quality woodworking typical of the German-American community around Philadelphia, but it also hints at the dilemma that plagued musicians playing the gut-string guitar for the next century and beyond. Scherr's patented innovation precluded the need for the musician to lean the guitar against the body, which, according to Scherr, muffled the sound. While the elegant, more harp-like design sacrificed the typical guitar's portability, Scherr was perhaps betting that guitarists would gladly carry a more cumbersome case if it held a guitar that offered more volume.

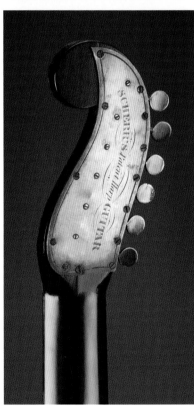

Top, Emilius Nicolai Scherr, who emigrated from Copenhagen to Philadelphia in 1822, was first listed in the Philadelphia directory in 1825 as a pianoforte and organ maker. Before coming to the United States, Scherr had trained in Linz, Germany (which was then Prussia).

Bottom, Scherr's ebonized neck with cone-shaped heel and in-line machine tuners is remarkably similar to that of Martin, Schatz, and other guitar makers on both sides of the Atlantic.

DIMENSIONS

TOTAL LENGTH	59.75"	1518 MM
BODY LENGTH	40.25"	1022 MM

WIDTH

UPPER BOUT	13.13"	333 MM
WAIST	NA	NA
LOWER BOUT	NA	NA

DEPTH

NECK	3.13"	79 MM
WAIST	3.44"	87 MM
END	2.25"	57 MM

NUT WIDTH	1.87"	48 MM
SCALE	25.44"	646 MM
SOUNDHOLE	3.25"	83 MM

BRACING CONFIGURATION

RELATIVE SIZE

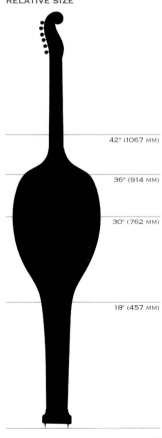

42" (1067 MM)

36" (914 MM)

30" (762 MM)

18" (457 MM)

The alternating ivory and ebony stripes in the neck of this guitar are rarely seen in instruments made in North America, but such decoration has a long tradition in earlier European instruments, many of them predating the six-string version of the guitar.

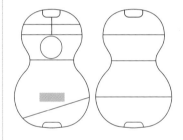

Martin opened his first shop at 196 Hudson Street just six months after his arrival in New York. Research indicates that the label was the first of the many different paper labels used in early Martin guitars.

This is the earliest known Martin guitar, and it displays many features found in Johann Georg Stauffer's Legnani model. These include a fingerboard clear of the guitar's top and a key-operated mechanical adjustment of the angle of the neck, which facilitated easy changes in the height of the strings. The neck, body shape, and interior construction are all typical of guitars made in Austria and Germany during the first half of the nineteenth century.

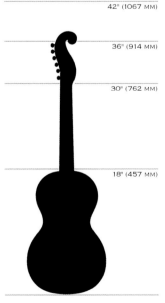

While this style of "moustache" bridge, which Martin called a "bridge with little hearts," was one of the typically European features retained on his early guitars, the decorative hearts at either end were more commonly found on guitars from Martin's homeland in Saxony rather than Vienna, the home of Stauffer, his mentor.

DIMENSIONS

TOTAL LENGTH	37.44"	951 MM
BODY LENGTH	17.25"	438 MM

WIDTH

UPPER BOUT	9.21"	234 MM
WAIST	6.93"	176 MM
LOWER BOUT	11.61"	295 MM

DEPTH

NECK	2.68"	68 MM
WAIST	3.23"	82 MM
END	3.31"	84 MM

NUT WIDTH	1.75"	44 MM
SCALE	23.78"	604 MM
SOUND HOLE	3.15"	80 MM

BRACING CONFIGURATION

RELATIVE SIZE

42" (1067 MM)

36" (914 MM)

30" (762 MM)

18" (457 MM)

Although the long scroll headstock is considered the signature of Martin's early New York guitars, we now know that slotted headstocks like this one, as well as simple headstocks with friction peg tuners, also were constructed. This design, with curved inner faces of the slots, is found on early nineteenth century guitars made in Saxony, in and around Martin's hometown of Markneukirchen. The machine tuners on this guitar were produced by James Ashborn, who manufactured his own machines in Connecticut, whereas Martin imported tuners from Germany. The Ashborn tuners no doubt replaced a set of German tuners, which were not as well made as Ashborn's.

This guitar was made shortly after Martin's arrival in New York, just months after the example shown in Profile 5, and it shares the same construction and dimensions of that slightly earlier model. Until recently, it was presumed that the headstock shown here was a later replacement for the usual "Stauffer style" scroll headstock with in-line tuners. However, there are references in Martin's earliest journals to guitars with machine tuners on both sides of the headstock, and a second early example with a similar neck has been identified.

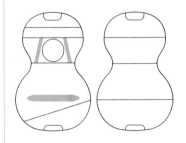

This is apparently the second label Martin used, and differs from the example seen in the slightly earlier guitar (Profile 5) only in the additional promotional text, "From Vienna, pupil of the celebrated STAUFFER." Both of these labels, as well as later labels used by Martin, state that he manufactured violins and guitars. However, while early Martin ledgers record many sales of violins, there is no other evidence that he ever made anything other than guitars.

DIMENSIONS

TOTAL LENGTH	35.88"	911 MM
BODY LENGTH	17.25"	438 MM

WIDTH

UPPER BOUT	9.16"	233 MM
WAIST	6.81"	173 MM
LOWER BOUT	11.43"	291 MM

DEPTH

NECK	2.50"	64 MM
WAIST	3.17"	80.6 MM
END	3.29"	83.7 MM

NUT WIDTH	1.75"	44 MM
SCALE	23.88"	606 MM
SOUND HOLE	3.15"	80 MM

BRACING CONFIGURATION

RELATIVE SIZE

42" (1067 MM)

36" (914 MM)

30" (762 MM)

18" (457 MM)

In both construction and decoration, this guitar is very much in the style of Johann Georg Stauffer, and the label visible through the sound-hole emphasizes that its builders are both "from VIENNA, Pupils of the celebrated STAUFFER." In just a few years, however, both Martin & Schatz would be building very different guitars that showed the influence of Spanish guitar makers.

This label, which was first used around 1835, marks the initial appearance of Henry Schatz's name in Martin guitars. Schatz emigrated from Markneukirchen to the United States in 1830, and in addition to influencing Martin to leave Saxony, he apparently also had a role in leading the Martin family to Pennsylvania. Another slightly different Martin & Schatz label was used in guitars constructed in the early 1840s.

This is one of nineteen guitars described in Martin ledgers as being made with "zebrawood" between 1836 and 1840, and although similar wood was used after that date the records have not survived. Zebrawood is one of several names for goncalo alves, a highly figured reddish brown species from South America that today would probably be misidentified as Hawaiian koa. The Martin company later made much use of koa, which was not yet being imported from Hawaii when this guitar was constructed.

DIMENSIONS

TOTAL LENGTH	36.05"	916 MM
BODY LENGTH	17.17"	436 MM

WIDTH

UPPER BOUT	9.13"	232 MM
WAIST	6.89"	175 MM
LOWER BOUT	11.57"	294 MM

DEPTH

NECK	2.60"	66 MM
WAIST	3.15"	80 MM
END	3.25"	83 MM

NUT WIDTH	1.75"	44 MM
SCALE	24.13"	613 MM
SOUND HOLE	3.11"	79 MM

BRACING CONFIGURATION

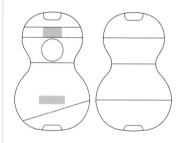

RELATIVE SIZE

42" (1067 MM)

36" (914 MM)

30" (762 MM)

18" (457 MM)

See page 47 for
Profile 8
C. F. Martin,
c. 1837

Figure 3-10. *The Times.* Lithograph by Edward Williams Clay, printed and published by H. R. Robinson, New York, July 1837. This caricature of the Five Points neighborhood in lower Manhattan offers detailed commentary on the depressed state of the American economy, particularly in New York, during the financial panic of 1837. The hat and spectacles floating in the sky represent former president Andrew Jackson, whose monetary policies many blamed for the panic.

Martin's ledgers from this period indicate that 196 Hudson Street was a busy location, and guitars were only a part of a complex web of music-related commerce. The number of shipments from Markneukirchen steadily increased, but Martin also purchased wholesale goods from domestic suppliers and stocked sheet music for a wide range of musical instruments besides guitar. He also took in instrument repairs, rehaired violin bows, and rented instruments either by the month or, in some cases, for just a few days. Jacob Hartman apparently did the repairs of brass instruments, and Schmidt, or perhaps Martin himself, repaired both violins and guitars. Henry Schatz continued to send Martin guitars, but the number of instruments sold in a similar price range suggests that Schatz could not have been responsible

for all of Martin's guitar production during this period.[17] By mid 1837, Henry Schatz had disappeared from Martin records. It is unclear why, but a notation in the ledgers regarding postage for a June 1838 letter sent to "Hein. Aug. Schatz" in Dresden hints that he may have made an extended trip back to Saxony.[18]

Schatz may also have been finding a market for his own guitars by this time, and it should not be assumed that all of his work was confined to instruments made in collaboration with Martin. Guitars very much in the same Austro-German style as late-1830s Martins, but with labels reading "Made by Heinrich Schatz, Nazareth, PA" have recently come to light, adding yet another layer to what was probably an unrestricted partnership between the two Markneukirchen expatriots.

By early 1837, Martin's business had apparently outgrown the Hudson Street storefront, prompting him to open a second location at 212 Fulton Street. By this time, Charles Bruno, also from Saxony and a recent immigrant to the U.S., was Martin's bookkeeper and in charge of the Fulton Street store.[19] Martin's expansion to a second location was poorly timed, through no fault of his own, as the Panic of 1837 hit New York City on May 10 and quickly caused a decrease in sales. Martin's ledgers show expenses for the purchase of "bank note lists," which were notices of which banks had failed, making their notes worthless (banks went so far as to accept payment only in gold or silver coinage). The last sale recorded for 196 Hudson St. is on June 9, 1837, but Martin apparently continued to live and maintain a workshop at that address.

The Panic of 1837 was caused in part by rampant speculation and inflation caused by the widespread introduction of paper currency by the banks. As in other periods preceding such dramatic corrections, there was a great deal of money floating around New York before the panic set in, much of it spent on luxury goods. Of course, it may be mere coincidence that the guitar shown in Profile 8, the most opulent example of a Martin made in the Austro-German style, was constructed just months before the Panic of 1837's corrections put a damper on most New Yorkers' ability to buy necessities, let alone such a luxurious instrument.

Yet, we can be sure this guitar was made before Martin began to do business from 212 Fulton Street, and, since the label makes no mention of Henry Schatz, he probably did not participate in its construction. Ivory fingerboards were an expensive option obvious to all, and one that a number of Martin's more wealthy customers requested over his first twenty-five years of guitar making in the U.S. This is the only example known that has the entire neck made of ivory, and the guitar also has the more typical ivory binding on the body edges, as well as an ivory bridge. By early 1837, Martin was already

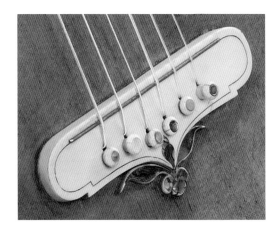

Left, top to bottom:
Figure 3-11. Bridge, C. F. Martin, c. 1837. (See Profile 8.)

Figure 3-12. Label, C. F. Martin, c. 1837. (See Profile 9.)

Figure 3-13. Label, Martin & Bruno, c. 1838. (See Profile 11.)

Figure 3-14. Label, Henry Schatz Terz, c. 1836–1838. (See Profile 12.)

See page 49 for Profile 9
C. F. Martin, c. 1837

See page 51 for Profile 10
C. F. Martin, c. 1837–1839

See page 53 for
Profile 11
Martin & Bruno,
c. 1838

See page 55 for
Profile 12
Henry Schatz Terz,
c. 1836–1838

moving beyond strict copies of Stauffer models, however, and the colorful (some might say gaudy) alternating dark and light half circles of pearl around the edge of the soundboard keep up the theme of extravagance signaled by the gleaming ivory neck. The earlier "steg mit herzchen" bridge has also been abandoned in favor of a larger shield-shaped bridge with a jewelry-like pearl pendant. This same bridge design is found on the plainer Schatz guitar with Nazareth label, which is more difficult to date but is probably from the same period (See Profile 12).

The back and sides of the guitar shown in Profile 8 are Brazilian rosewood, a more expensive option than maple. The guitar shown in Profile 9, which also has a rosewood back and sides bordered in herringbone purfling, has a virtually identical bridge and soundboard decorations, but a more typical black-stained wood neck supporting its ivory fingerboard. Judging by the handwritten address on its label, it is not much later than the example with the ivory neck, as the 196 Hudson Street location was still open. There are a few other surviving Martin guitars with nearly identical pearl and ivory appointments, but all remnants of this opulent style were abandoned almost as quickly as they had appeared, much like the fortunes of many New Yorkers of the same period.

The Panic of 1837 was by no means restricted to that year alone, suppressing commerce of all kinds and resulting in a dire business climate that probably contributed to the dramatic changes that were soon to follow for Martin. The year 1838 was a turning point in several ways and marked the beginning of his retreat from New York City. On May 1, Martin and his bookkeeper entered into a formal partnership as Martin & Bruno, and a new label was printed for guitars made after that date. The Martin & Bruno guitar shown in Profile 11 appears at first glance to be very much in the Austro-German style, but a closer look reveals that Martin was beginning to feel the influence of guitar makers far from Vienna. Although the body shape is only slightly altered, the fan-pattern top bracing is decidedly unlike that found in any of

Martin's earlier instruments and suggests that he had examined, or perhaps even repaired, guitars made in Spain.

Martin's life was also changing. Payments sent by Bruno in June to Mrs. Martin in Nazareth, Pennsylvania, with other payments to follow, suggest that the Martin family had already moved to the area that became their new home. That same summer, Louis Schmidt left Martin's employ, setting up his own musical instrument business on Chatham Street in New York, around the same time that any mention of expenses related to 196 Hudson Street disappear from surviving records. Perhaps because of moribund sales of both guitars and musical goods in general, the Martin & Bruno partnership ended about six months after it had begun, although Bruno continued to work for Martin and kept his books until the end of the year.[20] Martin was still taking orders for guitars and filling them efficiently, so perhaps there was a workshop at 212 Fulton Street, but it is not yet established where he constructed the last of the guitars with this label.

Martin probably expected Charles Bruno to continue the wholesale distribution and retail sales of musical merchandise that had begun in 1834, as well as serving as the New York outlet for Martin's guitars after he joined his family in Pennsylvania. The failure of this partnership is probably what led Martin to give up the wholesale and retail trade. He sold his entire inventory to Ludecus & Wolter in mid May 1839. Martin's substantial inventory included over 150 flutes and more than 100 violins, along with large numbers of brass and woodwind instruments and vast quantities of parts for instrument repair. The goods Martin had amassed were not all that Ludecus & Wolter acquired; from that point on, shipments of goods from T. F. Merz in Markneukirchen were addressed to them, indicating that they had inherited Martin's account with his primary supplier as well as his inventory. Although the price of this transaction was over $2500, it apparently did little more than relieve Martin of a debt. The terms of the sale directed payments, and any interest, to Merz in Prussian currency.

Once relieved of what had remained of his music business, Martin joined his family in or near Nazareth, and, in December, purchased eight acres outside town in Bushkill Township, an area known as Cherry Hill. The Martin's property was on a main road, and the fact that it was also one of the stagecoach routes between Philadelphia and New York was certainly not a coincidence. Martin was free to pursue guitar making with fewer distractions, and, although now at a considerable distance from New York, both he and his guitars would make that journey often. Although records for the following decade are missing, the same connections that had sustained him for the last several years would be ones he would continue to rely upon. Names like Beitel, Hartmann, Keller, Schatz, Schuster, Voigt, and Zoebisch appear often in surviving Martin records of the 1800s, and these families communicated by letter, loaned money to each other, and intermarried. Although Martin obviously felt most comfortable doing business with his Vogtland countrymen, there were highly trusted exceptions such as John Coupa and later, Justin Holland, among others.[21] Letters in the Martin Archives indicate that even years after C. F. Martin's death, the guitar company bearing his name would continue to seek experienced woodworkers willing to leave the Vogtland's instrument trade for better opportunities in its Pennsylvania factory.

In ledgers covering 1837, toward the end of Martin's New York period, the word *Spanish* begins to appear in descriptions of his guitars, although it is unclear what that word meant in these early notations. In June of that year, a guitar made by Martin was described as having a "Spanish bridge," and, in August, a guitar sold to John Coupa was noted as having a "Spanish bridge & neck." A "Spanish guitar" was sold in late December, and, by March of 1838, John Coupa's name begins to appear more often, and all his purchases from that date on are described as "Spanish" guitars or models. Although Ludecus & Wolter were assigned as Martin's agents in New York after the dissolution of the Martin & Bruno partnership, that agreement was also short-lived, and John Coupa filled the role instead. Coupa was certainly not a Vogtlander, and apparently had little interest in the time-honored Austro-German style of guitar Martin had been offering, but he proved to be a trusted friend and loyal business partner.[22] Henry Schatz and the comfortable familiarity of a Moravian community in rural Pennsylvania may have led Martin and his family out of New York, but John Coupa would prove to be an equally profound and even more long-lasting influence on Martin's guitars. ★

Figure 3-15. C. F. Martin c.1834 (Profile 5). A detail of the earliest known Martin guitar, showing its alternating ivory- and ebony-striped neck, the keyed mechanism that allowed the angle of the neck to be adjusted, and Martin's stamp. This "New York" stamp would continue to be used on the exterior of Martin's guitars until 1898, although on most later examples with cedar necks it was instead placed on the back of the headstock. Only an interior stamp would be changed in 1867 to read "C. F. Martin & Co."

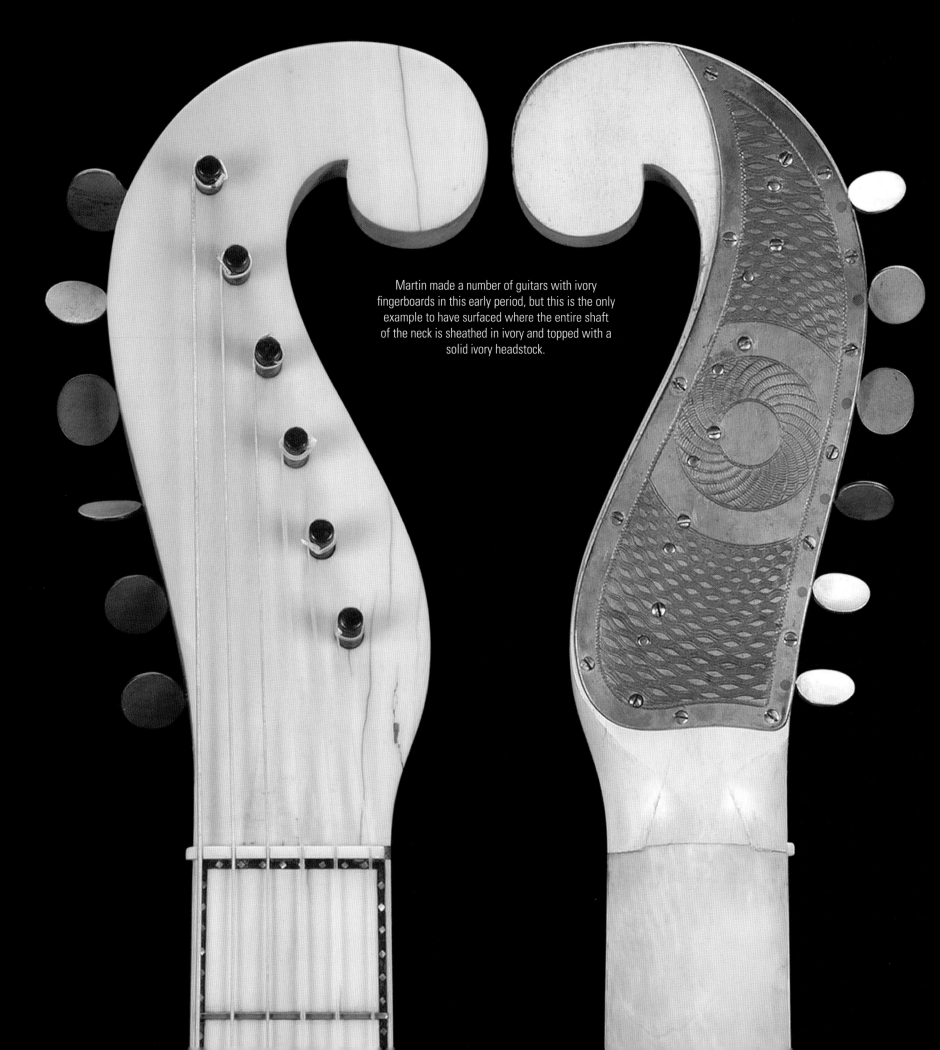

Martin made a number of guitars with ivory fingerboards in this early period, but this is the only example to have surfaced where the entire shaft of the neck is sheathed in ivory and topped with a solid ivory headstock.

From the first months after his arrival in New York, Martin made highly appointed instruments with expensive materials and decoration. The surviving records and correspondence in the Martin Archives make it clear that he did not build opulent guitars like this one on speculation, but that they were the result of special orders from wealthy clients requesting something that would be perceived as luxurious at first glance.

The colorful border around the top of this guitar, made up of half circles of alternating abalone and white mother-of-pearl, is found on several other surviving Martins from the 1830s. A button vendor near Martin's shop on Hudson Street may have been the source of the pearl discs.

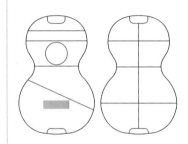

This is the first of only a few of Martin's earliest guitars to display a number on the label. The several references to numbers in surviving ledgers of the period suggest that these were inventory numbers, not actual serial numbers.

SERIAL NUMBER 1114

DIMENSIONS

TOTAL LENGTH	36.63"	930MM
BODY LENGTH	17.29"	437MM

WIDTH

UPPER BOUT	9.13"	232MM
WAIST	6.89"	175MM
LOWER BOUT	11.69"	297MM

DEPTH

NECK	2.60"	66MM
WAIST	3.35"	85MM
END	3.27"	83MM

NUT WIDTH	1.87"	48MM
SCALE	23.94"	608MM
SOUND HOLE	3.13"	79MM

BRACING CONFIGURATION

RELATIVE SIZE

42" (1067 MM)
36" (914 MM)
30" (762 MM)
18" (457 MM)

Martin was committed to a consistently high quality of construction for all of his guitars. He used the highest-grade materials on deluxe guitars like this one, including South American rosewood for the sides and back, and lavished both subtle and extravagant details on every edge and surface. Nevertheless, the interiors of instruments that cost far less were still given the same labor-intensive structure and design.

This is Martin's fifth style of paper label since his arrival in New York, and the first to mention the address of his second shop at 212 Fulton Street. The original shop at 196 Hudson Street was apparently still open, since that address was added to the lower right portion by hand.

While remarkably similar to the ivory-necked example in Profile 8, this slightly later guitar shows a top bracing pattern that strays from the Austro-German style, a harbinger of Martin's eventual adoption of Spanish fan bracing just a few years later.

The shield-shaped bridge was a short-lived design, apparently only lasting from 1836-37 until about 1840. The abalone and ivory decoration at the bottom of the bridge, however, was continued as an optional adornment on the rectangular bridge design that followed this one.

SERIAL NUMBER 1168

DIMENSIONS

TOTAL LENGTH	36.63"	930 MM
BODY LENGTH	17.13"	436 MM

WIDTH

UPPER BOUT	9.13"	232 MM
WAIST	6.85"	174 MM
LOWER BOUT	11.57"	294 MM

DEPTH

NECK	2.62"	67 MM
WAIST	3.35"	85 MM
END	3.27"	83 MM

NUT WIDTH	1.68"	43 MM
SCALE	24.21"	615 MM
SOUND HOLE	3.13"	79MM

BRACING CONFIGURATION

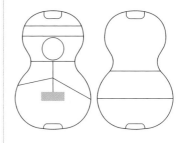

RELATIVE SIZE

42" (1067 MM)

36" (914 MM)

30" (762 MM)

18" (457 MM)

There is no ivory binding or decoration on this guitar and only a thin line of simple marquetry bordering the top, but the soundhole rosette and bridge ornament are identical to those found on far more costly Martin guitars from the same period.

While the previous profile shows a highly ornamented model, this example, which shares the same label from Martin's last years in New York, is far more representative of guitars that were still high grade and quite expensive. With the exception of the bridge, the construction of this guitar is nearly identical to earlier Martin instruments and shows very little variation from the Austro-German style.

SERIAL NUMBER 1188

DIMENSIONS

TOTAL LENGTH	36.75"	933 MM
BODY LENGTH	17.19"	437 MM

WIDTH

UPPER BOUT	9.13"	232 MM
WAIST	6.94"	176 MM
LOWER BOUT	11.69"	297 MM

DEPTH

NECK	2.62"	67 MM
WAIST	3.25"	83 MM
END	3.31"	84 MM

NUT WIDTH	1.81"	46 MM
SCALE	23.75"	603 MM
SOUNDHOLE	3.13"	79 MM

BRACING CONFIGURATION

RELATIVE SIZE

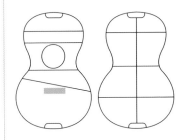

42" (1067 MM)

36" (914 MM)

30" (762 MM)

18" (457 MM)

Although this guitar is still firmly in the Austro-German tradition, Martin had moved beyond strict copies of Stauffer models by the time of its creation. The influence of Spanish guitars is primarily seen in the fan-pattern top bracing. There are remarkable similarities between this Martin & Bruno instrument and the Henry Schatz guitar shown in Profile 12.

Unlike his partnership with Henry Schatz, Martin's partnership with Charles Bruno was made to facilitate the sales of guitars, not their construction. The business union of Martin & Bruno was announced May 1838, but apparently ended late in the same year, so it is not surprising that only a few guitars with this label have surfaced.

The name Charles Bruno looms large in the history of early Martin guitars. Bruno had been Martin's bookkeeper for two years before the partnership indicated by the label in this guitar began, and many of the meticulous surviving expense records from the mid-to-late 1830s are in his hand. Those records suggest that the Panic of 1837 continued to stifle business of all kinds, especially in New York, and that sales of high-grade guitars such as this one were few.

DIMENSIONS

TOTAL LENGTH	36.38"	924 MM
BODY LENGTH	17.13"	435 MM

WIDTH

UPPER BOUT	9.06"	230 MM
WAIST	6.75"	171 MM
LOWER BOUT	11.19"	284 MM

DEPTH

NECK	2.63"	67 MM
WAIST	3.19"	81 MM
END	3.25"	83 MM

NUT WIDTH	1.75"	44 MM
SCALE	24"	610 MM
SOUNDHOLE	3.13"	79 MM

BRACING CONFIGURATION

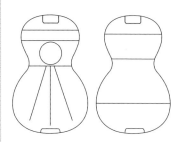

RELATIVE SIZE

42" (1067 MM)

36" (914 MM)

30" (762 MM)

18" (457 MM)

All the appointments found on this guitar can also be seen on various Martin-branded instruments from the same period. The soundhole rosette and shield-shaped bridge are the most obvious connection to Martin instruments, but even the delicate marquetry bordering the top is also a pattern shared by both Martin and Schatz.

Even the most knowledgeable connoisseur of early American guitars could be forgiven for mistaking this instrument for a Martin made in the mid-to-late 1830s. After all, Schatz was involved in building nearly identical guitars bearing Martin & Schatz labels, and both guitar makers emigrated from Markneukirchen, where they were steeped in the Austro-German tradition.

Henry Schatz settled near Nazareth well before Martin, possibly as early as 1830, upon his arrival in the United States from Saxony. We do not know if the Martins had close friends in the Nazareth area other than the Schatz family. However, we do know that as early as 1838, Martin's partner and bookkeeper, Charles Bruno, was sending money to Otillia Martin in Nazareth. She and the children were there well before Martin purchased the Cherry Hill property just outside the town that would become their first home and guitar-building workshop in Pennsylvania.

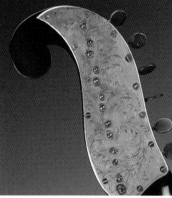

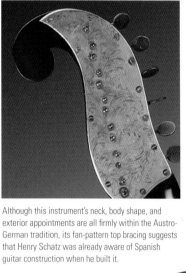

Although this instrument's neck, body shape, and exterior appointments are all firmly within the Austro-German tradition, its fan-pattern top bracing suggests that Henry Schatz was already aware of Spanish guitar construction when he built it.

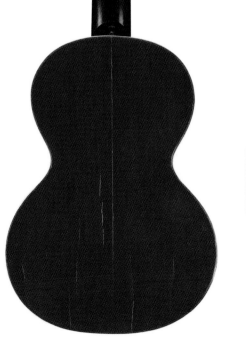

DIMENSIONS

TOTAL LENGTH	33.50"	851 MM
BODY LENGTH	15.44"	392 MM

WIDTH

UPPER BOUT	8.88"	225 MM
WAIST	6.56"	167 MM
LOWER BOUT	11.31"	287 MM

DEPTH

NECK	2.63"	67 MM
WAIST	3.19"	81 MM
END	3.38"	86 MM

NUT WIDTH	1.88"	48 MM
SCALE	22"	559 MM
SOUNDHOLE	2.88"	73 MM

BRACING CONFIGURATION

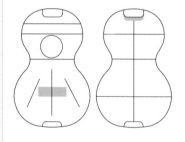

RELATIVE SIZE

42" (1067 MM)

36" (914 MM)

30" (762 MM)

18" (457 MM)

C. F. MARTIN,

MANUFACTURER OF

IMPORTER OF

GUITARS & VIOLINS

MUSICAL INSTRUMENTS

WHOLESALE & RETAIL.

C. F. Martin affixed paper labels in his guitars from the time of his arrival in New York in 1833 until the death of John Coupa in 1850. Since his journal entries are minimal and all his business records are missing for a period of ten years, the range of his label designs—and the addresses on the labels—provide some of the only concrete evidence available to help date Martin's early instruments.

The fifteen labels illustrated on the facing page include all ten labels found in early extant Martin guitars. Also pictured is the only extant label found in a Schmidt & Maul guitar (Chapter 3, Profile 7), labels affixed to the Cadiz-style guitars featured in Chapter 5, and labels affixed to two of the Stauffer guitars discussed in Chapter 1.

c. 1828–1830 (Profile 1)

c. 1831 (Profile 2)

c. 1834 (Profile 5)

c. 1834 (Profile 6)

c. 1835–1837 (Profile 7)

c. 1837 (Profile 8)

c. 1837–183 (Profile 9)

c. 1838 (Profile 11)

c. 1839–1840 (Profile 15)

c. 1839 (Profile 13)

c. 1853 (Profile 14)

c. 1842 (Profile 25)

c. 1843 (Profile 26)

c. 1840–1850 (Profile 16)

c. 1841–1843 (Profile 21)

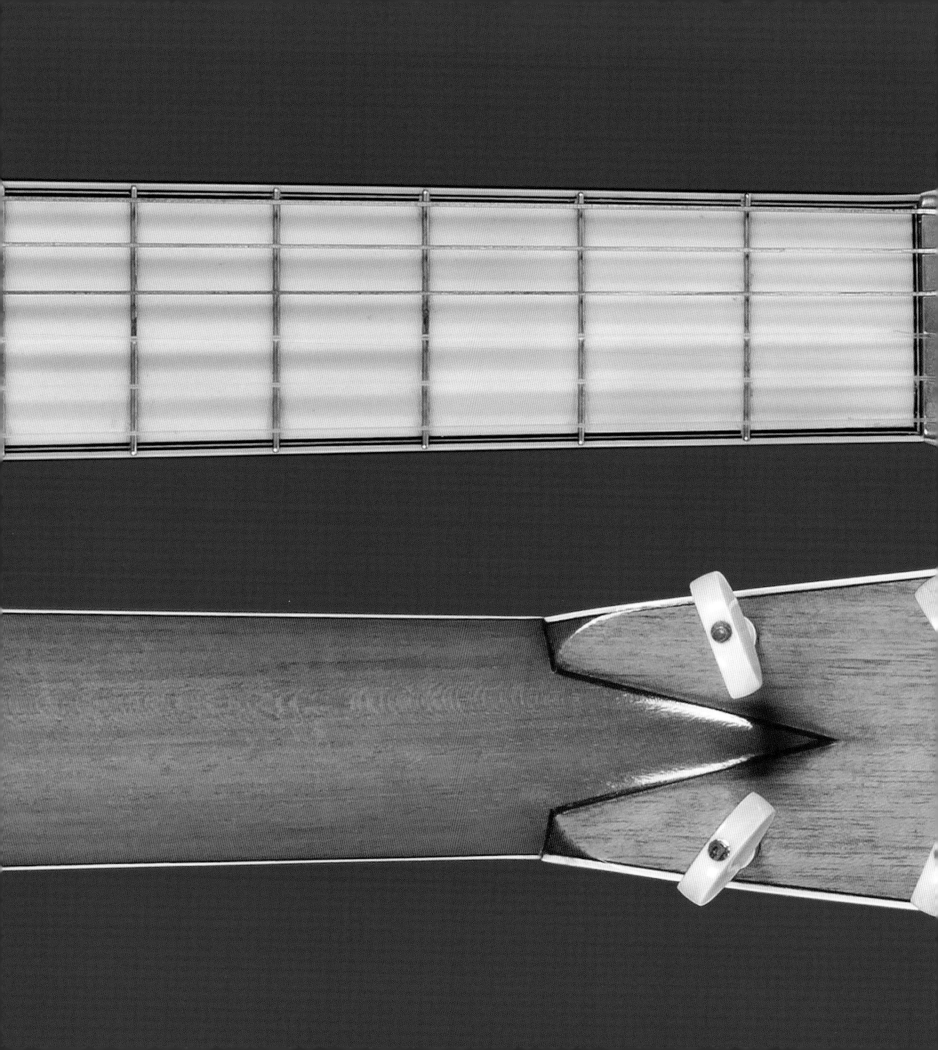

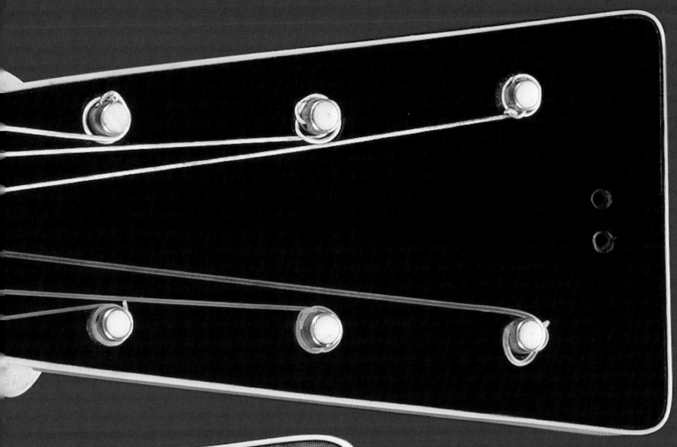
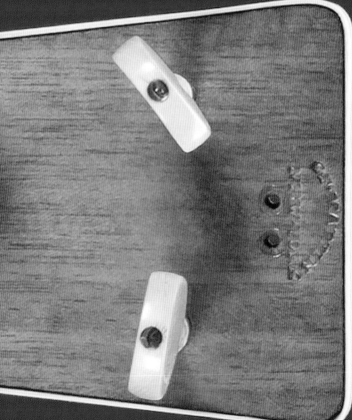

PART II SPANISH STYLE

CHAPTER 4

The Spanish Guitar in the United States Before 1850

DAVID GANSZ

Primarily because of the scarcity of surviving instruments and documents relating to them, little is known about the history of the guitar in America from colonial times through the first quarter of the nineteenth century, either in Anglo-American secular music or on the concert stage. It has been equally unclear how the North American public perceived the guitar and its associations, and how these became modified by and embedded in the emerging American cultural milieu.

By the eighteenth century, the guitar already had become "romantically associated with Utopian ideals, languor and romance, an escape from the ordinary world. These qualities are part of a certain kind of poetry, and the guitar often belongs to that area of the imagination in much of its history and repertory."[1] These qualities would be greatly enhanced as the American imagination came to associate the guitar more closely with things Spanish as the nineteenth century got underway.

The American colonists had inherited their English ancestors' Elizabethan prejudices against Spain, which were based on religious and political grounds and further fueled by such English/Spanish skirmishes as the War of Jenkins's Ear (1739–1743). This generationally entrenched English Hispanophobia culminated in the "Black Legend," in which Spain was contrasted with England (and thus America) as decidedly non-industrial and non-democratic; Muslim instead of Christian (and hence linked to the Orient); and, within the bounds of Christianity, seen as perpetrator of the Inquisition. "Hatred of Spain and

of all her ways burned deep and lasting in the minds of the English colonists of the seventeenth century on the Atlantic seaboard."[2] As late as the 1830s, while Anglo immigrants to America were called "American," Spanish immigrants were viewed as "European."

However, concurrent with freedom from England in 1776, a growing American intellectual discovery of and appreciation for Spain and things Spanish began to emerge. During the last quarter of the eighteenth century, libraries in Philadelphia, New York, and Boston—the three primary cultural centers of the early United States—added significant holdings of Spanish literature and history books to their collections.[3] Popular publications also made Americans aware that the guitar played a significant role in the life of Spain and the Spanish character. Thus, for example, as early as 1743, the following characterization appeared in the press (presumably written by someone who had traveled in Spain): "The proud Spaniard pretends to love to Distraction; He puts himself into an Agony, torments himself, and fights by Day in the Churches, and by night under his Mistress's Windows, where he plays upon the Guitar all the Carnival time, and lashes himself devoutly in Lent. 'Tis all for the sake of love."[4] Tellingly, this popular perception of the guitar in Spain was linked with common folk, romance, passion, and religious fervor, and doubtless reflected, at least in part, a swipe at Catholicity spawned by a puritanical Protestant mindset.

The natural home of the guitar at this time
[1750-1770] was in the humbler parts of Spanish

society: the bar, the street, and the barber's shop. In Madrid it was particularly associated with the poor but glamorous figures…who lived on the margins of society, playing, singing, and dancing in the streets at night, and the guitar…[was] an essential accompaniment to drinking sessions, not just for the lower classes but also for dissident artists and intellectuals…The instrument's day-to-day existence was inextricably interwoven with…the fandango…strongly disapproved of by polite society…because it supposedly encouraged licentiousness.[5]

While the late eighteenth- and early nineteenth-century American view of the Spanish character vis-à-vis the guitar was being formed by reports from travelers abroad, it was equally informed by travelers reporting from Spanish colonial domains west of the Mississippi River and not yet annexed by the United States. For example, one English traveler reported encountering a group of French and Spanish individuals north of St. Louis in 1806: "Here the guitar resounds, soon after sunset, with the complaints and amorous tales of the village swains; and the same hand which toils all day in the wilderness, strikes the tender notes of love in the evening. Every house has its group, and every group its guitar, fiddler, or singer."[6] Again, the "Spanish" guitar is portrayed as a "folk" instrument utilized to convey romantic love.

Finally, there were travelers' reports of the guitar in the emerging homogeneous culture "south of the border" in Mexico. As early as 1758, inhabitants in Mexico are described "dancing after the Spanish fashion to the music of the guitar."[7] Half a century later, an 1810 account of Mexican women states:

They are fond of music, singing, and dancing; the Spanish guitar, in particular, is universally played by them. Their favourite dances are el fandango, which is as much the rage here as it is in Old Spain; the young, the old, the brisk, the grave, the gay, nay, even the most stupid and dull

people, become all alive, and put themselves into motion the very moment the guitar strikes up and begins to play."[8]

This is the same folk portrayal, with further diminutives describing the passionate, "out of control" effects of the guitar as a potentially evil instrument of women used to arouse all manner of lowlifes.[9]

As the nineteenth century progressed, the popular American perception of the guitar as an Spanish musical instrument associated with ladies and romance won out over the cautionary tales.

For more general use with the voice, I know nothing comparable to the Spanish Guitar…It is in this country little valued, because little known; but as an accompaniment, its elegance and fluency appear to me to be unrivalled. In the moonlight of Spain, where it first floated on my ear, mingled with the fragrance of the orange grove through which it wandered, I could have fancied its low, rich murmuring, the minstrelsy of a spirit of love. The Spaniards, alone, know how to draw forth this hidden soul of harmony! Sometimes I have heard the strings ringing in such whispers of strange concord, that you would have thought they but echoed to the touch of the silken wings of the wild bees as they flew across them. Again the sounds rose like the sweet sighing of the south upon a bank of violets—lingered—faded—died away.[10]

It is important to note that this flowery, romantic description was written by an anonymous Englishman and reprinted in America in 1819. Such language exemplifies the "purple prose" of the romantic and picturesque movement sweeping the collective English imagination, inspired by the "grand tour" of Mediterranean countries. The guitar, with its sublime sounds, is posited in the hands of Spaniards who employ it in accord with love, nature, mysticism, and a spirit of universal harmony outdoors.[11] Also of interest is the fact that the author clearly distinguishes the Spanish guitar as a variety of the instrument little known on his side of the English Channel.

THE "ENGLISH GUITAR" VS. THE SPANISH GUITAR

Several studies have been published pertinent to the development of the gut-strung guitar (i.e. guitars utilizing strings made from dried sheep intestines, sometimes called "catgut") in Europe up through the nineteenth century.[12] While sufficient written documentation exists regarding European instruments, relatively little has been written regarding the presence of these guitars in colonial America.[13] The "English guitar" was by far the most popular guitar-family instrument in England and America from 1750–1810. These instruments were strung with wire (i.e. metal) strings and resembled the pear-shaped cittern more than the gut-strung instruments known in continental Europe.[14] Thus, the earliest eighteenth-century references to guitars in the northeastern United States are almost assuredly either English "guitars" or citterns.[15] In fact, "Citterns outnumber all other types of instruments in the inventories"[16] of colonial Boston households.

The first use of the word Spanish in reference to the guitar appears in print in 1703, when a French music dictionary states, "It is often called Spagnuola, because the instrument came from Spain to Italy, and into the other countries, and because it is very common in Spain."[17] Thereafter, Spanish seems to have been applied by Americans (as it had by the English) to any gut-strung guitar—whether of northern European or Mediterranean construction—and used solely to demarcate it from a wire-strung instrument. "Thus, in a generic sense not unlike that of 'French horn,' the name 'Spanish guitar' has generously embraced all guitars of normal pattern regardless of national origin: London, Paris, Vienna, various Italian cities, all produced such instruments during the guitar's heyday of popularity in the late eighteenth and early nineteenth centuries."[18] One scholar notes that when the terms Italian, French, Spanish, German, and English

Figure 4-1. English guitar (cittern), made by Thompson's in London, c. 1780.

appear in colonial American newspapers identifying different instruments, "In some cases the adjectives could be indicating the music being played rather than the instrument itself, but it seems likely that both types of guitar were current in colonial America, with the cittern-type guitar being the most common."[19] An 1819 government publication clearly indicates, however, that the United States was engaged in the importation of guitars directly from Spain as early as 1816.[20] Perhaps the earliest concert performed on a guitar of truly Spanish origin took place in Salem, Massachusetts, the year before, in 1815.[21]

Considerable confusion exists regarding exactly what gut-strung guitars co-existed beside the more popular English "guitar" and cittern in colonial times. Generally speaking, they were designated by the generic term "Spanish guitar." The earliest known distinction in print dates to 1708: "…do you believe there's no more in this Art than thrumming a Guitar, or scratching a Citern, which you boast you have learn'd without Instruction?"[22] Half a century later, in 1764, a German craftsman, having arrived in America after building musical instruments in London for nine years, advertised his ability to make both "English and Spanish Guittars,"[23] and, in 1768, a French guitarist "respectfully informs the public that he instructs…in the art…of playing on the Spanish and English guitars."[24] Another half a century later, in 1815, a Boston music store similarly advertised that it sold "English and Spanish Guittars [sic]."[25] As late as 1819-1820, a Boston music teacher continued to offer lessons on both "English & Spanish Guitars,"[26] and an advertisement for another Boston music store clearly delineated the availability of both "English and Spanish Guitars."[27]

Over the first two decades of the 1800s, the Spanish guitar replaced the English guitar in America as the preferred popular instrument played (mainly by women[28]) in the parlor of one's home (along with the flute and, for those able to afford it, the pianoforte[29]).[30] "In an era of nostalgia, the simplicity of the Spanish guitar…must have been attractive to those wishing to escape modern technology,"[31] and "The guitar as a feminine instrument stood in opposition to the inherently male world of the city and technological progress."[32] Spanish guitar method books first appeared in America in 1816 and increased in regularity through the 1820s. The Spanish guitar's popularity in America is further evidenced by the fact that a profitable music publishing business arose and flourished from 1830–1850, producing voluminous popular literature for the middle-class newly emerging from the industrial revolution.[33] By the 1830s, the English "guitar" had almost completely disappeared in both England and America.

Figure 4-2. Print showing the parts of a Spanish guitar and the proper position for playing one, from Dionisio Aguado's influential *Escuela de Guitarra (School of Guitar)*, published in Madrid in 1825.

SPAIN ROMANTICIZED IN ANGLO-AMERICAN LITERATURE

The stage was set for an appreciation of things Spanish among the literate American public when the writings of Cervantes, author of *Don Quixote de la Mancha*, reached their peak influence on American letters from approximately 1790–1815. "The vogue for travel to unknown places in the eighteenth century signaled a shift in Western mentality that further manifested itself in the ramifications of the exotic voyage or 'tour' in the romantic literature of the early nineteenth century."[34]

The popular American author Washington Irving (1783–1859) supplied some of the key writings that nurtured this shift. Already well-known to American readers for his 1819-1820 Hudson River Valley fables about such characters as Rip Van Winkle, Ichabod Crane, and the "Headless Horseman" (the latter pair appearing in "The Legend of Sleepy Hollow"), Irving's travels in Spain from 1826–1829 resulted in his 1832 publication, *The Alhambra: A Series of Tales and Sketches of the Moors and Spaniards.* "Oriental in coloring, intimate in spirit, it became for at least a generation…a guidebook for other American travelers."[35] To the northern European, English, and American imaginations, Spain represented a brush with Islam, hence with "the East" or "the Orient," exotic in its otherness. When

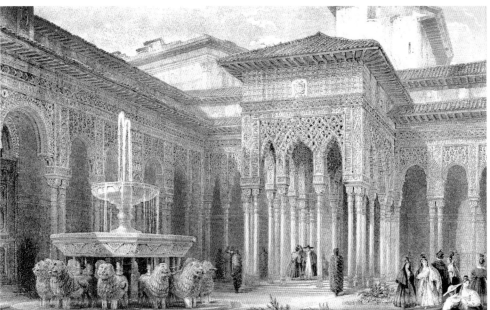

Figure 4-3. Patio Leones (Patio of the Lions) within the Alhambra, the fourteenth-century palace and fortress in Granada, Andalusia, Spain, that inspired Washington Irving's 1832 book *Tales of the Alhambra.* Irving stayed in the palace for some time while working on his book.

the Moors occupied southern Spain, northern Europeans perceived the Orient as beginning at the Pyrenees Mountains, which separate Spain from France. In addition, it should be remembered that Spain is a land from which, in places on a clear day, one can see the continent of Africa.

Irving's *Alhambra* was a wildly popular and often-reprinted book. It satisfied a deep yearning in the collective American psyche for romantic travel writing, especially regarding things Spanish. *The Alhambra* represented the magical ruins of a bygone era, stirring trans-Atlantic longings for a distant place and time, painting pictures in words before the age of photography. Irving's book "psychologically joins a distant Moorish Granada with nineteenth-century Spaniards and their American romantic guest in the Alhambra. Irving makes astute Yankee Protestant comments on Catholic and Moorish cultures, both of which had to appear exotic by comparison with New York." [36] "Washington Irving stands at the head of several nineteenth-century romantic trends in U.S. history, and he is the primary exemplar of popular history written on Spanish themes." [37] Although writing specifically about Andalusian culture in the south of Spain, Irving's characterizations were ascribed to Spaniards in general, regardless of regional or provincial origin or attribution.

Irving mentions the guitar on no less than two-dozen different pages in *The Alhambra*. [38] The associations he makes with it do not differ from those mentions made in the popular press before his time:

He touched the guitar with masterly skill, and afterwards danced a fandango with a buxom Andalusian damsel, to the great delight of the spectators...

Give a Spaniard the shade in summer and the sun in winter, a little bread, garlic, oil, and garbanzos, an old brown cloak and a guitar, and let the world roll on as it pleases. Talk of poverty! With him it has no disgrace. It sits upon him with a grandiose style...

Sometimes the dubious tones of a guitar and the notes of an amorous voice tell perchance the whereabout of some moonstruck lover serenading his lady's window...

...if he can play the guitar, he is sure of a hearty welcome among the peasant... [39]

For the impressionable nineteenth-century American public, Irving painted a lasting picture of the guitar as the portable travel instrument of Gypsies, much like the guitar in the hands of Woody Guthrie would come to represent the nomadic flight of the hobo on railway cars escaping the pressures of the modern, industrialized, cosmopolitan American world of the twentieth century.

Irving was not alone in this characterization. 1833—the year after *The Alhambra* appeared in print—saw the publication of *Outre-Mer: A Pilgrimage Beyond the Sea* by Henry Wadsworth Longfellow (1807–1882), the romantic American poet known for "Paul Revere's Ride" and "The Song of Hiawatha." He mentions guitars on five pages pertinent to Spain; the following is typically effusive:

When evening came, the merry sound of the guitar summoned to the dance; then every nook and alley poured forth its youthful company,— light of heart and heel, and decked out in all the holiday finery of flowers, and ribbons, and crimson sashes. A group gathered before the cottage door; the signal was given, and away whirled the merry dancers to the wild music of voice and guitar, and the measured beat of castanet and tambourine. [40]

TRINIDAD HUERTA, THE FIRST SPANISH GUITARIST TO CONCERTIZE IN THE NEW WORLD

The Monroe Doctrine of 1823 ended American isolationism and opened doors for additional travel, trade, and cultural contact with Old World Spain and the Hispanic New World. That same year, King Fernando VII exiled many liberal Spaniards after a failed revolution against him. Whether exiled or of his own accord, the Spanish guitarist Trinidad Huerta (1800–1874), then twenty-three years old, moved to Paris that year and arrived in New York City the following spring. [41]

Huerta was the first Spanish guitar virtuoso to concertize in the United States. In fact, Huerta's was "the first New York concert in which the main

Figure 4-4. The Alhambra, seen here in an 1856 American book illustration, fueled the public's romantic imagination for such Spanish exoticism as Gypsies, flamenco music, and the guitar.

artist on the program was a guitarist."[42] His contemporaries, the Spanish guitarists Fernando Sor (1778–1839) and Dionisio Aguado (1784–1849), did not travel to America. "While Sor, with Aguado and the European guitarists of their generation, represents civilization—a guitaristic product of the Enlightenment—Huerta represents barbarism (otherness, exoticism)."[43] Huerta was self-taught and unable to read musical notation, all of which served to reinforce the image of the Spanish guitarist as a "noble savage."[44] Sor reportedly referred to Huerta as the "sublime barbarian,"[45] and the famous composer Hector Berlioz exclaimed, "Nothing is more deliciously crazy than his Andalusian gaiety."[46] The guitarist and teacher Mme. Sidney Pratten, further described Huerta as "the restless child of wild Spanish nature."[47]

The French romantic author Victor Hugo waxed most poetically in response to hearing Huerta play:

The guitar, such a limited instrument, knows no bounds in your hands. You make it produce all sounds, all chords, all melodies. You know how to draw from those few strings the most varied notes: those that speak to the soul, to the mind, to the heart. Your guitar is an orchestra. I love Spain and the Spaniards very much, Señor Huerta, and therefore the guitar as well—but especially in your hands. There it is not only a string that breathes; it is a voice, a true voice that sings, that speaks, and that weeps: one of those deep voices that makes those who are happy think and brings those who are sad to meditation.[48]

Huerta gave his first New York concert nineteen days after his arrival in the United States in May of 1824,[49] and, three days later, announced in the press that he would teach guitar in the city.[50] Thereafter, he concertized in New York (June); Philadelphia (July); Baltimore and Saratoga, New York (August); back in New York City (September); and again in Baltimore (November through December).[51] 1825 saw him back in New York again, following the publications of two pieces of sheet music for the guitar.[52] His farewell concert took place on January 2, 1826, after which he is believed to have traveled first to Havana, Cuba, before arriving in London in 1827.[53] In 1828, he married a daughter of the famed London luthier Louis Panormo.[54] While it is impossible to say what guitar Huerta played on stage in America, his Panormo guitar from later in that decade—with Spanish plantilla and fan bracing—remains extant.[55]

While no direct evidence exists to indicate that Huerta's choice of instrument (which was, presumably, of Spanish style, if not manufacture) in any way influenced the American public, it seems likely that those more than casual observers in his concert audiences sought out such instruments from the New York importers/retailers of the day.

THE FIRST IDENTIFIABLE "SPANISH" GUITAR IN ANGLO-AMERICA?

While the Spanish guitar had made only modest inroads into English culture from 1785 to 1815,[56] Fernando Sor's presence in London from 1815–1823 and his public concertizing ensured a rise in the instrument's popularity.[57] Sor purportedly consulted

Figure 4-5. The virtuoso Spanish guitarist Trinidad Huerta, portrayed in a c. 1820 lithograph, several years before he played for American audiences.

Figure 4-6. An 1827 guitar by Louis Panormo, London. Although it is not known what guitar Trinidad Huerta played during his American concerts in 1824–1826, his main concert guitar from 1828 on was built by Louis Panormo. He married Panormo's daughter Angiolina that year, and Panormo also supported the publication of his son-in-law's compostions for guitar.

with the luthier Joseph Panormo (elder brother of Louis), advising him regarding innovations in guitar construction to suit his technique and tonal requirements. Given that Sor was fond of the makers from Cadiz, Spain, (namely Benedid and Pagés), and of the work of José Martinez of Malaga, it is not by mistake that instruments made by the Panormo family came to resemble those of Andalusia very closely, especially the Cadiz school of builders, both in plantilla and the utilization of fan bracing.

It is of no small consequence that perhaps the earliest known mention of a Spanish-style guitar in America attributed to a specific maker is a Panormo and dates to 1831:

We saw a few days since, at the music store of Mess. Firth & Hall, an improved Spanish guitar, manufactured by Mr. Panormo, of Philadelphia, combining many valuable improvements, and giving a strength and richness of tone not often found in those of usual construction. The neck of the instrument is not liable to spring, and thereby render the tones uncertain, as in old instruments, and the finish is certainly superb. When instruments can be manufactured in this country equal to the imported, every friend of improvement will feel himself bound to prefer them; but when they are evidently superior to those of foreign manufacture, there is an additional interest given to our national spirit. [58]

At first glance, one might assume that the guitar in question was made by the Panormo family in London and was imported into the United States for resale by Firth & Hall in New York City, who were known for their importation of European instruments of all types.[59] This would seem likely, given that Firth & Hall as well as other large music houses were known to carry guitars of Spanish, German, French, and Italian manufacture. One might further assume that the assignation of the builder to Philadelphia is attributable to a misunderstanding; that, in fact, the instrument

was merely imported first into Philadelphia and then on to New York, rather than originating in Philadelphia. However, the remainder of the notice states quite clearly the author's point that the guitar in question is of domestic—not European—manufacture.[60]

It is entirely possible that Firth & Hall pitched the Panormo to their unsuspecting customers as an instrument of domestic manufacture in order to assuage long-standing consumer fears regarding guitars of European manufacture; which were known to be unable to withstand the climate of New England. As an 1852 notice continued to warn, "Until within a few years, most of the guitars used in the United States were imported from France and Germany—some few from Spain. Those of French and German make, though very pretty in outward appearance, were weak in tone, and the severe changes in our climate caused them to crack and open. The Spanish guitar, though very much superior in point of tone, became also generally affected by the same cause."[61]

C. F. MARTIN SR. AND SPANISH INFLUENCES ON HIS GUITARS

In 1833, two years after the Panormo guitar was noted in New York, Christian Friedrich Martin Sr. arrived in New York City. Martin purportedly worked for Stauffer in Vienna (in some accounts as Stauffer's shop foreman). Whether or not he did, he initially produced guitars in America that closely resembled Stauffer's Viennese guitars in plantilla, scroll head-stock shape, and ladder bracing.

It cannot be known with certainty whether Martin encountered Spanish-made guitars (or guitars made in the Spanish style) before his arrival in the United States. The following report is from 1833, the year of Martin's arrival: "There is at Mittewald [sic], a small manufacture of guitars; three persons follow this trade, and produce from their workshops, neat looking, and well toned instruments: they…are all sent to Munich, and no doubt sold there, as Spanish guitars—which they exactly resemble in shape."[62] So, evidently, there was knowledge among

Germanic luthiers that guitars of Spanish design were a "hot commodity," and that it might be in their best business interests at least to attempt to emulate the Spanish plantilla.

According to ledgers in the Martin Archives,[63] the first known retailer for Martin's guitars outside of his own shop was Atwill's Music Saloon, which opened at 201 Broadway in 1834.[64] Martin sold seven guitars on commission to Joseph F. Atwill in 1834. He sold one more to him in April of 1835, and, the next month, Atwill advertised guitars for the first time.[65] Later that same year, Atwill's advertised, "Splendid Guitars of rosewood, birdseye maple and satin wood, with the patent screw heads and inlaid with pearl, ivory & c. of great variety of paterns [sic] and of all prices."[66] Atwill's was selling Spanish guitars as early as 1836, when they advertised, "Spanish GUITARS of every style and pattern, varying in price from $6 to $100."[67] Martin sold Atwill a Spanish model in 1837.

Like the similar firm of Firth & Hall, which sold the aforementioned Panormo four years earlier,

Atwill's was likely to have imported guitars of French, German, and Spanish design, alongside which Martin's Germanic instruments were offered. Martin surely would have seen and closely inspected these competing products. The fact that some extant Martin guitars from the mid-to-late 1830s bear labels claiming that Martin made "Spanish and Vienna" guitars attests to the fact that he was willing to construct instruments in both styles.

Some early Martin labels clearly state that Martin also was an importer of musical instruments. For example, a July 20, 1836, ledger entry reads: "Recd from Brauns & Focke Baltimore, 6 guitars." This firm was known to be "importers of German goods."[68] It comes as no surprise then, that a few weeks later, on August 30, 1836, Martin "sold a German guitar." Similarly, on October 17, 1838, Martin dutifully records having sold a "French guitar with a case." Obviously, he was selling imported guitars (or guitars of European manufacture taken in trade) in addition to the occasional guitar of his own manufacture. It follows that when, on December 30, 1837, Martin "sold a Spanish guitar," the instrument may very well have been made in Spain (or, perhaps, made in Germany in a Spanish style) and retailed through him, rather than being of his own manufacture.

This assumption seems to be borne out by an August 16, 1838, transaction: "Sold a Spanish guitar to Mr. Ballard…Mr. Ballard gave a guitar made by C.F.M. in exchange." (Martin goes on to add that he gave Ballard a $16 trade-in value towards the $35 guitar).[69] At first blush, it would appear that Martin is distinguishing between a guitar made in Spain and one he himself made. However, a few weeks later, on September 10, 1838, Martin notes a "Recd order for a Spanish guitar…(3-4 weeks to be done)," which makes plain that he was, in fact, willing to build in the Spanish style at this time. Nevertheless, the fact remains that Martin's own building techniques in the Spanish style may have been influenced by Spanish-made instruments that he himself imported and

Figure 4-7. Advertisement for Atwill's Music Saloon, the first known retailer to sell C. F. Martin's guitars on commission.

resold. When, on October 23, 1838, he sold a "Spanish guitar with Viennese screws," the guitar was probably one he made with fan bracing and his conventional Germanic headstock.

C. F. MARTIN AND THREE "SPANISH" GUITARISTS

Whether Martin first encountered truly Spanish guitars in the Old World or the New World, his personal and business relationships with three "Spanish" guitarists certainly affected his desire to experiment with Spanish design and building techniques. The three were, in chronological order of their appearance in Martin's life, John B. Coupa, Francisco Benedid, and Dolores Nevares de Goni, each of whom made his or her presence known on the New York concert stage of the early 1840s.[70]

While John Coupa has been called a "Spaniard," his country of birth remains undocumented. An 1830 Boston city directory lists him as an "instructor" who performed on guitar in a concert that year,[71] and he is known to have published a guitar instruction book and some sheet music pieces in Boston between 1824 and 1835.[72] However, the date of Coupa's first presence as resident in New York is unknown. When Martin, according to his ledger, first sold guitars to Coupa in New York on May 11, 1837, Coupa was already established as a guitar teacher who sold guitars to his students.[73] The first direct mention of a Spanish guitar in Martin's ledger is dated December 30, 1837. Spanish guitars began to appear in the ledger more regularly after March of 1838, and almost all the guitars sold to Coupa after this date were designated as "Spanish." One might conclude that Martin's guitars of Spanish design were built at Coupa's prompting. Coupa may either have owned Spanish guitars that he allowed Martin to inspect or directed Martin to Spanish guitars at Atwill's or elsewhere in New York.

Between 1838 and 1840, Martin sold Coupa nine guitars, and, when Martin moved to Cherry Hill, Pennsylvania in 1839, Coupa became Martin's sole retail selling agent in New York from 1840–1841. He probably continued in this role until his death in 1850.[74] Several extant guitars labeled "Martin & Coupa" feature a Spanish-style heel in their neck construction, tie (as opposed to pin) bridges, and fan-braced (as opposed to ladder-braced) tops.

Francisco Benedid, the second Spanish guitarist in New York who may have influenced Martin to build in the Spanish style, is described at his first concert on November 7, 1839, alternately as being a "guitarist from Cuba"[75] and being "from Spain."[76] Thereafter, he continued to perform concerts with some degree of regularity in New York through 1844.[77] One contemporary musicologist calls Benedid, "ubiquitous but obscure."[78] Indeed, virtually nothing is known about him. However, the probability of his lineage vis-à-vis the famous Benedid family of luthiers in Cadiz, Spain, is provocative.

An 1855 biographical entry in a Spanish publication (roughly translated herein to English) states:

Figure 4-8. Niblo's Garden, inside and outside, 1828. Niblo's Garden, named after its proprietor, William Niblo, was a New York theater and open air saloon on Broadway, near Prince Street, that presented a variety of entertainments, including musical concerts. In the evenings, Niblo's Garden was illuminated with hundreds of colored-glass lanterns.

D. José Benedid, born in Cadiz, was the son of a constructor of guitars who was a contemporary of the famous Pagés. He began in Cadiz and went with his father to Havana, where he perfected and mastered the instrument, becoming fluent in the schools of Sor, Aguado, and Ciebra. He has the admirable disposition to retain in memory and to repeat guitar music that he hears. He writes much, knows harmony, and has brought the guitar to much instrumental and vocal music. Luck called on Benedid to make our instrument heard with dignity in the United States of America.[79]

Although the name is given as José instead of Francisco, the fact that he is noted as a guitarist connected with Cuba who played in the United States perfectly fits the description of Francisco Benedid in 1840s New York newspapers. Moreover, the fact that he is described as the son of the famous Cadiz luthier Josef (also known as José) Benedid (1760–1836) is astonishing. Of the elder Benedid, it has been written, "later he went to Cuba and placed his tools in a workshop in Havana,"[80] so a Cuban connection is irrefutable.

The definitive biographical source on Spanish luthiers lists a Francisco Benedid as a son of Josef, and then goes on to note that another son, Josef Maria ("José") Benedid, born in Cadiz 1808, was declared a 'guitarist' in 1827.[81] Adding further intrigue, one son of the Cadiz luthier Juan Pagés (1741–1821)—namely Francisco Pagés (1773–?)—"worked in Cadiz and later in Havana."[82] This Francisco Pagés married Francisca Josefa Benedid (1769–?), sister of Josef ("José") Benedid (1760–1836), thus the aunt of the Josef Maria ("José") Benedid who is said to have concertized on the guitar in New York.

While there is an indisputable link—both professional and familial—between the Benedid and Pagés families, it is unclear exactly who the guitarist Benedid in New York really was and how he was related to the luthiers, either in Cadiz or Havana or both. It is interesting to speculate about what guitar or guitars he would have played, their origin, and whether or not Martin might have been aware of them. It seems highly likely that, if Benedid was in fact (as all evidence indicates) directly related to the famous Cadiz families of luthiers, his instruments would have been fan-braced in keeping with the Cadiz school. Recent study of letters in the Martin Archives reveals that Coupa purchased a "Paez" model guitar from Martin in 1849. This could possibly have been a phonetic spelling of the Spanish pronunciation of Pagés.

The Benedid in question achieved his greatest fame in the United States in 1843, when he performed a concert at Niblo's Saloon in New York that featured an orchestra made up of twelve guitarists, including John Coupa.[83] They played Rossini's Semiramide Overture, no less.[84] The spectacle created a bit of media frenzy, with one reviewer exclaiming, "The idea of an overture being played by twelve guitars would once have been considered as absurd as crossing the Atlantic in three days in a flying machine is considered now."[85]

While no direct connection can be made between Benedid and Martin, it is certain that Martin's interest in Spanish guitar construction in the New World was further inspired by his relationship with the Spanish guitarist Señora Dolores Nevares de Goni (1813–1892), from Madrid via Paris.[86] Madame de Goni, as she came to be known, arrived in New York in 1840[87] from London, where she had published guitar pieces[88] and concertized.[89] She made her presence known at—and thereafter-frequented—the aforementioned Atwill's Music Saloon.[90]

Her concertizing and successes were immediate. In addition to numerous New York appearances, she also performed in Boston (where Henry Wadsworth Longfellow heard her play in January of 1842),[91] Philadelphia, and Baltimore (where Ralph Waldo Emerson heard her in January of 1843).[92] Between these dates, she played a concert at the Bethlehem Female Seminary[93] in Pennsylvania on July 18,

1842,[94] within ten miles of C. F. Martin's Cherry Hill home and guitar production facility, and another in Bethlehem in 1843.[95]

Of significant historical importance, the 1855 account by New York guitar teacher James Ballard states, "In 1843 Madame De Goni brought to New York a large pattern Spanish guitar, from which a number have been made, and distributed over the United States, by Martin, of Pennsylvania, and Schmidt and Maul, of New York."[96] Indeed, De Goni wrote a letter to C. F. Martin on November 8, 1843, praising him for two guitars he manufactured for her.[97]

Thereafter, Martin offered the "De Goni" as a "model" of guitar—presumably designated thus to distinguish it as having a Spanish plantilla rather than a more figure-8 shaped, Germanic plantilla. John Coupa is known to have ordered Martin's De Goni model in some quantities for resale to his students. One might speculate further that, during the 1840s, the De Goni model was Martin's "Spanish" model with an X brace, whereas the Paez model was perhaps the Spanish model with fan bracing. Was Martin inspired to experiment with X bracing below the soundhole after having observed an X brace above the soundhole (i.e. under the fretboard extension) on a Cadiz-made, fan-braced guitar?[98] Or, had De Goni introduced Martin to the X-braced "guitar of the future" because she owned or had seen a Roudhloff (or other) instrument that exhibited such experimentation?

A thorough review of New York concert appearances by Coupa, Benedid, and De Goni from 1839–1844 sheds significant light upon their interrelationships.[99] (See chart below).

Note that Philip Ernst, the flautist and guitarist, performed (presumably on flute) with all three "Spanish" guitarists. The connection with Ernst is the one they all have in common. (While Benedid and De Goni performed with Coupa, Benedid and De Goni are not known to have performed together). What is known about Philip Ernst? Apparently, he arrived in New York via London (as did De Goni) in 1840, advertising that he had "several excellent Spanish Guitars to dispose of."[100] By 1843, Ernst was in partnership and selling guitars with former Martin employees Schmidt and Maul.[101]

Figure 4-9. New York concert appearances by guitarists John Coupa, Francisco Benedid, and Madame de Goni from 1839–1844.

Date			Venue	Guitarist/Other notable(s) on the bill
November	7,	1839	City Hotel	Benedid, Philip Ernst
January	18,	1840	City Hotel	Benedid
December	19 & 29,	1840	City Hotel	De Goni
January		1841	City Hotel	Benedid, Coupa, and Ernst
May	28,	1841	Society Library	De Goni, Philip Ernst
April	30,	1842	City Hotel	Ernst and Coupa perform at a concert headlined by Sophia Melizet.
June	21,	1842	City Hotel	Ernst and Coupa perform at a concert of various musicians.
March	14,	1843	Apollo Saloon	Benedid and Coupa
April	21,	1843	Niblo's	Benedid
April	22,	1843?	Unknown venue	Benedid and Coupa perform at a concert given by Kossowski.
October	27,	1843	Apollo Saloon	De Goni, Coupa
April		1844	Unknown venue	Benedid performs at a benefit.
June	4,	1844	Apollo Saloon	Benedid

Martin's ledgers indicate that Louis Schmidt had worked for Martin in 1834-1835, before he began building guitars under his own label in 1836 and formed the partnership of Schmidt & Maul in 1839.[102] (Evidence also suggests that George Maul might have worked for Martin before teaming with Schmidt and that the Schmidt & Maul partnership was closely associated with the long-time Martin friend and business associate Henry Schatz.) Schmidt & Maul, along with Martin, also copied Madame de Goni's Spanish guitar in 1843, and they were among the earliest experimenters—along with Martin and Roudhloff—with X bracing. Could it be that De Goni's Spanish guitar, reported by Ballard as being copied both by Martin and Schmidt & Maul, in some way employed an X brace or prototype thereof?

JAMES ASHBORN'S GUITARS OF SPANISH DESIGN

When one thinks of nineteenth-century guitars in America, a single name usually comes to mind—the aforementioned C. F. Martin. But James Ashborn (1816–1876), an Englishman who came to Connecticut by way of New York City, not only operated the first factory in the United States devoted primarily to making guitars, but also produced triple the number of guitars that Martin built in the decade before the Civil War.[103] Ashborn's were "among the earliest American guitars and those which could be found more commonly than any other."[104] Clearly, Martin and Ashborn were "the country's two most important antebellum guitar makers."[105]

James Ashborn was born a year before Antonio de Torres Jurado, who is considered the 'father' of the modern Spanish, classical guitar. Ashborn was living in New York by the 1830s, the same decade that C. F. Martin emigrated from Saxony to New York and began selling his guitars there.[106] Beginning probably in 1842, Ashborn made guitars in Connecticut and shipped them to New York for wholesale and retail by the firm of Firth, Hall & Pond, who had Ashborn stamp the guitars with its name.[107]

The earliest surviving Ashborn guitar, which dates from 1845, is serial number 207 and is branded "Firth, Hall & Pond." In addition to sporting a plantilla that is immediately recognizable as Spanish—differing, in fact, very little from that used by Panormo—it also employs fan bracing, a tie bridge, and a Moorish flourish design at the top of the peghead (a feature that would become increasingly common on Spanish guitars in the later nineteenth century). Although it is impossible to say what Spanish model Ashborn based his guitar on, the fact that his sole distributor, Firth, Pond & Hall, had been known for the Panormo guitar in their showroom fifteen years earlier is telling. As early as October of 1846, Firth, Hall & Pond ran an advertisement for their (i.e. Ashborn's) guitars, which read, "Guitars made from the best Spanish patterns,"[108] much as Louis Panormo had labeled himself as being the only builder in England in the "Spanish style."

Based on his known production figures,[109] it is possible to estimate that Ashborn produced almost 12,000 guitars in his twenty-one years of active factory production (1842–1863). Ashborn's guitars lacked the Spanish slipper (heel and foot) neck commonly associated with Spanish building, but their Spanish tie bridges (identical, by the way, to those used by Martin in the 1830s and 1840s), fan bracing (hence "authentically Spanish" tonal production), and plantilla (hence "authentically Spanish" appearance) appealed to the American guitar-buying public. Along with Martin's similarly shaped "Spanish" plantilla, these Ashborn features did much to influence how Americans would come to picture the guitar henceforth.

THE GUITAR IN AMERICA, 1850S AND BEYOND

After its heyday in the 1840s, the guitar took a back seat to the banjo, which, due to the popularity of minstrelsy, predominated as America's instrument of choice for the next three decades.[110] (Minstrels were Caucasian performers who darkened their faces with a burnt cork to appear Negroid and performed

"Ethiopian" songs, dances, and skits in "blackface" in Broadway engagements—some of which ran as long as nine years.)[111] However, the guitar continued to be played, primarily by women in the home, during the entirety of the Victorian Era (1837–1901). Consequently, "An informal survey of some 500 imprints suggests that the 1840s and 1880s may have been the decades of greatest guitar publishing in the United States."[112]

In 1880, a touring band of "Spanish Students" became wildly popular on the American stage, thus initiating a new wave of Spanish intrigue. The troupe sported guitars and steel-strung bandurrias, which, being mistaken for mandolins, ushered in a mandolin craze that led to the founding of numerous mandolin quartets, clubs, and "orchestras" utilizing guitar accompaniment.[113] Most notably, Orville Gibson capitalized on the idea of the guitar belonging to the mandolin family—along with the mandolin, mandola, mandocello, and mandobass—and consequently built his guitars exclusively with steel strings and carved, rather than flat, tops. These carved archtop guitars could be driven forcefully by a plectrum; they were considerably louder than their gut-strung, flat-topped counterparts and lent themselves to being heard in jazz ensemble and club playing in the 1920s. Mandolin-inspired guitars generally came to utilize violin-like f-shaped sound holes, rather than the more typical rounded, single soundhole beneath the strings. Furthermore, they were distinctly differentiated from the flat-topped, otherwise Spanish guitars that many players were beginning to outfit with steel strings to gain more volume or, as in Hawaii, stringing with steel to facilitate playing with a metal bar slid over the strings to produce glissando effects.

The 1915 Pan-Pacific Exposition in San Francisco triggered a Hawaiian music craze in America that would last for the next forty years.[114] Central to this genre was the ukulele, and, secondly, the aforementioned steel-strung, flat-topped guitar played on the player's lap with a metal "slide" bar. Thereafter, some groups advertised themselves as available to concertize in either Spanish or Hawaiian garb—with correspondingly suitable song repertoires—depending on the booking agent's choice for the audience. After some bracing experimentation, Martin discovered their Spanish-shaped, X-braced, flat-top guitar was perfectly suited to withstand the 100% increase in tension brought by steel strings. This, coupled with the demands of musicians who, craving volume, wished to be heard in mandolin orchestras or jazz combos, led Martin to build steel-strung guitars in 1916; switch from gut to steel strings on one of its regular production guitar models in 1922; and, by the end of that decade, switch to making steel-strung guitars exclusively. During the 1920s, Martin advertised guitar strings with the following assignations: Hawaiian=Steel, and Spanish=Gut.

The following Martin production figures are indicative of the impacts made by the mandolin and ukulele vis-à-vis the guitar.[115]

Years	Guitars	Mandolins	Ukuleles
1901–1915	44%	56%	0%
1916–1930	28%	9%	63%

Clearly, Hawaii had replaced Spain as the focus for America's foreign intrigue and exoticism. Remnants of the distinction persisted with the advent of electric guitars in the 1930s. Gibson's first electric guitar was a Hawaiian lap steel model, designated "EH," for electric Hawaiian. Shortly thereafter, the conventional electric guitar was released with the designation "ES," for electric Spanish. Gibson continues to offer ES model guitars to this day, although most consumers are unaware of the Spanish designation.

By the time Jimmie Rodgers and the Carter family recorded the first country and western tracks in Bristol, on the Tennessee/Virginia border, in 1927, using steel-strung instruments in the mix, the division between gut-strung and steel-strung acoustic flat-top guitars was essentially complete. Gut-strung instruments (since the 1940s, nylon) are currently known in North America as "classical" guitars to distinguish them from steel-strung guitars, and in Europe as "concert" or "Spanish" guitars. In Europe, steel-strung guitars are called "Western" guitars.

Martin's complete switch from gut strings to steel strings coincided with the 1928 American debut in New York of Andrés Segovia (1893–1987), the most influential twentieth-century Spanish guitarist, and a champion of the gut-strung "classical" guitar. Continental European guitar development had taken a wholly different direction than that pursued by Martin and Ashborn in America. Torres (1817–1892) defined the contemporary Spanish classical guitar with his considerably larger plantilla. "Broadly speaking, all of modern concert guitar construction technology rests on a foundation laid by Torres between about 1850 and 1870."[116] In other words, all modern "classical" and flamenco guitar shapes are modeled after his body design. Segovia's instrument was modeled after Torres. Thereafter, the Torres plantilla was associated with Spanish (i.e. concert classical) and flamenco (i.e. Spanish Gypsy folk) guitars, while Martin body shapes set the standard for steel-strung instruments.

The Anglo-American fascination with Spain and things Spanish was not merely a passing fad that swept the United States in the first half of the 1800s. A full century later, in 1937, one writer states, "Spain represents, above all, the supreme manifestation of a certain primitive and eternal attitude of the human spirit, an attitude of heroic energy, of spiritual exaltation, directed not chiefly towards comfort or towards gain, but towards the more fundamental facts of human existence."[117] Such superlatives and absolutes abound as the North American imagination pictures Spain.

THE SPANISH MYSTIQUE TAKES HOLD

New York City had an established tradition of gut-strung guitar playing before the arrival of C. F. Martin and James Ashborn, and these guitars were generically referred to as "Spanish"—whether the instruments were of German, French, or Spanish construction. This fact in itself is indicative of the association

Americans made, relating the guitar with the exotic intrigue of Spanish culture. The commercial possibilities inherent in that association did not escape Martin's attention. If Martin had not already examined guitars of Spanish manufacture (i.e. fan-braced, with Spanish heel construction) in the Old World before his arrival, he was certainly introduced to such instruments almost immediately through players (Coupa) and dealers (Atwill). He may well have imported them for resale.

It is a tribute to Martin's ingenuity and genius that he readily adapted his guitar building to suit the varied desires of his diverse clientele. Thus, for example, Martin's ledgers indicate his willingness to allow customers to choose among three styles of pegheads: 1) Vienna-style (six-in-line on one side, with a scroll at the top) 2) violin-style friction tuning pegs, and 3) patent-head screws (three on a side, as are commonly used today).[118] Additionally, Martin eagerly experimented with Spanish fan bracing, in contradistinction to his own northern European tradition of ladder bracing. Several extant 1830s Martin guitars are hybrids, employing fan bracing, tie bridges, and Spanish heel design—all consistent with Spanish construction—but fitted with the traditional Vienna scroll headstock.[119]

Apparently, Martin used the word Spanish as a generic term in the 1830s to distinguish a guitar built with fan bracing, while he continued to offer "Vienna" guitars with ladder bracing. In the 1840s, he experimented with X bracing (at least on his De Goni model, the plantilla of which also was Spanish). It seems possible that, during this time, Martin distinguished between the X-braced De Goni and the fan-braced Spanish guitars of similar proportion by referring to the latter as "Paez" (read Pagés). By the time that X

Figure 4-10. Cover of *Instructions for the Spanish Guitar* by Francis Weiland, published by G. Andre & Co., Philadelphia, 1853.

bracing was established in the 1850s, the generic term "Spanish" was again used in reference to fan-braced instruments. Thus, for example, an order recorded in Martin's ledger in 1851 indicates a "large Spanish with pegs, Ladies No. 2½, and small degoni [sic]."

"The Martin company continued to use a simple fan-braced pattern…into the 1890s."[120] Evidently, Martin used Spanish fan bracing on his "lower-numbered styles,"[121] while X bracing was used on "styles 20 and above."[122] This implies that Martin felt his X bracing to be more laborious, hence more costly (thus reserved for his more expensive models). Alternatively, perhaps Martin viewed X bracing as simply unnecessary to strengthen the tops on smaller-bodied guitars.

By 1846, Martin's plantilla was established as essentially Spanish. James Ashborn's guitars, introduced in quantity around the same time, were very similar to, if not modeled on, the Spanish plantilla as used by Panormo. Moreover, all of Ashborn's guitars were exclusively Spanish-fan-braced during his entire factory production run, from 1842–1863. Given that Ashborn's output was considerably greater than Martin's, this reinforced and ensured that the Pagés/Panormo/Spanish plantilla became the dominant

shape associated with the guitar in North America Moreover, the Spanish plantilla alone became associated with the Spanish mystique, whether the instrument was fan-braced or not. The only known portrait of Madame de Goni, said to have been executed in the 1840s, depicts her playing an instrument made possibly by Roudhloff in London in a French (i.e. Lacote-like) style.[123] The mere fact of a Spanish connotation was enough to satisfy the American imagination. America was sold on the idea of "Spanishness" in the guitar.

Martin's arrival in 1833 was particularly timely, because "Guitar playing in America reached its most prolific period in the 1840s."[124] In 1845, a gentleman was advertising his guitar store in New York City as the "Spanish Guitar Repository," selling both new and "Good toned second-hand Guitars to loan or hire."[125] In fact, the guitar had so captured the American imagination by the middle of the nineteenth century that Edgar Allan Poe's 1845 story "The Fall of the House of Usher" includes the line: "I listened, as if in a dream, to the wild improvisations of his speaking guitar."[126]

The tone produced by fan bracing—coupled with the mystique of Spanish exoticism—ensured that the Spanish guitar became the instrument of choice in the American parlor from the 1830s onward. While Sor and Aguado were establishing the guitar as a legitimate instrument of the concert stage in Europe, and Huerta's American concerts furthered public awareness of the Spanish flair for the instrument, Madame de Goni's presence in America set the stage for the Spanish guitar to be perceived as an elegant and alluring parlor instrument for ladies. As a writer had already noted during Huerta's American presence in 1824, "The Spanish guitar is an instrument wholly unfitted for a public concert room, where the exquisite touches of the most delicate hand are entirely lost. In an ordinary apartment, however, it is a most interesting instrument."[127] Thus the guitar secured a place in nineteenth-century American culture neither as a conveyor of art music for the concert stage, nor

Figure 4-11. Satisfying America's appetite for Spanish flair, this illustration from an 1851 edition of Washington Irving's *Alhambra* depicts Gypsies dancing to guitar accompaniment while framed by a Moorish archway.

folk music (as it would in the twentieth century) but, instead, as a vehicle for popular music.[128]

Newspapers and popular publications of the time furthered the romantic associations surrounding the guitar and its Spanishness. "It is possible that in referring to the guitar as the 'Spanish Guitar,' publishers and fiction writers were trying to stir up images of the seductive women as well as the romance and exoticism associated with Spain."[129] On the one hand, the guitar had become "feminized" as the instrument of choice for middle-class Anglo-American women[130]—a domestic direction sustained by a plethora of publications of light, easy to learn and play, "feminine" love songs and romantic solo pieces. On the other hand, the guitar was being marketed with connotations of "dark-eyed" seduction and otherness, representative of the northern European intrigue with things Mediterranean.

This is epitomized in an 1855 painting portraying two Spanish Gypsy women playing guitar, singing, and dancing. When reproduced the following year as an engraving that graced the cover of a popular Boston publication, the accompanying text, in part, read:

Fair they are not—these bronzed daughters of the sun—and yet theirs is a wild and gipsy style of beauty, not without its fascination. Dark hair, dark eyes, pearly teeth and rounded contours are their heritage. There is a charm about the Spanish women which the coldest hearts acknowledge. Their figures are generally supple and elastic; their movements full of grace and witchery.[131]

The description is intentionally titillating. It preys on the Anglo-American males' "Madonna/whore" complex, insinuating that the virginal innocence of his Victorian domestic housewife could simultaneously hold the potential for licentious abandon and beguilement simply by taking up the Spanish guitar. Nowhere is this more perfectly expressed than in personal letters written by Henry Wadsworth Longfellow describing Madame de Goni:

Figure 4-12. *Spanish Minstrels*, after a painting by John Phillip (1817–1867). Printed in *Ballou's Pictorial*, Boston, October 22, 1856.

There is a sweet Spanish woman here, playing the guitar, La Señora de Goñy,—delicious.[132]

...La Señora De Goñy, whose guitar delights me more, perhaps because it awakens sweet remembrances of early youth and Spain;—perhaps because a woman plays it, and the devil is in it.[133]

An anonymous reporter, just a few months later, notes of De Goni, "The Madame has a beautiful pair of black eyes, which of themselves are an attraction."[134]

In 1833—the year that Martin came to the New World—it could be said of the guitar that, "It lends charm to the graceful appearance of the one sex, and realizes the romantic ideas of the other."[135] Anglo-America's Spanish diversion at this time was a romantic antidote to the anxieties wrought by the industrial revolution.[136] One-hundred-seventy-five years later, few American guitarists would know that their instrument of choice—now overwhelmingly in the hands of males—resulted from such a fascination with the allure of Spanish culture. ★

CHAPTER 5

The Cadiz Guitar and Its Influence on C. F. Martin

DAVID LAPLANTE

By the first quarter of the nineteenth century, the guitar in Spain had developed both a beauty of form and a high level of structural sophistication. The instruments were evolving from the eighteenth century's six double-courses to a six single-string configuration, and the advent of fan bracing allowed luthiers to create a particularly flexible top that produced a sound quality unmatched by other European guitars.

At this time, before the work of Antonio de Torres Jurado redefined the Spanish guitar, the guitars of Andalusia, in the southern portion of the Iberian Peninsula, had become distinctive. Cadiz, a seaport on the southwest coast, had become a guitar-making center, and, by the turn of the nineteenth century, the Pagés and Benedid families were prominent in this endeavor. By the mid nineteenth century, other Cadiz makers, including José Recio and his son Enrique, Juan Perfumo, Manuel Lopez, Federico Danino, and Manuel Hernandez, along with Antonio de Lorca in the nearby city of Malaga, also were producing guitars in the Cadiz style.

The Cadiz makers developed a lightly built instrument by utilizing fan braces in the portion of the top below the harmonic bars[1] adjacent to the soundhole. In contrast to the transverse barring used in other parts of Europe, fan bracing lightly reinforced the top of the guitar in a longitudinal direction, against the pull of the strings, while leaving a high degree of flexibility across the width of the top. The braces were placed at varying angles to the grain direction of the top wood, which allowed more movement in response to the vibration of the strings but stiffened the top sufficiently to produce a bright, singing treble, enhanced bass, and greater volume.

The aesthetic shown in the Cadiz guitar of this period is also striking. The plantilla[2] was characterized by an elongated body, with the upper bout noticeably narrower than the lower one. The pegheads of these instruments, most often a simple, tapered, paddle shape with a "squared off" tip, were fitted with simple turned wooden pegs.

C. F. Martin Sr.'s emulation of the Spanish style was very specific to the Cadiz guitar in internal construction and form. The first Martin guitars to show both fan-braced construction and the archetypical Spanish plantilla were those produced, starting around 1838, for the New York City teacher, concert artist, and instrument retailer John B. Coupa.[3] These were labeled with Coupa's name and sold in his studio, which was first located at 198 and later at 385 Broadway "upstairs."

Martin was responding to Coupa's requests to produce guitars in this style. Letters from Coupa to Martin of January 15, and April 2, 1849,[4] request a "Paez" model and seem to refer (albeit phonetically) to the guitars that Martin was making in the Cadiz style of the Pagés[5] family and others. Based on extant guitars, Martin had been producing this style for at least a decade.

STRUCTURAL COMPARISONS
A. BRACING

The use of fan bracing is considered the hallmark of the Spanish guitar. By 1759, the Seville maker

Francisco Sanguino had built a large guitar using three fan braces.[6] Cadiz makers Juan Pagés[7] and Josef Benedid's[8] guitars of 1792 and 1794, respectively, also show this mode of construction .

These thin struts, most often made of spruce, as was the top, were arranged in a basic radial pattern below the lower harmonic bar, adjacent to the

the Spanish mode of construction, his number of fan braces was also increased to five. It is widely recognized that the guitars of the Pagés family influenced the London-based maker Louis Panormo, who, by 1822[12] was building "Guitars in the Spanish style" as proclaimed on his label. Panormo had taken his plantilla from the Pagés guitars,[13] although many

Figure 5-1. *Left*, Antonio de Lorca, Malaga, 1839 (Profile 13); *center*, Martin & Coupa, c.1841–1843 (Profile 21); *right*, José Recio, Cadiz, 1853 (Profile 14).

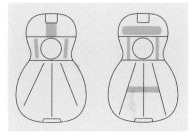

Figure 5-2. Fan bracing. *Above left*, Antonio De Lorca, Malaga, 1839 (Profile 13); *above right*, Martin & Coupa, c. 1841–1843, (Profile 20).

bottom edge of the soundhole. This arrangement often had a common apex along the centerline of the guitar. The higher the apex, the more nearly parallel the fans, while a lower apex created a more splayed arrangement.

The earliest Spanish-influenced guitars by C. F. Martin Sr. have from one to three fan braces.[9] These guitars exhibit a transitional body shape that retains some of the earlier rounded characteristics of the Austro-German style but features a more Spanish plantilla with significant size differentiation between the upper and lower bouts. Internally, and in other ways, these guitars were still quite similar to Martin's Austro-German guitars, with their large, rounded, spruce neck blocks and a "crescent-shaped" reinforcement plate under the block[10] and against the upper back. They also have solid, bent, internal linings.

By 1813, Josef Pagés had built a guitar with five fan struts.[11] As Martin progressed deeper into

of his other construction details are decidedly non-Spanish. In contrast, the guitars Martin built for John Coupa two decades later show a much purer and more direct Spanish influence, and it seems likely that his construction was influenced by first-hand exposure to Spanish-made instruments rather than by those of Panormo. Both in New York City and later in Nazareth, Pennsylvania, Martin was in a position to have been exposed to virtuosi of the Spanish guitar and to have seen and examined excellent examples of Spanish and Spanish-style guitars.[14]

Many of Martin's earliest Spanish-style guitars retained the scroll head and mechanical tuners of his Austro-German models. It seems reasonable to assume that a well-to-do clientele preferred (as many players still do today) the easier-to-manage geared tuners. However, many guitars with ebony or ivory friction pegs also were produced during this period, hinting at the extent of devotion to the Spanish

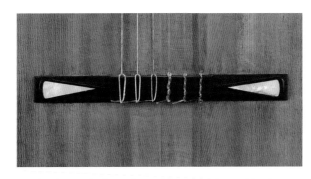

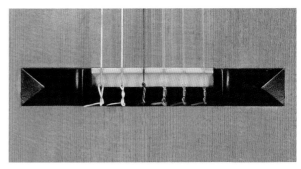

Figure 5-3. *Right,* bridge on Antonio De Lorca, Malaga, 1839 (Profile 13); *far right,* Spanish-style tie bridge on Martin & Coupa guitar, c. 1842–1844 (Profile 23). Note the "pyramid-shaped" ends.

See page 84 for Profile 13, Antonio De Lorca, c. 1839

See page 86 for Profile 14, José Recio, c.1853

aesthetic and that the pegs in many cases were actually preferred.[15] Coupa often requested the least expensive of these models in his letters to Martin,[16] which might also explain the use of the less-costly ebony pegs. Virtually all of the guitars built in Spain before 1850 were originally fitted with wooden tuning pegs.[17]

B. BRIDGES

The adoption of a tied bridge configuration (which was also the earliest appearance of the now familiar "pyramid" bridge) coincided with Martin's use of fan braces. Indeed, the tie bridge seems to have been widely accepted as the "proper" type during the 1840s; very similar examples can be found on the guitars of Martin (in both ivory and ebony variants), as well as on guitars by Louis Schmidt and George Maul and by James Ashborn.[18]

The tie bridge was certainly more compatible with the internal fan-braced configuration than the earlier (and later) pin-style bridges. A pin bridge used with three or five fans requires very careful placement of the required holes to avoid compromising a brace by drilling through it. Martin eventually simplified his fan bracing, reducing the number of braces to four, and crossing the inner two to form an "X."[19] This left a clear open space for the holes and allowed a return to the much-simpler-to-make pin bridge.

C. PLANTILLA

The Spanish guitars of this period, particularly those of the Cadiz school, are characterized by an elongated body profile, in which the lower bout is much wider than the upper bout (Profiles 13, 14). This plantilla also has a very rounded contour, often with an almost flattened portion at the butt end of the guitar that creates a distinctive "bell" shape.

D. SIDES ("RIBS")

Spanish guitar makers of this period had to process their own lumber,[20] and sufficient widths of timber in the proper vertical grain-cut were not always available. Thus, many early Cadiz school guitars show sides made up from two or more narrow slats of wood. This mode of construction actually seems to have been preferred from a decorative point of view; many existing instruments show an elaborate construction far beyond that of merely making up for narrow stock. These multi-pieced sides were joined together, bent over a hot iron heated with charcoal,[21] and then reinforced with strips of paper, which were glued over the joints.

C. F. Martin Sr. emulated this style in many of his instruments of the period. The sides of these guitars are often made in two pieces, which are bookmatched to each other, top and bottom (as opposed to bass and treble sides as seen in modern examples), and joined together with a simple line motif (or, in the case of many more-elaborate examples, a multicolored marquetry), that matches the back strip.

E. HEEL

During much of the 1830s, Martin used the Austro-German-style neck, which had a "separate" heel.[22] The neck and body were built separately and later joined by a double-tapered extension of the heel

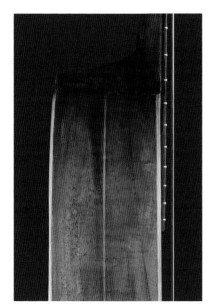 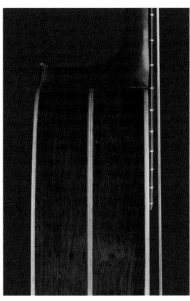 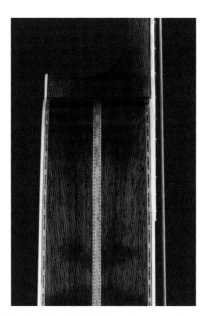

Figure 5-4. Side views. *Far left*, Antonio de Lorca, Malaga, 1839 (Profile 13); *center*, Martin & Coupa, c.1841–1843 (Profile 21); *left*, book-matched, two-piece sides, C. F. Martin, c. 1842-1844 (Profile 24).

("dovetail") fitted into a corresponding recess created in the front block of the instrument. The ebonized neck shaft was also attached to the "separate" heel by an even more elaborate dovetail and "key" joint. The major departure from Martin's previous neck construction was his adoption of the "Spanish foot" and smoothly sculpted "Spanish heel." First made in Cuban mahogany, these were later made from Spanish cedar.

When used in Spain, this style of construction featured the neck and internal block in one piece, often glued together from many layers of thinner stock, with the "foot" consisting of a piece at the bottom which extended along the inside of the back and created extra surface area for the glue joint. This decreased the tendency of the neck joint to rotate under string pressure. This Spanish mode of construction also featured slots cut in the block, into which the sides are inserted.

Martin's earliest Spanish foot designs are nearly identical to their Spanish counterparts, being roughly rectangular with rounded or neatly beveled edges. Similar "feet" can also be seen in the guitars of Schmidt and Maul during this period. Martin quickly asserted his own sense of design as he changed the shape of the foot to a graceful, pointed, "shield" shape, often

with the "C. F. Martin New York" brand appearing prominently at its tip. This foot shape persisted to the end of the 1840s.

When Martin closely emulated the Spanish foot design during this period, he recreated it using a dovetail joint that attached the neck to a footed internal block. This closely replicated the look of the one-piece Spanish construction but, in reality, retained the Austro-German-style construction, which was familiar to Martin and, perhaps, thought to be superior by him because it allowed the neck and body to be finished separately. This interesting and benign deception is further illustrative of the demand for a Spanish style of guitar at this time.

F. LININGS

Other internal features of the guitars reveal the extent to which Martin adhered to a Spanish mode of construction during this period. Earlier guitars, most notably those also associated with Heinrich Schatz, had simple, solid, bent, internal linings of the type found in the Austro-German-style guitars. The first appearance of separate glue blocks coincided with the advent of other Spanish features.[23]

In the Spanish mode of construction, the guitar is placed top down on a work board,[24] with the glue

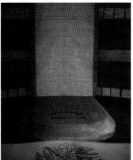

Figure 5-5. *Top*, Antonio de Lorca, Malaga, showing the Spanish-style foot extending along the inside surface of the upper back; *below*, c. 1840 Martin & Coupa Spanish foot nearly identical to the Antonio de Lorca in figure 13. The neck however is actually attached via a dovetail joint. Of particular note are the "dentellone"-style glue blocks, so-named for their tooth-like appearance.

blocks fastened individually to secure the top to the sides. It is not known whether Martin followed this assembly procedure. It seems likely that he, as his descendants did in later years, assembled the rim (sides attached at either end with the front and rear blocks) first to the back, and then attached the top last. Thus, the use of separate glue blocks seems more of a stylistic affectation than derived from any modification of his assembly sequence.

In addition, early Spanish-style Martin guitars employ horqueta[25] or "tuning-fork"-shaped brackets, which were typical of Spanish-made guitars of the first half of the nineteenth century. The two-piece sides needed additional support, and these brackets straddle the back braces as well as the top harmonic bars, extend onto the sides, and act as stiffeners providing reinforcement. In the Martin version, this joint was often covered with cloth twill tape, while the Spanish version often has blue paper tape reinforcement. Martin's use of the two-piece side seems to be another stylistic feature adopted from the Spanish aesthetic, although, as always, he refined the treatment, often by book-matching the pieces.

C. F. MARTIN AND THE CADIZ AESTHETIC

C. F. Martin Sr.'s emulation of the Spanish style was also very specific to the Cadiz guitar in external cosmetic design features. Although some early Cadiz guitars have wide rosettes with elaborate marquetry or an assortment of mother-of-pearl or bone shapes, Martin's rosettes most closely resemble those of later Pagés and Antonio De Lorca guitars, having three concentric rings of wood inlay, the center ring being wider and often containing an elaborate marquetry design.

In addition to Martin's use of Spanish-style center side-stripes and white wood bindings in holly or maple, the simple back stripes of these Martins consist of veneer lines and extend, Spanish-style, through and to the tip of the heel cap.

To modern eyes, the most striking feature of the pre-Torres Spanish/Cadiz style of guitar is the familiar square-topped headstock, now almost exclusively associated with Martin guitars. In fact, this elegantly plain design is first seen on Cadiz guitars of the later eighteenth and early nineteenth centuries, in particular those of Josef Benedid and Josef Pagés. José Recio, Antonio de Lorca, and a plethora of other Cadiz makers also used this design.

Also present at the neck juncture of these guitars is the now familiar raised dart-shaped volute. In an interesting turnabout, nineteenth-century Spanish makers actually copied this from earlier six-course guitars, in which it was a structural feature that defined the "V" joint used to attach the neck to the peghead. In Spanish guitars, this feature is purely cosmetic, because the pegheads themselves are usually joined to the neck with a Spanish-style "scarf" joint and the detail is then carved.[26] In Martin's version of this style, the sophisticated joint returns in the form of a modified bridle joint, but again emulates the raised carved dart of the Spanish style.

Note also the hole(s) in the headstocks of these guitars. This Spanish-derived feature was often used to attach a decorative ribbon or cord, which allowed the guitar to be hung on the wall, out of harm's way, when not in use. In Spain, cases were an additional and unwelcome expense to all but the most affluent. However, because virtually all Martin instruments were sold with a case, the inclusion of this otherwise

Figure 5-6. "Horqueta" or tuning-fork-shaped brackets. *Top*, Antonio de Lorca, Malaga, 1839 (Profile 13); *bottom*, Martin & Coupa, c. 1840s. The blue paper tape in the Antonio de Lorca guitar is original and seen in many Spanish guitars of this period. Similarly, cloth tape was used to reinforce the center-side inlay joint of the Martin.

Figure 5-7. Three-ring rosette details.
Far left, Antonio de Lorca, 1839 (Profile 13);
left, Martin & Coupa, c.1842–1844
(Profile 23).

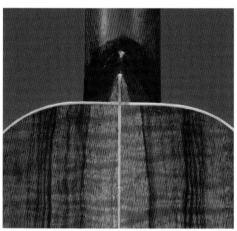
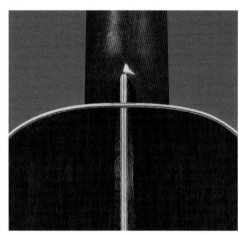

Figure 5-8. Heel cap details.
Far left, Antonio De Lorca, 1839 (Profile 13);
left, Martin and Coupa, c.1841–1843
(Profile 21).

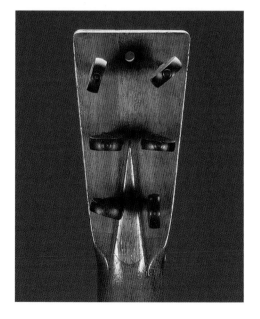
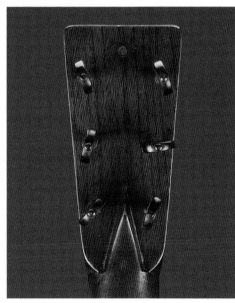

Figure 5-9. Headstock details.
Far left, Jose Recio,1853 (Profile 14);
left, Spanish-style C. F. Martin, c. 1846
(Profile 28).

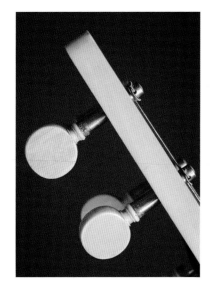

Figure 5-10. *Above*, ivory friction pegs, C. F. Martin, c. 1843–1848 (Profile 34).

Figure 5-11. Pegheads. *Right,* Antonio de Lorca, 1839 (Profile 13); *center,* José Recio, 1853 (Profile 14); *far right,* C. F. Martin, c. 1843–1848 (Profile 34).

Figure 6-12. *Oposite page, Una Seguidilla Guitanesca,* engraving after a painting by John Phillip (1817–1867), a Scottish artist best known for his portrayals of Spanish life. Rarely is a particular maker's guitar identifiable in a work of art, but this one, played by a lovely young woman, is, by virtue of the bridge detail, identifiable as the work of Antonio de Lorca of Malaga (see Profile 13).

useful feature on Martin guitars seems to be an additional detail that emulated the Spanish style but had little practical use.

Wooden pegs predominate on these early Spanish guitars and set the style for C. F. Martin's guitars of the 1840s. However, the ivory pegs most often seen on Martin instruments are far more elegant than the rather crude wooden types found on many Spanish-built guitars of this period, and they work surprisingly well. The use of Spanish-style friction pegs, albeit as a more expensive option when executed in Ivory, persisted on Martin guitars well into the early part of the twentieth century.

The appearance of the Martin and Schatz labeled "De Goni" guitar of 1842/3 marks the end of the distinctly Spanish period of development in C. F. Martin's guitar evolution, although he continued to produce Spanish models for a decade or so after

(and, indeed, Martin guitars with ivory friction pegs continued into the early twentieth century). The De Goni's prototypical "X" bracing, larger size,[27] and slotted head with "two-side-screw" machines heralded C. F. Martin's movement toward his signature American guitar design.

Though many of the influences on Martin's development of his guitar have been obscured by the passage of time, his elegant and sensuous plantilla as well as the now trademark simple square headstock with its carved dart were derived from the early-nineteenth-century Cadiz guitar. By responding to John Coupa's request to produce guitars in this style, Martin set on a path that took him forever away from the Austro-German style into an intense period of Spanish-style construction, and ultimately led to his mature, signature style of a decade later. ★

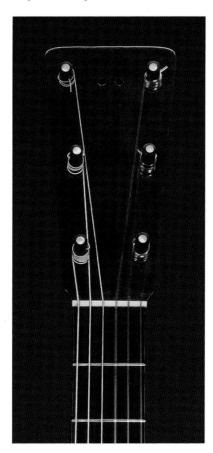 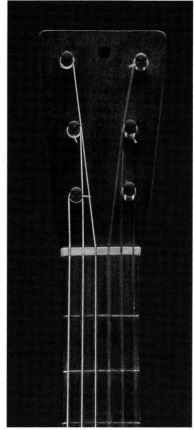 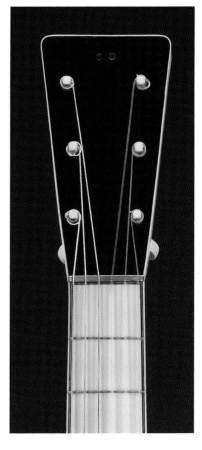

UNA SEGUIDILLA GITANESCA.

By John Phillip, R.A.

IN THE INTERNATIONAL EXHIBITION.

The elongated upper bout and "bell-shaped" lower bout, signatures of Cadiz guitars from this period, were emulated by C. F. Martin in his earliest Spanish-style guitars.

Antonio de Lorca Garcia (1798–1870) was the most noteworthy guitar maker working in the coastal city of Malaga in the south of Spain during the first half of the nineteenth century. His guitars were very similar in design to those made by the Pagés family, the most predominant makers in Cadiz during this period, with whom he is thought to have apprenticed.

This 1839 guitar by Antonio de Lorca demonstrates sophistication of construction lacking in most other instruments from Cadiz and may have been the sort of guitar played by Spanish guitar virtuosi on the New York stage. The two-piece sides and two-piece back are made from curly Spanish walnut, while the top is made of book-matched pieces of very high quality spruce. The guitar also has a three-ring rosette, a flat-ended peghead and a carved "dart," all of which became features of C. F. Martin's Spanish-style guitars.

DIMENSIONS

TOTAL LENGTH	36.63"	930 MM
BODY LENGTH	17.13"	435 MM

WIDTH

UPPER BOUT	8.06"	205 MM
WAIST	6.31"	160 MM
LOWER BOUT	10.69"	269 MM

DEPTH

NECK	3.5"	89 MM
WAIST	3.63"	92 MM
END	4"	101 MM

NUT WIDTH	1.81"	46 MM
SCALE	24.75"	628 MM
SOUNDHOLE	3.19"	81 MM

Decorative "pyramid" ends on a rectangular tied bridge, one of the characteristics of Antonio de Lorca's guitars, may have been a source for Martin's signature pyramid bridge design.

BRACING CONFIGURATION

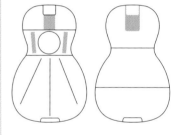

RELATIVE SIZE

42" (1067 MM)

36" (914 MM)

30" (762 MM)

18" (457 MM)

The flat-ended peghead and carved "dart" on the back of the neck joint are typical details of Cadiz guitars, which C. F. Martin emulated in the 1840s. Recio often included the hole in the upper portion of the headstock, a Spanish tradition used to hang a caseless guitar on the wall with a ribbon.

This guitar by José María Recio Beltrán (1806–c.1858) is typical of the Cadiz guitars made in the previous three decades. It is simply braced with four fans and has an almost-modern scale length. The back and sides were shaped from multiple pieces of locally available Spanish cypress, indicating that this was an inexpensive guitar made for a local clientele.

HECHA EN CADIZ
POR
JOSÉ RECIO,
calle de Sta. Elena, n. 330.
1853.

Recio and other Cadiz luthiers apparently produced enough guitars each year to warrant printing labels that included the specific year of production.

DIMENSIONS

TOTAL LENGTH	37.13"	943 MM
BODY LENGTH	18.31"	465 MM

WIDTH

UPPER BOUT	8.94"	237 MM
WAIST	6.88"	175 MM
LOWER BOUT	11.63"	295 MM

DEPTH

NECK	3.69"	94 MM
WAIST	3.88"	98 MM
END	4.19"	106 MM

NUT WIDTH	1.75"	44 MM
SCALE	23.81"	605 MM
SOUNDHOLE	3.19"	81 MM

BRACING CONFIGURATION

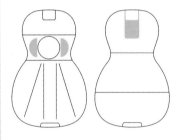

RELATIVE SIZE

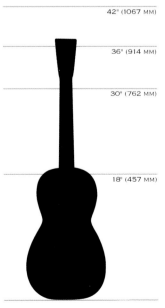

42" (1067 MM)

36" (914 MM)

30" (762 MM)

18" (457 MM)

CHAPTER 6

C. F. Martin in Pennsylvania, 1839–1850: A Period of Transition

RICHARD JOHNSTON

Figure 6-1. Martin & Coupa, c. 1840-1841 (Profile 16).

While moving to Pennsylvania after such a short period of time in New York was critical to securing his family's happiness, it proved an even more important step in establishing the business model that defined Martin's guitar company from that point forward. In New York City, C. F. Martin could rely on a close network of countrymen, craftsmen, retailers, and instructors who all helped him in both building and selling Martin guitars. Guitar instructors, for instance, could send their pupils to Martin to purchase an instrument and be paid a sales commission for their referral. Subcontractors could work on specific tasks in building Martin guitars, either in their own workshop or in Martin's, without needing to move or to demand full-time employment. Whether in building or selling guitars, Martin had many options open to him, depending on the customer and the instrument being requested.

Once in rural Pennsylvania however, Martin had to become more self-contained in the construction of his guitars, while, at the same time, he became more dependent on help from a distance to sell them. He had always known that he would need a sales outlet in New York City, and in John Coupa, an instructor to whom he had sold several guitars before leaving New York, Martin found a trusted business associate who would do much to shape both Martin's business and the guitars themselves in the next decade. This period has been glossed over in most previous studies of Martin guitars for a simple reason: there are essentially no surviving records for the 1840s. That Martin and Coupa were, respectively, the builder and the seller of instruments with a paper "Martin and Coupa" label has long been known, but there was little other information on this era until Philip Gura pieced together various fragments of communication to C. F. Martin, combining those letters with entries of expenses in Martin ledgers to craft a credible scenario. Although all that has survived are letters to Martin, with no communications from him to others, it is clear that he traveled to New York regularly, often spending weeks, not just days, in the city, and even delivering guitars to John Coupa in person. Thanks to Gura's research, previous visions of C. F. Martin as an isolated luthier struggling in a rural hamlet far from the city were abandoned. Instead, it is clear that during some years, Martin spent almost as much time in New York as he did at home in Cherry Hill.[1]

Advertisements placed in local newspapers in the 1840s by retailers or instructors offering Martin & Coupa guitars indicate that John Coupa was both a retailer and wholesaler of Martin guitars, as were Martin's later agents in New York City, Charles Bruno and C. A. Zoebisch & Sons. Not only did the paper labels in the instruments from this period list only Coupa's 385 Broadway address, the stamps on the guitars also continued to read "C. F. Martin, New York," just as they had in the mid 1830s. To a guitarist encountering such instruments and hoping to acquire one, or for an instructor or musical instrument retailer wishing to sell Martin guitars to their customers, all the markings point to New York, not Pennsylvania. Small ads placed in the New York Herald in 1842 and '43 list "Martin & Coupa, Guitar Manufacturers, 385

Broadway," and, even half a century later, all advertisements for Martin guitars give only the address of Martin's sales agent in New York City.

In recent years, a sizeable number of instruments with Martin & Coupa labels have been examined in detail, as have Martin guitars with so many similar characteristics to those with this label that it is clear they are from the same era. Martin's records from the late 1830s reveal how he entered the following decade, and the surviving records from the early 1850s offer a good sense of the larger Martin manufactory's production as it exited that period. Nevertheless, we have to rely on the surviving instruments themselves, many of which are illustrated in this volume, to tell us what happened between those bookends to Martin's 1840s production. Ironically, this period with no records is perhaps the richest in terms of the changes and development of instruments by C. F. Martin and his contemporaries. Labels in Martin guitars from the late 1830s and early 1840s mention "celebrated

Spanish and Vienna warranted Guitars...made in the best Italian style," and an 1842 ad reads, "Martin & Coupa Guitar Manufacturers...have constantly on hand a large assortment of Guitars, of French, German, and Spanish Model." While instruments from Europe were highly influential, what emerged after Martin's first two decades in Pennsylvania would be a uniquely American style of guitar.

In trying to track the evolution of Martin's guitars during the 1840s, we are fortunate that paper labels were still commonly used, and that the labels in many of these guitars have survived. These labels, and the fact that several "milepost" guitars with a unique history allow us to date their production within months, instead of years, means we can tentatively reconstruct the many changes to Martin guitars between 1839 and the early 1850s. The Martin & Schatz guitar (Profile 15) is a excellent example, as surviving records in the Martin Archives make it clear that before moving to Pennsylvania in mid 1839, C. F. Martin sold his

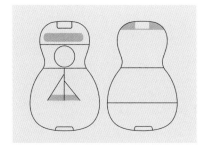

Figure 6-2. Tentative fan bracing in Martin & Schatz, c. 1839 (Profile 15).

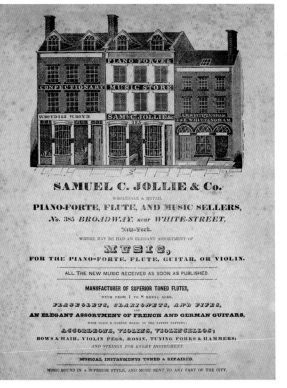

Figure 6-3. *Far left*. John Coupa's guitar showroom and lesson studio was upstairs from the Samuel C. Jollie & Co. music store, but there was probably little cooperation between the two businesses. Some of the ads Coupa placed in New York newspapers gave his address as "385 Broadway, upstairs," but also stated "No connection with the store below."

Figure 6-4. *Left*. Martin & Schatz, c. 1839 (Profile 15). The larger lower bout and fanned top bracing (figure 6-2) of this guitar produced shortly after Martin settled in Pennsylvania exemplify his early move beyond strictly Austro-German guitar design.

inventory to the New York City firm of Ludecus & Wolter, located at 320 Broadway, in the same block as Coupa's location. But Ludecus & Wolter were not Martin's sales agent for long, as their agreement ended in March of 1840, a convenient fact that makes it possible to date this guitar within a narrow time frame.

The second paper label in this instrument is one that appears in several guitars from Martin's early days in Pennsylvania. Soon after settling in Cherry Hill, Martin once again teamed up with Henry Schatz, his younger compatriot who had preceded him in leaving Markneukirchen for the New World.[2] The fact that Schatz made instruments with his own label that are virtually indistinguishable from mid-1830s Martins, and that at least two such guitars have labels indicating he was in Nazareth, make it easy to imagine a number of scenarios that resulted when the two friends lived only a few miles apart. While how this second wind in their partnership functioned is currently beyond our grasp, especially in terms of who did what on guitars bearing these labels, we do know Martin and Schatz produced guitars together until 1843, and perhaps later.[3] This particular Martin and Schatz guitar with two labels, which we know to be from 1839 or very early 1840, appears to be very much in the Austro-German style found in earlier Martin guitars made in New York, except for a distinctly larger lower bout and the more recently adopted "shield shape" bridge. Internally, however, it

See page 93 for Profile 15, Martin & Schatz, c. 1839

Figure 6-5. Below, guitars produced between 1839 and 1842 illustrate Martin's progression to a demonstrably Spanish-style instrument with a pronounced Spanish body outline, deeper sides and flat back, fan-pattern top bracing, and a rectangular tie-block bridge (Profiles 15–19).

has a small, three-brace pattern supporting the soundboard, instead of relying only on lateral braces, and we will see Martin's top bracing evolve quite quickly in the next few years

THE TRANSITION TO SPANISH STYLE

That the transition from building Austro-German style guitars to Spanish-influenced ones happened during Martin's Cherry Hill period has long been established, but only recently have we learned how early in the 1840s these changes in Martin guitars took place. All indications are that John Coupa, who replaced Ludecus & Wolter as Martin's primary sales agent, was the driving force behind Martin's rapid adoption of Spanish guitar elements. As David Gansz's essay has pointed out, Coupa, himself a performer on guitar, was very much in the center of the guitar concert scene in New York during this period, and Spanish guitarists made frequent appearances on New York concert stages.[4] More importantly, Coupa was a guitar instructor, and we know from later letters he wrote to Cherry Hill that many of the guitars sold with Martin & Coupa labels were ordered for specific customers. Since Spanish guitarists and their music were popular during this period, it is likely that in ordering guitars similar to those seen on the concert stage, John Coupa was simply supplying a demand for the type of guitars that were in fashion.

The guitars illustrated in Profiles 16, 18, 19, and 20 are telling examples of Martin's progression

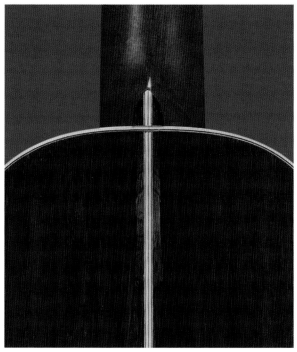

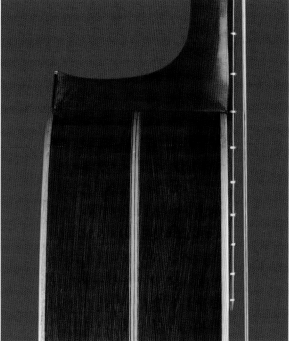

Figure 6-6. This small guitar (see Profile 21), with its mysterious "J. B. Coupa" label, is so thoroughly in the Spanish manner as to be an almost total rejection of the Austro-German style of Stauffer's Viennese instruments, and those Martin had been building in New York just a few short years earlier. But although guitars like this example prove Martin's skill and flexibility as a guitarmaker, the instruments that would make his reputation would be far less derivative of the guitars from Cadiz.

to a demonstrably Spanish-style instrument, and all have Martin & Coupa labels. The first (Profile 16), made with a bird's-eye maple back and sides, retains many Austro-German elements but has a more Spanish outline, plus deeper sides and a flatter back and a mature, three-strut fan bracing reinforcing the top. The next example in this transition (Profile 18) has both the Martin & Schatz and Martin & Coupa labels and is a similar amalgam of Germanic and Spanish elements, including three-strut fan bracing of the top. The critical difference on this example is the rectangular bridge with pyramid tips that would soon exemplify not only nineteenth-century Martins but also the more far-reaching American style of guitar in general. While later examples of the now-familiar "pyramid bridge" used ebony or ivory pins to anchor the strings beneath the guitar's soundboard, a "tie block" at the back edge of the bridge was used on Martin's earliest examples of this shape. This was a method of anchoring the strings found on all Spanish guitars and an indication of the origin of what was a new bridge outline for Martin when this guitar was made.[5]

The next Martin & Coupa–labeled guitar (Profile 19) shows much closer adherence to the style of early Spanish guitars, not only in its shape, which echoes guitars from Cadiz and is also almost exactly

the same size as Martin's later 2½ models, but also in its three-ring rosette, another feature borrowed from the Spanish that would define Martins and the American style guitar. The tie-block pyramid bridge and three-fan bracing pattern of the soundboard complete the Spanish package, making the guitar's Austro-German neck, even at this early date, seem almost an anachronism. The maple terz guitar (Profile 17), which has identical top and back bracing to the only slightly larger maple example, shows how Martin mixed and matched Spanish and Germanic styles during this period.[6] The terz guitar's shape and bridge predate Spanish influence, but the discrete three-ring rosette and straight-sided headstock with friction pegs soon became standard features on Martin guitars with pyramid-tipped bridges and the slimmer, Spanish-influenced body shape. The rough surface of the upper edge of this guitar's headstock suggests that the curved contour may not be original but was reshaped later from what would have been the tapered rectangular profile common in Spanish guitars. Although Martin had previously made a number of guitars with maple back and sides, he abandoned domestic hardwoods around this time, choosing instead to use tropical hardwoods from South America.

See page 94 for Profile 16, Martin & Coupa, c. 1840-1841

See page 96 for Profile 17, C. F. Martin, c. 1840-1841

See page 98 for Profile 18, Martin & Schatz– Martin & Coupa c. 1840-1841

See page 100 for Profile 19, Martin & Coupa c. 1840-1841

Continued on page 102

The shield shape shown here was Martin's second bridge design, at least on guitars made in the New World, replacing the more Austrian and German style of earlier models. This version was also short-lived, as the rectangular bridge with pyramid tips, inspired by Spanish guitars, replaced it within a few years. The ivory-edged abalone decoration was adapted for the later bridge shape and continued to be offered as an option until at least the mid 1850s.

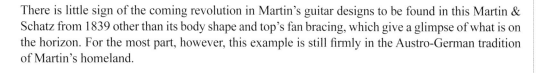

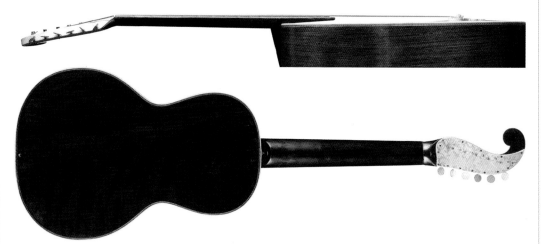

There is little sign of the coming revolution in Martin's guitar designs to be found in this Martin & Schatz from 1839 other than its body shape and top's fan bracing, which give a glimpse of what is on the horizon. For the most part, however, this example is still firmly in the Austro-German tradition of Martin's homeland.

SERIAL NUMBER 1296

DIMENSIONS

TOTAL LENGTH	37.44"	951 MM
BODY LENGTH	17.17"	436 MM

WIDTH

UPPER BOUT	9.21"	234 MM
WAIST	6.93"	176 MM
LOWER BOUT	11.61"	295 MM

DEPTH

NECK	2.68"	68 MM
WAIST	3.23"	82 MM
END	3.31"	84 MM

NUT WIDTH	1.77"	45 MM
SCALE	23.78"	604 MM
SOUNDHOLE	3.15"	80 MM

BRACING CONFIGURATION

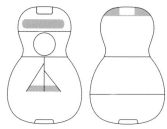

The Ludecus & Wolter label allows precise dating of this instrument, as the firm that purchased Martin's inventory of goods when he closed his New York shop was only the agent for selling Martin guitars for a brief time before being replaced by John Coupa.

Herringbone appears around the sides of this guitar, much as it does on earlier examples of Martins in the Austro-German style, but this is a very early example of the same marquetry used around the perimeter of the soundboard. Herringbone top borders would later become the signature of Martin's Style 28 guitars, a feature still in use today and widely copied by Martin's contemporary competitors.

RELATIVE SIZE

42" (1067 MM)

36" (914 MM)

30" (762 MM)

18" (457 MM)

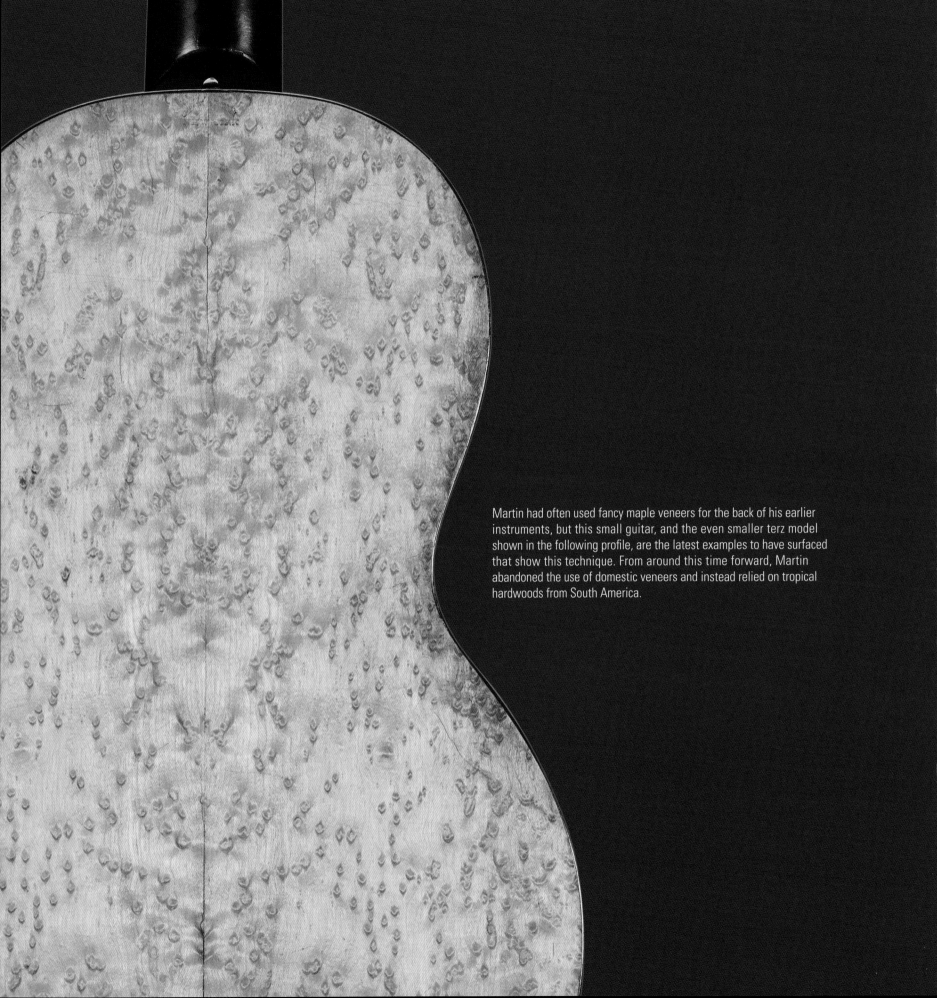

Martin had often used fancy maple veneers for the back of his earlier instruments, but this small guitar, and the even smaller terz model shown in the following profile, are the latest examples to have surfaced that show this technique. From around this time forward, Martin abandoned the use of domestic veneers and instead relied on tropical hardwoods from South America.

There is no surviving written record of Martin's transition from building pure examples of Austro-German style guitars, like those seen in previous chapters, to building close replicas of Spanish guitars just a few years later. This example, however, shows that transition in progress. The elongated body with a smaller upper bout and a three-ring soundhole rosette are hints of the changes that would follow, while the underside of the top indicates that Martin had already embraced the Spanish method of bracing the soundboard.

This is probably the earliest guitar shown in this volume with the Martin & Coupa label. By the time of Coupa's death almost a decade later, Martin guitars had been dramatically transformed and many of the features seen here abandoned.

DIMENSIONS

TOTAL LENGTH	36.38"	924 MM
BODY LENGTH	17.13"	435 MM

WIDTH

UPPER BOUT	8.56"	217 MM
WAIST	6.93"	176 MM
LOWER BOUT	11.56"	294 MM

DEPTH

NECK	3.13"	80 MM
WAIST	3.25"	83 MM
END	3.44"	87 MM

NUT WIDTH	1.75"	44 MM
SCALE	24"	610 MM
SOUNDHOLE	3.38"	86 MM

BRACING CONFIGURATION

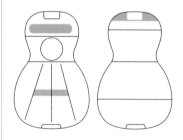

RELATIVE SIZE

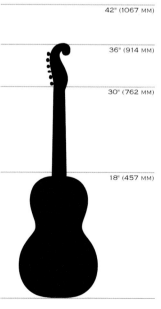

42" (1067 MM)

36" (914 MM)

30" (762 MM)

18" (457 MM)

The bridge, soundhole rosette, and binding on this guitar and the previous profile are almost identical. The bird's-eye maple is from the same flitch of veneers, and there are surviving records in Martin's archives of the purchase of this wood a few years earlier.

Although the materials, appointments, and construction details of this terz model and the guitar shown in Profile 16 suggest the two instruments were made at the same time, there is an important difference in their headstocks. This example shows a "peg head," rather than a headstock with "Vienna screws," and the rough surface of the upper edge suggests it may have been reshaped later. The original outline was likely to have been the now-familiar rectangle with tapered sides that Martin continues to use today.

DIMENSIONS

TOTAL LENGTH	32.00"	813 MM
BODY LENGTH	15.31"	389 MM

WIDTH

UPPER BOUT	8.38"	213 MM
WAIST	6.50"	165 MM
LOWER BOUT	11.38"	289 MM

DEPTH

NECK	3.38"	86 MM
WAIST	3.69"	94 MM
END	3.75"	95 MM

NUT WIDTH	1.75"	44 MM
SCALE	22.13"	562 MM
SOUNDHOLE	3.25"	83 MM

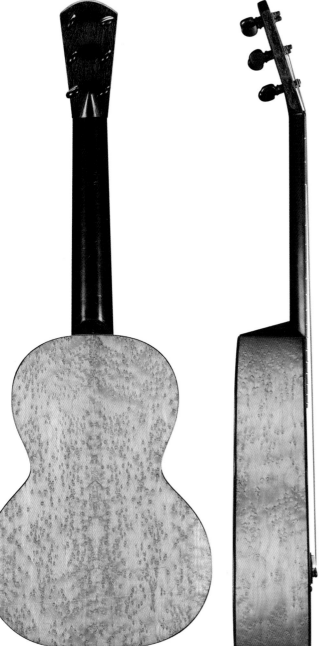

BRACING CONFIGURATION

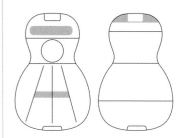

RELATIVE SIZE

42" (1067 MM)

36" (914 MM)

30" (762 MM)

18" (457 MM)

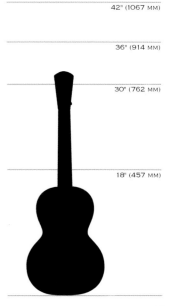

While later examples of the now-familiar "pyramid bridge" used ebony or ivory pins to anchor the strings beneath the guitar's soundboard, a "tie-block" was used on Martin's earliest examples of this bridge shape. Anchoring the strings by tying them to the back edge of the bridge was a method used on all Spanish guitars and was the origin of what was a new bridge shape for Martin when this guitar was constructed.

The rather confusing combination of both Martin & Coupa and Martin & Schatz labels suggests that this guitar was made shortly after Martin left New York for Pennsylvania in 1839. The top label represents Martin's off-and-on partnership in building guitars with his compatriot from Markneukirchen, Henry Schatz. The lower label signifies only a partnership to facilitate the sales of Martin guitars. Apparently, neither of these partnerships was exclusive; Martin also built and sold guitars without the assistance of either Schatz or Coupa around the same time.

DIMENSIONS

TOTAL LENGTH	36.75"	933 MM
BODY LENGTH	17.38"	441 MM

WIDTH

UPPER BOUT	8.31"	211 MM
WAIST	6.75"	171 MM
LOWER BOUT	11.38"	289 MM

DEPTH

NECK	3.50"	89 MM
WAIST	3.75"	95 MM
END	3.94"	100 MM

NUT WIDTH	2"	51 MM
SCALE	24.50"	622 MM
SOUNDHOLE	3.19"	81 MM

BRACING CONFIGURATION

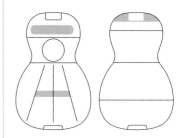

RELATIVE SIZE

42" (1067 MM)

36" (914 MM)

30" (762 MM)

18" (457 MM)

Even by mid-nineteenth-century standards, this Martin & Coupa guitar is very small. It shows a further step in blending Spanish elements into what had been an Austro-German design. Along with a decidedly Spanish body shape and top bracing, this example also has a rectangular bridge with pyramid tips that would soon exemplify not only nineteenth-century Martins but also the more far-reaching American style of guitar in general.

The engraving on the back plates of tuners that Martin sometimes referred to as "Vienna screws" show an almost endless variety of designs, from purely geometric to profusely floral. Perhaps some designs were repeated, but most of the engraving that has been encountered to date is unique. Butterflies were a common theme, but deer, parrots, and even a grasshopper were sometimes included as well.

This small Martin & Coupa is relatively plain compared to other Martin guitars shown in this volume, but it represents the upper end of what were more or less standard styles at the time. The appointments on Martin models were clearly still in flux, for although this example has a pearl rosette and ivory binding on both the body and the neck, there is no decoration up the middle of the two-piece rosewood back.

Martin is clearly leaning ever closer to Spanish guitar styles at this point, as indicated by the fan-braced top, tie-block bridge, and three-ring rosette, but the neck block has the same structure as found on Austro-German models. The use of more expensive "1 side screw" tuners may have been requested by the dealer or customer, as they would have made this instrument more costly than a guitar with friction pegs or three-per-side right angle tuners, both of which would have been more consistent with the Spanish style.

DIMENSIONS

TOTAL LENGTH	36.69"	932 MM
BODY LENGTH	17.36"	441 MM

WIDTH

UPPER BOUT	8.35"	212 MM
WAIST	6.81"	173 MM
LOWER BOUT	11.42"	290 MM

DEPTH

NECK	3.23"	82 MM
WAIST	3.43"	87 MM
END	3.62"	92 MM

NUT WIDTH	1.81"	46 MM
SCALE	23.94"	608 MM
SOUNDHOLE	3.39"	86 MM

BRACING CONFIGURATION

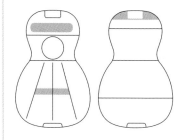

RELATIVE SIZE

42" (1067 MM)

36" (914 MM)

30" (762 MM)

18" (457 MM)

Figure 6-7. Spanish-style body shapes and tie block bridges can also be seen on the earliest extant guitars by two of Martin's competitors. *Right*, Schmidt & Maul, c. 1842; *far right*, Ashborn, c. 1845 (marked Firth, Hall & Pond, Profile 29). Both guitars also have fan-braced soundboards.

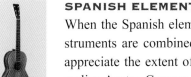

See page 102 for Profile 20, Martin & Coupa, c. 1841-1842

SPANISH ELEMENTS COMBINED

When the Spanish elements in these early 1840s instruments are combined in one guitar, we can truly appreciate the extent of the transformation from the earlier Austro-German style. (Profile 20) The delicately detailed pearl rosette, ivory bridge, and ivory-wrapped headstock of this instrument may be what first catch our attention, yet subtle touches are even more interesting in terms of Martin guitar evolution. These further advances toward the Spanish style include a cedar neck with a heel shaped like those on Spanish guitars, while the opposite end of the neck has a headstock volute and friction tuners borrowed from early Cadiz guitars as well.[7] While these elements are functional, two other features, one readily apparent from the outside and one only noticeable by looking through the soundhole, are solely cosmetic homages to the early Spanish style. As David LaPlante has pointed out, while two-piece sides were a functional necessity for early Spanish builders, this construction method represented extra effort with no structural gain for Martin, and the faux "Spanish foot" at the base of the neck block was a similar conceit.[8] This almost slavish attention to the Spanish guitar style is probably more indicative of Martin's response to consumer demand than his devotion to how those foreign guitars were constructed, for by the early 1850s, and perhaps earlier, the Spanish foot no longer appeared at the base of Martin's neck blocks, and constructing guitar bodies with two-piece sides was by then reserved for just a few models before being abandoned as well.[9]

For the next few years, however, all indications are that Spanish-style guitars were very popular, at least among fashionable New York guitarists, and tie-block bridges, fan bracing of the top, and heel blocks with Spanish-foot appendages at their base appear on other guitar brands from the 1840s. Again, John Coupa and the New York stages where Spanish guitarists appeared seem to have been the center of this

Figure 6-8. C. F. Martin, c. 1842–1844 (See Profile 24). Most of Martin's highly decorated Spanish style guitars are quite small, but this size 1 example is an exception. During this period, pearl inlay was usually reserved for only the rosette, even on deluxe models, while the rest of the body was decorated with colorful wood marquetry.

Figure 6-9. This is the only known photo of the Martin family's Cherry Hill home as it appeared in the mid-nineteenth century (although the building is still standing, it has been severely altered). As described in a family biography written in 1915, the Martin workshop was on the first floor, with living quarters above.

fascination with Spanish-style guitars, for the recently formed guitar-making partnership of Schmidt and Maul was in the same neighborhood as Coupa, and for a time in the same building.

But even as Spanish body shapes and structural elements swept through the New York community of guitar makers, the earlier Austro-German style was at times tenacious, as indicated by the Schmidt & Maul guitar shown in Profile 25. Despite its Spanish body and details, plus its cedar neck with Spanish heel, this early example from former Martin employees is topped with a scroll headstock and "Vienna" tuners, and the paper label inside shows what is clearly an Austro-German style guitar but with a Spanish-style rosette.

At least part of the demand for locally made guitars was no doubt driven by the poor survival rate of most Spanish-made instruments brought to the harsh climate of the northeastern United States. While the hot, humid summers may have been what made visitors uncomfortable, it was the cold winters, and the extremely low humidity produced by heating homes with coal or wood fires, that caused many guitars made in more temperate climates to shrink and crack until they were unplayable. While we do not know how Martin cured his wood supplies while in Cherry Hill, the workshop built in the 1850s in Nazareth had an extensive network of storage space in the rafters, making use of the rising heat in the winter and the roof's warmth in the summer, to thoroughly dry the wood before it was made into guitars. Martin's warranty of his instruments was probably reassuring, but it was their reputation for holding up over time, regardless of climate, which was one of the key attributes that made them in such demand.

John Coupa may have been the performer and instructor who helped fuel the demand for Spanish-style guitars, but he certainly did not have a monopoly on sales of Martins made in the Spanish fashion. This fact is demonstrated by two guitars (Profiles 23 and 24) that have typical stamped Martin brands, but no paper label mentioning Coupa, because those

See page 120 for Profile 25, Schmidt & Maul, c. 1842

See page 116 for Profile 23, C. F. Martin, c. 1842–1844

See page 118 for Profile 24, C. F. Martin, c. 1842–1844

labels were only applied to guitars sold, either retail or wholesale, through his 385 Broadway address. Martin had been selling guitars directly to a few instructors in Philadelphia since shortly after his move from New York, and was soon selling instruments to a small group of retailers and instructors in other cities such as Pittsburgh, Baltimore, Albany, and Boston. Unfortunately, the absence of labels, not to mention records, means it is impossible to know who ordered these particular instruments.[10] But it would appear that as Martin's reputation spread, so did the knowledge that, while the guitars were labeled as being from New York, they were in fact made in Cherry Hill, Pennsylvania, and their maker was not difficult to find.

While these guitars do not reveal where they were sold, they do indicate that Martin was progressing further into the Spanish style and already adding his own refinements. The top bracing is now a mature five-strut fan pattern, much like what became standard on later Spanish guitars, but the rectangular Spanish foot at the base of the neck block has been slimmed to a distinct point, with the Martin stamp prominent at the tip. The more elaborately decorated of these two instruments has an abundance of wood marquetry and ivory binding as well as a glittering pearl rosette and ivory bridge. Such opulence in pearl and ivory is rarely found on Spanish guitars, nor is the nickel-silver nut, a less showy feature that appears on many of the Martin guitars of this period but was an added effort and expense soon abandoned. This instrument, with a wide band of complex and highly colorful marquetry over

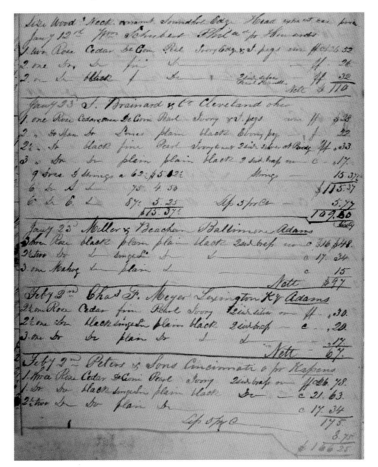

Figure 6-10. This ledger page from January of 1854 shows orders for six $26 size 1 models with "De Goni" ornament (bordering the top), pearl soundhole rosette, and ivory edge (binding). The example ordered by J. Brainard & Co. of Cleveland, however, lists "cedar, screw" in the "Neck" column and cost an additional two dollars. The adjustable "screw neck," once a standard feature on most of Martin's Austro-German models, was rarely requested by this time, especially on larger guitars. The order for Peters & Sons of Cincinnati, at the bottom of the page, includes half a dozen size 1 models, and this dealer would order the first size 0 model to appear in these records just four months later. Ohio guitarists were clearly fond of Martin's larger models.

the center line of the two-piece sides, and with additional marquetry next to the binding on the sides as well, represents a high point in the use of marquetry to decorate the sides of a Martin guitar. Henry Schatz apparently aided Martin in finding sources for such marquetry, and a detailed letter from him dated 1850 included samples, and their prices, from a supplier in Hamburg.[11] Even more telling is that this highly decorated instrument is a large guitar for the period, one of the few fan-braced examples to have surfaced, at least to date, with the dimensions of Martin's size 1. This was a concert-size guitar of the 1840s; one Martin would rely upon as his largest model for the rest of the decade and into the early 1850s.

Building what were quite credible Spanish-style guitars may have been Martin's goal for a time, but he did not stop there for long. Even when building an instrument for one of the most highly regarded performers of the period in 1843, the team of C. F. Martin and Henry Schatz made some significant departures from the Spanish guitars they had examined, and from their own versions of those models. Dolores Nevares de Goni, better known as Madame de Goni, was a highly regarded performer, especially in an era when female soloists on the guitar were unheard of.[12] While we do not know who

made the guitar Madame de Goni brought to the U.S. in the early 1840s, or how its top was braced, we do know that Martin & Schatz, and the New York City guitar-making partnership of Schmidt & Maul, both copied her instrument. Fortunately, one of the two guitars Martin made for De Goni has survived, and it gives us a firsthand look at what was almost certainly a turning point in the evolution of Martin guitars (Profile 26).

That the guitar Martin & Schatz made for Madame de Goni utilized X-pattern top bracing has been discussed in Chapter 5, but what is perhaps equally important is that fan bracing is not the only Spanish feature that this guitar lacks. The Cadiz guitars that had clearly influenced C. F. Martin a few years earlier all have wood friction pegs and tie-block bridges, while the guitar made for De Goni has a slotted headstock with mechanical right-angle tuners and a bridge with pins to anchor the strings. Although she was a stage performer, Madame de Goni apparently had little interest in the highly decorated guitars Martin often made in smaller "parlor" sizes, presumably for women. In terms of appointments, the De Goni guitar shown here is quite close to what would later be a middle-of-the-price-list style 21. However, another very similar Martin & Schatz labeled guitar, with the same headstock, bridge, and bracing, but with ivory binding and a pearl rosette, has also surfaced in recent years, suggesting that higher-priced versions were made at the same time as this one.[13]

In terms of the direction Martin guitar design would take in the next few years, it would be hard to overestimate the importance of the "De Goni model." Of all the mid–nineteenth century performers on guitar that Martin, or his agents, mentioned in promoting sales, the name "Madame de Goni" is by far the most prominent. Despite the fact that there is no mention of her in the music press just a few years after she was presented with the Martin & Schatz guitar, her name was the first listed among endorsers of Martin guitars in advertisements printed forty years later. The name "De Goni" was also frequently used in Martin's ledgers, intended only for his own use, and appears over two dozen times in the descriptions of "ornament" (around

Figure 6-11. Martin & Coupa size 1, c. 1846. The chain-like rosette pattern on this "large De Goni" model owned by Col. John Wilkins is similar to a marquetry pattern which has been found on early guitars made in Cadiz, Spain.

See page 122 for Profile 26, Martin & Schatz, c. 1843

See page124 for
Profile 27,
C. F. Martin,
c. 1843–1849

the top) and "soundhole" (rosette) for guitars sold in 1852 alone. We can assume that "De Goni chain" probably describes a pattern of wood marquetry often found on Martin guitars from this period; a similar "chain link" pattern for the back strip of style 28 Martin guitars is still in use today (See Profile 34). We are again hampered by a lack of records and correspondence from the 1840s, but it may be more than coincidence that Madame de Goni left New York for Cincinnati in 1844 and that ninety-four Martin guitars were sold to Cincinnati dealers in 1852-3 alone, far more than were sold in any other city, including New York.

An interesting Martin family footnote to at least one of the guitars made for Madame de Goni, and quite possibly the instrument illustrated in this volume, comes from a genealogy written by a granddaughter of C. F. and Otilia Martin, Clara Emelie Ruetenik Whittaker (1870–1958).[14] While much of the granddaughter's account regarding Martin guitars is marred by romantic errors, the description of an evening in her grandparents' Cherry Hill home, probably passed down to her from older relatives, is interesting because it was written long before Mike Longworth's first edition of *Martin Guitars: A History* was published, and her account could not have been influenced by historical views of Madame de Goni and her influence. After explaining that her grandfather took pleasure in having musicians at his house, Clara continues:

> In the day-time they often strolled into the orchard, read and amused themselves and in the evenings they gave little family concerts to Grandfather's infinite delight.
>
> Madame de Gorci [sic], probably the finest professional guitar-soloist of her time, in the South, was also there. It was she, I think, who clung to her Spanish guitar and would have no other. One evening when all were gathered together, Grandfather brought her a guitar that he had made in the exact shape of her Spanish guitar, but with his thin sounding board and other Martin characteristics. Quite casually, he asked her to try it. Madame de Gorci took the instru-

ment but displayed little interest. She struck a few chords, played a piece or two, then got up, took her Spanish guitar and set it in a corner. "I'm through with that," she said. "I don't care for it anymore. This is the guitar I want." That must have been a great triumph for Grandfather.[15]

Especially since this retelling of the "Madame de Goni switches to a Martin" story comes from another side of the extended Martin family, it suggests that De Goni's endorsement was a memorable milestone for the family as well as for the guitar maker, who at that time was probably marking his progress just ten years after leaving the homeland.

Of course, there is no way we can know the exact order in which many of the guitars in this section were constructed. With few exceptions, both the Martin stamps on these guitars, and the Martin & Coupa labels inside many of them, were unchanged for the entire 1840s decade.[16] We can assume that the interior construction of these instruments is a more reliable gauge when dating Martin's evolutionary stages in guitar design than are exterior details, however, simply because Martin's retailers and instructors were far more likely to make a request regarding tuners or decoration than they were to make demands about top bracing or the shape of the neck block.

An excellent example of the difficulty dating some of these instruments is the guitar shown in Profile 27, for although it has many structural details and appointments in common with the guitar made for Madame de Goni, and has very similar dimensions, the top shows a radically different experiment with X-pattern bracing: two X-bracing patterns, one on either side of the bridge. Was it made earlier or later? Was it a first-of-its-kind experim ent or simply one of only two extant examples of this bracing pattern found to date?

Fortunately, the differences between the guitar made for Madame de Goni and a similar instrument we know to have been purchased just a few years later give us a clear view of the direction Martin was

headed. It would be hard to imagine two more different Martin customers than the guitar-playing diva Dolores Nevaras de Goni and the young West Point graduate John Darragh Wilkins, but both of them received their Martin guitars as gifts. Wilkins, a career soldier who went on to spend forty years in the U. S. Infantry, was given his Spanish-style Martin when he graduated from West Point in 1846 (Profile 28). Both De Goni and Wilkins went to Mexico with their Martin guitars in the late 1840s, but for very different reasons. He traveled there to fight in the Mexican War, returning from Mexico City in 1848 after the treaty was signed defining the current border between the United States and Mexico. Madame de Goni went to Mexico City to perform the following year, leaving behind her young children, including an infant only four months old, and created a minor scandal as a result. After her concert career, Madame de Goni settled in New Orleans and wrote widely published guitar arrangements of popular melodies, while John Wilkins, who later rose to the rank of Colonel, fought in the Civil War battles of Fredericksburg and Bull Run. Unlike Madame de Goni, John Wilkins was probably never paid to play guitar, but his Martin, in its original wooden coffin case with added fortifications, traveled with him throughout his long military career.

Despite their considerable personal differences, these two guitarists owned similar instruments that are essentially the largest model Martin made at the time. The Colonel Wilkins guitar, as it has come to be called, is even more Spanish in style than Madame de Goni's; it has a friction-pegs headstock, two-piece sides, and centerline decoration of the back that is continued into the heel cap of the neck. Neither of these guitars has fan-pattern bracing supporting the top or a tie-block bridge, despite the prominent Spanish-style foot that cannot be missed with a casual glance into the soundhole. In terms of Martin guitar evolution, however, the most telling difference between these two guitars requires a mirror to detect. While the De Goni guitar has an early version of X bracing of the soundboard, it is a pattern only found on a limited

Figure 6-12. *Far left.* Case for the Martin & Coupa guitar that Colonel John Wilkins carried throughout his military career. Most Martin cases were built of poplar and stained black, but there are records of cedar and even rosewood cases supplied with deluxe guitar models. The faux wood grain finish on the standard Martin case seen here was probably added when it was given additional reinforcements to protect the guitar during Wilkins's travels.

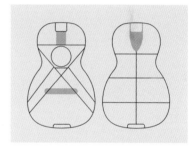

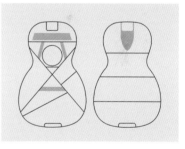

Figure 6-13. Bracing patterns of C. F. Martin guitars made for Madame de Goni (*top*), and Colonel Wilkins, (*above*), showing their different X bracing. The asymmetrical X bracing on the Wilkins guitar, made in 1846, three years after the De Goni, is almost identical to the bracing still used on the majority of Martin guitars.

See page 126 for Profile 28, C. F. Martin, c. 1846

number of extant guitars by Martin (and a few by his contemporaries) from this period. The Colonel Wilkins version, however, has the same asymmetrical X-pattern top bracing that is found on a vast majority of later Martin guitars, with the exception of inexpensive models, and this same X pattern is in use to the present day. While we cannot claim that this is the earliest Martin guitar with such bracing, it does point to the fact that while C. F. Martin would continue to produce instruments that were heavily dependent on the designs of Spanish guitar makers, by 1846 he had apparently already settled on a very different way of building them. All the parts of a guitar contribute to its voice, but the most critical element is the top, or soundboard. From around the time the instrument given to Colonel Wilkins was constructed, Martin's X-braced guitars would have a distinctly American accent.

It was not just the interior construction of Martin's guitars that was undergoing a series of changes by the mid 1840s, but also his entire way of doing business. The Martin family's move from New York City to Cherry Hill, Pennsylvania, had no doubt temporarily slowed the production of guitars, but the financial Panic of 1837, and the nation's slow recovery from it, was probably even greater reasons for sluggish sales. However, as the reputation of Martin guitars began to spread, so did the number of inquiries from guitar instructors and music retailers who wanted to sell his instruments. John Coupa was a loyal partner and close friend, but his was a relatively small business that could not grow as rapidly as the Cherry Hill workshop could, and did, expand its production. Letters from Coupa to Martin in the late 1840s indicate that during the hottest months of the summer, Coupa fled the city with his wife and children to a cooler country retreat, but the Martin workshop apparently built and shipped guitars year 'round, with the only concession to the summer's heat being a slightly shorter work week of fifty-five hours. Martin had begun selling guitars to instructors in nearby Philadelphia shortly after his move to Pennsylvania, and one, William Schubert, even placed ads in local papers a few years later announcing his "large assortment of guitars, from the celebrated manufactory of C. F. Martin." Increasingly, such ads by instructors and retailers outside New York City make no mention of Martin's partnership with Coupa. By around the time John Wilkins was given a Martin guitar as a graduation present, other retailers must have been carrying similar guitars, for the Wilkins instrument and others of like construction have no paper Martin & Coupa label, and instead have only Martin's typical stamps. A few surviving letters from the late 1840s to Martin include orders for multiple guitars from Jonathan Mellor of Pittsburgh (1848), and Thayer and Collins of Albany, New York (1849). While these letters do not show the highly personal tone of Coupa's correspondence, they show a familiarity with Martin guitar sizes, styles, and prices of the period that suggests neither firm was a new account.[17] While John Coupa continued to supply retailers in cities such as Baltimore and Boston with Martin & Coupa labeled guitars, by the late 1840s Martin was apparently also directly supplying new accounts in distant cities such as St. Louis, Nashville, and New Orleans. Ten years after leaving New York City, Martin was required to move beyond his highly personal method of selling guitars and do business with instructors and retailers he might never meet, instead relying solely on written communication. ★

Figure 6-14. *Opposite page*, Martin & Coupa, c. 1841–1843 (Profile 20). Martin's quest for simplicity, in keeping with the straightforward designs of most Spanish guitars, did not keep him from building instruments with a wealth of subtle details, obviously aimed at affluent customers. Despite this instrument's ivory binding, ivory bridge, and ivory-wrapped headstock, the body decorations are simple combinations of dark and light wood lines, including the top border. This simplicity shifts the viewer's focus to the goncalo alves back and sides, a figured South American hardwood with coloration that almost matches the Spanish cedar neck. Martin had used goncalo alves earlier on a few Austro-German models, but he would soon use only Brazilian rosewood for all but his least expensive guitars.

The goncalo alves used for the back and sides is a South American wood Martin had also used during his New York years (see Profile 7), but it has not been seen on Martins made after the 1840s. Note the extreme curve to the profile of the laminated Spanish cedar neck heel, the simple lines that border every edge of the sides and back and the light line along the center of the sides in the Spanish style. The top is also bordered in dark and light lines, rather than marquetry.

TOTAL LENGTH	36.25"	921 MM
BODY LENGTH	18"	457 MM

WIDTH

UPPER BOUT	9"	229 MM
WAIST	7.63"	194 MM
LOWER BOUT	12.25"	311 MM

DEPTH

NECK	3.75"	95 MM
WAIST	3.94"	100 MM
END	4"	102 MM

NUT WIDTH	1.88"	48 MM
SCALE	24.59"	624 MM
SOUNDHOLE	3.5"	89 MM

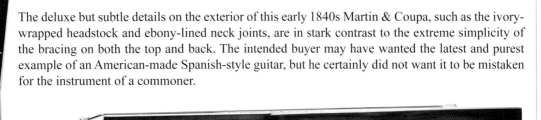

The deluxe but subtle details on the exterior of this early 1840s Martin & Coupa, such as the ivory-wrapped headstock and ebony-lined neck joints, are in stark contrast to the extreme simplicity of the bracing on both the top and back. The intended buyer may have wanted the latest and purest example of an American-made Spanish-style guitar, but he certainly did not want it to be mistaken for the instrument of a commoner.

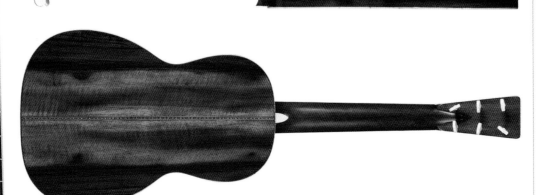

BRACING CONFIGURATION

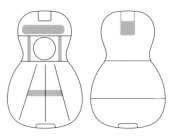

The bridge is of simple design, but even when crafted in ebony this form was more time-consuming to make than a bridge with ivory or ebony pins. Martin abandoned the use of ivory bridges with the Spanish-inspired tie-block just a few years after this guitar was constructed, but the rectangular shape with pyramid tips was continued until the early 1930s.

RELATIVE SIZE

42" (1067 MM)

36" (914 MM)

30" (762 MM)

18" (457 MM)

MARTIN & COUPA

Guitar Manufacturers

385 Broadway

up Stairs

NEW YORK

While the Martin & Coupa label was only affixed to guitars that John Coupa sold, Coupa handled a majority of Martin's production in the early 1840s, as the builder had not yet begun to sell large numbers of guitars to an expanded network of dealers in cities far from New York.

From the white holly binding and simple purfling lines to the widely spaced rosette rings, everything about this guitar's appointments suggests that the maker was closely following a Spanish example.

John Coupa crossed out his earlier address on Broadway, adding the address of the studio he occupied while representing Martin guitars until his death in 1850.

This small guitar is one of the most purely Spanish-style Martins to have surfaced to date. While prominently displaying Martin stamps on the faux Spanish foot at the base of the neck block, the paper label just below only lists J. B. Coupa, with no mention of the actual maker. We may never know the reason it does not bear the usual Martin & Coupa label, but it indicates Coupa's desire to present guitars with no sign of Martin's Austro-German origins.

Not only do the exterior details on this instrument seem purely Spanish, but its interior bracing is equally indebted to makers from Cadiz. Despite its small body, roughly equivalent to Martin's later size 2½, its neck is a full two inches wide at the nut, a dimension that has remained the standard for full-sized Spanish guitars to the present day.

DIMENSIONS

TOTAL LENGTH	35.43"	900 MM
BODY LENGTH	17.48"	437 MM

WIDTH

UPPER BOUT	8.44"	211 MM
WAIST	6.84"	171 MM
LOWER BOUT	11.52"	288 MM

DEPTH

NECK	3.64"	91 MM
WAIST	3.84"	96 MM
END	4.04"	101 MM

NUT WIDTH	2"	51 MM
SCALE	24.72"	628 MM
SOUNDHOLE	3.56"	89 MM

BRACING CONFIGURATION

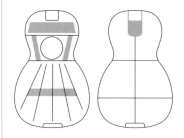

RELATIVE SIZE

42" (1067 MM)

36" (914 MM)

30" (762 MM)

18" (457 MM)

Martin may have borrowed the simple headstock shape of Cadiz guitars, but for a deluxe model like this one, the straight lines were given subtle decoration. Here the headstock edges are wrapped in ivory and a thin line of ebony, which also highlights the complex joint at its base.

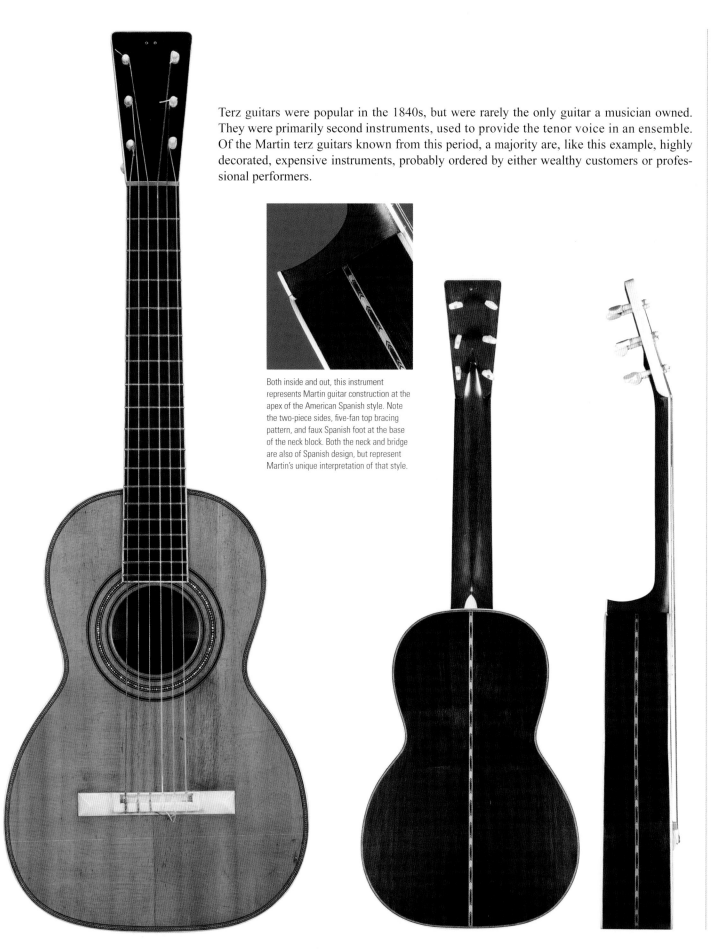

Terz guitars were popular in the 1840s, but were rarely the only guitar a musician owned. They were primarily second instruments, used to provide the tenor voice in an ensemble. Of the Martin terz guitars known from this period, a majority are, like this example, highly decorated, expensive instruments, probably ordered by either wealthy customers or professional performers.

Both inside and out, this instrument represents Martin guitar construction at the apex of the American Spanish style. Note the two-piece sides, five-fan top bracing pattern, and faux Spanish foot at the base of the neck block. Both the neck and bridge are also of Spanish design, but represent Martin's unique interpretation of that style.

DIMENSIONS

TOTAL LENGTH	33.25"	845 MM
BODY LENGTH	16.13"	410 MM

WIDTH

UPPER BOUT	8.44"	211 MM
WAIST	7.13"	181 MM
LOWER BOUT	11.56"	294 MM

DEPTH

NECK	3.5"	89 MM
WAIST	3.63"	92 MM
END	3.88"	98 MM

NUT WIDTH	2"	51 MM
SCALE	22.13"	562 MM
SOUNDHOLE	3.25"	83 MM

BRACING CONFIGURATION

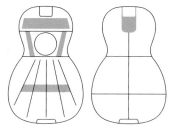

RELATIVE SIZE

42" (1067 MM)

36" (914 MM)

30" (762 MM)

18" (457 MM)

The two-piece sides, plain rosette, and simple light and dark lines for decoration indicate Martin's allegiance to the straightforward Spanish style. Despite the simplicity, ivory binding on both the body and neck suggest that this was not an inexpensive guitar.

Martin was deeply committed to the Spanish style by the time this guitar was constructed, and the bare minimum of back bracing is combined with a complex 5-fan pattern of top bracing, with additional "finger" braces on both sides despite the relatively small body size. Both the headstock and bridge are also the result of Martin fine-tuning what are essentially Spanish designs.

The nickel silver nut shown here is commonly found on Martin's higher models during the 1840s and early 1850s. It was a far more expensive material than ivory, and more difficult to shape. Considering these guitars were all strung with gut strings, not steel, this was probably a touch of luxury with little functional advantage.

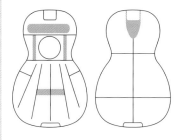

DIMENSIONS

TOTAL LENGTH	36.75"	933 MM
BODY LENGTH	18"	457 MM

WIDTH

UPPER BOUT	8.88"	225 MM
WAIST	6.44"	164 MM
LOWER BOUT	12.25"	311 MM

DEPTH

NECK	3.38"	86 MM
WAIST	3.68"	94 MM
END	4.13"	105 MM

NUT WIDTH	2"	51 MM
SCALE	24.69"	627 MM
SOUNDHOLE	3.44"	87 MM

BRACING CONFIGURATION

RELATIVE SIZE

42" (1067 MM)

36" (914 MM)

30" (762 MM)

18" (457 MM)

117

The profusion of wood marquetry located on the centerline and top and bottom of the sides and around the edge of the top has faded with time, and as a result displays muted colors. When new, however, the colors were more bold and bright, and when combined with gleaming ivory binding and a sparkling pearl rosette, the result would have been far less subtle.

DIMENSIONS

TOTAL LENGTH	37.38"	949 MM
BODY LENGTH	18.75"	476 MM

WIDTH

UPPER BOUT	9.25"	235 MM
WAIST	7.5"	191 MM
LOWER BOUT	12.75"	324 MM

DEPTH

NECK	3.62"	92 MM
WAIST	3.81"	97 MM
END	4.25"	108 MM

NUT WIDTH	1.94"	49 MM
SCALE	24.75"	629 MM
SOUNDHOLE	3.5"	89 MM

Compared to the previous profile, this larger size 1 model has far more opulent appointments, but with the exception of the pin bridge it is still very much in the Spanish style. This was Martin's largest concert model at the time, a size that is rarely found from this early period.

BRACING CONFIGURATION

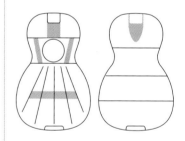

The curved profile of the neck heel, with its distinct upsweep to the heel cap, is a feature this guitar shares with other early Spanish-style Martins. However, while most of these models have simple purfling decorating the centerline of the back, with matching lines between the two-piece sides, the wide band of colored wood marquetry seen in this guitar is another example of Martin's willingness to spice up the Spanish style on guitars intended for his more affluent customers.

RELATIVE SIZE

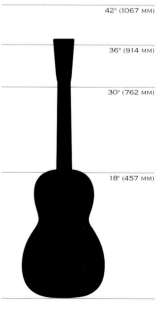

42" (1067 MM)

36" (914 MM)

30" (762 MM)

18" (457 MM)

G. L. SCHMIDT & C. MAUL
MANUFACTURERS of VIOLINS AND GUITARS
AND IMPORTERS of MUSICAL Instruments,
Broadway 412½ New-York.
All Kinds of Musical Instruments neatly repair'd.

— Faber

The label design chosen by Schmidt & Maul is decidedly different
from any of the paper labels used by Martin. Not only does it show a quite
accurate drawing of a guitar, it also states "All Kinds of Musical Instruments Neatly Repaired." Surviving records in the Martin Archives indicate
that the company founder took in many repairs, but there was never an
advertisement of that fact on any label appearing in Martin's guitars.

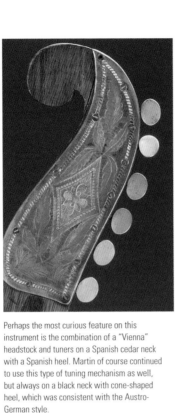

Perhaps the most curious feature on this instrument is the combination of a "Vienna" headstock and tuners on a Spanish cedar neck with a Spanish heel. Martin of course continued to use this type of tuning mechanism as well, but always on a black neck with cone-shaped heel, which was consistent with the Austro-German style.

DIMENSIONS

TOTAL LENGTH	36.13"	918 MM
BODY LENGTH	16.81"	427 MM

WIDTH

UPPER BOUT	7.94"	202 MM
WAIST	6.5"	165 MM
LOWER BOUT	11.19"	284 MM

DEPTH

NECK	3.44"	87 MM
WAIST	3.63"	92 MM
END	3.88"	98 MM

NUT WIDTH	1.88"	48 MM
SCALE	23.81"	605 MM
SOUNDHOLE	3.31"	84 MM

BRACING CONFIGURATION

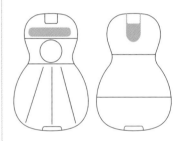

RELATIVE SIZE

42" (1067 MM)

36" (914 MM)

30" (762 MM)

18" (457 MM)

Louis Schmidt was the more experienced partner in the guitar-making team of Schmidt & Maul, having lived in the Martin household on Hudson Street in New York for at least five years. While he spent much of his time there helping construct guitars in the Austro-German style, by the time this guitar was made, its scroll headstock was about the only non-Spanish feature still visible. The fan-braced top and two-piece sides, plus the three-ring rosette and tie-block bridge, all indicate the extent to which the Spanish style dominated the New York guitar market.

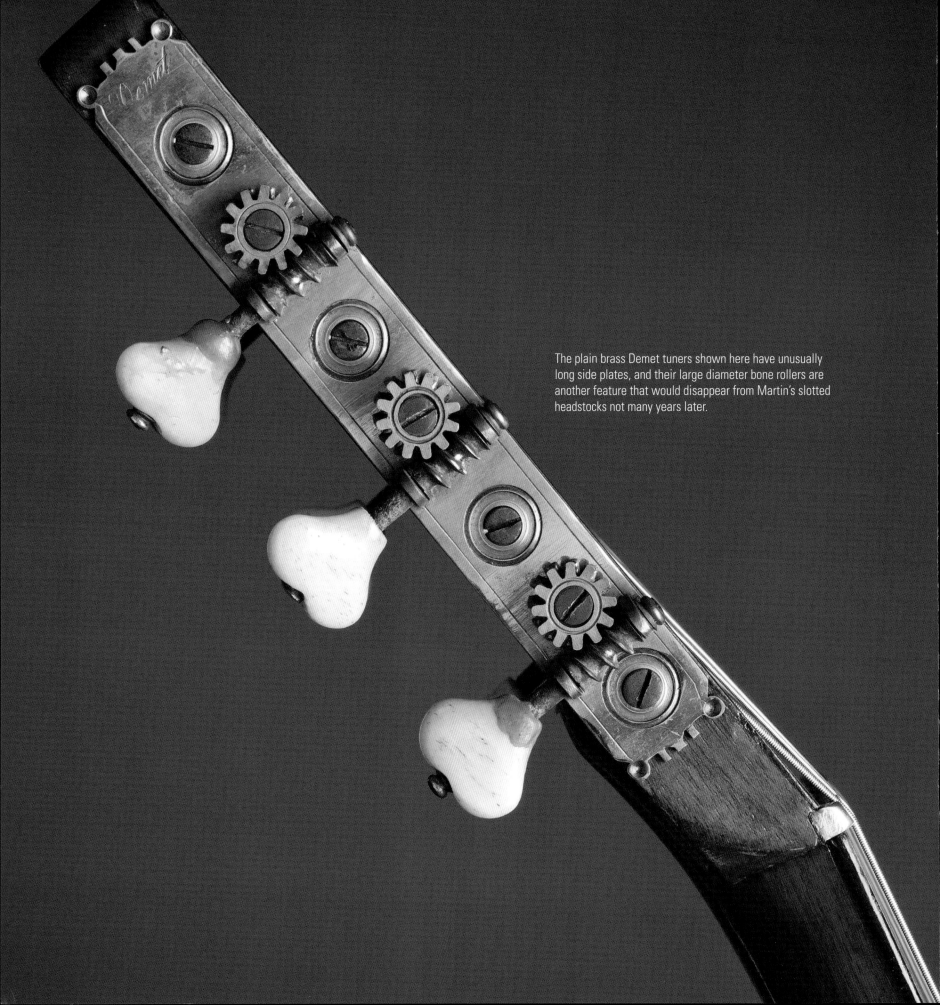

The plain brass Demet tuners shown here have unusually long side plates, and their large diameter bone rollers are another feature that would disappear from Martin's slotted headstocks not many years later.

DIMENSIONS

TOTAL LENGTH	37.13"	941 MM
BODY LENGTH	18.86"	479 MM

WIDTH

UPPER BOUT	9.29"	236 MM
WAIST	7.68"	195 MM
LOWER BOUT	12.80"	325 MM

DEPTH

NECK	3.62"	92 MM
WAIST	3.82"	97 MM
END	4.25"	108 MM

NUT WIDTH	1.85"	47 MM
SCALE	24.80"	630 MM
SOUND HOLE	3.43"	87 MM

At first glance, this guitar looks quite modern, as if it would fit comfortably with similar size 1, Style 21 Martin guitars made twenty-five or more years later. However, in addition to the label, this instrument's Spanish back bracing pattern, faux Spanish foot at the base of the neck block, and early hybrid of fan and X-pattern top bracing are indicative of its 1840s origin.

The inscribed Martin & Schatz label, and correspondence between Madame de Goni and Martin, date this guitar to 1843. The spelling of her last name on the label is curious, but not unusual in an age when phonetic spelling was common.

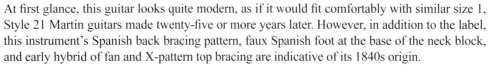

BRACING CONFIGURATION

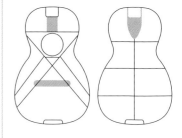

RELATIVE SIZE

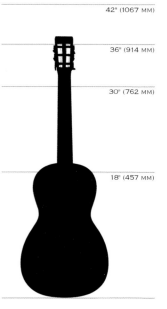

42" (1067 MM)

36" (914 MM)

30" (762 MM)

18" (457 MM)

The marquetry in the center of the rosette, a pattern of interlocking dark and light triangles, is found throughout Martin's Spanish period but disappeared well before the beginning of the twentieth century.

Stamped "C. F. Martin New York," this Size 1 guitar is large for its c. 1843 date. It is one of two currently known examples with two small X braces, which are located at either end of the bridge. The rosewood binding and dark and light purfling lines were later standardized as Style 21.

At first glance, except for its metal nut and early marquetry pattern decorating the rosette and centerline of the back, this size 1 model could pass for a typical mid-century Martin that sold to retailers for about $20. A look inside the guitar with an inspection mirror, however, reveals another of Martin's many experiments with bracing the soundboard as he moved away from Spanish fan patterns to the structure that would come to define the American guitar.

The bracing of the top, with X-pattern intersections at either end of the bridge plate, is certainly earlier than the modern X bracing of the Wilkins guitar shown in Profile 28 and may represent Martin's efforts to find a pattern that didn't conflict with the holes required by a pin bridge.

DIMENSIONS

TOTAL LENGTH	37.75"	959 MM
BODY LENGTH	18.82"	476 MM

WIDTH

UPPER BOUT	9.31"	237 MM
WAIST	3.88"	192 MM
LOWER BOUT	12.75"	324 MM

DEPTH

NECK	3.54"	86 MM
WAIST	3.88"	98 MM
END	4.38"	628 MM

NUT WIDTH	1.88"	48 MM
SCALE	24.75"	628 MM
SOUND HOLE	3.5"	89 MM

BRACING CONFIGURATION

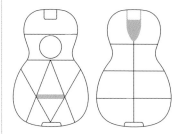

RELATIVE SIZE

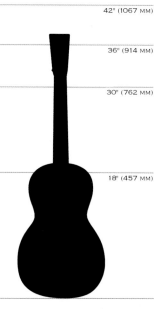

42" (1067 MM)

36" (914 MM)

30" (762 MM)

18" (457 MM)

Instead of ivory or rosewood, the body is bound in white holly, and, with the exception of the rosette, there is no patterned marquetry. Instead, all decorations are simple combinations of dark and light lines. Martin would abandon both of these features less than a decade after this guitar was constructed.

This guitar, which was given to John Darragh Wilkins upon his graduation from West Point in 1846, is a prime example of the influence of Spanish guitars on C. F. Martin's designs, although, by this date, he had already adopted the X-pattern top bracing that became the company's signature style in coming years.

Wilkins rose to the rank of Colonel in the U. S. Army, and, by all accounts, this guitar traveled with him in its reinforced case throughout his long career in the military.

The interior construction of Wilkins's guitar is another example of Martin's hybridization as the American style took form—the top bracing is American, but the back bracing and neck block are decidedly Spanish.

DIMENSIONS

TOTAL LENGTH	37.5"	953 MM
BODY LENGTH	18.75"	476 MM

WIDTH

UPPER BOUT	9.31"	237 MM
WAIST	8"	203 MM
LOWER BOUT	13.0"	330 MM

DEPTH

NECK	3.56"	90 MM
WAIST	3.88"	98 MM
END	4.38"	111 MM

NUT WIDTH	2"	51 MM
SCALE	24.75"	628 MM
SOUND HOLE	3.56"	90 MM

BRACING CONFIGURATION

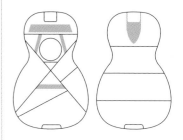

RELATIVE SIZE

42" (1067 MM)

36" (914 MM)

30" (762 MM)

18" (457 MM)

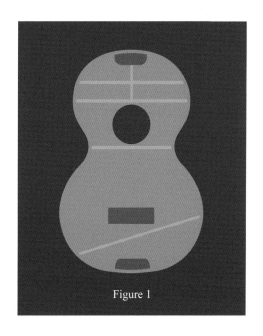

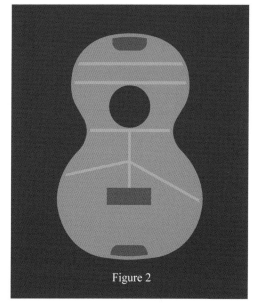

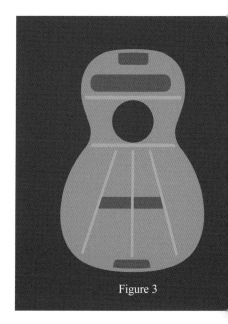

Figure 1   Figure 2   Figure 3

Figure. 1. Martin & Schatz c. 1835–1837 (See Profile 7).

Figure. 2. Martin c. 1837 (See Profile 9).

Figure. 3. Martin c. 1840-1841 (See Profile 17).

Figure. 4. Martin & Coupa c. 1842-1843 (See Profile 22).

Figure. 5. Martin c. 1843–1848 (See Profile 35).

Figure. 6. Martin c. 1859–1864 (See Profile 44).

The earliest guitars from C. F. Martin were braced in a simple transverse style (See Figure 1), which essentially had one or more angled braces across the lower bout.

With the advent of Martin's more literal interpretation of Spanish design, he began producing guitars that had five fan braces (See Figure 4). These guitars, as well as the three-fan models, often used an elaborate pyramid-ended, Spanish-style tie bridge in ebony or ivory, onto which the strings were tied and passed over an L-shaped ivory saddle insert that was laboriously fitted into the front of the bridge.

It seems reasonable that Martin would want to return to the simpler-to-make pin bridge that he had used from the beginning. However, the five-fan brace design required great precision in neck alignment in order to drill the necessary holes through the top without piercing one or more of the fans.

An apparent solution to this problem was Mar-

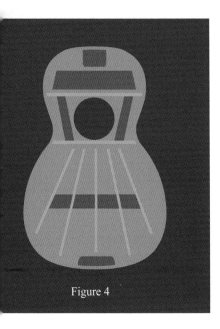

Figure 4

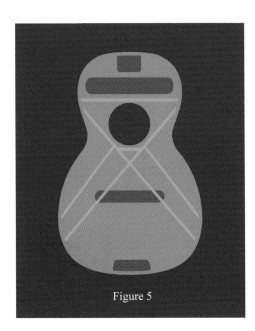

Figure 5

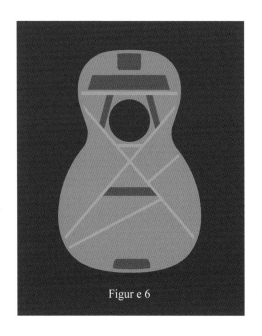

Figur e 6

tin's earliest form of X bracing, in which he eliminated the center fan of the five-fan pattern (fan #3), then splayed and extended the two inner fans (#2 & #4), so they crossed behind the sound hole. This cleared the bridge plate of any obstruction to the use of the simpler, and more efficient to make, pin bridge (see Figure 5). Note that the two outermost braces (fans #1 & #5) remain in a similar position to their placement in the earlier pattern seen in Figure 4.

In the mature form of the Martin X-bracing pattern, which was evidently first used just a few years later, an angled transverse brace below the bridge has been reintroduced, harking back to the early Austro-German style. The long outer braces that ran parallel to the lower portions of the X in Figure 5 have disappeared, replaced on the treble side by a short brace that runs perpendicular to the lower leg of the X, just above the bridge plate (see Figure 6). In later versions of this pattern, another short brace

was added on the opposite (bass) side, making the top bracing symmetrical except for the angled transverse brace below the bridge.

Martin also continued to fine-tune the three-fan pattern used on small, lower-priced models, adding an angled transverse brace above the tail block, between the two outer fan braces.

Although we now better understand the evolution of Martin's top bracing, the reasons for those changes given here are only informed speculation. There are no surviving written records or drawings by Martin, or any of his contemporaries, that give any information on such transitions in internal construction. ★

CHAPTER 7

MADAME DE GONI AND THE SPANISH-AMERICAN GUITAR

DAVID GANSZ

Arguably, the foremost extant instrument in the early history of the American guitar is one Martin built for Maria Dolores Esturias y Navarres de Goni (1813–1892) in 1843 (Profile 26). The guitar is exceedingly important historically not just because of its obvious personal association, but because its bracing is not typical of the Spanish fan design. Instead, it features a prototype of what Martin would develop into his famous X bracing during the 1840s. This revolutionary method was codified by 1850[1] and is used to this day.

The first known mention of the mysterious Madame de Goni dates from France in 1837, when she was twenty-four years old:

> *Madame Nevarez de Goni, who is distinguished by extremely beautiful black eyes, a head as Castilian as possible, and the most adorable thinness that one can wish, regaled us with a considerable number of sonatas and varied themes on the guitar.*[2]

Shortly thereafter, in 1840, she appeared on the London music scene (referenced as coming from Madrid) both as a composer of published waltzes for the guitar,[3] and concertizing with such luminaries as Luigi Sagrini[4] and Henri Herz.[5] While the impetus for her trans-Atlantic crossing to New York later that year is unclear, her arrival was heralded in the press:

> *A distinguished female, professor of the Spanish guitar, has just arrived from Europe. Her name is **Dona Dolores de Goni**, a Spanish lady of exquisite*

> *beauty, and still more exquisite accomplishments in Spanish music. During the last spring and summer she gave many exhibitions before the royalty and nobility of England, that brought forth great applause.*[6]

Evidently, according to a passenger manifest, she and her husband, who was also a guitarist, arrived in New York on November 2, 1840, on the ship *Sheffield*. Her first known American stage appearance took place on December 10, 1840,[7] at New York's City Hotel, and her second on December 23, 1840, when she performed at the annual benefit concert for the St. George's Society at the National Theatre in New York, with 3,000 spectators in attendance.[8] Six days later, she and her husband performed another concert at the City Hotel.[9] The press gave her a remarkably positive review, comparing her to Trinidad Huerta, the famous Spanish guitarist who had concertized in New York from 1824–1826:

> *Those who remember Huerta, the great Guitarist of the world, who was in this country some ten years ago, will be forcibly reminded of his extraordinary performances by the admirable execution of the very interesting Spanish lady, Madame de Goni, who gives a second Concert at the City Hotel, on Tuesday evening. If she does not equal Huerta in power, she is not behind him in rapid execution.*
>
> *Those who have not heard the Guitar in the hands of a Spanish lady, whose peculiar instrument*

Figure 7-1. *Opposite page,* Madame de Goni as she would have appeared in the 1840s. This portrait hung in the Louisiana State Museum from about 1920 until 1983.

ᴷ▶ DONA DOLORES NEVARES DE
GONI, Spanish Professor of the Guitar, begs leave re
spectfully to thank her friends and the public for their liberal patronage at her last concert, and to inform them that
her next concert will take place at the City Hotel, on
TUESDAY EVENING 29th December, at half past 7 o'
clock.

Figure 7-2. After her first New York concert appearance, Madame de Goni placed this notice in the *New York Evening Post* on December 19, 1840. "DONA DOLORES NEVARES DE GONI, Spanish Professor of the Guitar, begs leave to respectfully thank her friends and the public for their liberal patronage at her last concert, and to inform them that her next concert will take place at the City Hotel, on TUESDAY EVENING 29th December, at half past 7 o'clock."

Figure 7-3. Atwill's Music Saloon as it appeared when it opened at 201 Broadway in 1834. John B. Coupa's address that same year was 195 Broadway, just out of the picture to the left.

it is, are not aware how expressive and effective it may be made. The performance of the overture to *Semiramide, by Madame de Goni and her hus-band, at her late Concert, was a beautiful effort of art, and gave all the delicate shades and coloring that are generally expected from an orchestra alone. The patronage that this lady had received since she has been amongst us, will ensure her a numerous company.*[10]

She almost immediately made herself a fixture at Atwill's Music Saloon,[11] the first "retailer" of C. F. Martin's guitars in New York:

The fashionable music stores and lounges for musical people, at the date I am writing, were Atwill's Music Saloon, at the sign of the Golden Lyre, 201 Broadway; Millett's, Broadway (Mr. Millet still remaining in the same store); Firth and Hall, Franklin square; and Davis and Horn, of Broadway.

The first establishment, being next door to my place of business, I quickly became acquainted with its proprietor, Mr. Joseph F. Atwill, (now and for a long time past a resident of California), and many a delightful hour was passed by me there, and I was thus brought into immediate connexion, if not intimacy, with numbers of musical people.

Among the celebrities that in the year 1840 flashed for a while upon the musical horizon, and who were daily to be seen at Joe Atwill's, were... Madame Dolores de Goni (guitarist).[12]

Apparently not content to capture the New York audience alone, Madame de Goni began touring almost immediately. We know of at least one concert in Philadelphia in February of 1841.[13] In addition, the following description exists of a house concert in Philadelphia in April of that year:

I had yesterday quite a treat—listening to a Spanish Lady who played on the Guitar... She has extraordinary delicacy of touch and feeling... I was delighted to hear her...& shall always listen with pleasure to the tones which recall memories of by gone years...[14]

By the end of that year, she already enjoyed such notoriety that a piano composition was dedicated to her.[15] It was in Boston, however, that Madame de Goni made the greatest impression, as recorded in a letter regarding her house concert there in early 1842:

A Spanish woman with a guitar has furnished the sweetest, softest most expressive music ever heard in Boston. Everybody is amorous of the guitar, and this instrument despised bitterly by all but lovers and adventurers under balconies, is exalted in the estimation of the sober-minded. Last evg. Monday, Mrs. Ritchie had a graceful gathering where were violincello and guitar, guitar was the admired of all admirers. In this was hid a little Divinity. Allyne Otis waltzed with the Spanish woman, and Longfellow talked Spanish.[16]

Indeed, the famed poet Henry Wadsworth Longfellow was in attendance, and he was impressed enough to recount his experience of De Goni in separate letters two days apart:

There is a sweet Spanish woman here, playing the guitar, La Señora de Goñy,—delicious.[17]
...La Señora De Goñy, whose guitar delights me more, perhaps because it awakens sweet remembrances of early youth and Spain;—perhaps because a woman plays it, and the devil is in it.[18]

Beyond the confines of smaller parlor appearances in private homes, she also excited reviewers on larger, public Boston stages:

Madame de Gony is a most delightful performer on the guitar, and is certainly an artiste of high merit. She appears to have the most perfect command of the instrument. Her performances were distinguished for neatness, beauty, grace, sweetness, power, variety, finish, expression, and pathos. We have never heard anything like it. She was received by the audience with the warmest enthusiasm.[19]

This Boston concert was her first known in collaboration with the renowned cellist, George Knoop. Interestingly, in Baltimore in June of 1842 we learn that Knoop arrived with "the controversial Dolorez N. de Goni."[20] The controversy she stirred had to do with the nature of her relationship with Knoop, who had apparently replaced her husband, both on and off the stage.

De Goni's concert travels next brought her into close geographical proximity to C. F. Martin, when, on July 18, 1842, she gave a concert at the Moravian Women's School in Bethlehem, Pennsylvania, less than ten miles from Nazareth.[21]

The next month found her and Knoop departing New York "for Saratoga and Canada."[22] In upstate New York, they captivated audiences at concerts in Utica, Auburn, Rochester, and Buffalo:

Such music never before struck upon our ear... Senora de Goni flung her fingers across the strings of that sweet instrument, in a manner which showed we have never sufficiently appreciated the instrument. Fairies could not have more effectually chained us to the spot, as we listened to the notes of the 'merry guitar.'[23]
Madame De Goni is equally a mistress of Spanish Guitar. She touches it with most exquisite taste, and with a skill not to be surpassed. Its harmonies are no longer the curt, twanging harmonies commonly extort (sic) from that instrument but are produced with a combination, finish, and delicacy almost marvelous. While listening to her guitar and Mr. Knoop's violincello in concert, one is uncertain to which to devote his ear, agreeably distracted as it is by a display as rare as it is delightful of diverse skill so perfectly exhibited.[24]

Apparently, Madame de Goni's husband was no longer in the picture by this time, and, by the fall of 1842, the last recorded mention of him suggests he was a member of the Rainers, a touring family of northern-European folk singers who would be the immediate inspiration for the homegrown Hutchinson Family Singers in New Hampshire. (The Hutchinson Family Singers in turn presaged the appearance of the Weavers and Peter, Paul and Mary in the twentieth century).[25]

"After a journey west and through Canada," De Goni and Knoop were back in Utica, where again her guitar playing was lauded and applauded:

Madame De Goni has taught us, for the first time, that the Guitar may become a delightful solo instrument: that instead of being confined to accompaniment, by moonlight, of sentimental singers, for the gratification of sentimental hearers, it can be made, independent of such associations, to 'discourse most eloquent music.'[26]

In addition to having wowed Longfellow in Boston, De Goni also played for Ralph Waldo Emerson

Figure 7-4. An 1835 ad for Atwill's Music Saloon, which includes: "Splendid Guitars of rosewood, birdseye maple and satin wood, with the patent screw heads and inlaid with pearl, ivory, & c. of great variety of paterns [sic] and of all prices."

at a house concert in Baltimore on January 6, 1843.[27] Spring of 1843 saw Knoop and De Goni on a southern tour, playing in Washington, D.C., Richmond, Virginia, and Charleston, South Carolina.[28] An 1843 reviewer wrote:

This lady has a peculiar art of drawing from her instrument the tones of the human voice. Her playing is a song of continuous sweetness, and executed in a style at once exquisite and dramatic. This lady, indeed, succeeds in what guitarists generally are almost afraid to attempt…her performance is, in every respect, charming.[29]

See page 122 for Profile 26, Martin & Schatz, c. 1843

If Madame de Goni had not already encountered C. F. Martin in Atwill's Music Saloon in 1840 or shortly thereafter, or at her concert in Bethlehem in the summer of 1842, three pieces of historical evidence suggest she was in direct contact with Martin in 1843. The first is an 1855 recollection by James Ballard, a guitarist who, according to Martin's ledgers, was purchasing guitars from him in the 1830s, including a Spanish guitar on August 16, 1838. Ballard reports:

In 1843 Madame De Goni brought to New York a large pattern Spanish guitar, from which a number have been made, and distributed over the United States, by Martin, of Pennsylvania, and Schmidt and Maul, of New York.[30]

Martin was captivated by whatever Spanish guitar she had in her possession. One of his granddaughters recounts a family story of how he made a copy of her Spanish guitar and presented it to her while she was staying in his Cherry Hill home, presumably in the summer of 1843.[31] (See Chapter 6, p. 106.) The 1843 date is bolstered by the recollections of a writer who attended a concert by De Goni and Knoop in Bethlehem (again, just ten miles from Martin's Cherry Hill home) that year:

The greatest violincellist who ever performed in the United States was George Knoop, a pupil of the great Romberg. He possessed almost the powers of a Pagganini [sic]. He spent much time here, and the Bethlehem musicians were drawn towards him as by magic art. In 1843 he travelled with Signora De Goni, a Spanish lady, and a noted guitarre performer. They gave a concert, which I well remember; it was a treat. Never before was such enthusiasm manifested at a concert in Bethlehem as there was then.[32]

Finally, the date of 1843 is solidified by the fact that, later that year, "Madame de Goni was assisted in a duet by Signor Coupa, an excellent professor of the Guitar."[33] Coupa had the sole agency for Martin guitars in New York City. Not surprisingly, then, De Goni wrote a letter to Martin and Coupa on November 8, 1843, regarding the guitars they made for her

Messrs Martin & Coupa—Gentlemen: Before Leaving New York, I feel compelled to express my satisfaction and admiration of the two Guitars manufactured for me. I unhesitatingly pronounce them superior to any instruments of the kind I have ever seen in this country or in EUROPE for tone, workmanship and facility of execution. These remarks are not intended to apply solely to those you have made for me. Those which I have examined in your room are not less deserving of my praise, and I confidently recommend them to the public. DOLORES N. DE GONI, New York, 8th November, 1843.[34]

What is almost certainly one of the two guitars mentioned by De Goni in her letter has survived, and now resides in the collection of the Martin Museum in Nazareth (Profile 26). The guitar has a late style Martin & Schatz label inside with a remarkable endorsement: "Made for Madam De Gone [sic]."[35] Comparisons with writing by John Coupa from letters in the Martin Archives suggest that the endorsement on the label was probably penned by Coupa himself. This may well be the guitar

Coupa mentions in another letter to Martin. Dated November 29, 1849, it states:

I have a guitar to be repaired, it is broke in the back, can you tell me how I can send it, or if you can do it when you come in the city. It is a fine guitar, one you made for Mrs. Degoni. I had it here more than one month.[36]

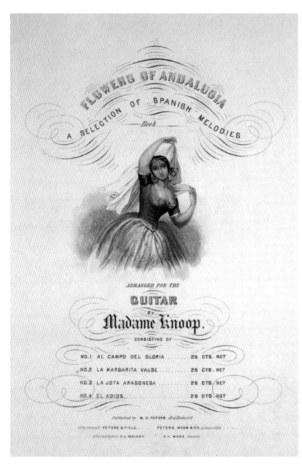

This description matches well with the condition of the guitar Martin built for De Goni, which has two cracks on the back. The repairs appear to be very old and may well have been executed by C. F. Martin Sr. himself.

Most likely with this guitar in hand, De Goni played with Knoop at his "farewell" concert in New York in January of 1844, according to the *New York Tribune*. "Not sufficiently appreciated," they sought a more hospitable clime in New Orleans[37] and Havana, Cuba, that spring, and:

In the fall of 1844, two artists came to Cincinnati to establish themselves as teachers and performers. Mr. Knoop modestly announced through the press that he was 'universally acknowledged both in Europe and this country as one of the greatest performers on the violincello that ever lived,' and that he would soon give a concert. The Cincinnati Gazette advised him to lower his price from one dollar to half a dollar, if he wished a full house.

The 'cellist's wife, Madame Knoop De Goni, who had 'few equals as a guitarist,' followed the Gazette's suggestion when she gave her first concert on October 24. Perhaps a woman could lower the price without loss of face. After the concert the Gazette reported that the guitar could not be played 'with greater sweetness.'[38]

Another Cincinnati newspaper reported, regarding her first concert there: "The tones she produces are as liquid and full of tenderness and pathos as the richest and most highly cultivated voice."[39]

Madame de Goni married Knoop in 1845,[40] and a most remarkable first-hand account exists of their living situation together in Cincinnati in 1846:

In February 1846 Gertrude James began to study with Madame Knoop. When she went to arrange for the lessons, she was much pleased with Madame Knoop but shocked by her obvious poverty. 'One of the greatest 'cellists that ever lived' could provide but one poor room for housekeeping. Madame Knoop had to earn her own living, going from house to house to give lessons.

A month later Gertrude wrote home that Madame Knoop had given a concert, assisted by local artists. Madame had played 'divinely,' and Gertrude had been completely 'enchanted.' Delia Carter had sung with her 'usual strength,' dressed in brightly striped stone-colored frock,

Figure 7-5. *Flowers of Andalusia: A Selection of Spanish Melodies* by Madame Knoop, W. C. Peters, Baltimore, 1850. Madame de Goni published three books of guitar music under her husband's name. The third, published in 1858, is the last historical record of her existence before her death in 1892.

Figure 7-6. The label of a guitar made by C. F. Martin for Madame de Goni in 1843 (Figure 7-8 and Profile 26). John Coupa is believed to have written the inscription on the label, which reads, "Made for Madam DeGone" (sic).

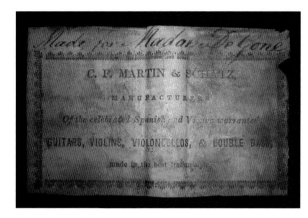

with a cherry-colored velvet headdress with gold fringe. Professors Tosso, Knoop and Goodson had 'produced most delightful sounds.' The concert yielded sixty-five dollars, but nearly all of it had to be paid to a pawn shop immediately to redeem sundry articles including Mr. Knoop's best violincello.[41]

In June of 1846, Leopold de Meyer performed a concert in Cincinnati, as a "benefit for Knoop and his singer-guitarist wife."[42]

From here, it is unclear what path De Goni's life took. A Cincinnati newspaper hints at her plans to go to Havana and South America late in 1847; she gave a concert in Cincinnati on April 4, 1848, and was not mentioned in any Cincinnati sources thereafter.[43] Meanwhile, Knoop took to the road with pianist Henri Herz and violinist Camillo Sivori for a concert tour in New York, Richmond, and Philadelphia in 1847-48. Evidently, he returned neither to Cincinnati nor to De Goni, as he was in Philadelphia from March of 1848[44] until his death there on Christmas day of 1849.

An October 1849 letter from John B. Coupa to C. F. Martin indicates that De Goni had gone to Mexico, abandoning her "children and 4-month old baby." According to biographical information contained in the Louisiana State Museum, De Goni was reported to be the wife of Juan Ignacio Laborde y Trueda, Interim Spanish Consul in New Orleans (1852-1853), and died there in 1892. Astonishingly, aside from the Coupa letter, the only record of her activities between 1847 and her death are three publications for the guitar, dated 1847,[45] 1850,[46] and 1858[47]—all published under the name Mrs. (or Madame) Knoop. However, Martin's late–nineteenth century distributor, Zoebisch, continued to mention her name in Martin guitar advertisements until at least 1893, the year after her death.

With its large plantilla and proto–X bracing, the surviving guitar that C. F. Martin made for Madame de Goni stands as the "missing link" between Martin's Spanish-influenced, fan-braced guitars and those that would become standardized, codified, and serve as models for all of his future production. Martin's grandson, C. F. Martin III, is quoted in 1973 as stating, "The big crossbar was my grandfather's idea and was modified from the fan bracing."[48] The X brace, as we know, would define the steel-strung, flat-top acoustic guitars of the twentieth century and beyond. Seen in this light, the "De Goni guitar" is perhaps the first true American—and modern Martin—guitar. ★

Figure 7-7. This Zoebisch & Sons ad for Martin guitars, published in 1892, the year of Madame de Goni's death, still puts her first in a list of "the best solo players ever known," whose testimonial to the quality of Martin's instruments "could be added" if it were necessary. Remarkably, De Goni had not appeared on the concert stage in nearly fifty years.

Figure 7-8. Martin & Schatz, 1843 (Profile 26). This guitar, one of two C. F. Martin made for Madame de Goni, carries a prototype of the X bracing that would ultimately help define his American-style guitars of the 1850s and beyond.

CHAPTER 8

The Spanish Guitar as Adopted by James Ashborn

DAVID GANSZ

The culture of the United States of America underwent significant changes between 1820 and 1850, which were driven by rapid population growth,[1] the invention of the telegraph, improved transportation of people and goods (via canals, railroads, and trans-Atlantic steamships), and the growth of urbanization and industrialization. These pivotal decades were particularly characterized by an incipient phase of mass production—itself an outgrowth of the industrial revolution—that quickly spread to the realm of musical instruments. Prior to the new, "manufactory" method of construction, instruments had been assembled literally piecemeal, following the age-old tradition of the guild system of crafts, known since medieval times. A master craftsman would work to turn out a product from start to finish, and imparted his knowledge to apprentices over many years of training. While an individual worker might specialize in a certain production task, or manufacture a discrete piece of the finished product, he was still expected to rise through the ranks of journeyman and apprentice to achieve the level of master, after which he could build a complete instrument unaided.[2]

C. F. Martin was a master in this Old World tradition, having apprenticed both in his father's workshop in Markneukirchen, Saxony, and, purportedly, in the workshop of Johann Stauffer in Vienna. Beginning in New York City in 1833, he built guitars with the occasional help of another craftsman or two, Henry Schatz, Louis Schmidt, and George Maul preeminent among them. After he moved to rural eastern Pennsylvania in 1839, he gradually employed more hands in the process, and his "factory" eventually utilized steam engines to power woodturning lathes and other machinery. At no time, however, could Martin's early operations be characterized as industrialized, whereby mass production resulted in the routinization of specialized activities in the service of expediency.

The English-born "mechanic" James Ashborn (1816–1876), on the other hand, seized on the industrial method of mass production and, between 1848 and 1864, utilized it exclusively to manufacture guitars in a factory of his own along the Naugatuck River in Connecticut. Ashborn's operation proved so successful that his output of finished goods was *triple* that of Martin during the same years.[3]

INDUSTRIALIZATION ALONG CONNECTICUT'S NAUGATUCK RIVER

Connecticut was especially notable for its many mechanically inclined thinkers who exploited rivers for waterpower to turn the machinery of their small-scale factories:

The system of interchangeable manufacture, which originated with two Connecticut gunmakers, Eli Whitney at Whitneyville, just outside New Haven, and Simeon North of Berlin, spread rapidly all over the state and was applied to the manufacture of clocks, hardware, and other articles. It gave order and direction to the labor-saving instinct and made it effective.

The interchangeable system can hardly be called an invention, but it comes near being one. It was a new method, and one which was far from obvious. That the corresponding parts of a mechanism, such as a gun, could be made interchangeable was thinkable, but that parts could be so produced not only commercially but actually cheaper than by old hand methods was incredible. Even if the system is not itself an invention, it is made possible only by a multitude of inventions covering the gauges, machines, and special jigs and fixtures to replace hand operations...

The next field to use the interchangeable method was that of clockmaking. Only a year or so after Whitney began his work at Whitneyville, Eli Terry at Windsor, later at Plymouth, began manufacturing wooden clocks in lots, first in twenties and hundreds, and within a few years by thousands...It is understood he did so on suggestions from Whitney. Terry's neighbors called him crazy, and said that such quantities could never be sold, but his new tools enabled him to lower the price of his clocks so that the market was more than able to absorb them. He was followed by Seth Thomas and Chauncey Jerome, both of whom worked for him.[4]

When the noted clockmaker Eli Terry diverted a Connecticut waterway and used a waterwheel to power his clockmaking enterprise in 1806, "This may have been the first instance in the United States of mass production of interchangeable parts by machinery of a domestic product."[5] However, Terry's son, recounting his father's biography, made a point of paying homage to another one of Connecticut's pre-eminent (yet almost entirely forgotten) innovators in early mechanical ingenuity—Asa Hopkins (1779–1838) of Litchfield County, which borders the Naugatuck River:

As part of this history, it should be here stated, that Asa Hopkins, of the parish of Northfield and

town of Litchfield, Connecticut, obtained a patent about the year 1813 on an engine for cutting wheels...Mr. Hopkins, whose factory was four miles or more north of Thomaston, profited little by the patent. He had few superiors as to mechanical skill, however, and really did more in the way of improvements in machinery than those whose names have become a trade mark...[6]

Asa Hopkins was intimately connected with the greatest names in early clockmaking in the United States. One undocumented story has Eli Terry duping Hopkins' wife into giving him the key to Asa's clock shop, with Terry consequently stealing an idea from a mechanism he saw and patenting it as his own.[7] Some believe that one of Asa's nephews, Orange Hopkins, "may have apprenticed to Eli Terry at one time."[8] More historically accurate is the recorded fact that, in 1836, Hopkins "sold a tract of woodland to Seth Thomas,"[9] a later student of Terry's who would have Thomaston, Connecticut, named for him and his clock factory. While Terry has been called "the last of the Craftsmen and the first of the Industrialists"[10] for being the first to utilize waterwheel power in the mass production of clocks in 1806, Asa Hopkins was not far behind when he opened his first waterwheel powered clock shop in 1812.[11]

Following a decade and a half of successful clock making, Hopkins next turned his ingenuity to the making of woodwind instruments, primarily flutes:

Hopkins was a mechanical genius, in the opinion of many of his contemporaries, and the first to distinguish himself in the highly competitive field of clockmaking, then turned to woodwinds. It seems possible that he was the first to introduce the principle of interchangeable parts for woodwinds, as his friend Eli Whitney had done in the mass manufacture of rifles and as Hopkins himself had taken steps to do in clock-making. His principal workshop stood until very recently and was about

*the size of a two-car garage. As his employees
gradually built their homes around this factory, the
village thus created became known as "Fluteville"
and is still so identified on maps of the area.[12]*

ASA HOPKINS' MUSICAL INSTRUMENT MANUFACTORY AT FLUTEVILLE, CONNECTICUT

Asa Hopkins incorporated his woodwind manufactory in 1829 and located it in what came to be called "Fluteville," near Northfield on the Naugatuck River, between Thomaston and Campville—a short distance downriver from the location of his second waterwheel-powered clock shop (which he operated from 1814 through 1825).[13] The main Fluteville manufactory building was most likely a two- or three-story structure. Remains of the foundation indicate that the waterwheel was located in the cellar.[14] In this regard, it probably very closely resembled the Hopkins & Alfred clock-making shop, co-owned by Asa Hopkins' nephew and located just a mile-and-a-half upriver.

Fluteville first appears in the Litchfield land records in 1831 merely as "buildings and machinery thereon…the stovepipe standing therein and all the tools and implements in the shop."[15] An accounting later that year reports $2,200 worth of "musical instruments" was produced there.[16] A report the next year, 1832, mentions a water-powered, joint-stock musical instrument 'factory' in 'Litchfield' (Fluteville being in greater Litchfield), with $7,000 of capital invested in the grounds, buildings, water power, and machinery, and an annual value of manufactures listed at $3,500. The manufactory employed seven men, who worked twelve-hour days, year-round. "Box w'd, Ebony, & c" are listed as "foreign" materials used in production. Regarding the viability of the business, the report states "No dividend yet," and "Can't speak of profit."[17] A year later, in 1833, Hopkins is noted as having exhibited a flute at the Sixth Annual Fair of the American Institute in New York, where the New York flute-makers Firth & Hall were awarded "first premium for the best flute."[18]

A quaint but, most likely, accurate picture of Hopkins' early method for distribution of his Fluteville goods appears in an obscure book. These words, sadly, are not footnoted, the source of the information having perished with the author (whose grandfather would have been of the generation who witnessed the events):

*Sheet Music and tracts, almanacs and cookbooks
were carried in pedlar (sic) packs to people who
had no printing presses. The man on horseback
from Fluteville, selling the woodwinds from Asa
Hopkins' little riverside shop in 1830, did more
than all the others to chase away the gloom. First
inspired by tales of the fifers of the Continental
Line, Hopkins drilled fifes and flutes from native
applewood, and made a profit. The pedlars
conceived the idea of playing a tune for their
prospects, giving concerts in roadside taverns,
and teaching the youngsters how to fife. The
product was light and valuable, easily packed in
the saddlebags, hard to copy and non-perishable.
One pedlar dressed himself in resplendent military
garb and draped his horse in a canopy advertising Fluteville Flutes, another trudged into town
afoot, tooting on a fife, and everybody bought.[19]*

Indeed, the 1860 census shows, amidst seven "flute makers" living in Fluteville, a twenty-six-year-old "pedler" named Charles Booth, son of the farmer Charles Booth, whose farm was immediately adjacent to the Fluteville enterprise to the south.

Moreover, this peddler tale goes on to state, "His company merged with J. Firth and Hall of New York," the woodwind instrument makers (and winners of the 'best flute' award in 1833 over Hopkins), who bought into Hopkins' Fluteville operation.

FIRTH, HALL & POND: NEW YORK CITY MUSIC DEALERS ACQUIRE FLUTEVILLE

Many standard biographical and music reference resources adequately cover the personalities and business ventures undertaken by John Firth (1789-1864),

William Hall (1796–1874), and Sylvanus Billings Pond (1792–1871) and their descendants.[20] None, however, captures them more vividly than an article published in 1855:

In 1801, Edward Riley commenced the musical traffic at No. 29 Chatham Street…In Mr. Riley's manufacturing department were two young, enterprising and ambitious men, named John Firth and William Hall, each of whom married a daughter of his employer. In 1821 (the year made memorable in history by the death of Napoleon at St. Helena) these young men were led to examine into the state of their finances, and finding a cash balance of ten dollars in their favor, they conceived the brilliant idea of starting business on their own hook. In addition to their (to them) inexhaustible supply of ready money, their wives possessed each a small quantity of sheet music; beside which, one had a piano-forte and the other a guitar, which they gave to their husbands; and which (the sheet music, the piano-forte, and the guitar) were considered an overwhelming contribution to the capital of the concern, and to ensure the success of the enterprise.

Messrs. Firth & Hall rented the store, No. 358 Pearl Street, known as a portion of the 'Clinton estate', carted thither the piano-forte, hung up the guitar, put the ten dollars in the till, spread the sheet music upon the shelves, and flung their banner to the breeze. In the basement, they fitted up a work-shop, and when it was in readiness, they went to the North River and invested their ten dollars in a log of Turkey box-wood, which they carried home on their shoulders, and worked up into flutes with their own hands. The new firm prospered. Nearly all the music sold in the United States at that time was imported; but after some two or three years, Messrs. Firth & Hall published one piece of sheet music, namely: Here we too, too soon to part. This was followed at long intervals by other publications, and the foundation of

a large and lucrative catalogue was laid. The business was then conducted on a very simple plan: if a violin cost the firm $10, they sold it at wholesale for $20, and at retail for $30; and every thing else was sold at a similar profit—one hundred per cent wholesale, and two hundred per cent retail: a most comfortable state of things, truly.

This firm underwent some changes, and in 1847 it was dissolved, and two large houses were formed from its elements, namely that of Wm. Hall & Son, and that of Firth, Pond & Co.; each of which has prospered immensely and deservingly, has at the present time a wide circle of constituents, and has contributed its share to bring the music trade of New York up to the vast sum of four millions of dollars in one year.[21]

Edward Riley was a flute maker, and he taught both of his sons-in-law to make flutes. Firth & Hall exhibited their flute-making handiwork widely, and to great acclaim. In addition to winning the award for "best flute" at the Sixth Annual Fair of the American Institute in 1833, beating out Asa Hopkins's submission, they were noted for exhibiting two "cocoawood" and silver flutes at the Seventh Annual Fair in 1834, where they were also awarded a silver medal for a pianoforte of their own manufacture.[22]

Firth & Hall "bought heavily into" Fluteville in 1839 and became its "General Partners," as they owned 39% of the operation compared to the 20% of Hopkins's successor, Jabez Camp.[23] Camp left in 1841, and Firth & Hall became "Controlling Partners" of Fluteville in 1842.[24] Firth & Hall gradually bought out the other partners and by 1846 "owned all stock" in the Fluteville musical instrument factory.[25]

Figure 8-1. The Hopkins & Alfred clock-making shop on the Naugatuck River at Harwinton, just one-and-a-half miles north of Fluteville. The Hopkins of this partnership was Edward, one of Asa's nephews. Hopkins & Alfred were active from June 1, 1831 through 1840, having signed an agreement with Eli Terry on March 14, 1833 to reproduce some of his "inventions and improvements."

Figure 8-2. John Firth, a founding member of the firm of Firth, Hall & Pond, New York's premier musical instrument and sheet music publishing firm of the nineteenth century.

There they had flutes manufactured for them and stamped with the name of their firm. The instruments were then shipped the one hundred miles to be sold in (and distributed from) their New York City showroom. "Hall & Son entered flutes in the American Institute Fairs of 1849, 1850, 1859, and 1869."[26] An article regarding the American Institute Fair in 1842 noted, "The specimens of brass and copper musical instruments from Firth & Hall's, N.Y., are of beautiful workmanship."[27]

The first instance of the word "Fluteville" known to have appeared in print dates to an 1854 overview of the business of Firth, Pond & Co.:

Their sales of violins, guitars, strings, and musical merchandise generally, reached about $30,000 annually. Under the above is included flutes and guitars of their own make—an establishment for the manufacture of which they have in Fluteville, Connecticut, and which they own jointly with Wm. Hall & Son.[28]

The most astonishing fact about this description is its mention that Firth, Pond & Co. was building guitars at Fluteville. A 1948 description of Fluteville—almost one hundred years later—makes the same assertion regarding guitar production there:[29]

...the business was purchased by the New York firm of Firth & Hall, who added guitar-making as a side-line... At one time the plant employed as many as 25 workers and was making a wide variety of musical instruments in addition to flutes and guitars—such things as flageolets, clarinets, fifes, drumsticks, castanets, bones, and so forth.[30]

Fluteville's "Organization of Partnership" (drafted early in 1831, but retroactively dated to its founding in 1829) states:

The business of the copartnership shall be that of manufacturing and vending musical instruments and other articles, instruments, implements and machines, the principal material whereof is wood, brass, or ivory.[31]

While "musical instruments" is a very broad and non-specific category, the 1848–1850 New York City directories explicitly state that Firth, Pond & Co. are "manufacturers of…guitars."[32]

Given that Firth & Hall became Controlling Partners of Fluteville in 1842, it is not surprising that the first known mention of a guitar manufactured by them dates from that year.[33] They were awarded a "diploma" for their guitar at the annual exhibition of the American Institute in New York City,[34] the press noting that, "The guitars of American workmanship are most splendid specimens of art. But a few years since, and we dreamed not of making these."[35] The following year, in 1843, their guitar entry was awarded a diploma for "best guitar" at the same exhibition.[36] Quick to capitalize on their success, by early 1844, they were already advertising "Guitars from the best Spanish patterns, for which they have received premiums from the American Institute over all other makers."[37]

While it is not known what Spanish guitar Firth, Hall & Pond modeled theirs after, the extant guitars are fully developed from design and manufacturing perspectives, with no evidence whatsoever of having gone through an evolutionary design phase as is seen in the instruments made by C. F. Martin in the late 1830s and early 1840s. Instead, these guitars exhibit Spanish features of plantilla (closely resembling instruments in the Spanish style by the London makers of the Panormo family), fan bracing, and tie bridges that belie no influences other than strictly Spanish design (save for the neck/heel joint, which was not Spanish).

The first advertisement in which Firth, Hall & Pond actually referred to themselves as "Manufacturers of Guitars" dates from 1845.[38] This is echoed in another ad from the same year, stating, "F. H. & P continue to manufacture all kinds of musical instruments. Their guitars are particularly recommended for workmanship, power, and brilliancy of tone."[39] 1846 being the year that Firth & Hall came to own all stock in Fluteville and could, therefore, produce whatever they wished, more vigorous advertising for their guitars began to appear.

In October of 1846, Firth, Hall & Pond ran their second known advertisement for guitars of their own manufacture, which read, "Guitars made from the best Spanish patterns which are remarkable for their power and brilliancy of tone."[40] Additionally, two single-page, printed broadside advertisements are extant, bound into the copy of Firth, Hall & Pond's catalogue of sheet music published in 1846 and held by the American Antiquarian Society in Worcester, Massachusetts.[41] The first reads: "Manufacturers of… Guitars, from the best Spanish models, and of very superior tone and finish, warranted to stand in any

F. H. & P. continue to manufacture PIANO FORTES of a superior tone and touch and warranted to stand in any climate. *Guitars* made from the best Spanish patterns which are remarkable for their power and brilliancy of tone. *Flutes, Clarionets, Flageolets, Kent Bugles, Post Horns, Tubas, Valve Trumpets, &c.,* all warranted; *Seraphines, Melodeons, Accordeons* and every article in the music line for Sale at the lowest rates. Orders from all parts of the country promptly attended to. *Military Bands* supplied.

climate."[42] The second broadside reads: "Firth, Hall & Pond, No. 239 Broadway, New York, Manufacturers of Piano Fortes, Guitars, (A very superior article, and made from the best Spanish Models)."[43] In May of 1846, Firth & Hall exhibited "1 Guitar in case" at the First National Fair for the Exhibition of American Manufactures in Washington, D.C.[44] The press reported the exhibited instruments in June 1846, as, "guitars by Martin and Frith (sic) & Hall, New York."[45]

Firth, Hall & Pond's Fluteville plant was robust enough to handle considerable output activity, as an 1845 statistical snapshot reveals: sixteen employees

Figure 8-3. Firth, Hall & Pond advertising guitars of their own manufacture in 1845.

(more than double the number in 1832), $15,000 in capital (again, more than doubled), and $8,000 in manufactures, an increase in production of almost 130%.[46] (An 1854 description states that fifteen men were employed at the time "In Fluteville, and with the aid of water power,"[47] essentially the same number as were employed nine years prior in 1845).

Clearly, Firth, Hall & Pond were manufacturing guitars in Fluteville as early as 1842 and, like the flutes, having them stamped with their proprietary "Firth, Hall & Pond" brand. Their earliest-known surviving guitar stamped thusly is serial number 207. Given that Firth, Hall & Pond ceased to exist by 1848, the guitar obviously predates the demise of the firm.

Regarding Fluteville's management, we know that "Thaddeus Firth was in charge of the plant for a while."[48] Thaddeus was the son of one of the firm's founders, thus indicating Firth & Hall's willingness to send its New York City personnel—even family— to Connecticut to oversee the business. The 1860 census shows one Isaac Pond, aged twenty-four, as a "flute manufacturer" boarding with Frederick S. Porter, then the Superintendent of the Fluteville plant. Although he cannot be found in censuses from other years, one would assume that he was in some way related to the family of Firth & Hall's business partner Sylvanus Pond, as he is listed as having been born in New York.

Furthermore, Firth & Hall "brought in skilled workers from elsewhere, possibly even from their own woodwind shop in New York City."[49] One example is Claudius Miller, who appears as a thirty-one-year-old "silver smith" living in New York City in

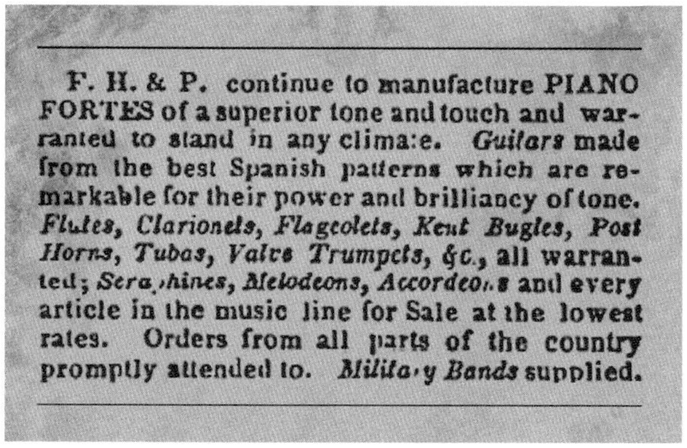

Figure 8-4. *Far left,* an October 10, 1846, advertisement for Firth, Hall & Pond's "guitars made from the best Spanish patterns."

the 1860 census, as a "flute maker" in Fluteville in the 1870 census, and once again as a "silver smith" back in New York City in the 1880 census, following the demise of Fluteville. It is entirely likely that another such workman the company "imported" from New York to Fluteville was James Ashborn, to whom they evidently entrusted the production of their guitars.

JAMES ASHBORN AT FIRTH, HALL & POND'S FLUTEVILLE?

Historical scholarship regarding the guitar maker James Ashborn has thus far assumed that he began building guitars at a factory of his own in Wolcottville (present day Torrington), Connecticut, sometime in

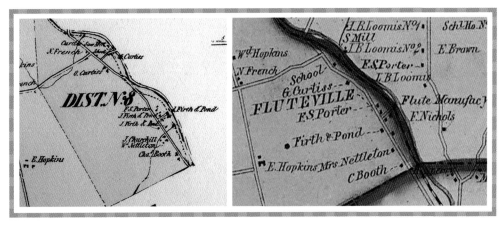

Figure 8-5. *Below left:* An 1852 map of Fluteville showing buildings owned by Firth & Pond, and the farm of Charles Booth, father of the Fluteville peddler, to the south.

Figure 8-6. *Above right,* an 1859 map of Fluteville.

the late 1840s, and that he relocated from New York to be associated with the thriving brass industry that had already attracted other English workmen there. Based on research into Fluteville's operations, these suppositions may now be seen in a new light. It is possible to surmise that James Ashborn produced guitars for Firth, Hall & Pond at their Fluteville manufactory from 1842 through 1847, or at least was heavily involved in their production during that time. The evidence is as follows:

- Firth, Hall & Pond were Controlling Partners of Fluteville in 1842.
- They exhibited the first known guitars with their brand stamp in 1842 (just as they had done with flutes previously).

- They were known to send craftsmen from New York to work in their Fluteville manufactory, as well as family members to administer the business there.
- Ashborn's extant sales ledger—which specifies serial numbers and dates of manufacture covering guitar production from April 1851 through December, 1855—allows us to extrapolate 1842 as the beginning date for production of "his" guitars (accounting for relatively slow production as the factory first got under way).[50]
- Firth, Hall & Pond owned Fluteville outright in 1846, but ceased to exist as a business partnership in 1847.
- Ashborn purchased his own factory and began producing guitars there in 1848.
- The surviving guitars stamped Firth, Hall & Pond from 1842–1847 are essentially identical to those later guitars known to have been produced exclusively by Ashborn at his own factory beginning in 1848.
- There is no evidence that Ashborn was producing guitars any place other than Fluteville before 1848, and certainly not in the "mass quantities" indicated in his ledger.

It is most likely that early in the 1840s, James Ashborn was associated in some capacity with Firth, Hall & Pond in New York City and that he moved to Connecticut, where the firm employed him as the guitar designer and maker in their Fluteville facility. Given the facts that Firth and Hall were controlling partners of Fluteville in 1842; that Ashborn (true to his English heritage) was one of the original "incorporators" of the Episcopal Church in Wolcottville in 1843;[51] that he was naturalized on March 8, 1844, in Litchfield;[52] and that his wife gave birth to a son of theirs in New York in 1844, it would appear that Ashborn was transitioning from New York to Connecticut during these years—probably so that he could participate in the revamping of the Fluteville manufactory to include guitar production. In the 1840s, one did not simply

leave New York City with one's family and relocate to a rural environment a hundred miles away without the promise of gainful employment (or, as was the case with C. F. Martin, without having a distribution arrangement with a New York firm for one's wares).

Fluteville produced guitars from 1842–1847, and Ashborn is registered as living in Litchfield when he remarried (in Wolcottville, at the Episcopal Church he helped found) the day after Christmas in 1847.[53] Inhabitants of Northfield and Fluteville were considered residents of greater Litchfield. Thus, for example, the only extant Firth, Hall & Pond flute made in Fluteville that is not stamped "New York" is stamped "Litchfield Conn."[54] Furthermore, all census records list Fluteville residents as being in "Litchfield." Thus, Ashborn was probably living and/or working in Fluteville at the time of his marriage in 1847. His proximity to Fluteville between 1842 and 1847 is evidenced by the burial of his infant son (b. 1841, d. 1842) and his first wife (d. 1847) in Plymouth, Connecticut, just three miles away.

Those who may remain skeptical that Ashborn was connected with Fluteville need only ponder the following fact: The 1860 Torrington census shows that Ashborn employed at his factory as a "guitar maker" the nineteen-year-old Julia A. Booth, younger sister of the Fluteville peddler Charles Booth noted above. The 1850 census had recorded her as living with her father and brother on the family farm next to Fluteville ten years earlier.[55]

At Fluteville, both Firth, Hall & Pond and Ashborn sensed a market for increased guitar production beyond the extant factory capabilities, given that it existed primarily to make flutes. Furthermore, the 1847

split of Firth, Hall & Pond into two separate and competing firms (Firth, Pond & Co., and Wm. Hall & Son) spurred Ashborn to seek financial backing for a factory of his own. He acquired monetary support from Austin Hungerford in nearby Wolcottville, Connecticut. (Hungerford's father, John Hungerford, owned the Wolcottville Brass Company, and hence possessed considerable wealth).[56] With him as a business partner, Ashborn opened his own guitar factory upriver from Fluteville in 1848. Ashborn proceeded to sell guitars exclusively to Firth, Pond & Co., and Wm. Hall & Son, "who advertised his guitars as their own."[57]

JAMES ASHBORN'S DAYTONVILLE, CONNECTICUT, GUITAR FACTORY

In 1848, Ashborn commenced making guitars— essentially identical to those made at Fluteville—at his own factory in Daytonville, a mile north of Wolcottville (a small town that the 1840 census describes as "about 40 dwellings")[58] and just 8.3 miles upriver from Fluteville, on the East Branch of the Naugatuck River.[59] Ashborn purchased a "modest frame building," an "unimposing structure,"[60] in Daytonville from one Lyman Clark, a carpenter and builder who belonged to his church.[61] The building was first erected as a homestead in 1792 and, thereafter, was used by various owners to make hay rakes and hoe handles,[62] after which it was used "in making German silver spoons."[63] It was located three buildings upriver from Arvid Dayton's structure, in which Dayton built melodeons and reed organs, beginning

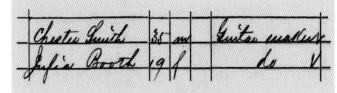

Figure 8-8. The 1860 census showing nineteen-year-old Julia Booth listed as a guitar maker (the "do" standing for ditto), rooming along with Chester Smith, another of Ashborn's guitar makers, in a farmhouse next to the guitar factory.

Figure 8-9. *Top,* John Hungerford, the father of Ashborn's business partner, Austin Hungerford. Hungerford achieved wealth in the brass industry in Wolcottville, Connecticut.

Figure 8-10. *Above,* "Ashburn (sic) & Hungerford" are named on this 1852 map as owning the structures just north of Arvid Dayton's melodeon manufactory. Note the Naugatuck Railroad tracks immediately to the north and the east branch of the Naugatuck River immediately to the west.

Figure 8-11. *Top right,* Wolcottville (present day Torrington), Connecticut, in 1836, as viewed from the northeast, depicting the town much as it would have appeared to James Ashborn when he first arrived there.

Figure 8-12. *Above right,* Arvid Dayton's organ and melodeon manufactory in Daytonville, Connecticut, as pictured in 1852. Ashborn's guitar manufactory was located just three dwellings upriver.

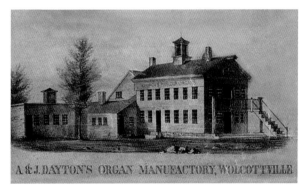

around 1840.[64] (Daytonville was, in fact, "named c. 1840 for Arvid Dayton, pipe organ builder").[65]

Ashborn would have been ill-advised to secure Hungerford's financial backing, purchase a factory building, hire half a dozen employees, and begin producing guitars in earnest if he did not already have an agreement in hand for the sale and distribution of his finished products. Unlike C. F. Martin, Ashborn did not start out on a small scale, hand build a few guitars and then look to "job" them himself to retailers a few at a time. Nor did he produce a few prototype units to entice large firms such as Firth, Pond & Co. and Wm. Hall & Son to order large quantities, thus increasing his production and enterprise over an extended period.

Instead, Ashborn already had established business arrangements with Firth, Pond & Co. and Wm. Hall & Son (arguably his employers up until that time) to produce guitars in large quantities specifically for them. Both firms would have wished to make exclusive arrangements to have Ashborn provide guitars solely to one house or the other. Indeed, a William Hall & Son advertisement from 1849 strongly infers that their firm was the recipient of Ashborn's most favored customer status over Firth, Pond & Co. It reads:

Guitars—W. H. & Son have made extensive arrangements for the manufacture of this instrument from the best Spanish models. They are made from the most seasoned material and warranted to stand the climate. They are much superior to instruments of foreign manufacture in tone, style of finish, and playability.[66]

Ashborn's account book, covering the years 1851–1856, seems to bear this out, as William Hall & Son account for 85% of his business, compared to only 15% for Firth, Pond & Co.

From 1848 through 1863, Ashborn operated the world's first known guitar factory, *per se*, with mechanized belts turned by a waterwheel.[67] "He built instruments of one standard size and adapted their manufacture to the strict division of labor that marked the earliest phase of the industrial revolution."[68] Ashborn's assembly-line production "simplified manufacture by making his guitars all the same size and shape, with a body 17¼ inches long and a lower bout 11 inches across."[69] Ashborn's instruments were so standardized that a late twentieth-century luthier who studied three Ashborn guitars built over a seven-year time span noted that all of the fretboard scale lengths were identical, and said, "There's less than 1/16th inch variance in almost all dimensions among them, which is a stricter tolerance level than many contemporary mass-produced shops require."[70] Thus, "Ashborn found his niche in the industrial revolution and produced large numbers of high-quality instruments in a factory run by operatives who performed set tasks in a division of labor established by a master 'mechanic,' Ashborn himself."[71]

By May of 1851, Ashborn had already built and shipped 2,113 guitars. Between April 1851 and December 1855, his factory produced approximately 3,260 instruments. By comparison, between 1852 and 1856, C. F. Martin turned out about 1,000 guitars, less than one-third of Ashborn's production.[72] "No other firm...rivaled Ashborn's production."[73] Thus in the 1850s not only was an Ashborn guitar half the price of a Martin,[74] but a customer was three times more likely to encounter an Ashborn-made guitar than a Martin. Based on his known production figures, it is possible to extrapolate and estimate that Ashborn produced almost 12,000 guitars in his twenty-one most active years of building. By comparison, Martin, on the other hand, built approximately less than 10,000 guitars in the sixty-five years between 1833 and 1898.[75]

THE NAUGATUCK RAILROAD AND ASHBORN'S GUITAR PRODUCTION

In addition to enjoying the advantages of close proximity to his business partner and other factories (some of which supplied him with raw materials), Ashborn's decision to locate his guitar factory near Wolcottville was almost certainly influenced by the construction of the Naugatuck Railroad. An 1848 account reads:

> *The charter of the Naugatuck Railroad company was granted by the Legislature of Connecticut, in the year 1845, and was altered and amended in 1847 and 1848. The company was organized in February, 1848...The whole road is to be completed and in readiness for the cars on or before the 1st day of September, 1849...[76]*

Figure 8-13. *Far Left.* Wm. Hall & Son's music store at 239 Broadway in New York as it appeared in 1848. They took over the premises from Firth & Pond following the dissolution of Firth, Hall & Pond the year before. This location was considered "a rendezvous for the musical community."

Figure 8-14. The Coe Brass Works (formerly John Hungerford's Wolcottville Brass Works) in 1864. This factory supplied the brass from which Ashborn machined his tuners and frets.

Figure 8-15. The Wolcottville Station of the Naugatuck Railroad c. 1870. From this depot, Ashborn shipped all of his guitars (as well as the banjos, strings, and capos he manufactured) to New York City.

At the Housatonic River, at Milford, the New York and New Haven connect with the Naugatuck Railroad—extending to the Naugatuck Valley, through Derby, Birmingham, Ansonia, Humphreysville, Naugatuck, Waterbury, Plymouth, Wolcottville, to Winsted; all of which are very thriving manufacturing villages, furnishing large amounts of freight and passengers destined for New York. This road is 56 miles long, and is now in course of construction. At New Haven the New York and New Haven connects.[77]

Doubtless, Ashborn would have known about the impending railroad construction while producing guitars at Fluteville from 1842–1847. While directly along the railroad line, Fluteville was not populated enough—nor did it produce enough cargo—to merit the trains stopping there. Fluteville goods in need of rail transport would have to be shipped by livery (horse-drawn wagon) to the first depot south (Plymouth), the first depot north (Camps Mills, named after Jabez M. Camp, Asa Hopkins's former Fluteville partner and successor who moved upriver), or the second depot north (Litchfield).[78] The third depot to the north was Wolcottville. So Ashborn, while his Daytonville guitar factory was similarly located immediately along the railroad (which followed the river), also similarly needed to have his guitars carted to the Wolcottville station, but just a little over a mile away.

Transporting goods a short distance to a rail station via livery was a minor and trifling inconvenience given the fact that, prior to the railroad's arrival, Ashborn would have shipped his guitars by "wagons and ox-carts" to "Plainville, where connections were made with the Northampton-New Haven canal"[79] in order for them to reach their ultimate destination in New York City. Ashborn's decision to locate in Wolcottville in 1848 was calculated to take full advantage of rail shipping. Indeed, and more or less on schedule, the first passenger train traversed the Naugatuck Railroad late in September of 1849,[80] and Ashborn began shipping his guitars directly from Wolcottville to New York City shortly thereafter.[81]

Obviously, the railroad was advantageous for Ashborn's business, as it was to the most prominent businessmen of the area.[82] Thus, for example, two of the four men in Wolcottville who were cited as being "of great service to the road"[83] (i.e. those who gave the most money in support of it and had the most to gain from it) were John Hungerford—the father of Ashborn's business partner—and George D. Wadhams—one of the two witnesses who would later, in 1852, sign in support of Ashborn's second patent.[84] "It would appear that Litchfield County had a distinct competitive economic advantage in that it was served at extremely early dates by railroads."[85] The Naugatuck Railroad, it should be noted, was completed twenty years before the trans-continental railroad was completed in 1869.

DESIGN ELEMENTS OF ASHBORN'S SPANISH GUITARS

Firth & Hall sold imported guitars when they opened their store in 1821,[86] and, in 1831, their newspaper advertisements flamboyantly declared that the instruments were Spanish:

GUITARS—SPLENDID—NE PLUS ULTRA!...
a MORE SPLENDID ASSORTMENT OF
Spanish Guitars than was ever before exhibited on
this side of the Atlantic. They need only to be seen
to be admired. Description would be useless—call
and inspect them...

UNPARALLELLED FOR SWEETNESS OF
TONE!!!...the most splendid assortment of
Spanish Guitars ever presented to the American
public. See them—touch them—and be convinced.[87]

The guitars may have been of Spanish manufacture, or made in the Spanish style by Panormo (or, perhaps, a French or German maker). It is unknown after which Spanish-style guitar or guitars Firth, Hall & Pond chose to model guitars of their own production (beginning in 1842), but they clearly advertised

them as being "from the best Spanish patterns"[88] or "from the best Spanish models."[89]

The guitars that Ashborn manufactured exclusively for them (beginning in 1848) were essentially identical to the 1842 Firth, Hall & Pond's models and were reviewed in the press in 1852 as being of Spanish design:

Until within a few years, most of the guitars used
in the United States were imported from France
and Germany—some few from Spain...

In manufacturing their Guitars, Messrs. Hall &
Son have taken the Spanish model, and they have
succeeded in preserving richness of tone, with all
the requisites of lightness, beauty, and power...[90]

The two earliest known guitars stamped with the Firth, Hall & Pond brand (bearing serial numbers 207, [Profile 29], and 235, dating from c. 1845) strikingly resemble the Panormo plantilla and size. Additionally, they utilize fan bracing (adopted either directly from guitars of the Cadiz builders or via guitars modeled after them) and traditional Spanish tie bridges.

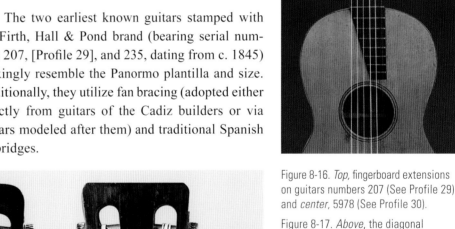

Figure 8-16. *Top,* fingerboard extensions on guitars numbers 207 (See Profile 29) and *center,* 5978 (See Profile 30).

Figure 8-17. *Above,* the diagonal fingerboard extension on an Ashborn model No. 1 is a Germanic design feature on an otherwise Spanish-style guitar.

Figure 8-18. The pointed headstock as found on Ashborn's earliest guitars including Firth, Hall and Pond number 207 (See Profile 29). *Center and right,* during the first "New Arrangement" transition in 1855-1856 Ashborn's higher numbered models had rounded corners (See Profile 32) whereas his lower numbered models had faceted corners.

See page 156 for Profile 29, Ashborn, c. 1845

Both guitars are immediately distinguishable by their abundance of veneer work. While it was not unusual for guitars of the period to feature veneered backs and sides, these instruments also have a thick wood veneer on their necks, as well as the back and sides of their headstocks—Circassian walnut on number 207 and satinwood on number 235. Such work is intricate, difficult, and time consuming, but matching back, side, neck, and headstock veneers in Brazilian rosewood would be a hallmark feature of all higher model guitars produced by Ashborn thereafter.

Numbers 207 and 235 share the identical shape, bridge, and tuners, and the next known guitar, serial number 648 (c. 1847), has these features in common with them as well. The three exhibit only slight differences in the numbers of ebony bands making up their purfling (eleven, seven, and nine, respectively) and inner rosette rings, also of ebony (eleven, nine, and eleven, respectively). In addition, the fingerboard extension on the two earliest examples, which is rounded at the outer rosette ring, is extended over the ring and terminates in a straight line on number 648.

Guitar number 648 displays all of the features that would be seen on the guitars made exclusively by Ashborn in his own factory the following year. The design flourish adorning the tip of the headstock on numbers 207 and 235—a slight curve culminating in a rounded point—has been done away with. Instead, the top of the headstock is completely flat, essentially the same as the paddle-shaped headstock being used by C. F. Martin on his Spanish-style guitars at the same time (except for the finely chamfered, rounded corners on Ashborn's). In addition, number 648 is branded internally with the number 4, designating a codified model number.

Unlike Martin's numbering system of a decade later, which was based on body size (followed by degree of ornamentation), Ashborn's guitars, being of uniform size, used numbers to designate models that differed primarily in degree of ornamentation (namely purfling, rosette, and tuner buttons). William Hall & Son's newspaper advertisements from 1851–1856 list their six available Ashborn-made guitar models.[91]

Ashborn's model No. 1 guitars were originally flamed maple, then featured a solid mahogany back and sides (although the neck and front, back, and sides of the headstock were veneered like all his higher numbered models). Their fingerboard extensions were cut at a diagonal over the body, this being a characteristic of Austro-German guitars (as evidenced by Martin's instruments of the 1830s, before he adopted a Spanish style). This feature stood out somewhat oddly on what was otherwise an entirely Spanish-influenced design.

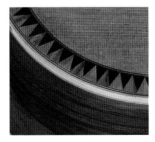  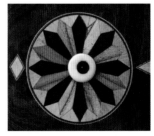 

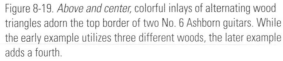

Figure 8-19. *Above and center,* colorful inlays of alternating wood triangles adorn the top border of two No. 6 Ashborn guitars. While the early example utilizes three different woods, the later example adds a fourth.

Figure 8-20. *Above far right,* extraordinary wooden inlays surround the endpins of early and late examples of No. 6 Ashborn guitars.

Figure 8-21. *Far right.* the multi-rosette of an Ashborn "New Arrangement" No. 3.

The back and sides of the model No. 2 were veneered with Brazilian rosewood. Ashborn's veneers were the most flamboyantly eye-catching examples of this exotic, imported wood ever used in the nineteenth century. The model No. 3, also veneered with rosewood, differed little except for additional purfling on the front and back of the body and a slightly more elaborate rosette (with inner and outer bands of rings, as opposed to just an inner band). The No. 4 was upgraded to ivory tuner buttons and had a modestly arched back intended to help project the sound.

The sole surviving example of a No. 5 Ashborn guitar features an intricate rosette utilizing a variety of wood inlays. There are five known examples of his No. 6, however. These are, as the advertisements stated, "elegantly inlaid." (See Profiles 31 and 32). Their rosettes consisted of an elaborate marquetry mosaic pattern in a variety of colorful triangular and kite-shaped woods, as did their top body purflings. Finally, an intricately inlaid circular pattern outlined the strap button on the butt ends of the No. 6 guitars.

Ashborn and Hungerford's business ledger indicates that a February 1, 1855, audit of "the accounts of W. H. & Son and A. N. Hungerford" found Hungerford owed Wm. Hall & Son $2,113.09. This represented more than 80% of a year's dividends for the factory, or the wholesale price of two hundred and fifty of Ashborn's least expensive guitars. As a result, Hall & Son quite possibly felt they were in a position to dictate the terms of their future arrangement with Ashborn, including the removal of Hungerford as Ashborn's business partner; he left the partnership shortly thereafter. Indeed, later in February of 1855, Firth, Pond & Co. returned eight guitars to Ashborn, and they ceased buying guitars from him for a period of five years, probably because of Hall gaining exclusive rights to Ashborn's production.[92] A few months later, in June, the Ashborn ledger indicates he shipped two new models to Hall & Son, including ninety-six maple guitars not specified by a model number.

By August 11, 1855, Hall was advertising a "New Arrangement" of Ashborn-made guitar styles, consisting of only three models instead of six.[93] The new model No. 1 was advertised as being superior to the old No. 2, the new No. 2 as the equivalent of the old No. 4, and the new No. 3 as the equivalent of the old No. 5. Additionally, Hall advertised

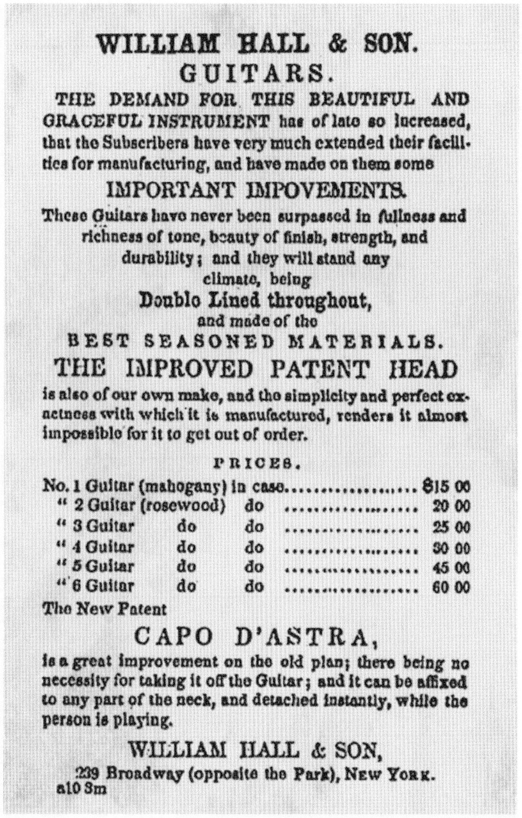

WILLIAM HALL & SON.

GUITARS.

THE DEMAND FOR THIS BEAUTIFUL AND GRACEFUL INSTRUMENT has of late so increased, that the Subscribers have very much extended their facilities for manufacturing, and have made on them some

IMPORTANT IMPOVEMENTS.

These Guitars have never been surpassed in fullness and richness of tone, beauty of finish, strength, and durability; and they will stand any climate, being

Double Lined throughout,

and made of the

BEST SEASONED MATERIALS.

THE IMPROVED PATENT HEAD

is also of our own make, and the simplicity and perfect exactness with which it is manufactured, renders it almost impossible for it to get out of order.

PRICES.

No. 1 Guitar (mahogany)	in case	....	$15 00
" 2 Guitar (rosewood)	do	....	20 00
" 3 Guitar	do	do	25 00
" 4 Guitar	do	do	30 00
" 5 Guitar	do	do	45 00
" 6 Guitar	do	do	60 00

The New Patent

CAPO D'ASTRA,

is a great improvement on the old plan; there being no necessity for taking it off the Guitar; and it can be affixed to any part of the neck, and detached instantly, while the person is playing.

WILLIAM HALL & SON,

239 Broadway (opposite the Park), NEW YORK.

a10 3m

Figure 8-22. A William Hall & Son guitar advertisement from 1852 specifies the six models of guitars Ashborn was producing for them.

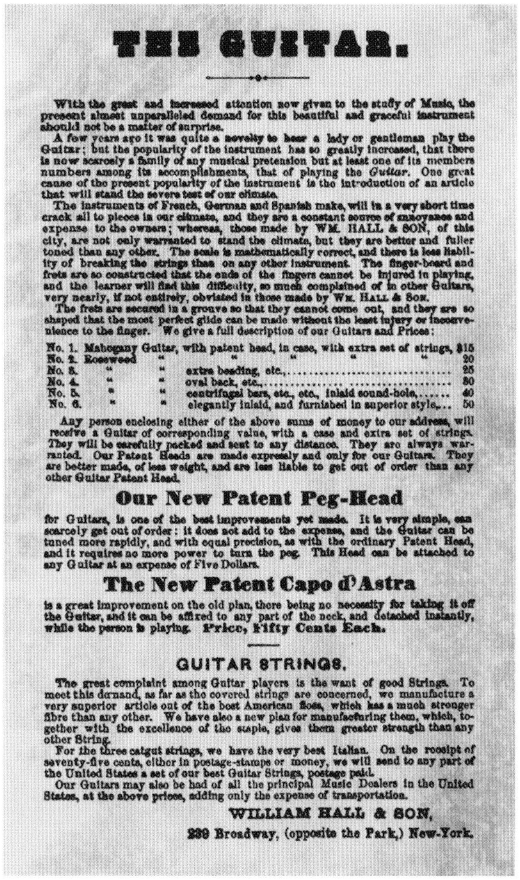

THE GUITAR.

With the great and increased attention now given to the study of Music, the present almost unparalleled demand for this beautiful and graceful instrument should not be a matter of surprise.

A few years ago it was quite a novelty to hear a lady or gentleman play the Guitar; but the popularity of the instrument has so greatly increased, that there is now scarcely a family of any musical pretension but at least one of its members numbers among its accomplishments, that of playing the *Guitar*. One great cause of the present popularity of the instrument is the introduction of an article that will stand the severe test of our climate.

The instruments of French, German and Spanish make, will in a very short time crack all to pieces in our climate, and they are a constant source of annoyance and expense to the owners; whereas, those made by WM. HALL & SON, of this city, are not only warranted to stand the climate, but they are better and fuller toned than any other. The scale is mathematically correct, and there is less liability of breaking the strings than on any other instrument. The finger-board and frets are so constructed that the ends of the fingers cannot be injured in playing, and the learner will find this difficulty, so much complained of in other Guitars, very nearly, if not entirely, obviated in those made by WM. HALL & SON.

The frets are secured in a groove so that they cannot come out, and they are so shaped that the most perfect glide can be made without the least injury or inconvenience to the finger. We give a full description of our Guitars and Prices:

No. 1.	Mahogany	Guitar,	with patent head, in case, with extra set of strings,	$15
No. 2.	Rosewood	"	" " " "	20
No. 3.	"	"	extra beading, etc., ...	25
No. 4.	"	"	oval back, etc., ...	30
No. 5.	"	"	centrifugal bars, etc., etc., inlaid sound-hole, ...	40
No. 6.	"	"	elegantly inlaid, and furnished in superior style, ...	50

Any person enclosing either of the above sums of money to our address, will receive a Guitar of corresponding value, with a case and extra set of strings. They will be carefully packed and sent to any distance. They are always warranted. Our Patent Heads are made expressly and only for our Guitars. They are better made, of less weight, and are less liable to get out of order than any other Guitar Patent Head.

Our New Patent Peg-Head

for Guitars, is one of the best improvements yet made. It is very simple, can scarcely get out of order: it does not add to the expense, and the Guitar can be tuned more rapidly, and with equal precision, as with the ordinary Patent Head, and it requires no more power to turn the peg. This Head can be attached to any Guitar at an expense of Five Dollars.

The New Patent Capo d'Astra

is a great improvement on the old plan, there being no necessity for taking it off the Guitar, and it can be affixed to any part of the neck, and detached instantly, while the person is playing. Price, Fifty Cents Each.

GUITAR STRINGS.

The great complaint among Guitar players is the want of good Strings. To meet this demand, as far as the covered strings are concerned, we manufacture a very superior article out of the best American floss, which has a much stronger fibre than any other. We have also a new plan for manufacturing them, which, together with the excellence of the staple, gives them greater strength than any other String.

For the three catgut strings, we have the very best Italian. On the receipt of seventy-five cents, either in postage-stamps or money, we will send to any part of the United States a set of our best Guitar Strings, postage paid.

Our Guitars may also be had of all the principal Music Dealers in the United States, at the above prices, adding only the expense of transportation.

WILLIAM HALL & SON,

239 Broadway, (opposite the Park,) New-York.

Figure 8-23. This 1855 advertisement for Ashborn's guitars spells out the six available models and briefly describes their stylistic differences. It goes on to mention Ashborn's patented tuners and capo, as well as strings of his own manufacture.

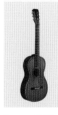

See page 160 for Profile 31, Ashborn No. 6, c. 1852

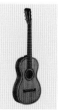

See page 162 for Profile 32, Ashborn No. 6, c. 1863

Figure 8-24. *Right,* the tuners of the three earliest known Ashborn guitars utilize elegant brass plates that are actually inlaid into the veneer on the side of the headstock. Those from Ashborn's factory (*below, right*) were a straight plate. While Ashborn usually used octagonally shaped tuner buttons, some later, lower-numbered examples used more conventionally shaped buttons. Higher numbers carried ivory buttons, while mid-range examples used ebony, and the most inexpensive models were rosewood. (See Profiles 29 and 31).

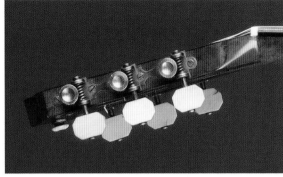

Figure 8-25. *Above,* the multi-colored wooden rosette rings around the sound hole of an Ashborn "New Arrangement" No. 3. (See Profile 32).

Figure 8-26. *Right,* The earliest Ashborn guitars have Spanish tie bridges with an ivory saddle, identical to the bridges C. F. Martin and Schmidt & Maul used on their Spanish-style guitars (See Profile 29); *bottom right,* Midway through 1851, Ashborn switched to, and settled on, an elegantly carved pin-style bridge that he then employed exclusively. It used a brass fret wire as the saddle, inset into a separate piece of wood in turn inset into the bridge (See Profile 32).

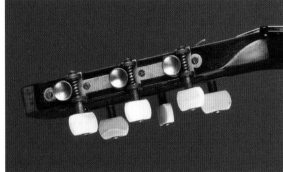

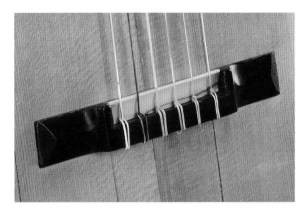

See page 158 for Profile 30, Ashborn No. 3, c. 1856

"Extra finished Guitars, varying in price from $40 to $100 according to the amount of work on them."

On October 29, 1859, Hall advertised yet another "New Arrangement."[94] This consisted of a model No. 0, described as maple and retailing for $7.50, a No. 1 of "Curl Maple" for $10, another No. 1 in rosewood at $18, the same No. 2 and No. 3 from the previous "New Arrangement," (see Profile 30), and the reintroduction of the No. 6. Again, "extra finished" guitars were offered from $40 to $100. The curly maple guitars are particularly elegant in their simplicity and are highly desirable among collectors, with few playable examples presently known.

A feature of all Ashborn guitars throughout their production that merits attention is their brass frets. The 1855 Hall & Son advertisement for Ashborn's guitars describes them in detail:

> *The finger-board and frets are so constructed that the ends of the fingers cannot be injured in playing, and the learner will find this difficulty, so much complained of in other Guitars, very nearly, if not entirely, obviated in those made by W. Hall & Son. The frets are secured in a groove so that they cannot come out, and they are so shaped that the most perfect glide can be made without the least injury or inconvenience to the finger.*[95]

These are the earliest known T-shaped frets in America, as opposed to the conventional "bar" frets of the day. C. F. Martin did not switch from bar frets to T frets until 1934, almost a century later.[96]

Ashborn's guitars were stamped on the back brace with the name of the wholesaler/retailer to whom he sold them, and nowhere bore Ashborn's name. The only exceptions were those guitars featuring Ashborn's patented friction tuners (the two known examples are both stamped "J. Ashborn/Patented 1852" on the tops of their headstocks), and some higher numbered guitars, whose brass tuner plates bear the "J. Ashborn" name.

All guitars built from 1842 through 1847 exhibit the Firth, Hall & Pond brand stamp (Profile 29). When

Model	Wholesale	Retail	% of Production
No. 1	$ 8.50	$15	29%
No. 2	$ 9.75	$20	32%
No. 3	$11.50	$25	18%
No. 4	$14.25	$30	13%
No. 5	$17.50	$40, $45, or $50	4%
No. 6	$25.00	$50 or $60	4%

Figure 8-27. *Left,* from 1851–1856 Ashborn offered six guitar models, which were identical in size but varied considerably in the amount of decoration they carried and their attendant prices. Their percentages of total production can be ascertained from Ashborn's ledger covering the time period.

Figure 8-28. One of two surviving Ashborn guitars featuring his patented friction tuning pegs showing Ashborn's name stamped on the top of the headstock. (Profile 30).

the firm split in 1848 and Ashborn's factory commenced production, numerous New York newspapers reported that, despite the dissolution, both new firms—namely William Hall & Son, and Firth, Pond & Co.—would continue to offer guitars of their own manufacture, in other words, they would continue to market guitars being made for them by Ashborn. (Profile 32). Thus, guitars made from 1848 through mid 1855 bear one of these two firms' names.

With the 1855 business realignment of Ashborn's factory to supply William Hall & Son exclusively, examples of guitars representing model numbers of either of the two "New Arrangements" were, of course, Hall's alone. Quite inexplicably, however, after a five-year hiatus, Firth, Pond & Co. would begin re-advertising "their" guitars, but the models were listed as the numbers 1–6, identical to those made for them from 1848–1855.[97]

When Firth, Pond & Co. further dissolved into Wm. A. Pond & Co. and Firth, Son & Co. in 1863, for the brief period of just two years, guitars were stamped with either one of these two new firms' names or Wm. Hall & Son, before Ashborn's factory closure in 1864. Some guitars from the 1859–1863 time period were additionally stamped internally on the neck heel with the name "J. Ashborn" for the first time.

ASHBORN'S FACTORY CLOSURE

James Ashborn was elected to Connecticut's House of Representatives in 1863 and began serving in 1864.[98] Consequently, he decided to close his Daytonville factory and presumably stopped making guitars there in 1864. Given that Firth, Pond, & Co. split into the two firms of Wm. A. Pond & Co. and Firth, Son & Co. late in January of 1863, and given that Ashborn assumed his seat in the State Legislature in January of 1864, it is most likely that any Ashborn guitars stamped "Wm. A. Pond & Co." or "Firth, Son & Co." were made in 1863. A March 1864 advertisement for Wm. Pond & Co. in Harper's Weekly mentions

Figure 8-29. This 1863 Wm. A. Pond & Co. flamed maple No. 1 model bears Ashborn's name stamped internally.

Figure 8-30. Four examples of Ashborn guitars with exquisite book-matched veneer on the backs. The one on the left is Circassian walnut (See Profile 29), while the other three are Brazilian rosewood. (See Profiles 30–32).

"accordeons," flutes, fifes, banjos, and drums—but no guitars.[99]

Beginning in 1864, Ashborn's factory "was rented for a time for the making of piano covers."[100] It seems entirely likely that the most swift and easy solution was for Ashborn to rent the factory to Wm. Hall & Son, who then utilized it to make covers for their pianos. We know that, in the 1850s, "he often sawed lumber for William Hall & Son's extensive piano factory in New York City."[101] Although Ashborn did not win re-election,[102] he chose to sell the factory building. "In 1866, the Excelsior Needle Company bought it"[103] shortly after their incorporation on March 2.[104]

In addition to the sole extant photograph of Ashborn's guitar factory as it appeared in 1866 when the Excelsior Needle Co. purchased it, the following written description exists of the sale transaction:

At the first stockholders' meeting, the directors voted to buy real estate from one James Ashborn of Daytonville, a satellite community at the north end of Wolcottville. At a price of $3,000, purchased with a $1,500 mortgage from the Litchfield Saving Society, the two-story, 16-room frame structure became the first factory site of the new enterprise.

Because each of the machines to be used in manufacturing would occupy little space, most of the original room partitions remained in place. As for the relatively small amount of power needed to run the light equipment, it was readily available from the nearby East Branch of the Naugatuck River.[105]

The account goes on to say that, in its first year, seven people worked in the building, similar to the size of Ashborn's workforce.

The renting of at least part of Ashborn's factory, if not the entire structure, in 1864, and its subsequent sale in 1866 are by no means indicative that Ashborn ceased making guitars. In fact, Internal Revenue Service Tax Assessment Lists indicate Ashborn produced from as few as a dozen to as many as thirty-one guitars in various months throughout 1865 and into early 1866. The Wolcottville census of 1870 continued to list him as a guitar maker (while no one else is listed as such), and his 1876 will enumerates unfinished guitars as well as guitar-making materials and tools.[106] It is unknown where he manufactured these instruments, but, as a later Wolcottville map shows, he owned several houses and properties,[107] any one of which might have been outfitted for guitar production. Suffice it to say, however, that his later years of production did not employ nearly as many hands, nor result in as many finished instruments. It also is unknown to whom he sold or supplied these instruments.

James Ashborn died in Wolcottville on December 7, 1876. His obituary in the local newspaper simply stated, "Ashburn [*sic*]—In this village, Dec. 7, 1876, James Ashburn [*sic*], aged 60 years," with a brief news notice on the same page elaborating:

There are but few of our readers who have not known James Ashburn [sic], who died at his residence in this village on the 7th inst. He has not enjoyed very good health for some years past, and a paralytic shock a month or two before his death was rather more than his old age could stand, and death soon after relieved him from his sufferings.[108]

ASHBORN'S ACHIEVEMENT

Ashborn's factory production ceased when it lacked its "master mechanic" (i.e. Ashborn himself) to run the operation, thus leaving its "assembly-line" workers without a leader knowledgeable regarding the finished product in its entirety. A decade later, in the 1870s, Thaddeus Firth corroborated that specialized line-production was the reason for Fluteville's eventual demise as a viable business enterprise: "You might send me the most capable machinist that you could find, and I would give him all the necessary tools to manufacture them, and he would not be able to make one of them unless he had previous experience in this line of manufacture."[109]

Moreover, Ashborn was, after Hungerford's departure, the factory's sole bankroller and, without his financial backing, the operation could not be sustained. The New York music houses that had enjoyed Ashborn's steady flow of guitars through their showrooms for eighteen years were left scrambling to replenish their stock. Some turned to C. F. Martin, but extant letters, in the Martin Archives in Nazareth, Pennsylvania, covering this time period indicate that dealers were impatient with Martin's relatively slow production and limited output compared to Ashborn's mass production.

Ashborn, in addition to being a mechanical genius (as evidenced by his patents),[110] was a shrewd judge of the market potential in his day. Location, for him, was everything. By choosing Daytonville, he placed himself alongside the Naugatuck River, which supplied the following:

- Waterwheel power to run his machinery.
- Close proximity to the timber resources necessary to produce his guitar tops (spruce), the necks, and some of the backs (maple).
- A close relationship with the brass works that supplied raw materials for his tuners.
- Easy cartage distance to the Wolcottville station for easy access to speedy railway transport.
- Reasonable closeness to New York City for sales and further distribution.

Building guitars of a consistently uniform, Panormo-like shape—varying solely by the augmentation of ornamental style—Ashborn further expedited the production process so that he made and shipped guitars literally in batches, by the dozens. It cannot be overly emphasized that, due to his mass-production factory methods, in the 1850s and into the Civil War, an Ashborn guitar was not only half the price of a Martin guitar,[111] but a customer was three times more likely to encounter an Ashborn-made guitar than a Martin. Ashborn accomplished this with a workforce roughly the same size as Martin's. "At its largest, Ashborn's workforce numbered about ten but more

regularly consisted of eight employees, two more than Martin had during the 1850s."[112]

One may glance back over the exhibits of the National Fair and understand how far, in 1846, the United States had already advanced in the World of Tomorrow... It meant a kind of factory production new to the world... It meant: the displacement of hand labor by machine labor to an ever-increasing extent, the application of machine labor to successive operations, increased precision, the production of finished objects by such an exact duplication of parts that the parts were interchangeable...and the development of straight-line manufacture and automatic machine tools. It meant that, by 1846,

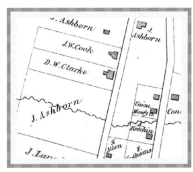

Figure 8-31. This 1874 map, drawn two years before Ashborn's death, shows some of his numerous property holdings in Wolcottville.

the American industrial order had so matured that it was manufacturing tools for the manufacture of the goods exhibited at the Fair—specifically that in various places, especially the Naugatuck Valley... the modern machine-tool industry was well established.[113]

From 1842 through the 1860s, in the example of Ashborn's guitar-making process, "It may be seen what a striking part one valley of the little State of Connecticut has borne during the Industrial Revolution."[114] ★

Figure 8-32. The only known photograph of James Ashborn's Daytonville, Connecticut, guitar factory, taken shortly after he sold it in 1866.

Ashborn applied highly figured veneer to all surfaces but the top soundboard on most of his guitars. The sides and back of this guitar are faced with Circassian walnut.

Over the sixteen most active years of his career (1848–1863) James Ashborn produced approximately 12,000 guitars, three times as many as Martin during the same period of time. Whereas Martin excelled in design innovation, Ashborn was the first American guitarmaker to employ mass manufacturing and distribution extensively.

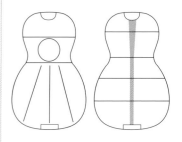

Firth, Hall and Pond were partners from 1832-47, but began making guitars in 1842. The serial number indicates that this guitar was produced c. 1844-1845.

While the design and decorative elements of Ashborn guitars are remarkably consistent, the complex shape of the top of this headstock and the curved profile of the machine plates are found on only his earliest examples.

SERIAL NUMBER 207

DIMENSIONS

TOTAL LENGH	36.50"	927 MM
BODY LENGTH	17.75"	450 MM

WIDTH

UPPER BOUT	8.87"	225 MM
WAIST	7.25"	184 MM
LOWER BOUT	11.37"	289 MM

DEPTH

NECK	3.75"	95 MM
WAIST	7.25"	184 MM
END	11.37"	289 MM

NUT WIDTH	1.87"	48 MM
SCALE	24.50"	622 MM
SOUND HOLE	3.37"	86 MM

BRACING CONFIGURATION

RELATIVE SIZE

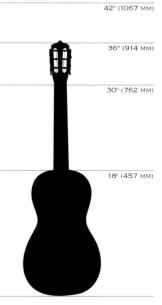

42" (1067 MM)

36" (914 MM)

30" (762 MM)

18" (457 MM)

Ashborn branded his guitars with the name of one of several wholesalers rather than with his own stamped brand. However the Ashborn stamp on the top of the headstock of this guitar announces his patented pegs, the second of two U. S. patents he obtained for increasing fine tuning capability.

Ashborn used the same two-piece pin bridge with a movable fret wire saddle in his later career. Elegantly detailed, it is best described by the architectural term "hipped roof," in contrast to Martin's pyramid bridge.

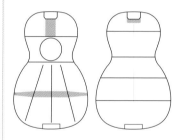

Ashborn's relationship with the wholesaler William Hall & Son in 1855 led to a new numbering system. This style 3 guitar would have been a style 5 under the earlier system.

Ashborn made all of his guitars the same size and shape so that they all fit into one size of coffin case. All surfaces except for the top soundboard were lined with veneer on most models, usually highly figured rosewood. Grades, which were numbered 1 to 6, were defined by the extent and complexity of the decoration around the soundboard, and, in the case of style 6, the addition of decoration around the edge of the top.

SERIAL NUMBER 5978

DIMENSIONS

TOTAL LENGTH	35.75"	908 MM
BODY LENGTH	17.69"	450 MM

WIDTH

UPPER BOUT	8.94"	227 MM
WAIST	7.25"	184 MM
LOWER BOUT	11.44"	335 MM

DEPTH

NECK	3.38"	86 MM
WAIST	3.75"	95 MM
END	3.63"	88 MM

NUT WIDTH	1.84"	47 MM
SCALE	24"	610 MM
SOUND HOLE	3.25"	83 MM

BRACING CONFIGURATION

RELATIVE SIZE

42" (1067 MM)

36" (914 MM)

30" (762 MM)

18" (457 MM)

Extraordinary inlay work on an example of an Ashborn No. 6 model (his fanciest), serial number 3,021, sold to Wm. Hall & Son in 1852.

An extant business ledger kept by Ashborn records the exact date this guitar was produced and left his factory. Serial number 3021 was the first of a batch of six No. 6 guitars made for William Hall & Son in November of 1852.

Unlike C.F. Martin, whose overall aesthetic adhered to a Germanic sense of austerity, Ashborn adorned his more expensive models with elaborate wood inlays. It is remarkable that he was able to execute such laborious and painstaking decoration within the context of a factory, yet keep his prices relatively low due to mass production—usually in batches of six or a dozen.

The No. 6 being his most expensive production model, Ashborn reserved his most flamboyant Brazilian Rosewood veneers for their bookmatched backs. The inlays on the top, while utilizing the simplest of oblique forms, nevertheless create the visual illusion of a swirling, ribbon-like pattern when viewed from a distance.

SERIAL NUMBER 3021

DIMENSIONS

TOTAL LENGTH	35.75"	908 MM
BODY LENGTH	17.62"	448 MM

WIDTH

UPPER BOUT	8.94"	227 MM
WAIST	7.25"	184 MM
LOWER BOUT	11.44"	335 MM

DEPTH

NECK	3.38"	86 MM
WAIST	3.75"	95 MM
END	3.63"	88 MM

NUT WIDTH	1.81"	46 MM
SCALE	24"	610 MM
SOUNDHOLE	3.25"	83 MM

BRACING CONFIGURATION

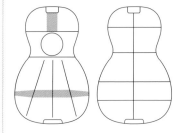

RELATIVE SIZE

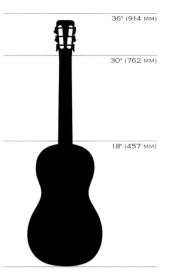

42" (1067 MM)

36" (914 MM)

30" (762 MM)

18" (457 MM)

Ashborn decorated No. 6 guitars, his highest grade, with complex marquetry patterns in the rosette and along the edge of the top. Consistent with Ashborn's rationalization of manufacturing and design, the patterns were constructed from only two shapes, a triangle and four-sided "kite" shape.

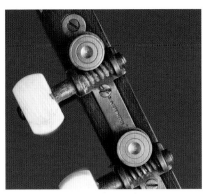

Unlike Martin, Ashborn fabricated his own machine tuners. They were elegantly designed and consistently set so that the surface of the plate was on the same plane as the face of the headstock veneer.

Ashborn's No. 6 guitar, advertised at $60, was an extremely high-priced instrument for its time. This example is stamped, "Firth, Son & Co," indicating that it was made between 1863 and 1865 as the firm existed for only two years after Firth, Pond & Co. dissolved in 1863. The guitar is additionally stamped "J. Ashborn" on the neck block, a rare example of the Ashborn stamp appearing on any of his guitars.

In addition to decoration on the top, the other visual element that defined the highest grade No. 6 was a decorative marquetry medallion surrounding the endpin. The medallion designs on each of the few extant No. 6 guitars are different.

DIMENSIONS

TOTAL LENGTH	35.75"	908 MM
BODY LENGTH	17.69"	450 MM

WIDTH

UPPER BOUT	8.94"	227 MM
WAIST	7.25"	184 MM
LOWER BOUT	11.44"	335 MM

DEPTH

NECK	3.38"	86 MM
WAIST	3.75"	95 MM
END	3.63"	88 MM

NUT WIDTH	1.84"	47 MM
SCALE	24"	610 MM
SOUND HOLE	3.25"	83 MM

BRACING CONFIGURATION

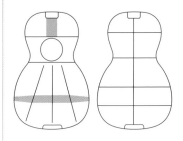

RELATIVE SIZE

42" (1067 MM)

36" (914 MM)

30" (762 MM)

18" (457 MM)

Ashborn employed workers who built all of his guitar cases in-house. Of uniform size (as were the guitars), the cases featured hinges and latches fashioned from brass supplied by the local brass works owned by his business partner's father—the same brass he used for tuners and frets on the guitars.

Although a painted black exterior was practical for shipping as well as storage, Ashborn's cases were usually lined with fancy fabrics in a range of dazzling colors and patterns. This unusual custom example has a grain-painted surface that imitates expensive rosewood and a bold calligraphic treatment of the owner's name in gilt.

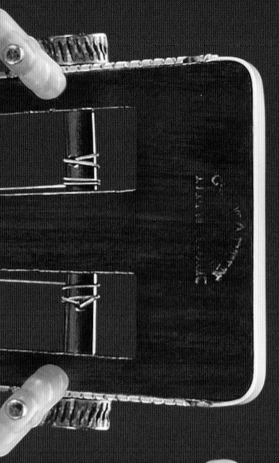
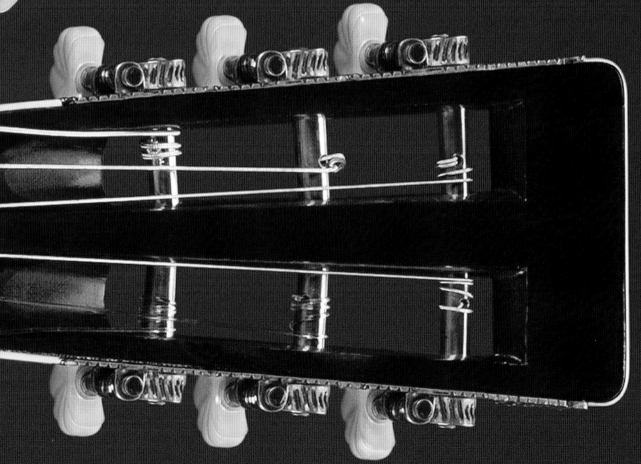

CHAPTER 9

MARTIN IN PENNSYLVANIA, 1850–1867: FINE-TUNING

RICHARD JOHNSTON

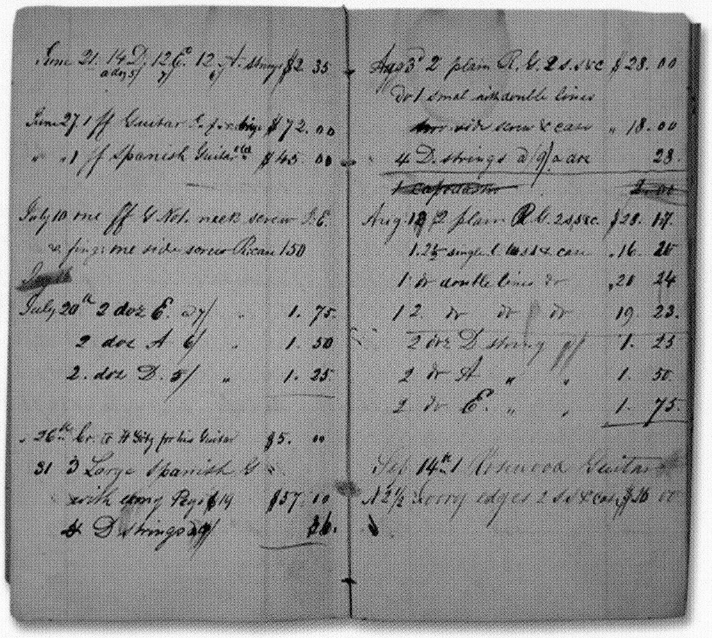

The mid-point of the nineteenth century represents a pivotal year both for C. F. Martin and for our understanding of how his production of guitars and his business operated. One of the reasons for change was no doubt a sad one for Martin at the time, as John Coupa, his New York retailer and distributor, died in May of 1850, bringing their decade-long partnership to an end.[1] Fortunately, C. F. Martin Jr., usually referred to as Frederick or Fritz, was by then in his mid twenties and able to help fill what must have been a challenging gap in how Martin moved his instruments from manufactory to market. Surviving expense ledgers show that young Frederick was in New York less than a month after Coupa's death, staying until the end of that year to continue selling Martin guitars from the 385 Broadway address, including shipping guitars to retailers in other cities. Along with guitars, he also sold many guitar strings, and Martin's sales ledgers that follow also show a brisk business in strings and even capos.[2] A daybook kept by Frederick in 1850 has survived, and, although some of its pages are missing, one

Figure 9-1. After John Coupa's death, young Frederick Martin took over the Martin sales-room at 385 Broadway. Shown here are two pages from his 1850 daybook.

page covering June and July, a portion of which is illustrated here, gives a rare glimpse of the sales of two guitars with prices far above the cost of even the most expensive styles that Martin usually made.

These prices are remarkable when compared to other listings from these same pages, which show costs identical to the prevailing wholesale prices in the more complete sales records for 1852, such as "rosewood guitar, ivory edges, 2 s s [side screws, meaning patent tuners] & case, $26.00," and "large Spanish G [guitar] with ebony pegs $19." (These wholesale numbers represent roughly two-thirds the projected retail price.) While we have no way of knowing if one of the small Martin & Coupa–labeled guitars shown here is the $72 model Frederick describes as "ff [very fine] Guitar I. [ivory] f. [fingerboard] & bridge," this listing does give us a sense of what such deluxe models cost at the time.[3] The "No. 1" model described farther down the same page as having "neck screw" [adjustable neck heel], ivory edge and fingerboard, plus "one side screw" [Vienna headstock] and rosewood case, was listed here at $150 but was sold by Frederick to John Heath at the slightly discounted price of only $142.50.[4] We can only imagine the other luxurious appointments Mr. Heath had requested and which resulted in an instrument that cost twice as much as the fancy guitars shown in Profiles 33 and 34.

C. F. Martin Jr. also performed many of the chores his father had often assumed while visiting John Coupa, such as purchasing the rosewood and ebony logs and ivory tusks needed to build and trim

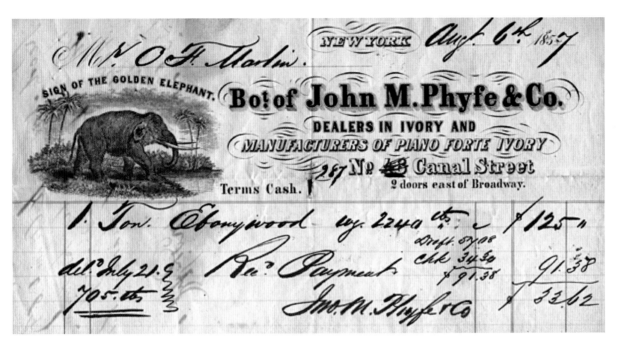

Figure 9-2. John M. Phyfe & Co. invoice for one ton (2240 lbs.) of ebony purchased by C. F. Martin, August 6, 1857. Unlike some of his competitors, Martin imported most of the materials used to build his guitars, and Phyfe was one of Martin's several New York sources of both ebony and ivory. By this date, all of Martin's guitars were made with Brazilian rosewood back and sides, which he also purchased from hardwoods dealers on Canal Street.

guitars. Martin's earliest guitars had often been made with maple, and the black-stained necks were of maple or birch, but that had changed with the pursuit of more Spanish-styled models. Well before Coupa's death, Martin had come to rely on imported parts and materials, with the exception of the spruce used for guitar tops and internal bracing. Besides Brazilian rosewood and smaller amounts of Cuban mahogany, the company was increasingly dependent on Spanish cedar, which soon replaced the black-stained necks on all but the least expensive models. Spanish cedar is curiously named, as it grows in South America, not in Spain, and is not a true cedar but part of the mahogany family. Martin's choice of this wood for guitar necks is almost certainly because it was the wood favored by Spanish guitar builders (and that is quite possibly where the name originated).

Domestic North American hardwoods such as cherry would have been both cheaper and more readily available. One of the reasons his competitor James Ashborn's guitars were considerably less expensive than Martin's was that he used more domestic woods. Ashborn also manufactured his own tuners (even Martin's ebony or ivory friction peg tuners were purchased). But unlike James Ashborn, a do-it-yourself Connecticut Yankee who went on to

become a state legislator, C. F. Martin had come to the United States at age thirty-seven after spending his formative years in Vienna, widely recognized—along with London and Paris—as one of the centers of Western art, music, and culture. While there is no indication that Martin was averse to using domestic materials, his choice of woods and materials from international rather than domestic sources, despite the considerable extra cost, suggests that, even after twenty years in the United States, his critical view of his own instruments was decidedly cosmopolitan. Not until Martin's grandson, Frank Henry Martin, took over in 1888 would the guitar company in rural Pennsylvania have an American-born captain, one who would change the brand stamped on each instrument to reflect where Martin guitars were actually made rather than listing the family name over New York, the one American city anyone in the world would recognize.

When taking an evening on the town in New York, Frederick made note in his expense book of the cost of tickets to the newly rebuilt Niblo's Garden, a venue that offered a variety of musical entertainment and a stage where Madame de Goni had performed a few years earlier.[5] While the twenty-five-year-old probably enjoyed a break from rural Pennsylvania,

See page 178 for Profile 33, Martin & Coupa Terz, c. 1845

See page 180 for Profile 34, C. F. Martin, c. 1843–1848

Figure 9-3. C. F. Martin Jr., known as Frederick or Fritz, at age twenty.

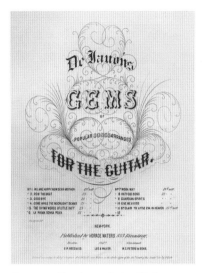

Figure 9-4. The close relationship between Martin's roster of dealers and the publishing of sheet music, especially arrangements for guitar, is indicated by the publisher and distributors of this 1854 collection of popular songs by Charles de Janon. Horace Waters was a Martin dealer in New York, and G. P. Reed, Lee & Walker, and W. C. Peters were Martin dealers in their respective cities.

Figure 9-5. Sheet music cover for the popular song "The Spider and the Fly," published by W. C. Peters, Martin's dealer in Louisville, Kentucky.

the Martins wasted no time searching for someone to fill Coupa's role, and, on New Year's Day 1851, a detailed contract was signed with Charles de Janon, a young teacher of piano and guitar who took over the 385 Broadway address and served as Martin's agent. While the contract gave Janon a commission of one-third the price of a retail sale, he made little or no profit on wholesale orders forwarded to Martin, who then shipped those orders directly to the retailer or instructor. This indicates that Martin was indeed switching his point of distribution to Cherry Hill, despite the fact that the guitars would still be marked as if they had originated in New York.

We can get a glimpse of Martin's production from the information he provided for the June 1850 census, in which he claimed a capacity to build 250 guitars annually and six workmen in his employ. This was almost certainly no exaggeration, for records in the Martin Archives from 1852 show production of 225 guitars that year, and over 300 in 1853. A new steam engine to power saws in the workshop was installed in late 1850 by Philip Deringer of Reading, Pennsylvania, but this was to replace an earlier steam-powered saw listed in the census report, so the Martin workshop had been enjoying the advantages of at least a few stationary power tools for some time. An even stronger indication of Martin's production capacity as the 1840s drew to a close are the two dozen dealers and instructors listed in the 1852 sales ledger, for such a complex web of retail accounts could not have been established in a short period. After a decade with little surviving correspondence and no information on production, records remaining in Martin's Archives from 1852 through mid 1864 allow us to track which types of guitars were sold, the size and level of decoration of those instruments, and how much they cost.

Charles de Janon did not turn out to be a suitable replacement for John Coupa, and his contract was not renewed for the following year. After one year in business as the "principle agency" for Martin guitars in New York, he owed C. F. Martin over $200, and

letters between Janon and Martin five years later reveal that a significant portion of that debt was still unpaid. In such cases Martin seems to have been remarkably forgiving, for Janon remained on good terms with his former employer and still ordered about a dozen guitars over the next several years under a wholesale arrangement similar to that granted to several other instructors who had accounts. Janon was one of the last Martin dealers who continued to order what were listed in the ledgers as "Spanish models," described as size 1 guitars with white holly binding, a style similar to the guitar played by John Wilkins. (See Profile 28). The last record of such models appears in 1856; after that date, the simpler Martin guitar styles continued to be bound in rosewood, while higher styles were given ivory "edges," (binding), and the use of light-colored wood binding was discontinued.

Without Coupa or Janon to serve as a primary sales agent in New York, Martin assumed a far greater role in the sales and distribution of his guitars in the early 1850s than he had previously. While we cannot be certain who made this far more complex and demanding business model work, it seems safe to assume that C. F. Martin Jr. probably played a significant role. Shipping guitars and receiving payment for them was far more complex during this era, as both the transportation and banking systems were still in their infancy even in the eastern U.S. Martin's Cherry Hill location was no doubt chosen partly because it was on a stage line, which made shipments and transportation to New York City, often by Hope's Express, relatively easy.[6] But Martin's web of retailers in distant states was expanding more rapidly than were the railway lines that later served them, so in some cases guitars were shipped by a combination of stage, railway, and canal boats or coastal steamers.

The ways in which Martin collected payment for the guitars he had delivered to distant customers was at times even more complex, for he could often only collect payment from the bank where his customer had an account or had established credit. When banks

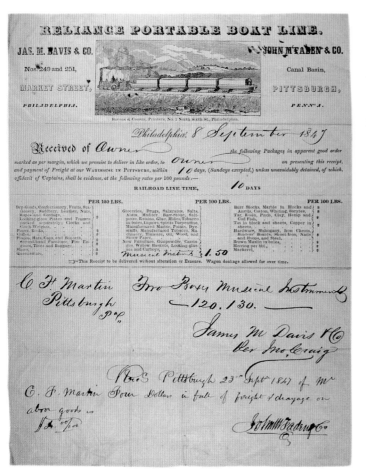

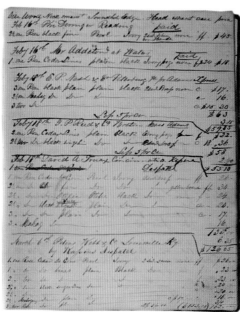

Figure 9-7. Philip Deringer, who supplied Martin with a new steam engine in late 1850, first wrote about purchasing a guitar in May of 1851 and again in March of 1852. This listing of a retail sale to Deringer in February of 1854 suggests that Martin made him wait a long time.

Figure. 9-6. *Left,* billhead for the Reliance Portable Boat Line, which Martin used to ship two boxes of guitars to Pittsburgh in 1847. The line transported goods by both land and canal in boats that could be loaded unto flat railroad cars without reloading their contents.

were in New York City or Easton, Pennsylvania, such limitations were not much of an inconvenience because either he or Frederick had reason to visit those cities often. To collect payment from the banks used by other customers in more distant cities, however, Martin relied on a network of trusted associates and even relatives. For example, "sight draft" payments from J. Brainard, Martin's retailer in Cleveland, Ohio, were collected with the help of his son-in-law, Reverend Ruetenik.[7]

However, if arranging shipping and receiving payment from over two-dozen different accounts was time consuming, this effort probably paled compared to the amount of time Martin spent corresponding with retailers. Letters in the Martin Archives reveal that along with the usual entreaties to speed delivery of the guitars they had ordered, he juggled constant

squabbles among his dealers over territory and pricing, and a constant clamoring from instructors wanting a sizeable portion of the profit in exchange for recommending Martin guitars to their pupils. These battles over exclusive "agency" (what would today be called a "dealership") for a particular city grew especially heated when an instructor who had been purchasing Martin guitars for his pupils directly from Cherry Hill was replaced as Martin's agent by a retail music store. Such a change was usually little more than a response to the city's growth and the guitarmaker's attempt to put his instruments in front of a wider audience, but to a Martin-loyal instructor, it was seen as betrayal. Of course, we are reading only the letters to Martin, as his replies have all been lost, but it seems that smoothing the ruffled feathers of retailers must have occupied much of his time.

See page 216 for Profile 43, C. F. Martin 2½–32, c. 1852–1867

See page 218 for Profile 44, C. F. Martin 2½–34, c. 1850–1862

Figure 9-8. *W. C. Peters & Co.*, one of Martin's largest dealers, published the *Baltimore Olio and Musical Gazette*, which contained concert news, printed music, educational and biographical essays, articles, and ads. C. F. Martin placed this ad in an 1850 edition of the journal.

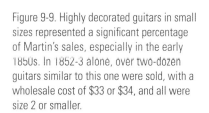

Figure 9-9. Highly decorated guitars in small sizes represented a significant percentage of Martin's sales, especially in the early 1850s. In 1852-3 alone, over two-dozen guitars similar to this one were sold, with a wholesale cost of $33 or $34, and all were size 2 or smaller.

The complaints from retailers regarding slow delivery of orders for Martin guitars were apparently a constant; in fact, the oldest surviving letters from John Coupa voice the same "hurry up" refrain. A November 26, 1851, letter from Peters, Webb & Co. includes the postscript, "Please don't fail to send us 6 guitars every month...I have not one handy," but Martin's sales ledger shows that the Louisville, Kentucky, dealer received only twenty guitars the following year. It seems unlikely that Martin intentionally kept his retailers on a starvation diet, and pages from the 1850s ledgers describing the guitars

> **C. F. MARTIN,**
> **Guitar Maker,**
>
> Respectfully informs the Musical public generally, that the great favor bestowed on him has induced him to enlarge his Factory, in order to supply the increasing demand for his instruments.
>
> A full supply of each pattern, always on hand, at the Music Stores of W. C. Peters, Baltimore; Peters & Field, Cincinnati; and Peters, Webb & Co., Louisville, Ky.   tf

completed for each account make Martin's dilemma in filling orders easy to understand. With so many guitar sizes, and a seemingly endless list of different appointments, much of Martin's production was essentially building custom guitars (with the exception of a few plain, lower-priced models that he rarely altered). In the first six months of 1852 alone, Martin

sold eighteen distinctly different models with different prices, despite total sales for that period being only ninety-five guitars shipped to a dozen different retailers. The vast majority of the models made in numbers above a half dozen from January through June of that year were lower priced, and only the $17 size 3 (eighteen sold) and the $20 size 2 and 2½ (twenty-four combined) made it into double digits. The more expensive the model, the more potential there was for options, and, unlike the lower-priced models that were only available in the two smallest sizes, the higher models could be ordered in any size, often with no change in the cost. The $26 size 1 often called a "large De Goni," for example, might have either a pearl soundhole rosette or one of ivory, "2 side screw" brass tuners in a slotted headstock or ivory friction pegs in a solid headstock—both changes that had to be planned for in the earliest stages of construction. The most expensive models shown as being sold in 1852 had a wholesale cost of $34, and their description in Martin's ledger matches the features found on the size 2½ model with ivory bridge (Profile 44). A similar guitar with ebony bridge that probably sold for two dollars less (Profile 43) displays the additional pearl ornament below the bridge often found on these models. Judging by the numbers and sizes of these high-grade models sold, women may have represented a majority of Martin's customers in the early 1850s, and the importance of this market is suggested by an 1850 advertisement in the *Baltimore Olio.*[8]

With few exceptions, Martin's guitar models came in four sizes in the early 1850s, from size 3 to the largest, size 1, which, at less than thirteen inches wide at the lower bout, would hardly qualify as a full-sized guitar today.[9] The larger size 0, which at thirteen-and-a-half inches wide is the smallest model the C. F. Martin & Company offers today, was apparently first ordered by a dealer in Cincinnati in early 1854 but did not sell in significant numbers until a few years later. By the end of the 1850s, however, this larger size, with appointments similar to the $26 large De Goni but costing one dollar more, had replaced the size 1 as Martin's "concert size." The even larger 00, which is roughly the size of a modern classical guitar, was ordered by the same Ohio dealer in early 1858, but, for reasons unknown, Martin chose to essentially ignore this body size; although a few were made, the company would not list its availability until the end of the century.

All indications from surviving records and the guitars that have surfaced suggest that Martin's infatuation with Spanish guitars had waned by the mid 1850s. The Spanish influence had certainly left its mark, as the body shapes, soundhole rosettes, headstock and bridge designs, and many other features first adopted during the early 1840s would remain central elements of the Martin style. But two-piece sides, tie-block bridges, and faux Spanish feet at the base of the neck block were left behind, along with other smaller touches. For the rest of the 1850s, the changes to Martin guitars were for the most part subtle refinements. For good reason, more of Martin's energy seems to have been devoted to the business of distributing his guitars; by this time, his web of dealers stretched across fifteen states and from Chicago to New Orleans, along what was then the country's settled western frontier.

C. F. Martin also had more distractions at home in Pennsylvania, for in mid 1857 his son Frederick purchased what would later amount to an entire block of vacant land on the northern outskirts of Nazareth. The Moravian church, which had owned and controlled Nazareth since it was founded and allowed only members of the church to live there, had loosened its grip a few years earlier and had begun to sell land to nonmembers. As if in reciprocation, the Martins joined the Moravian congregation in Nazareth once they owned property there. The route from Cherry Hill toward Nazareth is down the hill itself, and the Martins took their time making the move, as Frederick first constructed a new home at the southernmost corner of the lot, closest to Nazareth proper. This became the intersection of North and North Main streets, and a new Martin workshop at the rear of Frederick's home, facing North Street, was built next. It seems that Martin guitars were not constructed at this new location until at least 1860, and the senior Martin did not make the move from Cherry Hill to Nazareth until 1862.

Figure 9-10. *Above left,* C. F. and Otilla Martin, c. 1859.

Figure 9-11. *Above right,* North Main Street, 1859. Frederick Martin's home, with the workshop in the back of the main building, is at left. Although not visible here, the Martin factory faced what became North Street, which intersected North Main, hence the later name "North Street factory." To the right of the large home and factory was the residence of C. F. Hartmann. At the far right of this photo is the home occupied by C. F. Martin Sr. until shortly before his death in 1873.

At this point, Martin, now past the age of sixty, seems to have lost interest in making frequent trips to New York. Since a majority of his dealers were now men he had not met, and probably never would, he may have realized that it made more sense to have his guitars distributed from New York again and leave the duties of taking orders and collecting payment to someone else. This may have been prompted by a financial panic in 1857 that left several retailers unable to pay Martin what they owed, while others, such as longtime Washington D. C. dealer Hilbus & Hitz, simply went out of business altogether. In the past two years, Martin had already seen C. A. Zoebisch & Sons of New York become his largest dealer, and that firm took eighty-seven of the annual total of 231 guitars in 1857. Zoebisch & Sons, a major wholesaler of brass instruments and other musical goods and a far larger business than Martin, would certainly be better able to weather such financial storms. As if to hedge his bets even further, by 1858, Martin had not just one large dealer in New York who sold guitars both wholesale and retail, but two of them, and both were long standing acquaintances of Martin's with strong connections to Markneukirchen.[10] The second agent for Martin in New York was his old partner and bookkeeper Charles Bruno, and, for the next several years, Zoebisch and Bruno seemed to be battling for

the role of exclusive agency for Martin guitars. From 1858 on, Martin's sales ledgers no longer show the widening distribution of his guitars, because virtually all new accounts—and many of the old ones as well— had to purchase their guitars from one of these growing firms in New York.

One of the advantages of having distributors who were also importers of European goods was that Martin could take payment for guitars in materials and parts that he needed to make more instruments, eliminating the hassles and delays of ordering such supplies himself. Procuring supplies needed for guitar making had always been one of the roles of Martin's agent in New York, but the family pantry as well as the workshop was stocked by Zoebisch in exchange for guitars received; bottles of wine were one of the Martin family's most consistent requests. The greatest expense for Martin in building a majority of his instruments was the tuners, and these were always imported from France or Germany. The notation "Bruno G mashines" or "Z (for Zoebisch) G mashines" followed by a dollar amount is one of the most frequent entries in Martin's journal of shop expenses, but it seems he was always looking for more. The wide range of sources probably accounts for the fact that a number of different styles of tuners appear on Martin guitars from the same period. Higher

Figure 9-12. The machine tuners used on Martin's early guitars show a wide range of tuning button and metal plate designs, even on guitars of the same model. The second and forth tuners shown here (*from the left*) are by Jerome, a French manufacturer Martin seems to have preferred for many years, but his use of this brand ended before 1870. Left to right: De Goni guitar, 1843 (Profile 26); 2 1/2-34 (Profile 44); 2 1/2-40 (Profile 45); 3-24 (Profile 35).

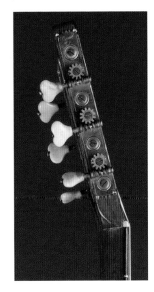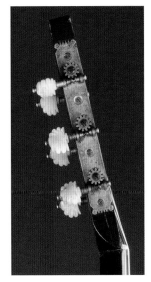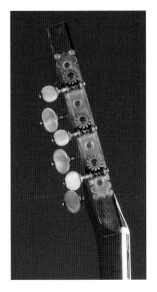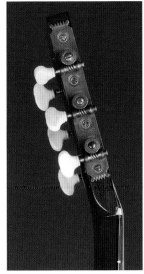

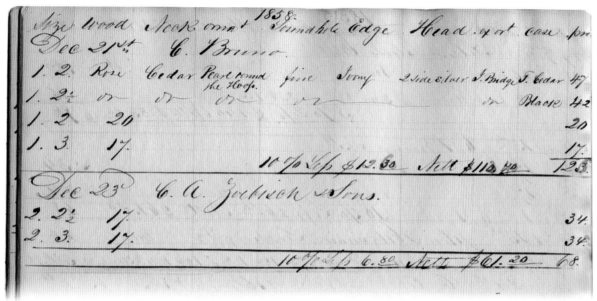

Figure 9-13. The last page in Martin's 1858 sales ledger, noting guitars sold to Charles Bruno. The first two listed, size 2 ½ and 2, each had "pearl round the hoop," silver tuners, and an ivory bridge The headings across the top detail the instruments' size, wood, neck, ornamentation, soundhole, edge, head, extra ornament ("ex ort"), case, and price. The $47 size 2's fine cedar case lifted it above the slightly smaller $42 size 2 ½ with a plain black case.

models were given more expensive tuners, often German silver with mother-of-pearl buttons on guitars with a wholesale cost of $30 and higher, but there is much variation even among the plain brass tuners with bone buttons found on $17 guitar models. Even as Martin guitars began to settle into distinct models that were sold year after year with few changes, not every element in their decoration, or, as Martin called them, "trimmings" or "ornament," remained the same. This is especially true of the wood marquetry (sometimes called "purfling" today) used around the soundhole, the face of the guitar, and up the center of the back. Different patterns and colors are often found on the same models from this period, and although the marquetry around the soundhole and the face of the guitar became less variable by the late 1860s, a wide variety of back strips continued to appear until late in the century. There is little indication that certain patterns or colors were requested by dealers or their customers or that anyone complained about the inconsistency; it appears instead that Martin's craftsmen had a free hand in making certain choices.

Thanks to use of the recently adopted size/price shorthand for what had become standard models, Martin's ledgers from the late 1850s do not offer quite the wealth of information about each

guitar as records from earlier years, but there are still entries outside the norm. Pearl bordering of the face of the guitar, which had previously been reserved for presentation models, apparently became a more standard top-of-the-line feature, setting the stage for what would later become Martin's signature style of decoration for its most expensive models (Profile 45). On December 21, 1858, perhaps just in time for Christmas, Charles Bruno received two small guitars, with the ornament described as "pearl round the hoop," plus silver tuners and an ivory bridge. This more expensive version of Martin's long-standing $34 model had an extra dose of flash and cost an additional eight dollars, while a fine cedar case brought the wholesale price of the second example to $47. We don't know if the size 2½ guitar illustrated in Profile 45 is one of those sent to Charles Bruno in 1858, as earlier examples are also described as having "ivory & pearl" edges, but this example does have more simple lines bordering the abalone band around the face than is found on later examples from the 1870s. Another similar model does not appear in Martin's records for another two years, but pearl-bordered style 40 and 42 guitars would appear on Martin's first price list a decade later. Few were made until late in the century, when they came to symbolize Martin

See page 220 for Profile 45, C. F. Martin 2½-40, c. 1859–1864

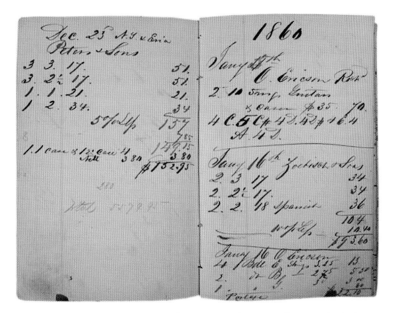
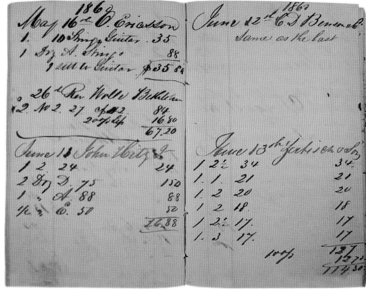

Figure 9-14. Martin ledger pages showing the sale of two 10-string guitars to Olaf Ericson on January 5, 1860, with the final order that followed four months later. Note the June 12th order to Benson & Co. on the following page, who took the easy route to restocking the Martin guitars they had sold by simply ordering "same as the last."

Figure 9-15. *Opposite page,* Martin & Coupa size 5 (terz), c. 1843–1845 (Profile 33). The ivory fingerboard and ivory-wrapped headstock of this terz guitar are features found on other Martins of the period, but the top border is decorated with additional ivory lines as well as the ivory binding. This use of bold black and white lines around the top, rather than marquetry or pearl, would be repeated over half a century later for the Style 44 guitars made for Vahdah Olcott Bickford, who was Martin's twentieth-century version of Madame de Goni.

elegance and were often made in larger sizes. These were precursors to the now-famous "pearl-bordered Martins" that glittered under stage lights in the hands of Gene Autry, Tex Ritter, and other cowboy stars during Martin's steel-string era.

An even more startling Martin guitar model from this period was clearly a special order and first appears in the daybook for 1859, when Olaf Ericson of Richmond, Virginia was sent a "2 neck guitar & case" for $32 in late September, plus a "bundle of best Italian strings." On January 4, 1861, he was sent two more "10-string" guitars, with an unusual selection of extra strings that included "4 C, 5 C#, 4 D, 4 D#, 4 G, 4 A, & 4 D." This time the price had gone up to $35 each, the same price Olaf was charged for yet another ten-string guitar shipped on May 16. Not much is known about Mr. Ericson or his music, but he was clearly spreading the joy of playing guitars with four additional bass strings.[11] Barely six months after Olaf Ericson took delivery of the last ten-string guitar Martin sent him, eleven states seceded from the Union, and, since Olaf was in Richmond, the capital of the Confederacy, he probably could not have taken delivery of another Martin guitar after shots were fired at Fort Sumter in April of 1861.

The war took an early and heavy toll on Martin's business; he was only able to sell eighty-two guitars in 1861, less than a third the sales of the previous year, and only eighty-five in 1862. However, business rebounded in 1863, with over two hundred guitars sold, and one hundred sixty-five guitars had been sold by mid 1864, when Martin's records again go missing and our trail runs cold. Such a rapid rebound in sales seems remarkable considering that the war was far from over and Martin's factory was not far from it. Although the battle of Gettysburg was fought only about 140 miles away, that was a formidable distance in the mid–nineteenth century, and, because the Moravians were pacifists, the war had far less impact on the community surrounding the Martins' new home and factory than many similar towns in the rest of the eastern United States. When Martin's records have again survived, beginning in mid 1867, it is clear that the standardization of models has continued, along with an increased dependence on C. A. Zoebisch & Sons and Charles Bruno as distributors. There is less communication with individual dealers and instructors by this time, and C. F. Martin, his son Frederick, and their small band of craftsmen are settling in to a long period of fine-tuning the models developed over a decade earlier. ★

Both the back and sides of this instrument are edged and divided by three different patterns of highly colored wood marquetry. Oddly, the face of the guitar carries no marquetry at all but is instead adorned with a double row of ivory binding around the perimeter and a similar ivory ring around the rosette that is bordered by glittering rings of minute pearl diamonds.

DIMENSIONS

TOTAL LENGTH	33"	838MM
BODY LENGTH	16.13"	410MM

WIDTH		
UPPER BOUT	8.43"	214MM
WAIST	6.97"	177MM
LOWER BOUT	11.34"	288MM

DEPTH		
NECK	3.39"	86MM
WAIST	3.62"	92MM
END	3.86"	108MM

NUT WIDTH	1.93"	49MM
SCALE	22.00"	559MM
SOUND HOLE	3.25"	83MM

This custom-grade size 5 is one of the most highly decorated terz guitars with a Martin & Coupa label to have surfaced to date. Terz guitars were a popular tenor voice for guitar duets or small ensembles of the period, and surviving correspondence from John Coupa suggests that he played one himself and recommended them to concert artists and students alike.

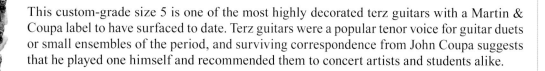

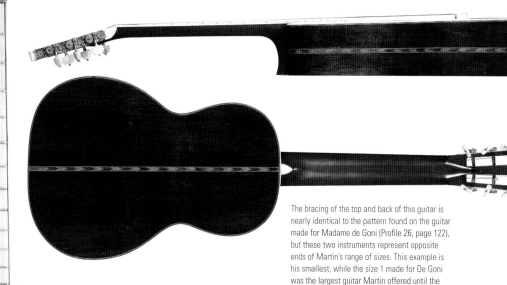

The bracing of the top and back of this guitar is nearly identical to the pattern found on the guitar made for Madame de Goni (Profile 26, page 122), but these two instruments represent opposite ends of Martin's range of sizes. This example is his smallest, while the size 1 made for De Goni was the largest guitar Martin offered until the early 1850s.

BRACING CONFIGURATION

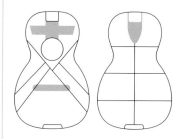

The extra ivory details, fancy tuners, and lavish use of marquetry suggest that this guitar was a special order, and one far more expensive than Martin's highest priced standard model. Along with the more obvious ivory fingerboard, the sides of the headstock are wrapped in thin ivory. It would be decades before Martin bound the headstocks of deluxe models with a narrow band of ivory at only the upper edge.

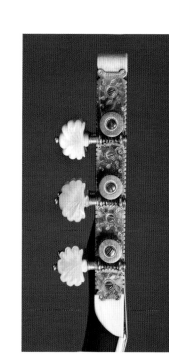

RELATIVE SIZE

42" (1067 MM)

36" (914 MM)

30" (762 MM)

18" (457 MM)

Many early Martin guitars have ivory friction pegs, but this is the only known example on which the shafts of the ivory pegs are sheathed in German silver.

TOTAL LENGTH	35.75"	908 MM
BODY LENGTH	17.36"	441 MM

WIDTH		
UPPER BOUT	8.23"	209 MM
WAIST	6.89"	175 MM
LOWER BOUT	11.42"	290 MM

DEPTH		
NECK	3.39"	86 MM
WAIST	3.62"	92 MM
END	3.86"	98 MM

NUT WIDTH	1.85"	47 MM
SCALE	24.5"	622 MM
SOUND HOLE	3.46"	88 MM

Small even for its day, this elegant guitar was almost certainly made for a woman, and the ivory fingerboard and other deluxe appointments suggest it was a special order of considerable cost. From the ivory-wrapped headstock to the tie-block bridge, most of the features found on this guitar were discontinued well before C. F. Martin's death in 1873.

Only the hybrid of X and fan-pattern top bracing puts this guitar in the newly evolving American style. All its other features are pure Spanish. Some of these details, such as twin holes in the headstock for hanging the instrument from a wall peg, only lasted for a few years.

This guitar does not conform to Martin's later specifications for each size. The body is size 3 but the scale length is the same as normally found on the slightly larger size 2½. Note that the back has only two braces, a feature found on only a few Martins, all with the faux Spanish foot at the base of the neck block.

BRACING CONFIGURATION

RELATIVE SIZE

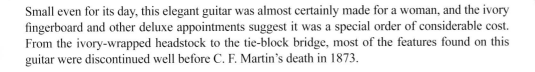

42" (1067 MM)

36" (914 MM)

30" (762 MM)

18" (457 MM)

The distinctive marquetry bordering the top, which was far more colorful before it faded with time, is more elaborate than found on lower Martin styles that used rosewood binding on the body's edges rather than ivory. The marquetry was imported from Saxony, and although Martin later settled on about a half dozen patterns he used repeatedly, there is far more variation during this period.

Tuners with bone rollers like those seen here were only used for a short period. Despite continuing to use gut strings, Martin later opted for brass rollers of a much smaller diameter. This is an early version of Martin's slotted headstock, with wider slots and a narrower horizontal portion at the top.

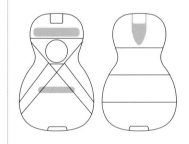

With no pearl or ivory appointments in sight, this little guitar looks quite plain compared to most of the Martins profiled in this volume, but it is actually representative of the majority of the Cherry Hill workshop's 1840s production. The appointments suggest this instrument probably had a wholesale cost of about $24, putting it in the middle of Martin's line of standard models, which cost retailers from $16 to $34.

Although the top is braced with an early hybrid of fan and X bracing, this is a very Spanish model, with a tie-block bridge, sparse back bracing, and a faux Spanish foot at the base of the neck block. Note that the bracing is nearly identical to Profile 26, so this is probably what both Martin and his dealers referred to as a "small De Goni." Despite the small size of the body, the neck is a full two inches wide at the nut.

DIMENSIONS

TOTAL LENGTH	35.25"	895 MM
BODY LENGTH	17.38"	441 MM

WIDTH

UPPER BOUT	8.38"	213 MM
WAIST	6.81"	173 MM
LOWER BOUT	11.38"	289 MM

DEPTH

NECK	3.5"	89 MM
WAIST	3.69"	94 MM
END	3.88"	98 MM

NUT WIDTH	2"	51 MM
SCALE	24"	610 MM
SOUND HOLE	3.44"	87 MM

BRACING CONFIGURATION

RELATIVE SIZE

42" (1067 MM)

36" (914 MM)

30" (762 MM)

18" (457 MM)

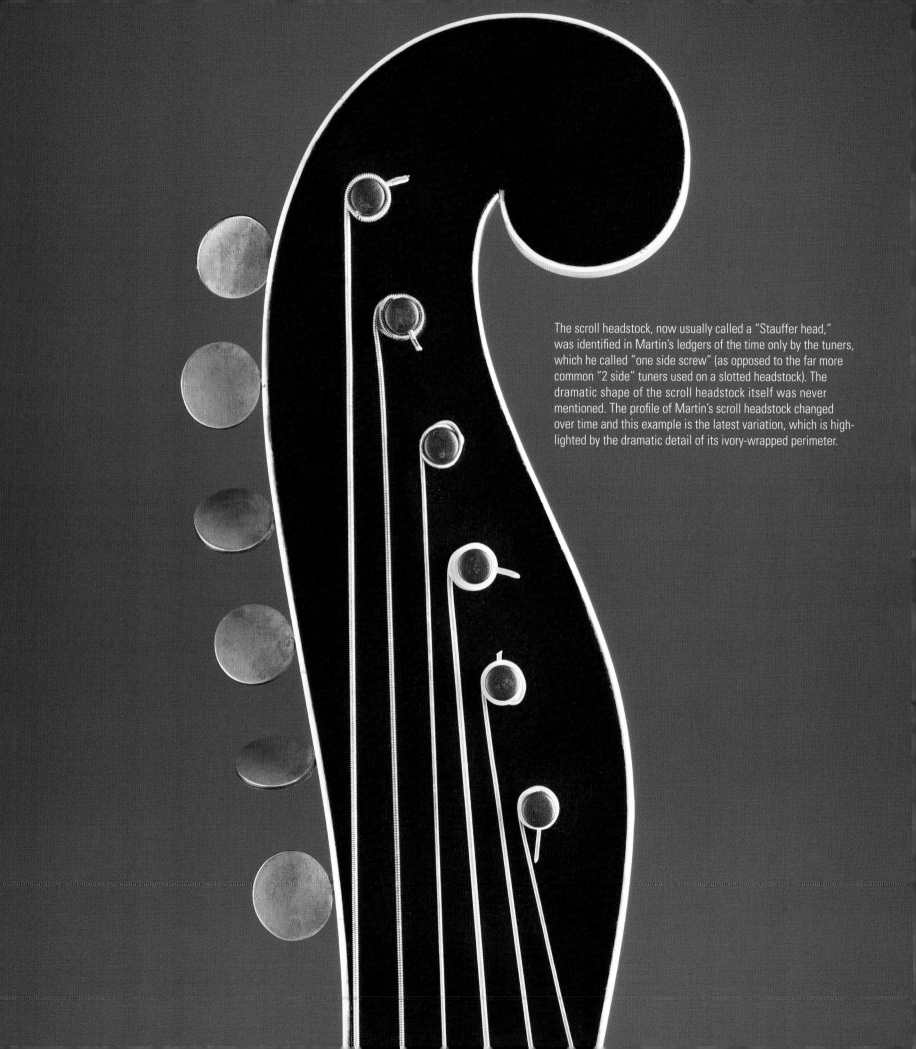

The scroll headstock, now usually called a "Stauffer head," was identified in Martin's ledgers of the time only by the tuners, which he called "one side screw" (as opposed to the far more common "2 side" tuners used on a slotted headstock). The dramatic shape of the scroll headstock itself was never mentioned. The profile of Martin's scroll headstock changed over time and this example is the latest variation, which is highlighted by the dramatic detail of its ivory-wrapped perimeter.

This size 2 Martin & Coupa is a classic example of Martin's willingness to combine elements of the Austro-German style, the more fashionable Spanish style, and his own newly evolving American style, all in one guitar.

The body of this instrument is nearly identical to the popular 2-34 models that were Martin's most expensive standard guitars until the late 1850s. The black neck with scroll headstock, however, is nearly identical to Martin models from the mid 1830s.

Although the X bracing, with a treble side "finger brace," appears quite modern, note that this example lacks the long angled brace below the bridge. The back bracing is still thoroughly in the Spanish style, with only two braces, both in the lower bout.

DIMENSIONS

TOTAL LENGTH	37.75"	959 MM
BODY LENGTH	18.31"	465 MM

WIDTH

UPPER BOUT	8.63"	219 MM
WAIST	7"	178 MM
LOWER BOUT	12"	305 MM

DEPTH

NECK	3.69"	97 MM
WAIST	3.81"	97 MM
END	3.94"	100 MM

NUT WIDTH	1.88"	48 MM
SCALE	24.5"	622 MM
SOUND HOLE	3.56"	90 MM

BRACING CONFIGURATION

RELATIVE SIZE

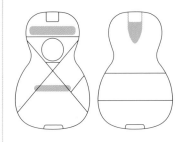

42" (1067 MM)

36" (914 MM)

30" (762 MM)

18" (457 MM)

Although the elaborate rosette first catches the eye, it is only one of a number of unusual features found on this guitar from Henry Schatz's period in Boston. The pearl figures are embedded in mastic, a technique used for the rosettes on many Martins from the New York era, but in this case the pearl is more widely spaced and the mastic is white instead of black, resulting in a highly decorative effect very different from the soundhole decoration on Martin guitars.

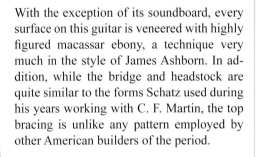

With the exception of its soundboard, every surface on this guitar is veneered with highly figured macassar ebony, a technique very much in the style of James Ashborn. In addition, while the bridge and headstock are quite similar to the forms Schatz used during his years working with C. F. Martin, the top bracing is unlike any pattern employed by other American builders of the period.

DIMENSIONS

TOTAL LENGTH	35.25"	895 MM
BODY LENGTH	17.38"	441 MM

WIDTH

UPPER BOUT	8.13"	206 MM
WAIST	6.5"	165 MM
LOWER BOUT	11.31"	287 MM

DEPTH

NECK	3.25"	83 MM
WAIST	3.44"	87 MM
END	3.5"	89 MM

NUT WIDTH	1.87"	48 MM
SCALE	24.62"	625 MM
SOUND HOLE	3.37"	86 MM

BRACING CONFIGURATION

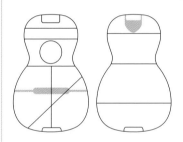

RELATIVE SIZE

42" (1067 MM)

36" (914 MM)

30" (762 MM)

18" (457 MM)

Henry Schatz was listed as making guitars in Boston between 1845 and 1850, when he traveled back to Saxony. He returned to the United States eight years later and died between 1866 and 1868.

Like several of Martin's highest-grade guitars, this instrument has an ivory facing that wraps around the top and sides of the headstock. The German-silver machine tuners with pearl buttons, similar to those found on Martin's Style 40 guitars, are set into the ivory surface.

Martin's scroll headstock had by this time been retired, but its shape was mirrored here to provide an artful lyre-shaped home for ten ivory friction pegs, four of them lining up neatly above the additional bass strings to the left of the conventional six-string neck.

Martin made a number of harp guitars shortly after 1900, but that was during the era of mandolin "orchestras," when virtually every fretted instrument manufacturer was offering harp guitars. This instrument predates those examples by forty years, and we know very little about the music it was used to play. The only hints are that Olaf Ericson of Richmond, Virginia, received at least four examples and that in Martin records, some are described as "10-string" and others simply as "2 neck guitar."

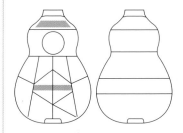

The body shape of this unusual instrument is closely related to the guitar shown in Profile 40. The primary changes to accommodate the additional strings are the extra top bracing added to the three-fan pattern and the deeper body to augment the bass response.

DIMENSIONS

TOTAL LENGTH	38"	965 MM
BODY LENGTH	18.62"	473 MM

WIDTH

UPPER BOUT	8.66"	220 MM
WAIST	7.6"	193 MM
LOWER BOUT	12.83"	326 MM

DEPTH

NECK	3.54"	90 MM
WAIST	4.05"	103 MM
END	4.37"	111 MM

NUT WIDTH	1.85"	47 MM
SCALE	24.8"	630 MM
SOU ND HOLE	3.66"	93 MM

BRACING CONFIGURATION

RELATIVE SIZE

42" (1067 MM)

36" (914 MM)

30" (762 MM)

18" (457 MM)

CHAPTER 10

MARTIN'S EVOLUTION TO AN AMERICAN GUITAR

RICHARD JOHNSTON

By the early 1850s, Martin guitars were well on their way to evolving into a truly American style. While the many surviving Martin guitars from the latter half of the nineteenth century show the end result of this evolution, and the far more rare ones pictured in this volume show many of its intermediary steps, there is, unfortunately, little historical evidence regarding why C. F. Martin made the changes he did.

The primary reason for these gaps in our knowledge is the lack of surviving Martin records, of either guitar orders and sales or business commerce in general, for the period between 1839 and 1850, when the majority of Martin's innovations in the transition from Austro-German style guitars to Spanish styles, and then beyond, took place. After reveling in the wealth of detail the records from the 1830s provide, we enter a period where the paper labels in some of the guitars and a few late 1840s letters from dealers are all the documentary evidence that has survived. We have a good idea of what Martin was building before he left New York, and we have fairly complete production and sales records showing what the much larger Martin workshop in Cherry Hill, Pennsylvania, was making in the early 1850s, but what took place between those dates, and exactly when, is still a mystery.[1] Since C. F. Martin reported a staff of six workmen and an annual production potential of 250 guitars for the 1850 census, even allowing for a slow start after leaving New York, his workshop at Cherry Hill almost certainly produced well over a thousand guitars during the 1840s.[2]

Another reason for our inability to pin down the exact dates when many of the changes to Martin guitars took place is that even when Martin's day books and sales ledgers have survived, they contain very little information regarding construction details of the guitars recorded. We might learn about the soundhole decoration for a particular guitar made in 1852, for instance, whether its neck was cedar, what type of tuners were used, and how much the guitar sold for, but there is never any notation regarding internal construction. This means that an over-$20 size 2 guitar with fan bracing of the top and a tie-block bridge could appear in Martin's records with the same description given a similar size 2 guitar that had X-pattern top bracing and a pin bridge. The first guitar would of course represent the lingering influence of the Spanish style, while the second would be more or less like the Martin models that were continued into the early twentieth century. However, because both guitars had similar binding and decoration and sold for the same price, Martin's records rarely give us any indication of such differences.

To make following the transition from Martin's Spanish-influenced period to the later American style even more confusing, the changes we know were afoot were not applied to all models at the same time and were not applied to some models at all. For instance, we think of long body shapes with narrow upper bouts, fan bracing of the tops, tie-block bridges, cedar necks with Spanish heels, and individual piece "dentellone" linings as all being signs of the Spanish influence. However, by the time this period of rapid evolution was drawing to a close, Martin's smaller, less expensive model s—Styles 18 and below—were still given fan-braced tops, while Style 20 and above were X-braced, regardless of size. Not many years later, the lower-priced, fan-braced models were the only ones still displaying the black necks that we associate with Martin's Austro-German influence, while the higher, X-braced models were given a more Spanish-style cedar neck.[3] Such rules certainly did not apply during the Martin & Coupa years, however, as exemplified by the ornate size 2 shown in Profile 36. This example has a neck that is nearly identical to the style used on high-grade Stauffer models of the late 1830s, but with the same slim body shape and X-braced top with pin bridge that was continued into the next century. The inside back of the guitar, however, shows the pointed foot at the base of the neck block and the sparse two-brace design of Martin's more Spanish-influenced models. This mixing of Germanic and Spanish elements makes it clear that, while Martin's models were evolving, their designer had little allegiance to one particular style or region.

Yet, a strict division between X-braced and fan-braced models is apparent by the mid 1850s, when Martin guitar evolution seems to have slowed. The same differences between a size 2 guitar with a wholesale price of $20 and the smaller size 2½ sold to dealers for $17, for example, are still evident thirty years later in Martin's 2-20 models compared to 2½-17 models. Today, the relatively plain Style 17 guitars get little attention, partly because they are so small that modern guitarists have little use for them, but also because they turn up so often. It is important to remember that those drab little Martins, with their simple binding and black necks with cone-shaped heels, are relatively common today because they were extremely popular in their time. In fact, decades after Martin had adopted X bracing, these small, fan-braced models represented almost a third of the company's annual production.[4]

Some of the reasons for Martin's retreat from more purely Spanish features, especially on higher

models, may indeed have been that the way Martin made guitars was never quite compatible with true Spanish guitar construction.[5] In other words, Martin embraced the aesthetic of the Spanish builders from Cadiz but not their methods, and eventually, the demands of practical production won out over features that even today are considered trademarks of a true Spanish guitar, regardless of where it is made. Although the faux Spanish foot at the base of the neck block disappeared, the Martin workshop did not abandon fan bracing of the top even when it stopped using the Spanish-style tie-block bridge. The three-fan bracing pattern was apparently deemed quite adequate on small guitars, and a center fan running between the third and fourth string bridge pin holes apparently wasn't enough of an obstacle to warrant the extra effort required by Martin's interlocking X pattern of top braces. That Martin considered X bracing to be superior is suggested by the fact that, by the mid 1850s and probably earlier, higher styles were always given X-pattern top bracing, even when those styles were ordered in the same small sizes found on the less costly Style 17. The Martin "package of features" associated with X-braced models, which included a cedar neck, more binding, and individual block linings, resulted in a significantly higher price tag, and customers were apparently not allowed to order larger examples of the relatively inexpensive Style 17.[6] Martin was more than willing to make smaller examples of his higher styles, but no larger Martin models, such as a size 1 with the features found on a 2½–17, appear in the ledgers or have come to light.

While Martin did not continue using several of the more Spanish-like features, especially after John Coupa's death in 1850, the influence of Spanish body shapes, necks, bridges, and even soundhole rosettes, had become part of what was already a fairly consistent American style of guitar, and those features were, by mid-century, firmly in place. This is especially evident in the instruments made by former Martin employees Louis Schmidt and George Maul, as shown in Profiles 41 and 42, both of which are from

See page 184 for Profile 36, Martin & Coupa, c. 1846–1850.

See page 212 for Profile 41, Schmidt & Maul, c. 1853.

See page 214 for Profile 42, Schmidt & Maul, c. 1858.

Figure 10-1. George Maul, 1859. A remarkably modern-looking guitar by one of C. F. Martin's former employees. Both Louis Schmidt and George Maul, who worked as partners for many years, made guitars that are virtually indistinguishable from their mentor's work.

the 1850s. An even more modern-looking example by Maul is shown above, and, although it was built in 1859, it looks as if it would easily fit into any late 1800s catalog of American-style guitars.

Martin offered a more diverse line of guitars than his competitors, but he still differentiated his models—which spanned a wide range of sizes, appointments, and prices—with variations of an essentially fixed set of designs. The ornate bridges found on earlier high-grade Martins, for instance, had been left behind thanks to the Spanish influence, and the most costly Martins now had ivory bridges, less expensive models had bridges of ebony, although both the ivory and ebony bridges were the same rectangular shape with "pyramid" tips. Pearl ornaments were sometimes added to higher models, but these "flowers," as they were sometimes called in Martin's ledgers, were affixed to the soundboard, under or on either side of the bridge, and did not alter its shape.

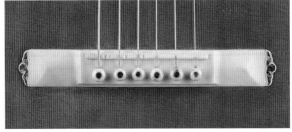

Figure 10-2. Pearl "flowers" were sometimes added to higher models, either below or on the side of the bridge.

With only a few exceptions, Martin's soundhole rosettes consisted of three rings with the inner and outermost rings identical, while the center ring was wider and more ornate. The vast majority of Martin headstocks were simple rectangles with tapered sides and no decoration, except for a diminishing number of requests for the long scroll-shaped headstock with tuner buttons all on one side. What we now call a "Stauffer head," which was noted in Martin's ledgers as "Vienna screws" or "one-side screw," was, with the exception of the black neck and cone-shaped heel, the most tenacious visual element of the Austro-German style

Once this "Stauffer head" disappeared in the mid 1850s, all Martin guitars shared similar straight-sided headstocks, although the slotted version with "two side screws" (geared tuners, three on a side with knobs facing back) had less flare at the top than did the "peg head" (head with friction pegs) that had been adopted as part of the Spanish style.[7] With the exception of a few specially ordered "presentation models," which had ivory-wrapped headstocks, even the most expensive of Martin's standard guitar models had very plain necks with no decoration except for ivory binding on the fingerboard, and Martin guitar necks continued to remain unadorned for the rest of the century.[8] The black neck with cone-shaped heel continued to be used on many small guitars with pearl rosettes and colorful marquetry long after the cedar neck became standard on larger, but plainer models, such as the De Goni. The 1850s guitar shown in Profile 44 has all the features of Style 34, including an ivory bridge and German silver tuners with fancy mother-of-pearl buttons. However, with the exception of "ivory to the nut,"—Martin's way of describing a guitar with a bound fingerboard—its black neck and plain headstock are not much different from the necks used on Style 17 models that sold for half the price.

MARTIN GUITAR BODY SIZES

Because of the almost total lack of records or correspondence from the 1840s, we do not have many details to explain how the wide range of Martin's guitar sizes evolved. Since Martin listed Spanish models in his ledgers beginning in late 1837, some of the smaller sizes, perhaps with shapes similar to those found in the early 1850s, were already being made. The last notations before the extended record-less period are from early 1840 and list a number of sales to John Coupa of "Spanish guitars," with mention of "size 2" for some and "size 3" for others. Unfortunately, of course, we cannot be certain how those shapes compare to later Martins with a similar designation.[9] There is considerable variety in the overall dimensions of the guitars from the Martin & Coupa era, and noticeable asymmetry is not unusual, as evidenced by the differences between the right and left halves of the high-grade Spanish-style Martin model shown in figure 10-3.

Martin body sizes were identified with a numbering system that makes sense to machinists and electricians—the larger the number, the smaller the size—but can be confusing to the rest of us.[10] From the first listings of guitar sales in Martin's ledgers from mid 1834 through 1836, there are details about the instruments regarding wood, tuners, inlay, and cases, but no mention of sizes. Beginning in 1837, some guitars are described as "large," but there is no size description for most, with the exception of a few listed as "ordinary size." The first appearance in Martin's ledgers of the word "size" followed by a number (either 2 or 3) is in the group of orders for John Coupa in March 1840 (mentioned above), but then the trail disappears, as there are no more surviving records until almost a decade later. Letters from retailers in 1849, however, mention both size 3 and

Figure 10-3. *Left,* C. F. Martin, c. 1841-45. This Spanish-style guitar's body is asymmetrical, with right and left halves of slightly different contours.

Figure 10-4. *Above,* fancy fan-shaped mother-of-pearl buttons were reserved for styles 30 and higher, and were apparently only used for a few years.

size 2½, plus the "large De Goni" (size 1) and "small De Goni" (size 2), so we know Martin was making at least four sizes of regular guitars before 1850, plus the smaller terz model frequently mentioned by John Coupa[11] (See Profile 33).

It is safe to assume that most, if not all, of the guitars mentioned in the earlier portions of the 1830s records are of the Stauffer-like Austro-German shape. By 1837, however, the phrase "Spanish guitar" appears, and, for the next few years, the Austro-German shapes and the newer Spanish-influenced guitars apparently existed side by side, for some of the earlier style have surfaced with Martin & Coupa labels. What was described as a "large" Martin guitar

See page 218 for Profile 44, Martin 2½–34, c. 1859–1864.

See page 178 for Profile 33, Martin & Coupa Terz, c. 1845.

Figure 10-5. *Far right*, illustration of violas de gamba from *The Division Viol, or the Art of Playing upon a Ground* by Christopher Simpson, published in 1659. The viola de gamba is a bowed, fretted instrument, usually with six strings, that was extremely popular in the Renaissance and Baroque periods. As its name suggests, the viola da gamba (literally viol of the leg) was played held between the knees. It was tuned like a guitar, and, like lutes of the period, had moveable frets made from gut strings that were tied round the neck.

in 1840 was probably roughly equivalent to the size 1 made for Madame de Goni a few years later, with size 2 and size 3 being respectively smaller. A quick glance at the guitars shown in this volume and their measurements, however, will make it clear that the instruments presumed to be early examples of the Spanish influence have body shapes and proportions that are slightly different from the later nineteenth-century Martin models that were continued with little change into the next century. There are several guitars in this volume, for instance, that measure 12¼ inches across the lower bout, but before 1860, Martin's size 2 was slimmed down slightly to a 12-inch width.

This decade of experimentation and development resulted in a range of body shapes unmatched in their day and even more exceptional when compared to the offerings of modern guitar companies of far greater size. By the early 1850s, Martin was producing significant numbers of five different body sizes, ranging from size 5 terz guitars to the size 1 championed by Madame de Goni, a remarkable number of options considering that there was only a 1½-inch difference in body width between the smallest and largest models.[12]

Whether by conscious design or simply by way of habit, Martin guitars display a remarkable aesthetic consistency by the early 1850s. When looking at these guitars in photos it can be difficult to gauge their size, because the dimensions of the bridges, headstocks, and soundholes, and even the spacing of the rings in the rosette, were all minutely adjusted to suit the size of the body (although size 5 is easier to identify because of its much shorter body and neck). This consistency was achieved with considerable effort; it meant there were far fewer standard parts that could be used on more than one or two sizes, but the result was guitars with the same pleasing proportions between their respective parts regardless of their size.[13] This variety is in marked contrast to James Ashborn, who only offered one size and shape, but with several levels of appointments.

MARTIN'S "RENAISSANCE" GUITARS

Martin produced at least three distinctly different versions of the unconventional body shape shown in Profile 39 and 40, and seven examples have come to light with varying features, suggesting that their production spanned as much as a decade, and perhaps longer, before they disappeared around 1860.

In recent years, these models have been lumped together under the catchall "Renaissance" title, despite the fact that they have little in common with any known guitars from that era. The narrow but elongated upper bout, usually with a flattened shelf where the neck attaches, echoes early members of the viol family, and some German makers produced guitars that have bodies clearly inspired by the shape of a viola da gamba.

Forma Chelyos utravis Minuritonibus apta, fed Prima refonantior.

Although somewhat similar European instruments with reduced upper bouts preceded them, such as the wappengitarre, Martin's efforts were probably inspired by guitars with sloping upper shoulders made by highly regarded European builders such as

Lacote in Paris or D & A Roudhloff of London.[13] Even Stauffer had experimented with a different-shaped upper bout near the neck joint, perhaps while a young C. F. Martin was still in his employ, and one of those guitars is shown in figure 10-6. (Also see Profile 2).

Considering Martin's frequent correspondence with European suppliers to acquire tuners or marquetry, and his association with a number of well-traveled performers such as Marco Aurelio Zani de Ferranti (once guitarist to the king of Belgium), it seems likely that these oddly shaped models are further proof that Spanish guitars were not Martin's only sources of influence in the years after he left New York.[14]

Judging by highly decorated examples that have survived, Martin apparently had high hopes for this quite different, and decidedly un-Spanish design. (No reference has been found suggesting what this body shape was called at the time, either by Martin or anyone else, perhaps due to missing records covering the 1840–1852 period). The example with abalone pearl fingerboard shown in figure 10-12 was specially ordered in 1852 by Peters & Son in Cincinnati, for a customer who presented it as a wedding gift.

An equally elaborate version with an ivory fingerboard, presumed to have been made around the same time, is shown in Profile 39 and came with a rosewood case bordered in fancy marquetry.

See page 208 for Profile 39, C. F. Martin Renaissance Style, c. 1843–1852.

See page 210 for Profile 40, C. F. Martin Renaissance Style, c. 1850–1860.

Figure 10-6. This Stauffer guitar (see Profile 2) suggests that building a guitar whose upper bout flowed into the contours of the neck heel was not unique to Martin. Stauffer and other European makers experimented with similar body shapes.

Figure 10-7. Despite the advantage it gave to guitarists reaching for the upper frets, the extra effort required to build a design as radical as the Martin shown above probably explains why this guitar shape was not continued. (See figures 10-9, 10, 11, and 12).

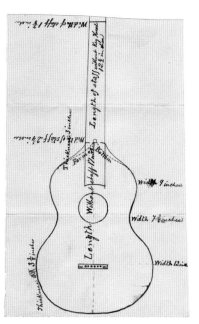

Figure 10-8. This working drawing, found in the Martin Archives and with handwriting that suggests it was drawn by Henry Schatz, shows the same shape and dimensions as the Martin guitar illustrated in figure 10-7.

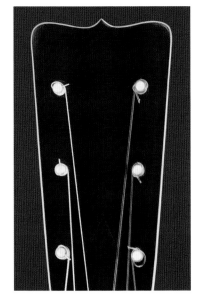

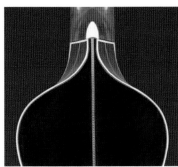

Figure 10-9. *Top.* The peaked headstock has only been found on some of Martin's short-lived "Renaissance" models. Among Martin's post-New York guitars, it is the only exception to his use of the curved "Stauffer" headstocks or the more common Spanish-style rectangular shape.

Figure 10-10. *Above.* By blending the sides of the guitar into the contour of the neck heel, this design allows the player far easier access to the upper frets.

Figure 10-11. *Right.* This "Renaissance" model has the full compliment of Spanish features, despite its very un-Spanish shape. It has Martin's early tie-block bridge, a faux Spanish foot neckblock, two-piece sides, and a fan-braced soundboard. The fretboard is both wider and has a steeper radius than Martin's standard models.

These are the most highly decorated guitars yet to have surfaced from Martin's post-New York era. Models with more pearl inlay would not appear until 1902.[15]

Another even more rare feature that appeared and disappeared around the same time is a straight-sided headstock with a small peak at the top. This shape is found on two of the above-mentioned models with different versions of the "Renaissance" body shape, one with a slotted headstock and another, shown in figure 10-11, with ivory pegs. This peaked headstock, which is not known to have been used on any of the Martin models with a more standard body shape, is one of the most ephemeral elements to appear on Martin guitars and only heightens the mystery surrounding these unusual instruments.

One possible reason for the unorthodox body shape of these models is that the much smaller upper bout, with a very narrow section nearest the neck heel, was intended to allow the guitarist easier access to the upper frets. Three of these guitars have twenty-fret fingerboards, while De Goni models Martin made during the same period have only eighteen frets total.

While one of these models has a fan-braced top and tie-block bridge, the others are more in the newly-emerging American style, suggesting that the unusual shape may have been part of Martin's effort to construct instruments that were very much his own, rather than continuing only to build what were essentially Spanish-shaped guitars made in America.

While these models indicate Martin's willingness to innovate during this critical post-Spanish period, they apparently did not spark much demand, and the result was an evolutionary dead-end. These short-lived experiments and hybrids are further proof that C. F. Martin was well aware of international trends in both the aesthetics and structure of the modern guitar, and in terms of guitar design, his small workshop was, much like his adopted country, a melting pot.

Figure 10-12. *Far left.* Among surviving examples of Martin's "Renaissance-shape" guitars, this highly decorated presentation model has numerous unique features, including gold frets, that allow us to link it to letters in the Martin Archives from 1852.

Figure 10-13. *Left.* Martin's "Renaissance" models were made in at least two sizes, with three different top bracing patterns. This size 2 example has the same appointments and X-pattern bracing as Martin's later guitars; its only unusual feature is the shape of the body.

Figure 10-14. *Below.* This deluxe rosewood case housed the elaborately decorated "Renaissance" model shown in profile 39, but similar cases have been found with other presentation-grade models such as shown in figure 10-12. This example features binding, marquetry, and a French polish finish of the same quality as found on Martin guitars.

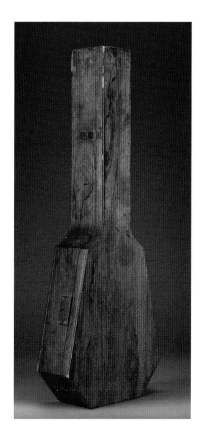

EARLY MARTIN GUITAR STYLES

Most of the long standing controversy about Martin's guitar styles and how they evolved can be traced to Martin's habit of deriving style numbers from the prices charged for a guitar with a specific list of appointments, a shortcut commonly found in other retail goods and practiced by both C. F. Martin & Co. and its competitors in recent times.[16] Even in Martin's earliest ledgers, from the mid 1830s, the price of a guitar was used as an identifying code. This was the retail price, which meant that the number assigned to the guitar and the price Martin was paid for it did not match, because of discounts or sales commissions. Once Martin records appear again in the early 1850s, the Cherry Hill workshop is primarily selling to retailers and instructors, not guitarists, and the reference has become the wholesale price. Prices for both materials and labor were stable for over a decade, allowing a numbering system based on each guitar's cost in dollars to become thoroughly entrenched.

Although records for the period when most of Martin's Spanish-influenced styles were developed have been lost, there are a few letters from dealers in the late 1840s listing guitar orders, in which several of the styles and sizes, and their cost, are a close match to listings found in Martin sales ledgers a few years later. Since these letters clearly assume that the reader, in this case C. F. Martin himself, knows what guitar is being ordered when the price is mentioned, they confirm that well before 1850 the wholesale price was already a familiar code that described the level of decoration. Martin later called this a "number of quality," or at least that was the term used on the paper labels affixed to the underside of the case lid where customers could see it.

The very small, plain guitars for which dealers paid $17, for instance, are already a staple; an 1848 letter from Martin's Pittsburgh dealer, Jonathan Mellor, includes an order for three of them. Although the size is not mentioned, they were probably size 3, because the majority of the $17 guitars sold in 1852 are described as being that size.[17] Another guitar listed in

Figure 10-15. *Far right*, this volume primarily shows Martin models that were quite expensive, but plainer guitars like this one from the 1840s represent the level of decoration found on the majority of Martin's production.

Mellor's order is "1 guitar fine, ivory edges, double side screw & ff case" that cost $27, and guitars of this description and price also appear in the 1852 ledger. The $26 "large De Goni" mentioned in this same order and in Coupa's letter from the following year, is probably similar to more than a dozen size 1 models, all with the same description and "ff" (extra fine) case, sold to several dealers in 1852 for $26. Although it had been nine years since Martin had made two guitars for Madame de Goni, models linked to her name were still frequently requested.

Some of the appointments on the guitars described in these late 1840s letters may have differed slightly from later models that had the same cost, but readers familiar with Martin's first printed price list from the early 1870s will recognize several model codes that appear repeatedly in the early 1850s ledgers.[18] The $17 size 3, $27 size 2, and $26 size 1 guitars that appear in Mellor's 1848 order and which also appear often in the 1852 ledger, suggest that although certain details would change, the move towards standard models was already in progress. At the end of an 1849 letter from Mayer & Collier of Albany, New York, which included an order for "3 g like the last 3 you sent us" is the request: "Will you please send us a list of prices and descriptions of each kind of guitar you make." To the frustration of many retailers, it would be two decades before Martin complied with such requests.

Although Martin was already moving towards standardization, not all the guitars mentioned in these late 1840s orders, or even in the early 1850s ledgers, were precursors of later popular Martin models. Some of the instruments described in this period would soon disappear. These instruments are often versions of similar guitars that had evolved earlier in the 1840s, but with features that were left behind. Coupa's letters mention small guitars with "double back," a term repeated in C. F. Martin Jr.'s journal entries after he traveled to New York to keep the 385 Broadway sales studio in operation after Coupa's death in 1850. "Double back" almost certainly refers

to the interior lamination of spruce on the backs of many surviving Martin guitars from this period, a feature apparently reserved only for higher models in smaller sizes.[19]

Although we cannot be sure when this feature disappeared, it was certainly well before 1867. Mellor also ordered low-priced mahogany models in the same 1848 letter, and size 3 guitars of mahogany with a cost of $15 or $16 also appear throughout ledgers of the early 1850s. These guitars sold to dealers for less than half the price of a rosewood Martin that was only slightly larger, but had "ivory to the nut," a pearl rosette, "extra fine" ornament (wide multicolored marquetry around the top), and "German silver

See page 216 for Profile 43, C. F. Martin 2½–32, c. 1852–1867..

See page 218 for Profile 44, C. F. Martin 2½–34, c. 1850–1862.

Figure 10-16. Spruce lining on the inside of the back on a size 2 with Style 34 appointments. Many of Martin's higher models from the 1840s and '50s share this feature, which John Coupa described as a "double back".

two side screw" tuners with mother-of-pearl buttons (right-angle gears mounted on the sides of a slotted headstock). Such a $34 model differed from a nearly identical $30 guitar of the same size only in that it included an ivory, instead of ebony, bridge (Profiles 43 and 44). Although special orders, such as for the presentation-grade guitars described on pages 196–197 were even more costly, in the years before "pearl around the hoop" (abalone bordering the perimeter of the face) pushed the prices of deluxe standard models even higher, small guitars like the one shown in Profile 44 were the most expensive standard Martins and would survive with few changes into the next century.

The inexpensive mahogany models, however, would see an opposite fate. Mahogany Martin guitars disappeared altogether before the 1860s, but returned in the early years of the twentieth century under

Frank Henry Martin (C. F. Martin Sr.'s grandson) and soon dominated Martin production, especially during the Great Depression.[20]

SUMMARY OF MARTIN GUITAR STYLES AS RECORDED BEFORE THE CIVIL WAR

$14, $15, & $16 MODELS

While it is difficult to differentiate these three styles based on the descriptions in Martin sales ledgers, all are mahogany and have appointments similar to the $17 models described below.[21] Guitars sold for these prices are all listed as size 3 or 2½, with either ebony pegs or brass tuners. At least one Martin matching this description has surfaced with no binding on the top edge, but other extant examples have rosewood binding on the top only. They do not appear in the records after 1856.

GUITARS SELLING FOR $17-$35

All models listed below have rosewood bodies. Wooden cases were available in three grades—common ("c"), fine ("f"), and extra fine ("ff"). If a model normally supplied with a fine case was supplied with the higher grade, the guitar's price would go up, while if a guitar that normally came with the ff case was instead shipped with the lower grade, the price paid for the guitar would drop (all models with prices above $25 were usually listed with the "ff" case). Some models were ordered with either ebony or ivory friction pegs, which could also affect the price (ebony pegs cost less than ivory and often less than geared tuners). While many models were described as having brass tuners, the brass tuners supplied with a $27 guitar were more costly than the brass tuners supplied on $17 models, and, because getting an adequate supply of these imported parts was often a problem, guitars may have been shipped with different grades of tuners, which could also have affected the price. These fluctuations probably account for the confusing listings, especially of guitars that cost between $20 and $23, and those with prices between $30 and

$34. Although Martin apparently did not consistently charge a higher price for a larger size guitar with the same appointments during this era, almost as many ledger entries contradict this rule as confirm it.

Once the size/wholesale price shorthand became a standard for Martin's bookkeeping in the late 1850s (see below), trying to determine the differences among some of the more obscure models becomes almost impossible, as there is usually no mention of the grade of case or tuners, and no description of the appointments. Some dealers apparently had standing orders that certain models be shipped with a different grade of case or tuners than was typical, and this would, of course, affect the price. This could have resulted in 2-20 models sent to one dealer being identical to guitars entered in the ledgers as 2-21 models when sold to another account. Martin intended these records, which were clearly not always entered by the same person, only to be for his company's own use. The Martin workshop had intimate knowledge of the preferences of a small group of instructors and retailers, and so did not feel it necessary to write down details for Martin guitar devotees to ponder a century and a half later.

The code in parenthesis following many of the models below are the models that appeared on Martin's first price list, a rough draft of which was prepared by Charles Bruno in 1868.[22] While other sizes of these style numbers were sold, once the price list was issued an overwhelming majority of Martin's sales was of these standard models.

$17 MODELS (LATER 2½-17 AND 3-17)

Offered only in size 3 and size 2½, with black neck, plain purfling around the top and soundhole, rosewood binding on top edge only, and common case. By far the most popular Martin style, with over a thousand sold between 1852 and 1862, Style 17 appeared on the first price list and continued to sell well, with essentially no changes, for the rest of the nineteenth century. To the best of our knowledge, most, if not all, have three-fan top bracing and solid linings.

Figure 10-17. Martin sold guitars like this size 2 for $20–$21 (wholesale) through out the 1840s and '50s. They were the least expensive models that were routinely given X-pattern top bracing.

$18 MODELS (LATER 2-18)

Usually seen in size 2, but also listed occasionally in size 2½ and 3. Black neck, brass tuners or ebony pegs, no binding on back edge, usually fan-braced top, common case. It can be difficult to distinguish these models from Style 17, but Martin ledgers list $18 size 2 models as having "single line ornament" (top purfling), while, in the same order, a $17 size 2½ model has only the word "plain" in the same column. Part of the difference in price may be that Style 18 was given "dentellone" (individual block) linings, a more time-consuming way of assembling a guitar body. In the early 1860s, listings for 2-18 models often include "Sp" or "Span" or "Spanish," but it is not clear what the late use of that term meant. The 2-18 model appeared on the first Martin price list, but the widespread recognition Style 18 has today is based upon the X-braced mahogany models made for steel strings from the early 1920s through to the present.

$20 MODELS (LATER 2-20)

Most commonly found in size 2 and 2½. Initially had black necks, but cedar necks on $20 models became standard by the late 1850s or earlier. Similar appointments to Style 18 above, but with binding on the back edge (later Style 20) models get a marquetry back strip, often of a herringbone pattern, usually with a matching center ring in the rosette). $20 models usually came in a common case, most have X-braced tops, and by the late 1860s, Style 20 is essentially the size 2 version of the 1-21 model. Both were quite popular.

$21 MODELS (LATER 1-21)

Usually found in size 1 but also made in smaller sizes, with rosewood binding, fine case (some listings with common), and appointments similar to Style 20 above (black neck only on earliest examples, cedar neck far more common). This was the least expensive size 1 guitar Martin regularly offered, and although it appears only rarely in the early 1850s ledgers, it

was far more popular by the 1860s and was made in large numbers for the rest of the century. Although other marquetry patterns appear on the early versions, Style 21 would soon display a herringbone back strip and soundhole rosette, and this pattern would define Style 21 until the mid 1940s, when Martin ceased using herringbone marquetry.

$22 AND $23 MODELS

Although over two hundred $22 and $23 size 2 models were sold in the decade before the Civil War, they were soon left behind, even if they had been considered defined styles. This is probably because the descriptions of $22, $23, and $24 models are so close that they were consolidated into one model, the 2-24, by the late 1860s, when the first Martin price list was organized. All are listed with a cedar neck, brass tuners, fine case, and purfling patterns around the face and soundhole that were given a variety of names including "De Goni," "Otilia," or "Spanish." It is quite possible that the only difference between the $22 and $23 versions was a price difference created by different grades of cases or tuners.

$24 MODELS (LATER 2-24)

Size 2½ models costing $24 show up fairly often in the 1850s but, by the 1860s, guitars with this price are usually size 2.[23] $24 models were the most expensive style with rosewood binding. The 2-24 was included in the first price list, and these models usually show a light line on the sides below the dark binding and were the last style to display marquetry at the endpiece. The name "Otilia" is more often shown in descriptions of the soundhole and top ornament of this model than any other, leading to speculation that the guitar made for C. F. Martin Sr.'s wife may have been similar.

$25 MODELS

A number of $25 size 1 models sold in the early to mid 1850s are described as having white holly binding with "Spanish ornament" (purfling or marquetry

Figure 10-18. The primary difference between this model and the guitar shown in Figure 10-17 is the addition of marquetry around the top, instead of dark and light lines. Later versions of this model were given a pin bridge and sold to dealers for between $22 and $24. (See Profile 35.)

Figure 10-19. Size 1 guitars with holly binding (described at left), the last of Martin's larger Spanish-style models, were discontinued before 1860.

Figure 10-20. Martin's more Spanish-styled $25 models with white holly binding had only dark and light lines as decoration for both the rosette and the top edge of the body.

Figure 10-21. For Martin models that cost $30 or more, a pearl rosette was combined with wide multi-colored marquetry around the perimeter of the top.

Figure 10-22. Models with a wholesale cost of $40 or $42 were given an abalone border around the top as well as the soundhole.

around the face), a "Spanish soundhole" (referring to the rosette), and extra-fine (ff) case. It seems that by this time, "Spanish" meant a decoration of dark and light parallel lines, rather than a complex marquetry pattern. These were the last of the more Spanish-influenced size 1 models; a style that was dying out. Binding of white holly, like two-piece sides, was a holdover from the period of Spanish influence that would soon disappear, leaving all Martin guitars bound in either rosewood or ivory.

$26 MODELS (LATER 1-26)

A very popular style similar to the $25 size 1 models described above, but with ivory binding. Although the size 1 versions far outnumber all others combined, size 2½, 2, and even 0 versions were also sold at this price (about 250 guitars are listed between 1852 and 1862 with a cost of $26). Until 1858, most $26 size 1 models are described as having a pearl soundhole, while from then on they usually have the same "5-9-5" rosette with ivory center section that has defined many of Martin's higher styles ever since. [24] There is a great deal of variation in the top purfling found on early $26 models, but by the early 1870s, the 1-26 usually has a "half-herringbone" or rope pattern around the edge of the top. That feature and the smaller size are all that distinguish it from the larger 0-28 model of the same period.

$27 MODELS (LATER 2-27)

Although there are $27 models listed in other sizes, the vast majority in the 1852–1858 period are size 2. The biggest difference compared to the $26 size 1 is a more elaborate (and usually multicolored) purfling around the face, as both came with brass tuners and an extra fine case. This feature and the pearl soundhole and bound fretboard continued to characterize Style 27 into the next century. Beginning in the late 1850s, there are $27 size 0 models listed in the records, but none has surfaced with the same features as the smaller Style 27 models. It is presumed that for this new larger guitar, "27" was a price, not a style

code indicating appointments identical to the size 2 guitar sold for the same amount.

$28 MODELS (LATER 0-28)

Although there were small guitars that cost $28 before the size 0 was first given that price in 1862, their list of features (pearl soundhole, German silver tuners, etc.) make it difficult to distinguish them from the same size guitars that cost $30. By 1864, Style 28 was apparently reserved for Martin's large "Concert Model," the 0-28, which was a relatively plain guitar with no binding on the neck and brass tuners (many were ordered with ivory friction pegs). Except for the herringbone marquetry around the top, this model was virtually identical to the smaller 1-26. Although a herringbone-pattern top border is the most common, size 0 models made before the late 1860s often show other patterns of narrow marquetry.

$30, $32, AND $33 MODELS (LATER 2-30)

With a very few exceptions, guitars with the above prices were size 2 and 2½. When compared to a $27 size 2, these have wider multicolored purfling around the face, as well as German silver tuners, often with mother-of-pearl buttons. Most have ivory-bound fretboards, and those priced at $32 or $33 often have a pearl ornament below the bridge that Martin sometimes referred to as a "flower" in the "extra ornament" column of the ledger. The model 2-30 appeared on Bruno's first draft of a Martin price list in 1868, by which time the pearl ornament option had disappeared.

$34 MODEL (LATER 2-34)

Usually seen in size 2 or 2½ with the features described for the $30–$33 models described above, but with an ivory bridge. Despite their high ranking, these models retained the black neck long after styles that cost $20 to $26 were given cedar. There are several years in the early 1850s when these were the most expensive Martins listed. The 2-34 model survived to appear on the first Martin price list, but it was far more popular in the 1850s than it was later in the century, when it was superseded by models with pearl bordering around the edge of the face as well as the soundhole (see Profile 44).

$40 AND $42 MODELS
(LATER 2-40 AND 2-42)

The first appearance in surviving records of what later became Style 42 are size 2½ guitars described as having a "pearl edge" (in 1853) or "pearl around the hoop" (in 1858), that were sold to Martin dealers for $42. The number "40" appears as the style code for a size 2 model sold to Zoebisch in late December of 1863 (cost of $44) and a size 0 model was also sold to Zoebisch in May of 1864, for $45 (after the "style as price" rule had been abandoned because of war-time inflation). The 2-40 model appears in the earliest Martin price list a few years later, with a "screw neck" version, which had additional pearl bordering around the end of the fretboard, listed as model 2-42, the most expensive standard Martin style.[25]

THE CONTINUING MOVE TOWARDS STANDARDIZATION

Since both wages and the cost of materials used in guitar making were stable for most of the two decades preceding the Civil War, it is easy to see how the size of a guitar and its wholesale price evolved into a code that both Martin and his retailers could use to avoid lengthy descriptions of the many different Martin models.

When a large batch of similar guitar models such as $17 and $18 models were being ordered by the same dealer, the result was a lot of "dos" (meaning ditto), which often became a trailing horizontal line across the page that meant "these features are just like the guitar listed above." For the first guitar described in a new order for another account, the process began again. In February 1855, for example, the entry for a dealer named H. Parson is stated simply as "six guitars same as the last $155."

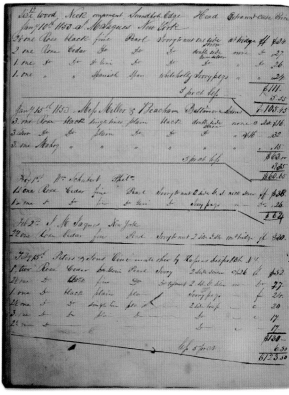

Figure 10-23. This sales ledger from January 1853 shows Martin's typical headings at the top of ten columns: "size" "wood" (back and sides), "neck" (black or cedar), "ornament" (purfling around the top edge), "soundhole" (rosette), "edge" (binding), "head" (tuners), "extra ornament," and "case" are briefly described before the price is given on the far right.

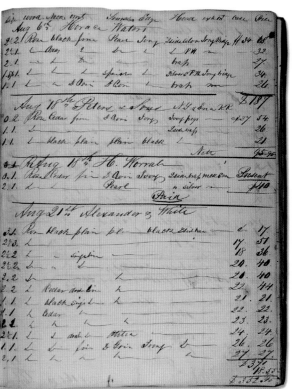

Figure 10-24. By 1856, whoever was charged with entering all those orders was clearly tiring of his job. The entry of 18 guitars for Alexander & White is little more than a sea of squiggles, but those filling the order at Martin's shop clearly knew what models were requested simply by the price.

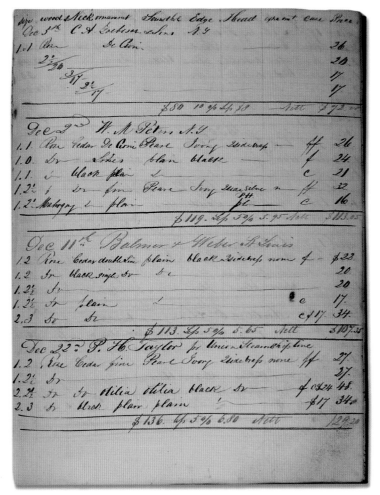

Figure 10-25. This page from December 1856 shows the newly adopted size/price model code in use for a simple order of lower-priced Martin models being shipped to C. A. Zoebisch & Sons, New York. The rest of the page, however, is in the more descriptive style Martin had used previously. Note the Dec. 2 listing of a $24 size 0 model with "plain" soundhole (rosette) and "black" edge (binding).

In October 1856, a short order of four guitars for C. A. Zoebisch & Sons was recorded in a kind of shorthand that eliminated the descriptions and instead identified each model with just the size followed by the price. This method was used again for another simple Zoebisch order a few weeks later, but the old written descriptions were retained for all of Martin's other accounts, and for Zoebisch's orders of more expensive models.

By 1858, however, these same abbreviations were used for virtually all ledger entries. It is probably no coincidence that at this time a majority of the orders for Martin guitars were coming from Charles Bruno and C. A. Zoebisch, the two New York dealers who also served as Martin's distributors and were given an additional 10% discount. Bruno and

Zoebisch were, in effect, middlemen who needed an efficient way of transferring orders from the retailers they served to the manufacturer. Shown in figure 28 is a portion of the ledger page from December 1858 that includes only one guitar style, a 2-22, which was not listed in the first Martin price list drafted by Charles Bruno a decade later. Ledger pages from just a few years earlier, however, showed a much more diverse list of sizes and prices.

This is not to suggest that a $26 size 1 Martin guitar from 1852 was the same as a 1-26 model from a dozen years later, as features on many of these already recognized models were still in flux. This "large De Goni" guitar, for instance, had usually been given a pearl soundhole rosette, but by the 1860s more often displayed the same "ivory" rosette with the familiar "5-9-5" pattern of black and white lines now associated with Style 28. Black necks no longer appeared on higher styles; from the 1860s on, they were used only on the least expensive Martin models. The purfling or marquetry around the top edge of Style 24 and higher guitars continued to vary, as did the pattern found in the back strip, but, while the rosettes and other decorative marquetry were not fixed, little else would change. This was true of the interior construction as well.

EARLY RECORDS OF LARGER MARTIN GUITARS

The first surviving record of a Martin guitar larger than size 1 is a size 0 shipped to W. C. Peters & Sons of Cincinnati in May of 1854. Another size 0 model was shipped less than a month later to G. P. Reed & Co. in Boston. The cost was $24 for the first and $26 for the second, and the description of their appointments makes it clear both models were plainer than smaller Martin guitars of the same price. Peters & Sons ordered two more in August 1856, this time of higher grade with ivory binding. Sales of this larger model were slow until 1858, when eleven were sold, including five more to Peters & Sons. This Cincinnati dealer seems to have had a market for larger guitars, as they also ordered the first 00 size Martin on record in February of 1858.[26]

Although the 00 size only appears twice before Martin's records of guitar sales again start to go missing in July 1864, size 0 began to sell briskly to many Martin dealers in this same period.[27] The 0-28 was described as Martin's "Concert Size" in the price list that followed a decade later, suggesting that it had usurped the role formerly held by the size 1 "De Goni" models. While the 0-28 went on to become the quintessential nineteenth-century Martin guitar, and the "New York Martin" model most likely to be played in modern times (because it was large enough to avoid being branded with "parlor guitar" status), the 00 model did not appear on a price list until 1898. A few were made—one in 1861, another in 1873, a pair in 1877, and then a few others—but, for reasons unknown, both C. F. Martin Sr. and Jr. seemed content to leave the 00 largely a secret. Frank Henry Martin, who took over company leadership in 1888 after the death of his father (C. F. Martin Jr.), gave this larger model a prominent place in the first Martin catalog and introduced an even larger 000 size in 1901.

STYLE NUMBERS AND PRICES DIVERGE AT LAST

As wartime inflation took its toll, the Martin company finally began to raise its prices in March 1863. This ended the convenience of style designations that were determined by a guitar's wholesale cost, the handy code that had been used by Martin and its distributors and retailers for at least the previous fifteen years. At first, rather than multiplying the old cost by a fixed percentage and winding up with the right hand column of the page awash in decimal points and cents for each model, Martin instead opted to raise the price of each guitar a dollar or two. The popular 2½-17 and 3-17 models, for instance, went from $17 to $18 dollars, while the 2-18 went up to $20 and the 1-21 went up to $23. Although Martin opted to cap the increase at $2 per guitar even on the far more expensive 2-34 models, size 0 guitars received the largest increase, rising from $27 to $30. Some size 0 guitars were recorded as 0-28 models in 1862 (with a cost of $28), which may indicate that inflation was having an even earlier effect on what Martin paid for wood.[28]

By 1864, Martin was forced to raise prices again, and, by June of that year, inflation was causing such havoc that Martin went back to the original shorthand of the size followed by the earlier price and then used a multiplier for each dealer's entire order. For reasons unknown, these percentage increases were not consistent, and, at this point, Martin's daybook of guitars sold is a confusing blur of prices and percentages. After an entry of a half dozen guitars for C. Bruno on June 28, 1864, the records disappear

Figure 10-26. This ledger page from late 1858 shows the effects of the standardization of models that had long been brewing at Martin's workshop. Only two styles are shown here which were not included in the early draft of Martin's first price list from a decade later.

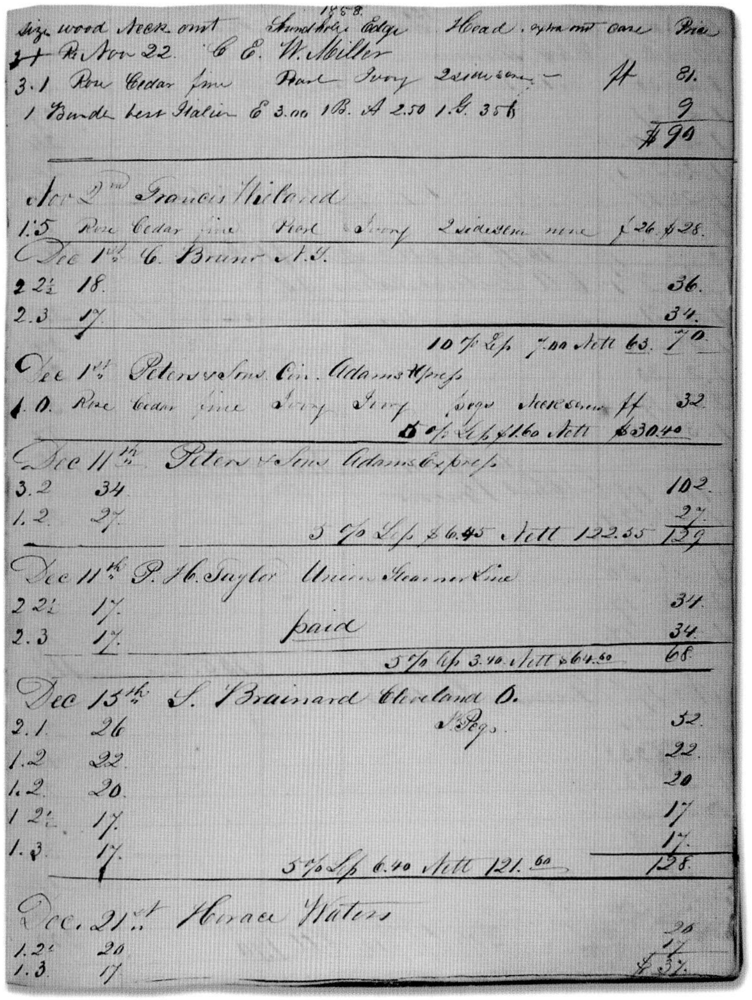
1858.
Size wood Neck ornt Sound hole Edge Head extra ornt Case Price
Nov 22. C. E. W. Miller
3.1 Rose Cedar fine Pearl Ivory 2 sidescrew — ff 81.
1 Bundle best Italian E 3.00 1 B. A 2.50 1 G. 3.50 9
$90
Nov 2nd Francis Weiland
1.5 Rose Cedar fine Pearl Ivory 2 sidescrew none $26. $28.
Dec 1st C. Bruno N.Y.
2 2½ 18. 36.
2.3 17. 34.
10 % Lep 7.00 Nett 63. 70.
Dec 1st Peters & Sons Cin. Adams Express
1.0. Rose Cedar fine Ivory Ivory pegs Neckscrew ff 32
5 % Lep $1.60 Nett $30.40
Dec 11th Peters & Sons Adams Express
3.2 34. 102.
1.2 27. 27.
5 % Lep $6.45 Nett 122.55 129
Dec 11th P. H. Taylor Union Steamer Line
2 2½ 17. 34.
2.3 17. paid 34.
5 % Lep 3.40 Nett $64.60 68.
Dec 13th S. Brainard Cleveland O.
2.1 26 52.
1.2 22. 22.
1.2 20. 20
1 2½ 17. 17
1.3 17. 17.
5 % Lep 6.40 Nett 121.60 128.
Dec. 21st Horace Waters
1.2½ 20 20
1.3. 17 17
$37.

again, but reappear beginning in August 1867. When the records resume, the multiplier is 35 or 45 per cent of each order, and an even greater majority of Martin guitars sold are going through New York distributors C. Bruno or C. A. Zoebisch & Sons, importers who reciprocated by supplying Martin with guitar tuners and strings from Europe.

With few exceptions, the models that appear in these 1867 records are the same ones that appear on Martin's first price list, which followed soon after.

Unlike during the 1850s, each style, with the exception of Style 17, is offered in only one size, and the 0-28, the only Martin model from the pre–Civil War era to survive to modern times, has its own identity at last. While Martin continued to take special orders for these numbered styles in sizes other than those mentioned in the price list, the end result of the standardization that had begun over twenty years earlier would define the styles of Martin guitars for the rest of the century. ★

Figure 10-27. *Right.* C. A. Zoebisch & Sons was the New York firm that eventually won out over C. Bruno to become the sole "wholesale depot" of Martin's guitars. This invoice, for 50 sets of "patent heads brass" (meaning geared tuners for slotted headstocks) would have given Zoebisch enough credit to pay for several Martin guitars, which he then sold to Martin's retailers. Note that since both the Zoebisch and Bruno invoices are from late 1867, a couple of months after Martin had taken his son and cousin, C. F. Hartmann, as partners, the bills are addressed to "C. F. Martin & Co. *Far right,* Charles Bruno's letterhead indicates that "C. F. Martin's Guitars" was only one of several instrument brands he represented. Along with requesting credit for the strings he supplied to Martin, this invoice includes a complaint about Martin making the "cut" in front of the high E string bridge pin too large, which allowed the small knot at the end of the gut string to slip through.

Figure 10-28. *Opposite page.* Lavishly decorated guitars such as this one suggest that twenty years after his arrival in New York, the reputation of Martin guitars was attracting extremely wealthy customers who wanted far more than just a high quality musical instrument. Although other guitar manufacturers would successfully compete with the Martin Company decades later, in the years leading up to the Civil War Martin was clearly the most prestigious brand of what was emerging as an American style of guitar distinctly different from the instruments made in other countries.

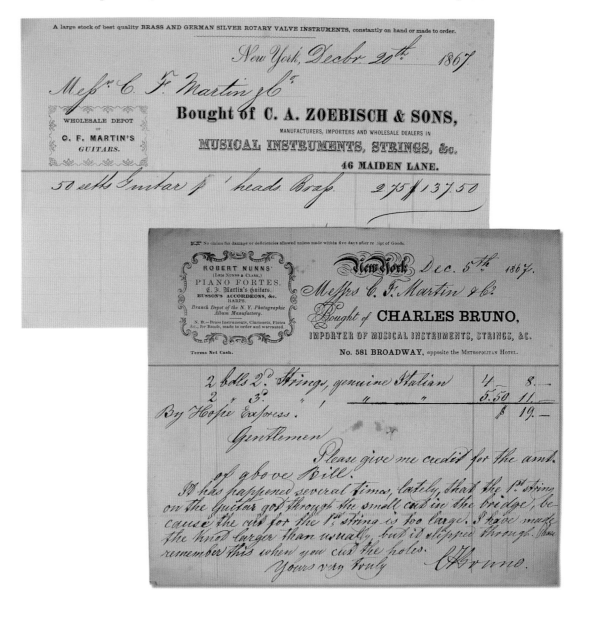

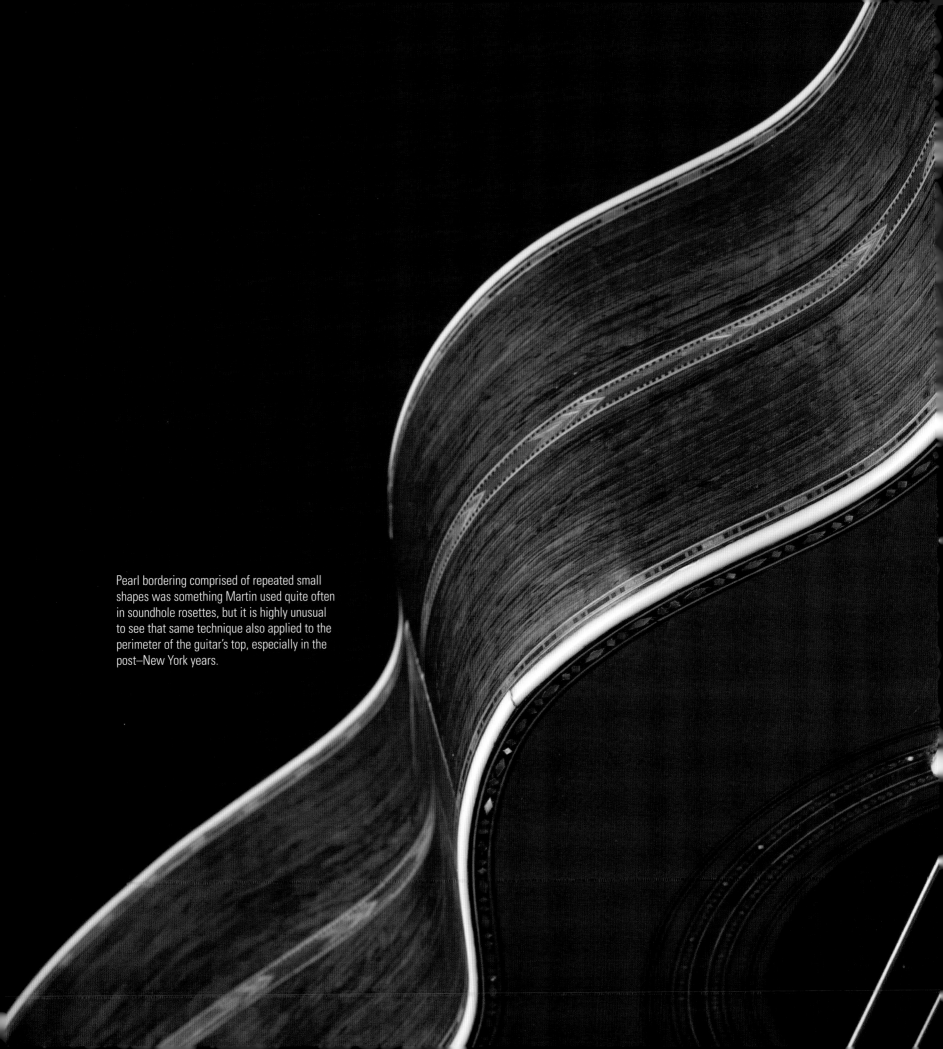

Pearl bordering comprised of repeated small shapes was something Martin used quite often in soundhole rosettes, but it is highly unusual to see that same technique also applied to the perimeter of the guitar's top, especially in the post–New York years.

The wealth of detail lavished on this instrument is remarkable, but how it was decorated is even more telling. There are no ornamental flowing vines, flowers, or butterflies; instead, all the pearl, ivory, and marquetry is adornment of the guitar's form and structure. While the guitar is clearly of presentation grade and expense, it is not known exactly when it was constructed or for what purpose.

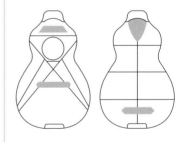

While unusual, the shape of this guitar is not unique. Other, plainer examples that are also size 1 have survived, as have smaller versions with the same outline in size 2. The top has the same hybrid of fan and X-pattern bracing as the guitar made for Madame de Goni (see Profile 26), and the back bracing shows similar Spanish influence on what is otherwise a very non-Spanish Martin guitar.

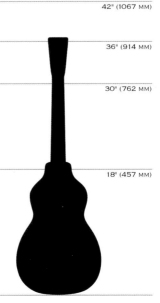

Both the headstock joint and the area where the neck joins the body are lined with ivory and ebony. The guitar's end bout (not shown) is given similar treatment.

DIMENSIONS

TOTAL LENGTH	37.88"	962 MM
BODY LENGTH	19.44"	494 MM

WIDTH

UPPER BOUT	8.75"	222 MM
WAIST	7.69"	195 MM
LOWER BOUT	12.75"	324 MM

DEPTH

NECK	3.63"	92 MM
WAIST	3.88"	98 MM
END	4.31"	110 MM

NUT WIDTH	1.87"	48 MM
SCALE	24.5"	622 MM
SOUND HOLE	3.62"	92 MM

BRACING CONFIGURATION

RELATIVE SIZE

42" (1067 MM)

36" (914 MM)

30" (762 MM)

18" (457 MM)

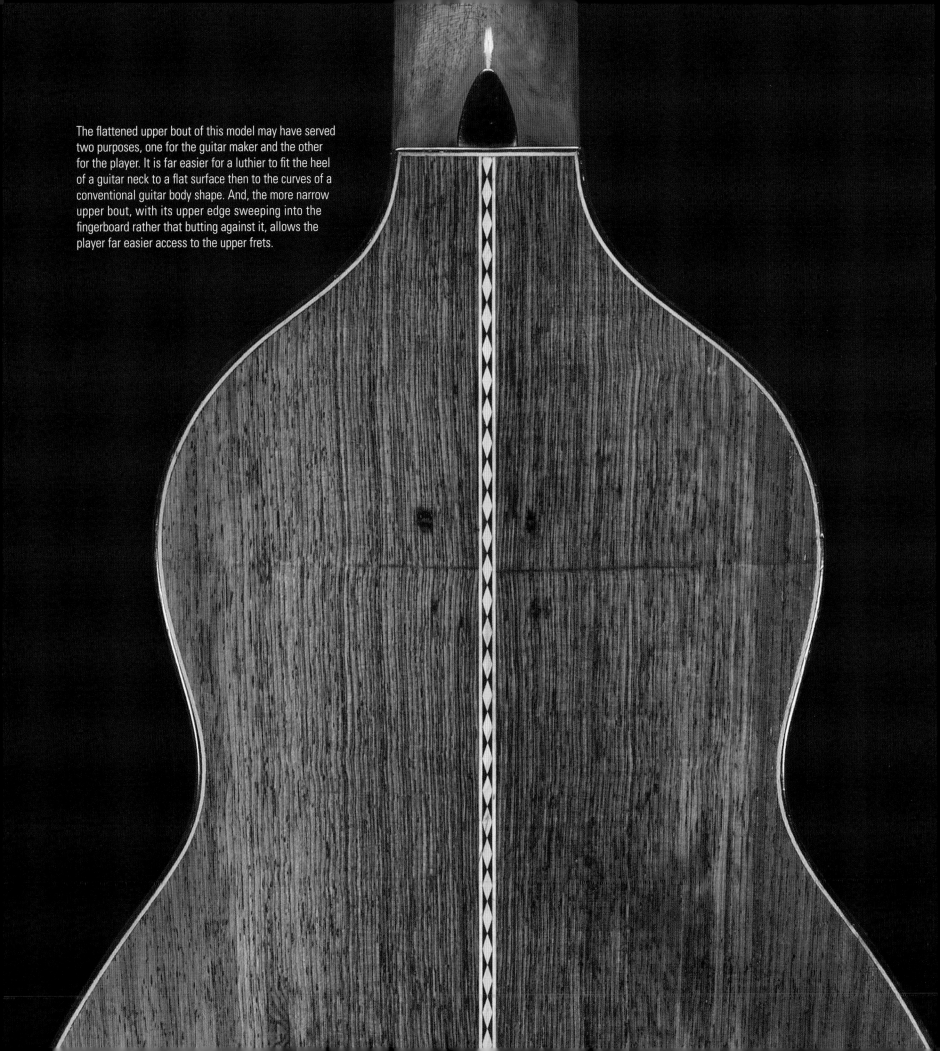

The flattened upper bout of this model may have served two purposes, one for the guitar maker and the other for the player. It is far easier for a luthier to fit the heel of a guitar neck to a flat surface then to the curves of a conventional guitar body shape. And, the more narrow upper bout, with its upper edge sweeping into the fingerboard rather that butting against it, allows the player far easier access to the upper frets.

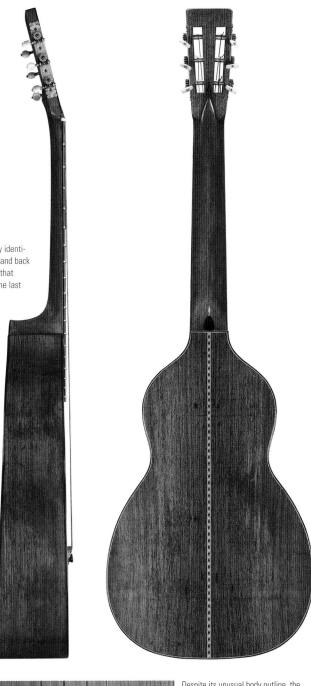

The appointments of this guitar are nearly identical to Martin's Style 21, and both the top and back bracing are the same as size 1 models of that style that were very popular throughout the last decades of the nineteenth century.

DIMENSIONS

TOTAL LENGTH	37.13"	943 MM
BODY LENGTH	18.31"	465 MM

WIDTH

UPPER BOUT	8.66"	220 MM
WAIST	6.97"	177 MM
LOWER BOUT	12.01"	305 MM

DEPTH

NECK	2.68"	68 MM
WAIST	3.23"	82 MM
END	3.31"	84 MM

NUT WIDTH	1.85"	47 MM
SCALE	24.41"	620 MM
SOUND HOLE	3.43"	87 MM

BRACING CONFIGURATION

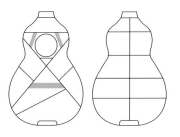

RELATIVE SIZE

42" (1067 MM)

36" (914 MM)

30" (762 MM)

18" (457 MM)

Despite its unusual body outline, the most curious thing about this guitar is its unique metal bridge, which, while clearly original does not look like something Martin would have used. The bridge, which is simply screwed to the top, is small, plain, and quite practical. Although the guitar is shown here with steel strings, it was originally strung with gut.

This is both the plainest and, apparently, the last of the unusually shaped Martin guitars now called "Renaissance" models. Unfortunately, there are no surviving records to inform us how they were described in their time. Except for its odd body shape and even more unusual metal bridge, this is a conventional mid-century Martin guitar.

The multi-colored marquetry around the perimeter of the top is identical to one of the patterns often found on similar Martins from the same era.

Martin had many competitors, but the guitarmaking partnership of his former employees Louis Schmidt and George Maul produced guitars that were so close to the form and style of Martin's models as to be almost indistinguishable. For a time in the early 1840s, Schmidt & Maul were tenants in the same 385 Broadway building that housed John Coupa's showroom and lesson studio.

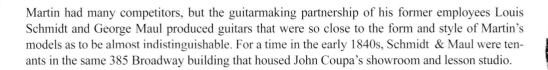

The bracing of the top and back is very close to that used on the guitar Martin and Schatz made for Madame de Goni a decade earlier. Schmidt and Maul reportedly made a guitar for De Goni around the same time.

Even the stamp used by Schmidt and Maul bears an uncanny resemblance to the stamp on the center back strip of Martin guitars. Such instruments may have been the first to come so close in appearance to Martins, but they wouldn't be the last. This example is dated 1853 and signed by Louis Schmidt

DIMENSIONS

TOTAL LENGTH	36.88"	939 MM
BODY LENGTH	17.6"	447 MM

WIDTH

UPPER BOUT	8.59"	218 MM
WAIST	7.09"	180 MM
LOWER BOUT	11.7"	297 MM

DEPTH

NECK	3.46"	88 MM
WAIST	3.7"	94 MM
END	3.9"	99 MM

NUT WIDTH	1.97"	50 MM
SCALE	24.02"	610 MM
SOUND HOLE	3.43"	87 MM

BRACING CONFIGURATION

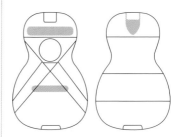

RELATIVE SIZE

42" (1067 MM)
36" (914 MM)
30" (762 MM)
18" (457 MM)

Although the straight-sided headstock with ivory friction peg tuners utilizes the same joint as found on Martins and earlier Schmidt & Maul instruments, the long and almost rectangular profile chosen by Maul for this guitar is distinctly different.

George Maul was one of several New York guitar makers who worked in the transitional Spanish-to-American style after C. F. Martin had resettled in Pennsylvania. This guitar has a "Schmidt & Maul" stamp on the neck block, but it is signed in pencil "G. Maul 1859" below that stamp. A second pencil inscription—"G. Maul/New York/August 3, 1858/ U. S."—appears on the underside of the top. These suggests that Maul, who later built guitars that display only his own name, may have already separated from his former partner (and former Martin employee), Louis Schmidt.

George Maul's top bracing on this guitar shows yet another variant of the intersection between true Spanish fan patterns and the recently evolved X bracing Martin had adopted several years earlier. This instrument has a harmonic bar below the soundhole, as on Spanish guitars, but it carries an abbreviated X brace with fan braces on either side. This pattern accommodates the bridge pinholes, which are not shown in the drawing.

Slightly smaller than a Martin size 1, this guitar's body shape, bridge, and rosette would make it easy to mistake for one by the much larger workshop in Pennsylvania. While the maker was probably not attempting to copy Martin's instruments, it does show how pervasive the American style had become well before the Civil War.

DIMENSIONS

TOTAL LENGTH	37.81"	960 MM
BODY LENGTH	18.7"	475 MM

WIDTH

UPPER BOUT	9.13"	232 MM
WAIST	7.09"	180 MM
LOWER BOUT	12.56"	319 MM

DEPTH

NECK	3.62"	92 MM
WAIST	3.81"	97 MM
END	4.06"	103 MM

NUT WIDTH	1.85"	47 MM
SCALE	24.02"	610 MM
SOUND HOLE	3.58"	91 MM

BRACING CONFIGURATION

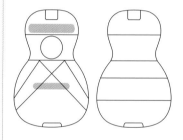

RELATIVE SIZE

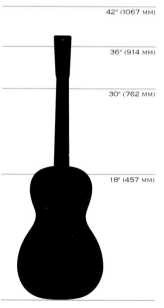

42" (1067 MM)

36" (914 MM)

30" (762 MM)

18" (457 MM)

By the time this guitar was made there is more consistency in both the structure and appointments of Martin's guitar models, but their evolution was still continuing. The spruce lining of the back, seen through the soundhole, and the optional pearl decoration below the bridge would both disappear several years before Martin's death in 1873.

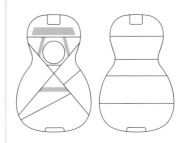

These engraved nickel-silver tuners were shared by other ornate models, and were the finest Martin offered. While " 2 side silver P.H." (for pearl handles) would continue to appear in the descriptions for the "head" of such guitars, these fan-shaped buttons were later replaced with less ornate designs.

There is much variety found in Martin models that sold for wholesale prices between $30 and $34, yet all are highly decorated and were usually only sold in small sizes. The ivory bridge found on the similar model in the following profile was an optional feature that commanded the top price, while the pearl bridge ornament was a less costly upgrade. Both options appeared in the "extra ornament" column of Martin's daybook descriptions of each guitar. (This example was almost certainly supplied with ivory bridge pins with abalone dot originally).

The black neck seen here, and the cedar neck as seen in Profile 45, apparently existed side by side for several years on Martin's more expensive small models like this one. In the mid 1850s some dealers would order both black neck and cedar neck versions of these models in the same order. The size 2 1/2 versions like this sold for the same price as the slightly larger size 2, which eventually won out and only size 2 was listed on Martin's first price list a decade later.

DIMENSIONS

TOTAL LENGTH	36.63"	930 MM
BODY LENGTH	17.88"	454 MM

WIDTH

UPPER BOUT	8.38"	213 MM
WAIST	7"	178 MM
LOWER BOUT	11.69"	297 MM

DEPTH

NECK	3.25"	83 MM
WAIST	3.5"	89 MM
END	3.94"	100 MM

NUT WIDTH	1.69"	43 MM
SCALE	24.38"	619 MM
SOUND HOLE	3.5"	89 MM

BRACING CONFIGURATION

RELATIVE SIZE

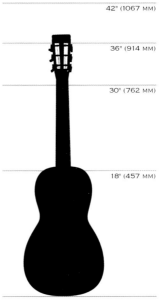

42" (1067 MM)

36" (914 MM)

30" (762 MM)

18" (457 MM)

Two features visible here would not survive into the 1860s: the colored wood marquetry on the sides below the ivory binding, and the "scooped" back edge of the pyramid-tipped ivory bridge.

Despite their role as Martin's most expensive standard models, these small guitars with a wealth of ivory binding and multicolored marquetry retained the black-stained neck with cone-shaped heel long after models from the middle of Martin's price range were consistently given necks of Spanish cedar.

Martin's American style had fully evolved by the time this guitar was constructed, and both the X-pattern top bracing and the back bracing shown here are very much like what would be found on similar models made a half-century later.

DIMENSIONS

TOTAL LENGTH	36.63"	930 MM
BODY LENGTH	17.88"	454 MM

WIDTH

UPPER BOUT	8.63"	219 MM
WAIST	7.13"	181 MM
LOWER BOUT	11.75"	298 MM

DEPTH

NECK	3.31"	84 MM
WAIST	3.56"	90 MM
END	3.94"	100 MM

NUT WIDTH	1.94"	49 MM
SCALE	24.5"	622 MM
SOUND HOLE	3.5"	89 MM

BRACING CONFIGURATION

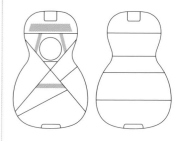

RELATIVE SIZE

42" (1067 MM)

36" (914 MM)

30" (762 MM)

18" (457 MM)

The appointments on this ladies guitar represent Martin's highest stock model in the early 1850s, a period from which a remarkably complete set of daybooks that list production have survived. It sold to dealers for $34 wholesale.

Martin used pearl decoration around the perimeter of the top from the very beginning, but it was comprised of small shapes, such as small squares or trefoils, repeated and set in black mastic to form a continuous border. In the 1850s, this practice gave way to a solid band of abalone pieces, the joints made almost invisible by the natural variations in the nacreous layers of the pearl itself. In Martin's ledgers, this option was called "pearl round the hoop," and in later examples, additional thin black and white lines were added on either side of the abalone.

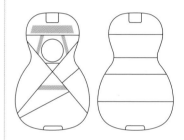

German silver tuners with mother-of-pearl buttons were the most expensive option for Martin guitars with a slotted headstock and were used on Styles 30 and higher.

Martin guitars with pearl bordering were considered the holy grail as guitar collecting gathered steam during the 1960s folk revival, especially since Martin had discontinued this type of decoration during World War II. Although the glittering iridescent bands of abalone had been ideal for 1930s stage performers like Gene Autry, this style of adornment had begun almost a century earlier with very small guitars like this one, usually played in the parlor by women seeking something even more eye-catching than the multi-colored marquetry that appeared on Martin's highest standard models (see Profile 43).

DIMENSIONS

TOTAL LENGTH	36.25"	921 MM
BODY LENGTH	17.88"	454 MM

WIDTH

UPPER BOUT	8.38"	213 MM
WAIST	7"	178 MM
LOWER BOUT	11.75"	298 MM

DEPTH

NECK	3.38"	86 MM
WAIST	3.63"	92 MM
END	4"	102 MM

NUT WIDTH	1.69"	43 MM
SCALE	24.38"	619 MM
SOUND HOLE	3.5"	89 MM

BRACING CONFIGURATION

RELATIVE SIZE

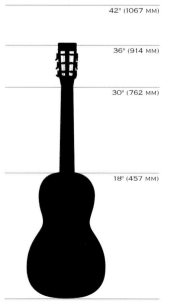

42" (1067 MM)

36" (914 MM)

30" (762 MM)

18" (457 MM)

CHAPTER 11

EARLY MARTIN DESIGN AND CONSTRUCTION: WHAT SURVIVED

RICHARD JOHNSTON

Figure 11-1. The "figure 8" body shape, with upper and lower bouts of almost equal proportions, was a feature of the Austro-German guitar that Martin abandoned less than a decade after his arrival in New York.

Figure 11-2. The bridge shape shown here, which followed the design shown on the guitar above, was apparently only used for about five years or less, before it was replaced by the rectangular bridge.

Much of this volume has focused on when Martin first adopted a Spanish-influenced body shape, first used X-pattern top bracing, or the earliest dates of many other features that mark the evolution from Austro-German to Spanish style, and then to a unique and fully American style. However, as new features were adopted, others were left behind, and we have paid far less attention to when key elements found only on earlier guitars disappeared. This is of little consequence for guitar makers like Ashborn or Schmidt and Maul, as their production ended not many years after they had started, but the Martin company survived and carried many features found on guitars made in the 1840s into modern times. However, while there is no doubt that the company abandoned other details, both stylistic and structural, before C. F. Sr.'s death in 1873, pinning down when these features were phased out is often difficult. Dating early Martin guitars, especially those without paper labels, is problematic because, unlike the stamps inside James Ashborn's instruments, Martin guitars from the mid 1860s display the same stamped markings that were first used over thirty years earlier. Thankfully, the "C. F. Martin & Co." stamp, first used in October 1867, when C. F. Martin Jr. and his cousin C. F. Hartmann were made partners with the founder, gives us a dependable marker that roughly corresponds to the transition between generations of Martins leading the company (C. F. Sr.'s health was failing before his death, so C. F. Jr. was more or less running the Martin workshop by 1871, and probably earlier).[1] The more we look at pre-"& Co." stamped guitars in comparison to similar examples made

after 1867, the more obvious it becomes which features were deleted in the years before the stamp was changed.

Some of the features Martin abandoned first are readily noticed, and their disappearance is easy to justify. The most important of these would include (in approximate order of their disappearance):

- The figure-8, or Austro-German, body shape (Profiles 5–11)
- Elaborate Austro-German bridge (Profiles 5–7)
- The wide "shield-shaped" bridge with rounded ends that followed the style described above (Profiles 8–10, 15–17)
- Lateral bracing of the soundboard (Profiles 5–10)

The disappearance of these features can probably be attributed to the change in guitar fashion away from what had become outdated styles, or, at least, a turn toward the simpler, more purely functional aesthetic of the Spanish builders. David Gansz's research on America's fascination with "things Spanish" during this period makes these changes easy to understand, especially considering John Coupa's role in representing Martin guitars in New York and the competition John Ashborn's guitars presented.[2]

But Martin's fascination with many Spanish guitar elements was short lived, and very few of the following visual and structural details of early guitars from Cadiz that had so profoundly influenced him are seen on Martin guitars made after the mid 1850s:

- Tie-block string anchoring at the bridge
- Two-piece sides with decorative marquetry or lines between the two halves
- Back strip decoration that is continued into heel cap on neck
- Faux "Spanish foot" appendage to interior bottom of neck block
- Laminations in cedar neck heel (sometimes called "stacked heel")
- Nickel-silver nut (instead of ivory)
- Side brackets, often yoke shaped, supporting top and/or back braces (See Chapter 5, Figure 5-6)

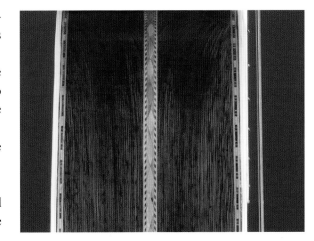

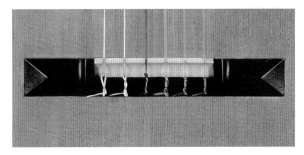

Figure 11-3. *Left,* Of all the elements Martin borrowed from Spanish guitar makers, the use of two-piece sides was probably the most time consuming and problematic. For Martin, its advantage was purely cosmetic.

Figure 11-4. *Below left,* Neck heel caps with the same design as the center seam of the back were another decorative conceit emulating Spanish guitar builders. It was retained on some of Martin's models, especially those with holly binding, but soon disappeared along with other Spanish appointments.

Figure 11-5. *Center,* The faux Spanish foot at the base of neck block, like two-piece sides, was another visual homage to the Spanish style that Martin left behind as the American style of guitar began to take shape.

Figure 11-6. *Bottom,* Martin's use of tie-block bridges to anchor the strings lasted barely a decade, but the bridge pin version of this design, still with "pyramid" tips at each end, would last almost a century and its use has been revived in recent years.

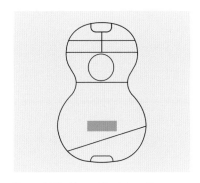

Figure 11-7. *Above,* Martin's earliest guitars had soundboards reinforced with simple lateral braces, but this pattern was soon left behind in favor of fan bracing as used on Spanish instruments.

Figure 11-8. The dramatic curve in the profile of this Spanish-style Martin neck heel is almost a half-circle, but such an extreme shape was only used by Martin for a few years. Note the laminated heel, another characteristic of Spanish guitars that Martin abandoned well before 1860.

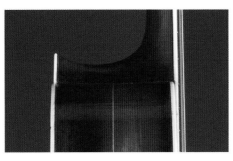

Figure 11-10. *Left and below.* The adjustable neck is found on Martin's earliest guitars, but by the late 1850s it was rarely requested. The "screw neck" was still a listed feature on Martin's highest model on the first price list, however, yet very few were made.

Figure 11-9. Martin's use of metal nuts is one of the more mysterious, and tenacious, features found on many of the higher-grade guitars he built in the 1840s and '50s, as this practice seems to offer little advantage on gut-string instruments. Making nuts of nickel silver was certainly more difficult than fashioning them of ivory, and this may have been the primary reason for their disappearance. The solid ivory fingerboard shown here is another feature that Martin apparently did not continue to offer after the 1850s, but we do not know if that change was because of the cost or supply of ivory or was the result of a lack of demand for presentation-grade guitars.

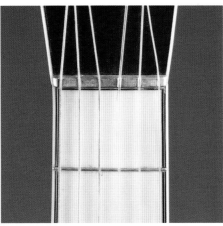

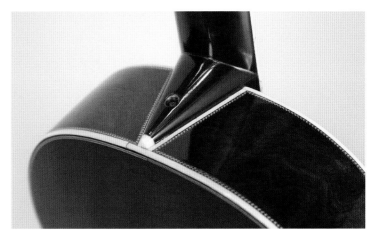

While John Coupa was probably the driving force behind the adoption of Spanish guitar styles that revolutionized Martin's construction and design in the early 1840s, the Spanish influence on Martin guitars had already begun to wane even before Coupa's death in 1850.[3] Surviving records in the Martin Archives indicate that more of Martin's production began to be sold in cities other than New York, where dealers and guitar instructors were less enthralled with things Spanish, or at least were less demanding about small details that would only be noticed by those who had actually seen genuine Spanish-made guitars in person. Perhaps even more important, Martin's New York distributors, C. A. Zoebisch & Sons and Charles Bruno (later Bruno & Morris), were primarily concerned with maintaining a steady stream of commerce (and their own survival) in an increasingly cutthroat music industry, rather than in the characteristics of individual guitars.[4]

Unlike the retreat from the Austro-German style that had taken place in the 1840s, far more of the Spanish influence remained in Martin's instruments during the transition to what became a more purely American guitar. The long body with narrow waist and small upper bout survived in a series of graduated sizes, as did the tapered rectangular headstock and three-ring rosette. The rectangular bridge shape with pyramid points at each end remained the standard for all models regardless of price or size, although Martin returned to using pin bridges without exception rather than also offering a tie block bridge. From the outside, at least, the changes to Martin guitars after abandoning the more purely Spanish styles would have been far less noticeable to the average American guitarist. Curiously, three elements from the earlier Austro-German style outlived many of the more purely Spanish components: the long, curved "Stauffer head" was apparently last used around 1854, but the black neck with cone-shaped heel continued to be used on Martin's lowest-priced styles until the late 1890s, and the adjustable "screw neck" has been seen on at least one guitar with a serial number on the neck block that dates it after 1900.[5]

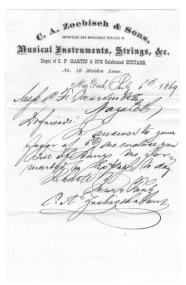

Figure 11-11. *Far left.* This 1870s Zoebisch & Sons advertisement is curious because the only illustration is of a horn, and the list of "best soloists known" who endorse Martin guitars is sadly out of date: Madame de Goni hadn't appeared on the concert stage in over a decade, and J. B. Coupa had been dead for over twenty years. All of the guitarists' names listed here, plus a few others, would still appear in Zoebisch advertisements for Martin guitars published decades later. (See Chapter 7, figure 7-7). *Left.* By 1869, C. A. Zoebisch & Sons had won its long-running contest with C. Bruno & Son and was the sole New York "depot," or distributor, of Martin guitars, which probably prompted the change in the firm's letterhead. A few years later, Zoebisch would print the Martin price list shown in Figure 11-13, on the back of its stationery.

DECADES OF REPETITION

It would be easy to blame the lack of variety or innovation found in post-1867 Martin guitars on C. F. Martin Sr.'s fading health and old age, or on C. F. Martin Jr.'s unwillingness to be involved in anything other than consistent production of standard models. In truth, however, Martin's move towards a more unified line of guitars began two decades before "& Co." was added to the C. F. Martin stamp. Research into this transition is hampered by the early stages of standardization evidenced in Martin's abandoning its descriptions of each guitar in the mid 1850s, instead relying on a simple code of the body size followed by the style number, which for a time was apparently based on the wholesale price of the same guitar. (For years, Martin and its dealers had referred to guitars by their price, and some researchers have confused this abbreviation with defined style numbers, despite the fact that such numbers are often unique to a single journal entry.)

Although a price increase in the early 1860s removed the direct connection between the style number and the wholesale price, the ratios between the costs of different styles remained much the same. Thirty years later, Martin's New York distributor paid the same amount for a pair of 2-20 models as it paid for a single 2-40; a 2-34 was twice as expensive as a 3-17 model, etc. By the late 1860s, and perhaps earlier, this style number was what Martin referred to as the "number of quality" that also appeared on labels affixed to the interior of the case.[6]

Before the mid 1850s, the descriptions of each guitar in the company's ledgers, although highly abbreviated, make it far easier to spot the interesting differences in Martin's production, such as high-numbered styles that still had a black neck or which models were given a pearl rosette or had bound fretboards ("ivory to the nut"). However, by the late 1850s, Martin's ledgers give us page after page of model codes and little else, making the decade preceding the 1867 change to the "& Co." stamp a period of considerable mystery regarding the details found on the actual instruments. We know how many guitars of each style were sold, but we cannot determine how those examples compare to earlier, or later, versions of the same model.

It is no coincidence that Martin's first accounts to have their orders described with just a list of size/style codes were C. A. Zoebisch & Sons and Charles Bruno, the two New York dealers that vied to monopolize the distribution of Martin guitars to other retailers. Since Martin's ledgers were only for their own use, this change suggests that Bruno and Zoebisch were Martin's first customers to focus on a selection

Figure 11-12. *Right.* In April, 1868 this draft of a wholesale price list for Martin guitars was drawn up by Charles Bruno, and since he included Tilton guitars at the bottom it was probably intended to be distributed to Bruno's retail dealers. All the sizes and styles of Martin guitars shown here are identical to those included in the Zoebisch retail price list that first appeared about five years later.

Figure 11-13. *Far right.* This price list appeared on the back of the C. A. Zoebisch & Sons stationery beginning in 1874, and was still in use over twenty years later. Unlike the earlier C. Bruno list (*right*) this one shows retail prices. Both of these lists only made official what had been Martin's standard models, with very few exceptions, for the last decade.

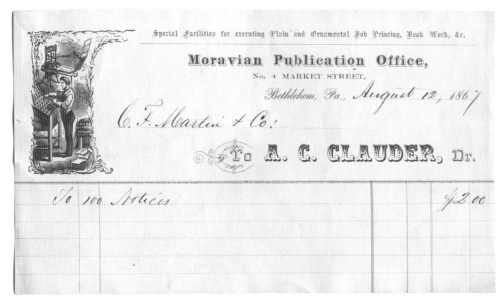

PRICE LIST
OF

C. F. MARTIN & CO'S GUITARS.

No	3–17	Rosewood, plain,			$36 00
"	2¼–17	"			36 00
"	2–18	"	double bound,		37 50
"	2–20	"	Cedar neck,		42 00
"	1–21	"			45 00
"	2–24	"	" fancy inlaying,		50 00
"	1–26	"	inlaid with Pearl, Ivory bound,		54 00
"	2–27	"	"	"	58 50
"	0–28	"	"	"	60 00
"	2–30	"	"	"	63 00
"	2–34	"		" Ivory bridge,	72 00
"	2–40	" richly	"	" "	84 00
"	2–42	"	"	" Screw neck,	90 00

No. 3.	**No. 2¼.**	**No. 2.**	**No. 1.**	**No. 0.**
Small Size.	Ladies' Size.	Ladies' Size.	Large Size.	Larg'st Conc't Size.

All the above numbers, with Patent Head or Peg Head and any size desired made to order.

If not specially ordered with Peg Head, Guitars with Patent Heads will be sent.

The prices above include wood case.

Figure 11-14. The Moravian Publication office printed the notices which explained to Martin's business accounts that "C. F. Martin, Senior, has associated with him as Partners C. F. Martin, Junior, and C. F. Hartmann, for the manufacturing of Guitars, under the firm of C. F. Martin & Co.". This co-partnership notice went on to explain that C. F. Jr. and Hartmann "have been employed...over a quarter of a Century. We can therefore guarantee our customers a first-class article, and would respectfully solicit your future patronage." These notices were inserted in all correspondence for six months, but there's no indication such an announcement had any negative effect on the number of orders for Martin guitars.

of guitars with fixed appointments, resulting in models that could be quickly summarized and orders easily duplicated. By 1868, Bruno had drawn up a price list of thirteen different Martin models, and, although the list lacks any descriptive text, it seems safe to assume that the appointments found on those models had probably been fixed much earlier. Although we do not know the exact sequence of changes that resulted in the stock price-list models, many guitars bearing the earlier stamp have identical appointments, suggesting that the standardization of Martin models took place well before 1867.

Although Zoebisch had won the battle for exclusive distributorship of C. F. Martin guitars by 1870, the printed price list that appeared on the verso of Zoebisch stationery, beginning the year after C. F. Sr.'s death, is identical to the earlier list drawn up by Bruno.[7] This list of stock models had a number of advantages over the price-equals-style-number shorthand used previously. With the exception of Style 17, all Martin styles were only offered in one size, so if a customer wanted a larger example of a 2-20, for instance, they could order a 1-21 (there was a similar relationship between the 1-26 and the slightly larger 0-28). Another advantage was that duplicate style numbers (because the guitars described sold for the same price) were eliminated. In the mid 1850s, a $27 size 2 and a $27 size 0 Martin guitar had quite different appointments, but on the Zoebisch price list they were defined as a 2-27 and a 0-28. While we may lament such standardization today, it is easy to understand why it would have been a tremendous advantage to Martin dealers and customers at the time.

This mid–nineteenth century evolution in Martin guitars is subtle, and changes to their interior construction cannot be credited to Civil War–era equivalents of the Strat versus Les Paul swings of a guitar fashion pendulum. There is no evidence in surviving correspondence to suggest that Bruno or Zoebisch requested or selected the appointments of what became the price-list models. However, being distributors, their emphasis would have been on an efficient way of marketing a Martin guitar to more than one buyer by making certain that guitar's replacement was identical to the one sold before it, and to the next example they might receive. By electing to sell an increasing majority of its guitars through distributors, those distributors selected what would become stock models simply because their orders represented a growing majority of Martin's production. For example, while Martin may have chosen to eliminate the bother of making guitars with a spruce lamination on the inside of the back, other features, such as pearl rosettes, may have disappeared from certain models because the distributors targeted a slightly lower price by leaving off that option.

FEATURES THAT DISAPPEARED BEFORE 1867

Following is a short list of the features that have, at least to date, not been found on Martin guitars with the post–1867 "& Co." stamp. Most of these features apparently disappeared before the 1860s.

Laminated backs: This feature appears on some Austro-German style guitars from Martin's earliest production in New York and has also been found on models from the 1840s (Coupa apparently referred to this feature as a "double back.") However, spruce-lined backs also appear on many size 2 and 2½ guitars with features that suggest they were made at least as late as the 1850s, usually in Style 24 and higher. To date, no size 1 or size 0 models with spruce-lined backs have surfaced. Martin also used guitar backs lined with mahogany and other hardwoods, but these laminations were apparently only used on quite early examples, usually with the Stauffer headstock. As far as we know, the later laminated-back Martins all had spruce for the interior layer.

Pin bridge with "scooped," as opposed to rounded, back edge: For a time before 1867, the pin bridges still displayed a concave back edge, presumably a remnant of the tie-block style that was used during Martin's more purely Spanish period. We do not know when Martin went from the scooped back edge of its pyramid bridge to the now familiar rounded back edge, and we do not know if it was a simple across-all-models change, or a more typical Martin transition that involved some models first and others later. Pyramid-tip bridges with the later, rounded back edge certainly appeared before 1860.

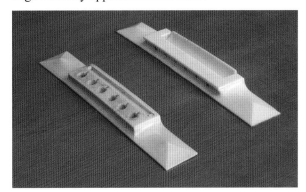

Figure 11-15. These two ivory bridges for size 2 models both show the "scooped" back edge. On the tie-block bridge (right), this concave surface both secures and conceals the tied ends of the strings. On the pin bridge (left), however, this feature served no functional purpose and was later abandoned, replaced by a smooth curve from the top of the bridge to its back edge.

Figure 11-6. *Below.* We now know that Martin's use of what his customers usually called "patent heads" on a slotted headstock did not begin with his move to more Spanish-inspired guitar styles, but the tuners shown below quickly replaced the Stauffer-style headstock whenever the convenience, and accuracy, of geared tuners was requested. Throughout the 1840s, Martin apparently sought tuners with bone rollers, which were more in keeping with the Spanish style. As other Spanish elements were abandoned, tuners with smaller diameter brass rollers became the standard. This may have been primarily because the bone rollers were more fragile, and, since tuners were often replaced, we can't be sure when the use of bone rollers was phased out. Martin may have continued to use tuners with bone rollers for a time on his more Spanish models, but, to date, they have not been found on guitars known to be from the mid 1850s or later.

Figure 11-17. *Left to right:* All three of
the soundhole rosette patterns shown
here were in use by the 1850s and were
continued into the twentieth century. The
pearl rosette at right was used on Styles
27, 30, 34, 40, and 42 as listed on the first
price list. The "5-9-5" rosette shown in
the center was used for Styles 26 and 28,
with the herringbone rosette on the far
right used on Styles 20 and 21 Although
the materials have changed—ivory disappeared before 1920—the Martin Guitar
Co. still uses these designs today. Most of
the other soundhole rosette patterns seen
in this volume, however, were discontinued before C. F. Martin's death in 1873.

Figure 11-18. Marquetry endpiece decorations were common in the 1840s, but by
the 1860s are rarely found except on Style
24 models. Note that this size 1 example,
like many of Martin's more Spanish-influenced guitars, was not given an endpin.

Soundhole rosettes with complex pearl pattern in the center ring or with marquetry for the innermost and outermost rings: Even after the 3-ring rosette was standard on virtually all Martin guitars, there was still considerable variety. But by 1860 or even earlier, the only soundhole decorations still in production were the same ones seen on late 1800s Martins, and the marquetry used for the center ring of the rosette is the only thing that varied within any given style (the same can be said for the marquetry used for the backstrip). To date, no post-1867 Martins have surfaced on which the innermost and outermost rings of the 3-ring rosette are anything other than a plain dark line or a pattern of from three to five alternating dark and light lines. The variety of soundhole rosettes was also pared down to five styles for all twelve models: 17/18, 20/21, 24, 26/28, and 27/30/34/40/42 (this last group all had the same pearl rosette). Note that Style 24 is the only model with a unique rosette. The classic "5-9-5" rosette pattern of black and white lines, first used in the 1840s and found on most 0-28 and 1-26 models from the late 1850s on, has remained in continuous use to the present day.

Standardization of body binding: Not only do two-piece sides with marquetry down the middle disappear, but any decoration other than the actual binding itself is also eliminated from the sides of all Martin models by 1867. As with soundhole rosettes and end pieces, the lone exception is Style 24, which retains a simple light-colored line on the sides

beneath its rosewood binding. Decoration on the sides of Martin guitars in addition to binding would not reappear until after 1900, with the introduction of Style 45.

Marquetry strip, instead of end wedge, where the sides are joined over the tail block: This feature appears somewhat haphazardly on pre-1867 models; about the only qualifier is that the guitar has to have a backstrip of marquetry, instead of simple lines. This marquetry end piece apparently survived only on Style 24 models made after 1867, but it was used on plainer models as well in the earlier period. Ivory or solid wood end pieces that are rectangular (instead of wedge-shaped) also disappear well before 1867.

Deluxe neck and bridge details: This includes ebony or ivory lining of the joinery on cedar necks, ivory binding that covers the entire edge of the headstock, and pearl decorations just below, or at the ends, of bridges. Binding only the upper edge of the headstock seems to have been an idea that didn't occur to Martin until decades later, after more heavily inlaid versions of Style 42 were renamed Style 45 (headstock inlays and binding first appeared on Martin mandolins introduced in 1895). Throughout the post-1860 period, Martin apparently did not put binding on their guitar headstocks at all; Style 42 was given essentially the same headstock as lower models but with fancier tuners. The only decoration found on necks of post-1867 guitars are small silver plaques attached to the face of the headstock, often bearing an engraving of the owners name or initials. (see Figure 11-19).

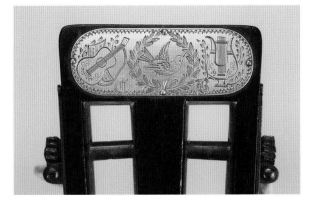

Figure 11-19. *Far left*, Engraved metal plaques like this one appear on some of Martin's guitars from the late 1860s and '70s. Some show the owner's name, and some are dated, but the plaque found on this 1-26 model is the most elaborately engraved version to have surfaced. Because the engraving includes two musical instruments, sheet music, and the initials "C. B," it may have been made for, or at least sold by, Charles Bruno, and/or Charles Bruno Jr., but of course we can't be sure. C. Bruno & Son were Martin's second largest account at the time this guitar was built.

Solid—not kerfed or individual block—linings. Although solid linings are found on early Austro-German models, they appear to have been relegated to only the lower styles by the 1850s. Martin continued to use solid linings during the "& Co."–era on size 2½ and 3 guitars in Style 17, and these models were continued, virtually without change, into the 1890s.

Inconsistent back bracing: Back bracing patterns vary widely on some, but certainly not all, pre-1867 Martins. Bracing patterns range from two to five braces, with different combinations of narrow blade-shaped and wider low-rounded bracing profiles. The only consistency is that low-rounded back braces are never used above the waist, but backs with all braces blade-shaped are common. In contrast, all post-1867 Martin guitars have either four or five back braces, and the braces below the waist are always the low-rounded shape, with only the upper two back braces being blade-shaped (the number of back braces is not necessarily related to the size of guitar).

Figure 11-20. *Above left*, This is the earliest printed version of the paper label that Martin glued to the inside lid of his black wood "coffin" cases, although retailers had often added their own labels before this date. Considering the "10/9/1867" inked on this label, the 1-26 model (headstock shown at left) was shipped shortly after the partnership between Martin, his son C. F. Jr., and cousin C. F. Hartmann was finalized.

Figure 11-21. C. F. Martin Jr. enlarged his small factory in Nazareth in the late 1880s, investing in new saws and machinery. He did not live to enjoy the results of those efforts, however, and died November 15, 1888, at the age of 63.

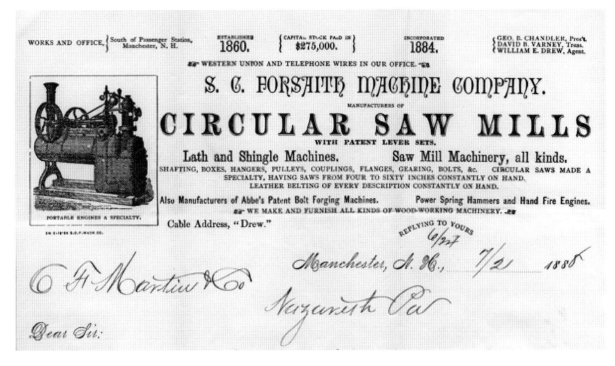

THE PERILS OF A MONOPOLY ON DISTRIBUTION

With distribution being almost entirely handled by New York City wholesalers Zoebisch and Bruno (and only Zoebisch after 1869), innovation in Nazareth was apparently ending. Sales books from the C. F. Jr. era reveal that only a few guitars were sold directly to instructors or other long-standing Martin accounts, with all the rest sold through C. A. Zoebisch & Sons.[8] A quick glance through records for the ten-year period following C. F. Sr.'s death shows the almost absolute monopoly that Zoebisch had on Martin's production, receiving over 1450 guitars while less than 200 were shipped to all other accounts combined (most of these went to two nearby Philadelphia dealers or an occasional instructor with long-standing connections to the Martin family). Many successful retailers who had previously purchased guitars directly from Martin had to adapt to ordering from a middleman instead. While some of these dealers had sold only a few guitars during the 1850s, others were quite successful and served emerging economic powerhouses such as the cities of St. Louis, Cincinnati, Petersburg and Richmond (Virginia), and New Orleans.

This additional firewall between Martin and its retailers probably kept communication with anyone who wanted something different to a minimum. While such an efficient arrangement allowed the workshop in Nazareth to concentrate on quality and consistency, it also kept Martin more isolated from the larger guitar scene, especially in emerging markets not beholden to New York City. Compared to the 1850s, very few guitars were shipped from Nazareth as single-purchase orders, and Zoebisch apparently did little to persuade Martin retailers to carry higher-priced models, although sales of the more expensive Martin styles did improve somewhat in the 1880s. More importantly, the only frequent variation was for guitars with "peg head" (friction pegs in a solid headstock instead of right-angle "patent heads" in a slotted headstock), an option stated on the price list. In fact, any exceptions from price-list models were rare during this period; a few terz models, also mentioned on the price list, and an occasional 00, which even

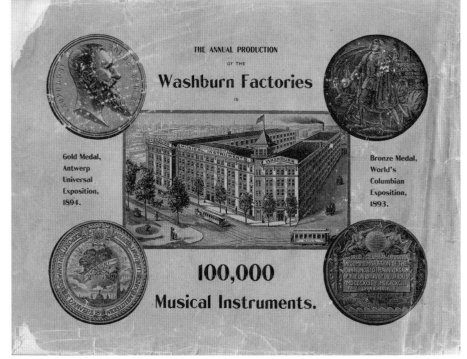

Figure 11-22. In the early 1870s, Lyon & Healy was vying with Zoebisch & Sons to distribute Martin's guitars, and ordered expensive models, including Style 42, for their lavishly appointed sales rooms in Chicago. But twenty years later, mass-produced Washburn brand guitars were the most troublesome competitor Martin's grandson, Frank Henry, had to face in the rapidly expanding marketplace. Along with a wide range of guitars, this questionable '100,000 instruments annually' claim included a full line of mandolins and banjos.

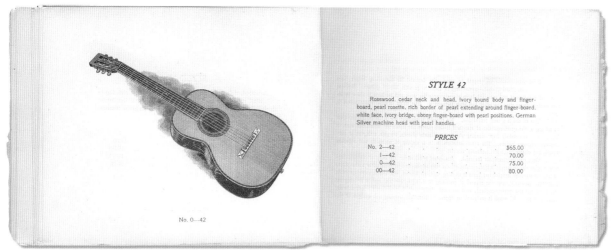

STYLE 42

Rosewood, cedar neck and head, ivory bound body and finger-board, pearl rosette, rich border of pearl extending around finger-board, white face, ivory bridge, ebony finger-board with pearl positions. German Silver machine head with pearl handles.

PRICES

No. 2—42	$65.00
1—42	70.00
0—42	75.00
00—42	80.00

No. 0—42

Figure 11-23. Martin's first catalog showing its guitars was issued in 1898, and although there were fewer styles offered than in the price list from twenty-five years earlier, each style was available in several sizes. The styles themselves, however, were little changed except for the addition of position markers on the fretboard

twenty years after its introduction was still never advertised or listed. Only occasional upgrades appear in Zoebisch orders, such as a 0-28 with fretboard binding. The advantage of this lack of variety in Martin's production was, of course, that its half-dozen workmen could build instruments in anticipation of demand because future orders were more predictable. This is not to say that C. F. Jr. wasn't interested in progress—he built an addition to its factory and invested in new saws and equipment in 1887—but there were no changes to the guitars themselves and no new or different models. While the 1840s and '50s were characterized by change and innovation, production during the 1870s and '80s was characterized by a lack of either. Unfortunately for the Martin company, while what it made and how those instruments were sold during C. F. Jr.'s tenure did not change, the same could not be said for the American guitar market in general.

In 1880, less than seven years after C. F. Martin Sr.'s death, the lure of "things Spanish" again changed the American guitar scene when the new decade was rung in with the Figaro Spanish Students' arrival in New York City. Despite the fact that this exotic-looking group's signature sound of tremolo melodies was achieved with bandurrias, the resulting mandolin craze that swept the continent would forever change the role of the guitar, which quickly became the preferred accompaniment instrument for everything from mandolin soloists to full sized "plectral orchestras" in which every bowed instrument in a standard

string orchestra was replaced with an equivalent size mandolin.[9] While guitar clubs were nothing new, the guitar's role in this thriving mandolin scene helped move even average players out of the parlor and onto the stage, or at least into group settings where the gut-strung guitar's quiet tone put it at a distinct disadvantage compared to even a single mandolin. As a result, guitar players' occasional pleas for more volume grew to a clamorous roar. While Martin's model selection had been adequate in 1850, even its

Figure 11-24. The Milwaukee Mandolin Orchestra, 1908. Note the five guitarists standing in the back row, and among the many mandolinists is at least one mandola, and a 12-string mandolin as well. Even much smaller towns in rural America would often have a mandolin club with a dozen or more members.

Figure 11-25. Martin's first printed catalog was issued in 1896, but only showed the company's new Italian-style mandolins (now more often called "bowl-back"). Only four styles were shown, and. by 1898, they had been replaced with slightly different models that had tuners mounted from the back of the headstock. The earlier G styles, like the G 3 shown here, had tuners that were mounted from the front of the head.

Figure 11-26. *Below.* This unusual mandolin from 1901 was not Frank Henry Martin's idea, but he agreed to build it and at least one other version based on an 1895 patent held by C. H. Gaskins of Shamokin, Pennsylvania. Always in search of additional sales in the first years of the new century, Frank Henry accepted commissions to build several unorthodox stringed instruments for inventors, including double-bodied guitars. Once the Martin company's production soared as it began building ukuleles and steel-string guitars, however, such requests from inventors were routinely refused.

MARTIN MANDOLINS

*T*HE manufacturers ask attention to some special points of excellence in the Martin Mandolin.

Only a few styles are here pictured, but the same principles are observed in all. The framework is built up by a system at once neater and more durable than any other in use; the tone is superior because of careful work on the sound-board, which is the life of the instrument; the neck and head are shaped to fit the hand for easy and rapid execution, and the strings are regulated with the same end in view. In the ornamentation artistic simplicity has been observed, and in brief, the methods which have made and kept the Martin Guitar without a peer, have been applied to the Martin Mandolin throughout.

Other and finer styles will be made to order. The prices quoted are net cash.

STYLE G 3. Rosewood, ivory bound, 27 ribs with continuous binder, mahogany neck and head, both bound in ivory, ebony fingerboard with finer position dots, white face inlaid at sound hole and border with pearl, finely inlaid guard plate, ivory bridge, finely engraved machine head and tail piece.
Price . . $40.00

largest 0-28 "Concert Model" could not hold its own in this newer and louder environment.

Another louder environment was the promotion of new brands as America's age of advertising and catalog sales gathered steam. The promotion of Martin guitars had not changed in decades and was hopelessly out of date compared to Lyon & Healy's compelling cute-kids-and-pets advertisements of its popular Washburn brand instruments. By 1890, after decades of being the preeminent American guitar company, Martin found its sales sagging below pre–Civil War levels, while sales of competing brands, especially Washburn, soared to many times Martin's annual output. Ironically, most of these competitors' guitars had body and headstock shapes, and even rosettes, that were clearly patterned after Martin's now-familiar style, which had evolved almost half a century earlier. By 1900, even Martin's X-pattern top bracing was being widely copied.

There is no surviving correspondence to indicate that C. F. Martin Jr. saw this cloud looming over his company's future before he died suddenly in 1888 at age sixty-three. Fortunately, C. F. Jr.'s son, Frank Henry Martin (1866–1948), was more like his grandfather, and it was Frank Henry's flurry of innovations in both what Martin made and how it was priced and distributed, that resulted in the Martin company of the early twentieth century. Less than a decade after Frank Henry took over the company at age twenty-two, he began to streamline Martin's list of guitar models. The 1897 price list is the earliest surviving record suggesting what was in store; it shows that Styles 24 and 40 had already been discontinued. The following year, Martin distributed its first guitar catalog, in which Styles 20 and 26 had also been left behind, with Styles 27 and 34 deleted as well by the release of the next catalog in 1901.

Instead of offering distinctly different styles, Frank Henry chose to present more models, offering each of the surviving styles in several sizes. This meant that instead of a 1-26, customers could order a 1-28, which was essentially the same guitar, while

Styles 17 and 18 were combined, with Style 18 offered in five sizes. One distinct advantage to this simplified system was that a small Martin dealer could represent Martin's entire line of guitar styles and sizes with only a half-dozen instruments in stock. As was (and still is), typical of the company, these early catalogs only made policies that had been in effect for some time official; Martin had been offering a wider number of sizes in any given style, rather than one size for each style shown on the 1870s Zoebisch price list.[10] And the fancier styles, such as 30 and 42, which had initially only been offered as "ladies models" (size 2) were now available in larger sizes, including the 00. The styles that survived this consolidation, especially 21, 28, and 42, looked much as they had in the 1850s, and remain with us even today.

Shuffling styles and sizes of guitars was only a small part of Frank Henry's changes. Under his energetic leadership, we see a full line of Martin mandolins (1895), larger 000-size guitars (1901), harp guitars (1902), fancier pearl-bordered models that soon became the legendary Style 45 (1902), and even bizarre double-bodied "Model America" guitars in 1906. Not all the additions to the Martin line were fancy or unusual; as Frank Henry sought new markets and greater sales, lower-priced mahogany guitar models were introduced in 1906 with a retail price of only $20 (Martin's earlier mahogany guitars had a retail price of $24 in the late 1840s). While this new variety of instruments and more modern and open-minded approach to innovation made Martin's production far more interesting, it still was not enough to insure the company's survival. Demand for guitars wasn't the problem in the new century; instead. it was competition, especially from big factories in Chicago, New York and New Jersey, which could produce instruments more quickly, and at far cheaper prices, than the old-fashioned Martin workshop in Nazareth.

Frank Henry saw a potential life-line being tossed to Martin when the Hawaiian music craze

Figure 11-27. This 1908 mandolin was played by Herbert Keller Martin, who often performed in guitar & mandolin duets with his older brother, C.F. Martin III. It has remained in the Martin family since Herbert's untimely death in 1927. Martin's bowl-back mandolins were the most ornate instruments the company produced, this example has double rows of pearl around both the top and the sound hole.

Figure 11-28. *Far left,* While Frank Henry Martin tried to make the most of America's infatuation with mandolins and mandolin orchestras, this 18-string harp guitar from 1902 was probably the most complex engineering challenge he had to face. Several other harp guitars were made by Martin, like this one on the new larger 000-size body, but most had only ten strings.

Figure 11.29. The influence of the mando-lin style of decoration is clearly seen on this 00-42 "Special" from 1902, one of a number of similar models Martin made that year. The inlaid pickguard, centered beneath the strings, and elaborate vine-pattern fretboard inlay would not survive, but the additional pearl bordering on the sides and back, and the inlaid headstock, were features Frank Henry Martin contin-ued on Style 45 models introduced in the 1904 catalog.

Figure 11.30, (below), and Figure 11-31 (opposite page). C. F. Martin & Co. 0-28, c. 1870s. Of all the Martin models that originated before the Civil War, the 0-28 is the most iconic, with an over seventy-five year run in continuous production with few visual changes. (It has recently been reissued by the current Martin Guitar Co.) The original "Martin herringbone," it was already so well known by the late 1800s that at least one competitor gave their copies paper labels that read "0-28 Model." This early, undated example of the model may have been made not long after the formation of the C. F. Martin & Co in 1867 and almost certainly dates before 1880.

began in the mid teens, and the radical Dreadnought built for Ditson, all-koa guitars made for Southern California Music, and Martin's own wildly suc-cessful line of ukuleles were all introduced in less than two years. Most of these new instrument types were the direct result of requests from Martin deal-ers or instructors.[11] All that progress in such a short time would have been impossible if not for one of Frank Henry's first important decisions; shortly after he took over leadership of the Martin company, he ended the exclusive distribution agreement with C. A. Zoebisch & Sons and began shipping directly to new accounts, especially in the newly emerging markets in the western United States. While the resulting success of the C. F. Martin Co. in the twen-tieth century is another story, and one focused on guitars with steel strings, the Martin guitar models themselves would retain many structural and visual details that first appeared over half a century ear-lier, when C. F. Martin Sr. distilled and blended a wide range of influences to create what became the uniquely American guitar. ★

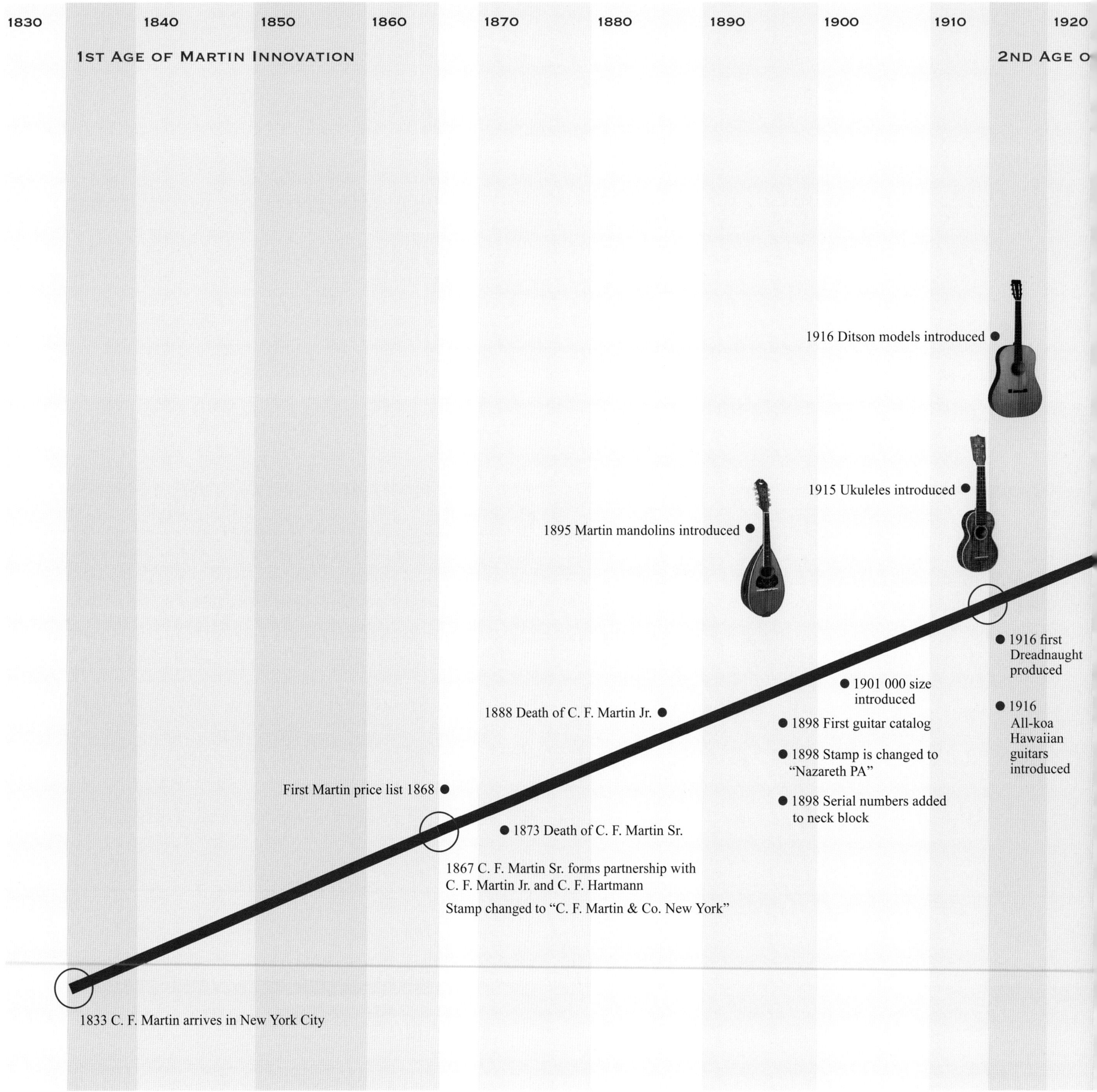
1830
1840
1850
1860
1870
1880
1890
1900
1910
1920
1st Age of Martin Innovation
2nd Age o
1916 Ditson models introduced
1915 Ukuleles introduced
1895 Martin mandolins introduced
1916 first Dreadnaught produced
1901 000 size introduced
1916 All-koa Hawaiian guitars introduced
1888 Death of C. F. Martin Jr.
1898 First guitar catalog
1898 Stamp is changed to "Nazareth PA"
1898 Serial numbers added to neck block
First Martin price list 1868
1873 Death of C. F. Martin Sr.
1867 C. F. Martin Sr. forms partnership with C. F. Martin Jr. and C. F. Hartmann
Stamp changed to "C. F. Martin & Co. New York"
1833 C. F. Martin arrives in New York City

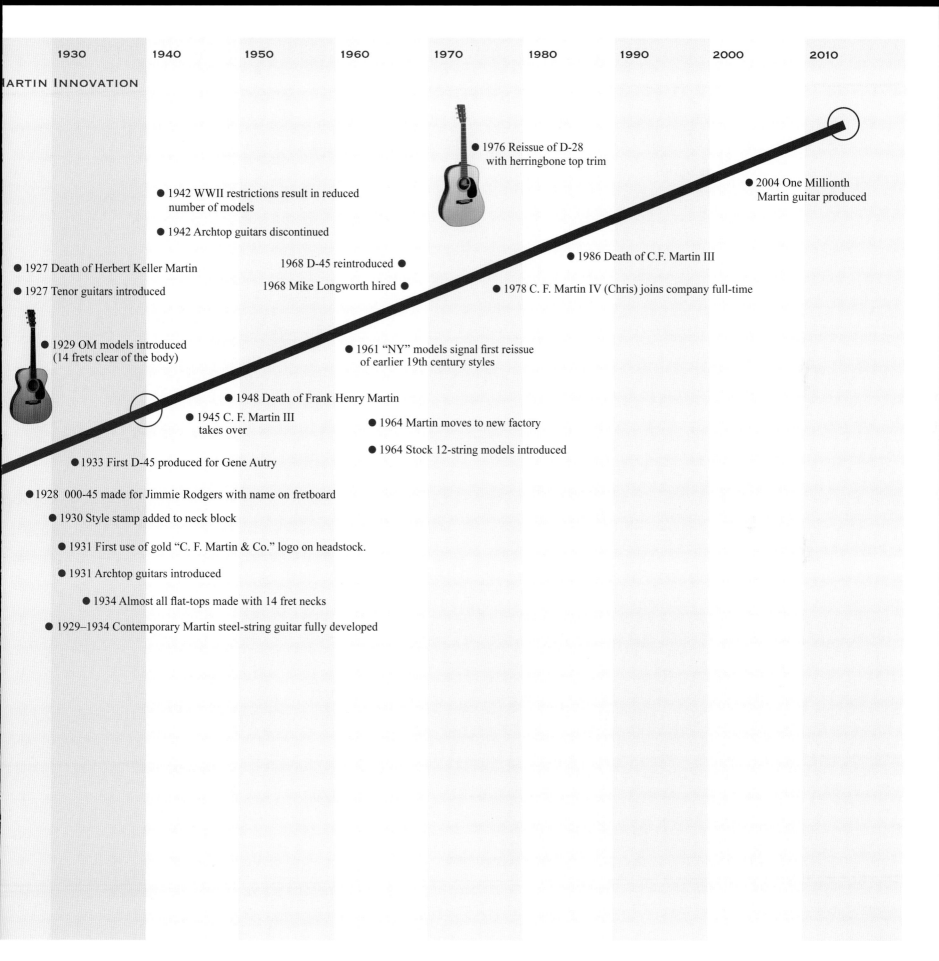

1930   1940   1950   1960   1970   1980   1990   2000   2010

MARTIN INNOVATION

● 1976 Reissue of D-28 with herringbone top trim

● 1942 WWII restrictions result in reduced number of models

● 1942 Archtop guitars discontinued

● 2004 One Millionth Martin guitar produced

● 1927 Death of Herbert Keller Martin

1968 D-45 reintroduced ●

● 1986 Death of C.F. Martin III

● 1927 Tenor guitars introduced

1968 Mike Longworth hired ●

● 1978 C. F. Martin IV (Chris) joins company full-time

● 1929 OM models introduced (14 frets clear of the body)

● 1961 "NY" models signal first reissue of earlier 19th century styles

● 1948 Death of Frank Henry Martin

● 1945 C. F. Martin III takes over

● 1964 Martin moves to new factory

● 1964 Stock 12-string models introduced

● 1933 First D-45 produced for Gene Autry

● 1928 000-45 made for Jimmie Rodgers with name on fretboard

● 1930 Style stamp added to neck block

● 1931 First use of gold "C. F. Martin & Co." logo on headstock.

● 1931 Archtop guitars introduced

● 1934 Almost all flat-tops made with 14 fret necks

● 1929–1934 Contemporary Martin steel-string guitar fully developed

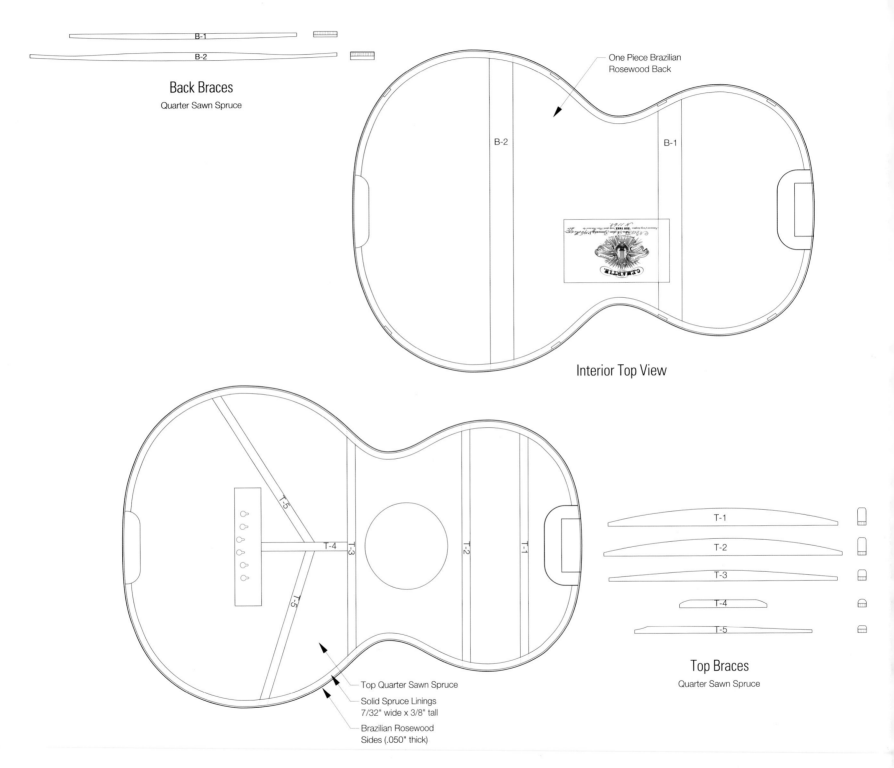

Back Braces
Quarter Sawn Spruce

B-1

B-2

One Piece Brazilian
Rosewood Back

B-2

B-1

Interior Top View

T-5

T-4

T-3

T-2

T-1

Interior Bottom View

Top Quarter Sawn Spruce

Solid Spruce Linings
7/32" wide x 3/8" tall

Brazilian Rosewood
Sides (.050" thick)

Top Braces
Quarter Sawn Spruce

T-1

T-2

T-3

T-4

T-5

MEASURED DRAWING—AUSTRO-GERMAN STYLE MARTIN GUITAR, C. 1837

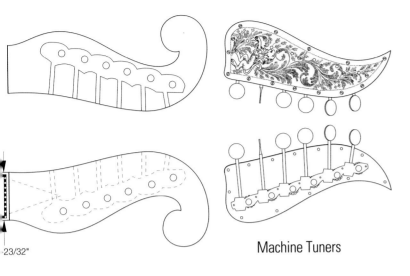

Machine Tuners

·23/32"

·760"

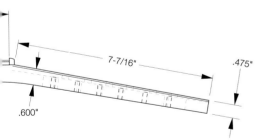

7-7/16"   ·475"

·600"

The design and construction of this example of one of Martin's earliest American-made guitars is solidly based on the guitar-making tradition of his Austro-German homeland. It also suggests an intimate knowledge of the guitars of Vienna's most successful luthier, Johann Georg Stauffer, especially his patented Legnani model, which featured:

- Scroll-shaped headstock with machine tuners on one side
- Key-operated mechanically adjustable neck
- Raised fretboard that extended clear of the guitar's top

This guitar has additional features that are uniquely Martin's and draw attention to his capacity for aesthetic and technical innovation. The top bracing shows a tentative move away from Austro-German lateral bracing toward the fan bracing that would become the norm in Martin's Spanish-style guitars a few years later.

Martin created the elegant shield-shaped bridge design on this guitar and used it for a brief period between abandoning traditional Austro-German moustache bridge designs and embracing the pyramid bridge that remains the standard on Martin guitars to the present day.

While the extensive use of herringbone trim will be immediately familiar to modern eyes, other decorative motifs are unique to C. F. Martin's earliest Austro-German period. The rosette design consisting of alternating crescent and trefoil shapes, as well as the pattern of half circles that embellishes the perimeter of the top, are examples of Martin's earliest motifs. His creative and tasteful use of opulent materials such as mother-of-pearl, abalone, and Ivory is lavish but never gaudy or garish.

See Profile 9 on page 48 for more details.

A full-scale construction plan of this guitar can be purchased from Stewart-MacDonald at www.stewmac.com.

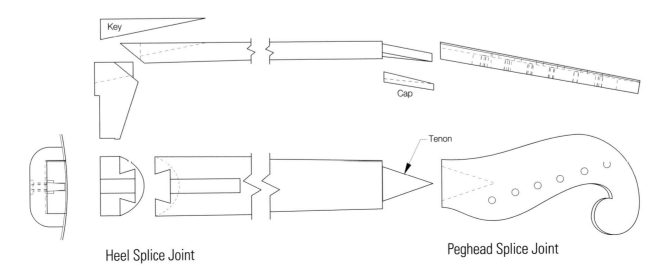

Key

Cap

Tenon

Heel Splice Joint   Peghead Splice Joint

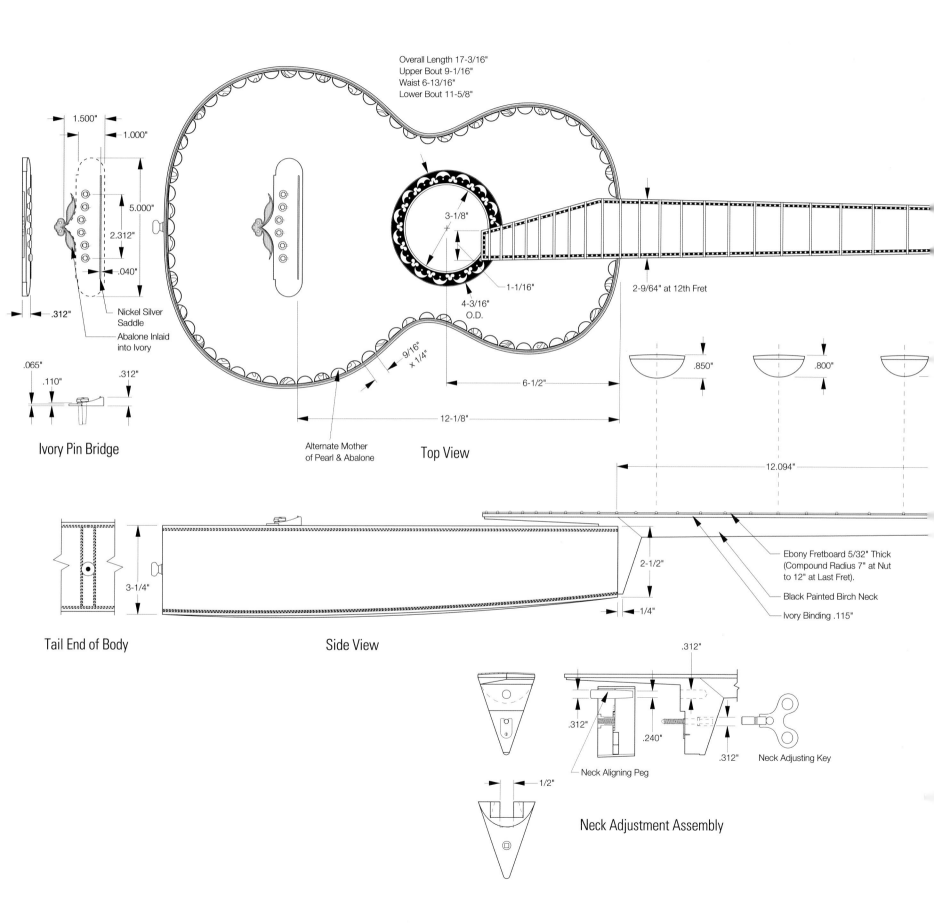

Overall Length 17-3/16"
Upper Bout 9-1/16"
Waist 6-13/16"
Lower Bout 11-5/8"

1.500"
1.000"
5.000"
2.312"
.040"
.312"

Nickel Silver
Saddle

Abalone Inlaid
into Ivory

.065"
.110"
.312"

Ivory Pin Bridge

9/16"
x 1/4"

3-1/8"

1-1/16"

4-3/16"
O.D.

2-9/64" at 12th Fret

6-1/2"

12-1/8"

Alternate Mother
of Pearl & Abalone

Top View

.850"
.800"

12.094"

Tail End of Body

3-1/4"

2-1/2"

1/4"

Ebony Fretboard 5/32" Thick
(Compound Radius 7" at Nut
to 12" at Last Fret).

Black Painted Birch Neck

Ivory Binding .115"

Side View

.312"

.312"

.240"

.312"

Neck Aligning Peg

Neck Adjusting Key

1/2"

Neck Adjustment Assembly

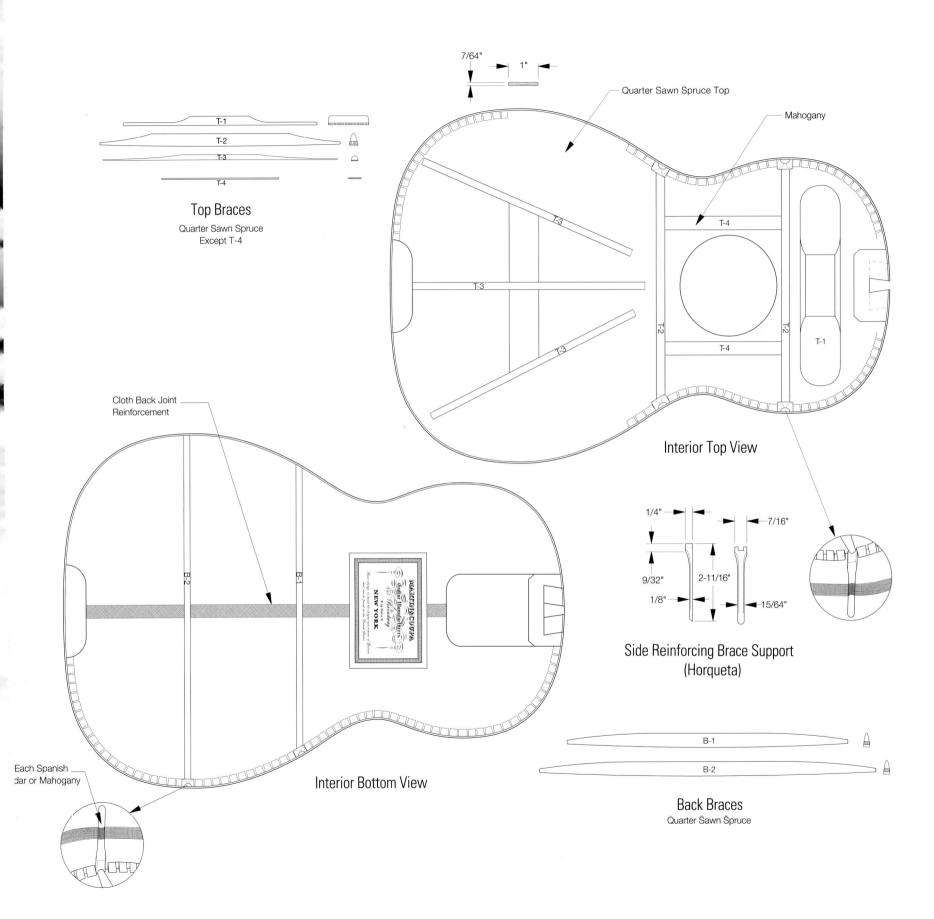

7/64"

1"

Quarter Sawn Spruce Top

Mahogany

T-1

T-2

T-3

T-4

Top Braces

Quarter Sawn Spruce
Except T-4

T-3

T-3

T-4

T-4

T-2

T-2

T-1

Interior Top View

Cloth Back Joint
Reinforcement

B-2

B-1

1/4"

7/16"

9/32"

2-11/16"

1/8"

15/64"

**Side Reinforcing Brace Support
(Horqueta)**

Interior Bottom View

Each Spanish
dar or Mahogany

B-1

B-2

Back Braces

Quarter Sawn Spruce

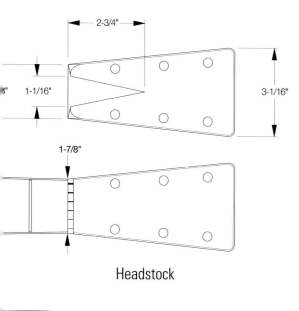

Headstock

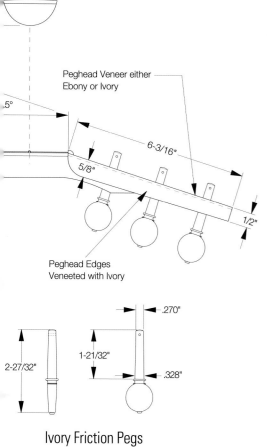

Peghead Veneer either
Ebony or Ivory

Peghead Edges
Veneeted with Ivory

Ivory Friction Pegs

This guitar is an example of an early Spanish design that C. F. Martin Sr. produced for John Coupa at the beginning of the 1840s. It represents the intermediate style that Martin developed between the Austro-German guitars he produced upon his arrival in New York City in 1833 and the American-style guitars that he and the company he founded produced from the 1850s to the present.

Typical "Spanish" features, which Martin was applying to his guitars for the first time, include:
- Three fan braces
- Elongated body shape
- Pronounced size differential between upper and lower bouts
- Distinctive flat-ended "peg" headstock copied from Spanish-made examples of this style

Several additional features that served a functional purpose on early Spanish guitars are entirely nonfunctional design elements of Martin's Spanish-style guitars. For example, although a typical Spanish foot appears on the interior of this guitar, the neck is still attached using a dovetail joint. Another non-functional

Spanish feature is the instrument's two-piece sides with inlay on the centerline. These details reveal that Martin was designing in the Spanish style while still relying on familiar Austro-German construction techniques.

This is also the first of Martin's guitar designs to regularly use a variant of the "pyramid" bridge on which the strings were tied to a raised rear portion in the Spanish style.

The wood Martin used in his Spanish style guitars usually consisted of spruce for the top, solid Brazilian rosewood for the sides and back, and Cuban mahogany or cedar for the neck. This particular high-grade example has an ivory bridge, ivory binding, and ivory veneer facing the sides and top of the peghead. It is also one of only two extant Spanish-style examples with sides and back of goncalo alves in place of Brazilian rosewood.

See Profile 20 on page 110 for more details.

A full-scale construction plan of this guitar can be purchased from Stewart-MacDonald at www.stewmac.com.

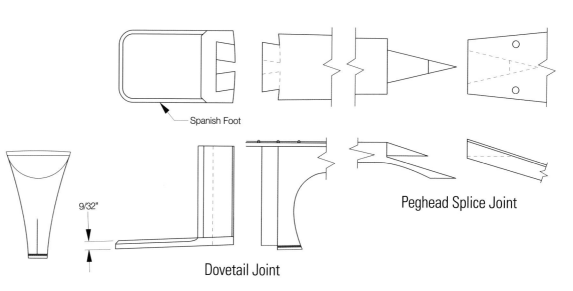

Spanish Foot

Peghead Splice Joint

Dovetail Joint

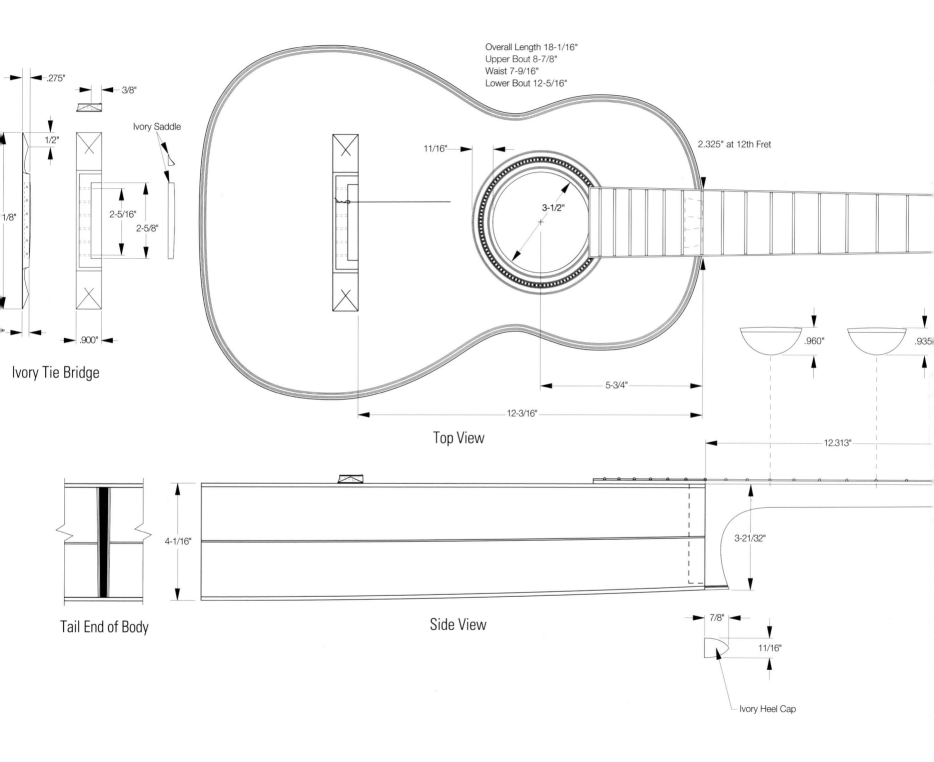

.275"

3/8"

Ivory Saddle

1/2"

1/8"

2-5/16"

2-5/8"

.900"

Ivory Tie Bridge

Overall Length 18-1/16"
Upper Bout 8-7/8"
Waist 7-9/16"
Lower Bout 12-5/16"

11/16"

2.325" at 12th Fret

3-1/2"

5-3/4"

12-3/16"

Top View

.960"

.935"

12.313"

4-1/16"

3-21/32"

Tail End of Body

Side View

7/8"

11/16"

Ivory Heel Cap

C. F. Martin used a limited variety of simple and finely scaled herringbone, ladder ,and rope marquetry patterns for purfling on his earliest Austro-German style guitars. However, by the time he was creating his Spanish-style guitars, he was incorporating a wide range of multicolored decorative marquetry patterns in soundhole rosettes, to border the top, and for fillets and decorative purfling located on the centerlines of the back and two-piece sides. Until Martin began to establish specific uniform styles later in the1840s, there appears to be no continuity in the selection of his marquetry patterns and which ones he combined to decorate a single instrument.

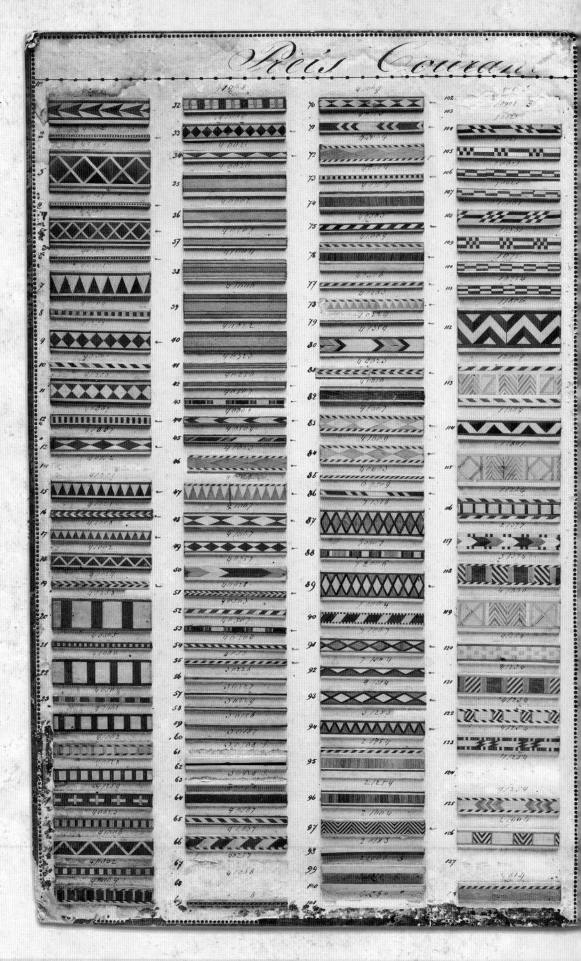

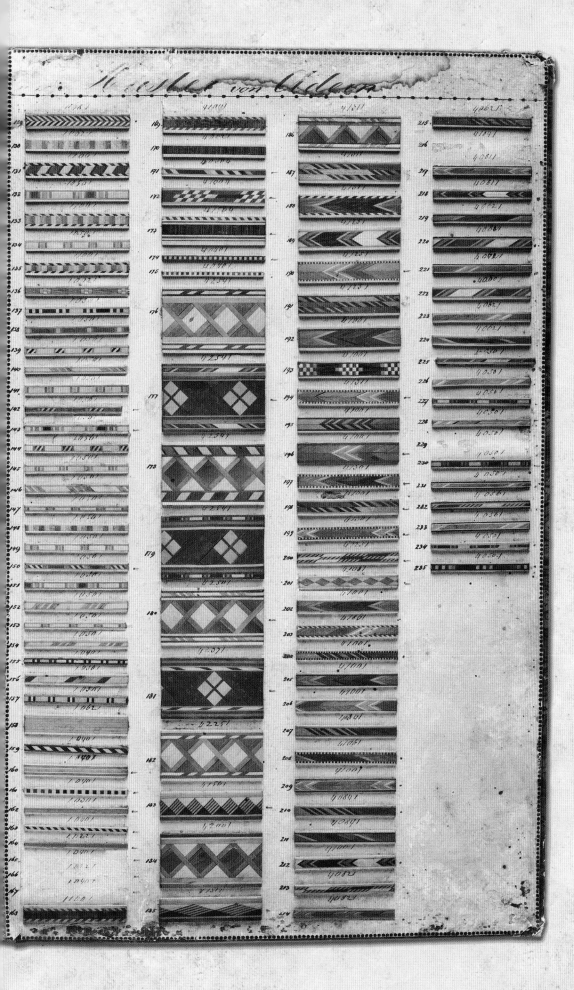

C. H. Burdorf in Hamburg, Germany, was an early marquetry source for Martin, and many of the patterns on this rare Burdorf marquetry sample card can be found on extant examples of early Martin guitars. But many patterns commonly seen on early Martins are missing from the sample card, and many numbered spaces on the card are missing the marquetry samples those numbers would have identified. One possible explanation is that Martin pried examples of the marquetry he wanted to order off this card and pasted them onto letters sent to Burdorf, or to Zoebisch or another third party who was placing the order for him. Considering how long it would have taken before Martin would receive such an order from overseas, it is understandable that he would want to avoid any chances for error.

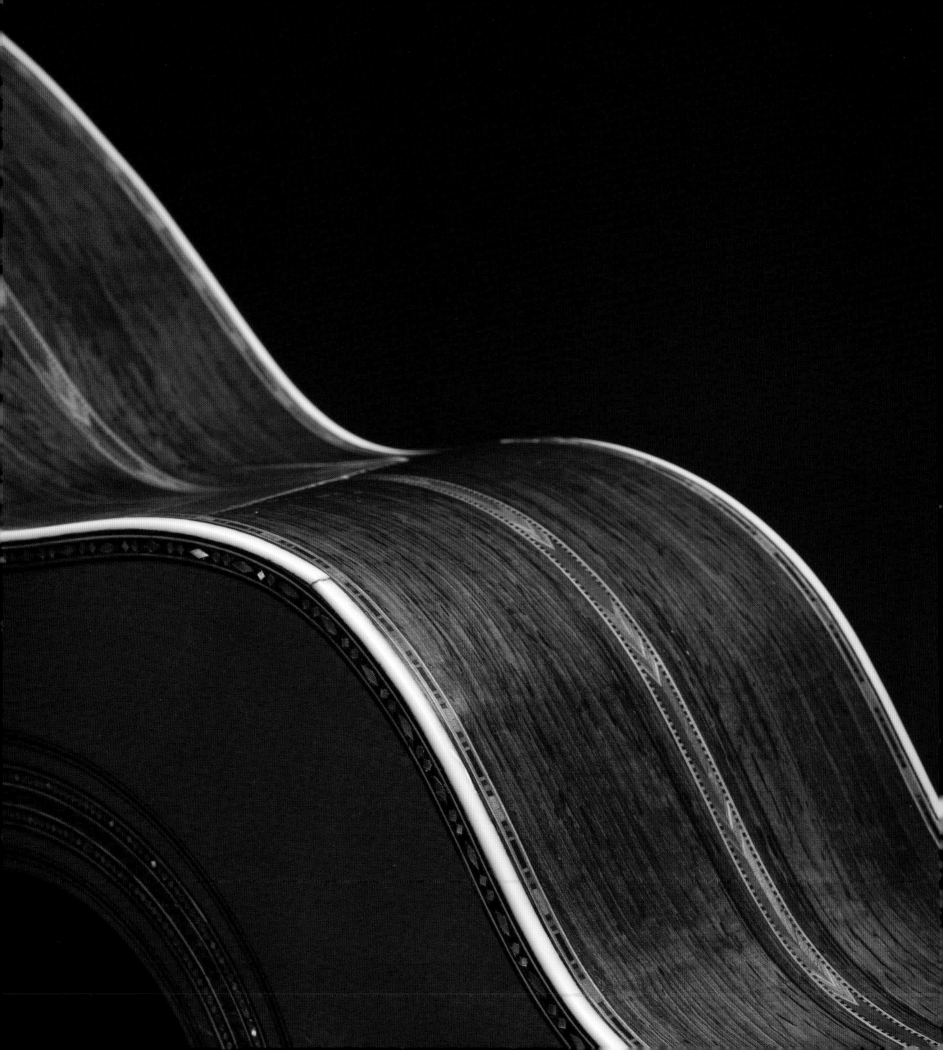

Acknowledgments

I am grateful for the opportunity to collaborate with the team that produced this book. They include designer Steve J. Hill, editor Bob Shaw, and writers David Gansz, Richard Johnston, David LaPlante, Arian Sheets, and James Westbrook, all of whom have been fully engaged throughout the multiple years of this project. It has been an enriching and inspiring experience.

Thanks to Greg Adams, Chris Andrada, Jim Baggett, John Bernunzio, Jim Bollman, Richard Brunkus, Don Bryson, Bill Capell, Bob Carlin, Christie Carter, Walter Carter, Tony Creamer, Tom Crandall, Frank Finocchio, Frank Ford, Robert Goetz, Philip Gura, George Gruhn, Erik Pierre Hofmann, Jay Hostetler, Greig Hutton, Stan Jay, Peter Kohman, Steve Kovacik, Bernard Levine, Dean Levy, Walter Lipton, Perry Margouleff, Kevin McCormick, Shawn McSweeney, Roddy Moore, David Oakes, Fred Oster, John Peden, Norm Peterson, Marc Silber, Mark Simon, Steve Spodaryk, Steve Uhrik, Matt Umanov, Ian Watchorn, Stan Werbin, and George Wunderlich.

Thanks also to Darcy Kuronan at the Museum of Fine Arts, Boston; Kenneth Moore, Jayson Kerr Dobney, Joseph Peknik, Susanna Cadeira, and the staff in the Musical Instrument Department of the Metropolitan Museum of Art; John O'Neill at the Hispanic Society of America; Heidrun Eichler at the Markneukirchen Musikinstrumenten-Museum, Markneukirchen, Germany; and Kerry Keane, Musical Instruments, Christie's.

Don MacRostie at Stewart MacDonald created excellent construction plans of early Martin guitars from which we developed our measured drawings. If readers are inspired to construct a replica of an early Martin guitar, full-size plans can be purchased directly from Stewart MacDonald.

John Sterling Ruth's outstanding photographic documentation of the profiled guitars enabled us to achieve our objective of "allowing the guitars to tell their own stories."

John Cerullo at Hal Leonard understood the scope and breadth of our intentions from the beginning and has been supportive throughout the project.

Thanks to Chris Martin, Amani Duncan, and Mike Dickinson, at C. F. Martin & Co. for their indispensable encouragement and cooperation.

My collaborators and I reserve special thanks to Dick Boak, Director of the Museum, Archives and Special Projects at C. F. Martin & Co., who provided inexhaustible vision and support for this project even before the idea for this book was fully conceived.

Finally, as always, I wish to thank my wife Kathryn for her love, tolerance of my idiosyncrasies, and wisdom in insisting that there be guitar- and banjo-free zones in our home.

PETER SZEGO

NOTES

CHAPTER 1. JOHANN GEORG STAUFFER AND THE VIENNESE GUITAR

1. Ian Watchorn, "Inventing the Modern Guitar: Johann Georg Stauffer and the Viennese School of Guitar Making" (Lecture Series, 5th Darwin International Guitar Festival, Music School, Northern Territory University, 2002), 2. The author wishes to extend special thanks to Ian Watchorn for most generously placing this paper and two others—"The Guitar in the 19th Century—Technology & Technique" (1999), and "C. F. Martin – Origins and Early influences in Guitar Making" (2011)—at his disposal.

2. *Ibid,*. 2.

3. Erik Stenstadvold, *An Annotated Bibliography of Guitar Methods*, 1760–1860 (Hillsdale, New York: Pendragon Press, 2010), 9.

4. See Jukka Savijoki, *Anton Diabelli's Guitar Works: A Thematic Catalogue* (Columbus, Ohio: Editions Orphée, 2004).

5. Giovanni Accornero, Ivan Epicoco, and Eraldo Guerci, *The Guitar: Four Centuries of Masterpieces* (Torino, Italy: Edizioni Il Salabue, 2008), 42-3 and 156-7.

6. W. L. F. v Lütgendorff, *Die Geigen und Lautenmacher vom Mittelalter bis zum Gegenwart* (Tutzing: Hans Schneider, 1975).

7. Ferdinand Prochart, *Der Wiener Geigenbau im 19. und 20. Jahrhundert* (Tutzing: Hans Schneider, 1979), 44 and 156.

8. Thomas Heck, *Mauro Giuliani: Virtuoso Guitarist and Composer* (Columbus, Ohio: Editions Orphée, 1995), 116.

9. Vincenz Schuster, *Anleitung zur Erlernung des von Hrn. Georg Stauffer neu erfundenen Guitarre–Violoncells* (Vienna: A. Diabelli, 1825).

10. Erik Pierre Hofmann, Pascal Mougin, and Stefan Hackl, *Stauffer & Co.: The Viennese Guitar of the 19th Century* (Germolles-sur-Grosne, France: Editions des Robins, 2011), 93.

11. Prochart, 152–157.

12. Accornero, Epicoco, and Guerci, 66.

CHAPTER 2. C. F. MARTIN'S HOMELAND AND THE VOGTLAND TRADE

1. Other violinmakers' guilds were founded the nearby towns of Graslitz (Bohemia) in 1669 and Klingenthal in 1716.

2. The Erzgebirge were a major historical European source of silver, iron, copper, cobalt, zinc, and nickel. Nickel silver or Argentan, made from copper, nickel, and zinc, was invented in the region in 1823.

3. Innungsprivilegium der Geigenmacher zu Markneukirchen, 1677, as transcribed in Bernhard Zoebisch, *Vogtländischer Geigenbau: Biographien und Erklärungen ab 1850,* (Zurich: Geiger-Verlag, 2002), 9–14.

4. Marnkeukirchen *Hausbesitzerverzeichnis* of 1812, Johann Georg Martin, father of Christian Martin, listed as "Martin, Melchetischer, Pianofortebauer."

5. In 1837, new articles were adopted by the violinmakers' guild, listing the required masterpieces as the following: violin, alto viola, guitar, viola d'amore, mandolin, lute, harp [meaning the local folk type without pedals], pedal harp, zither, violoncello, and violone [double bass], all unvarnished. In 1853, guitars were named as a special guild article of the furniture makers. On January 1, 1862, a new Trade Act in Saxony stripped the craft guilds of all legal authority. In 1881, a reversal of the previous *Gewerbeordnungen* (trade ordinances) allowed once again for guilds. A combined instrument and furniture makers' guild was established in 1887 and functioned through 1899 in Markneukirchen. The changes in guild legal ordinance was a recognition on the part of the federal German government (founded in 1871) that structured training was beneficial for national competiveness and worker development, but in no way was the intention to resurrect the power of the medieval guild structure. The revived guilds were entrusted with the operation of vocational schools and continuing education, the issuing of certifications, the provision of

health, disability, and death insurance for guild members, disciplinary action, and mediation. Guilds had informally continued as community service and social institutions even after their restriction in various German states in the mid-nineteenth century.

6. See *The Guittar and its Makers in the British Isles, 1750–1810*, Panagiotis Poulopoulos, Ph.D. dissertation, U. Edinburgh, 2011; Lanie Graf, "John Frederick Hintz, Eighteenth-Century Moravian Instrument Maker, and the Use of the Cittern in Moravian Worship," *Journal of Moravian History* 5, FALL 2008, 7–39.

7. Johann Georg Albrechtsberger, *Gründliche Anweisung zur Composition*, (Leipzig, 1790), 417. "Die Cither (Chitarra) ist dreyerley: die deutsche, die welsche und die spanische. Jede wird anders behandelt. Importa niente."

CHAPTER 3. C. F. MARTIN IN NEW YORK, 1833–1839

1. See Chapter 2 for more information.

2. C. F. Martin's father, Johann Georg Martin (1765–1832), was the son of Johann Adam Martin (1744–1808) and was married to Eva Regina Paulus.

3. While there are no surviving records of communication between Schatz and Martin while Martin was still in Saxony, they had an off-and-on partnership in America for about a decade, and the two families continued to share correspondence even after Schatz's death in the late 1860s. Their intermittent partnership was apparently the result of Schatz returning to Saxony for an extended period on more than one occasion.

4. The earliest record of Martin working for Kuhle is 1825, but, since C. F. Martin Jr. was born on October 2, 1825, it seems safe to assume that he was acquainted with the Kuhles well before that first surviving record.

5. Schmidt's name appears often in Martin's 1830s ledgers, but he had apparently left Martin's employ and started his own music business by 1838. It was not known that Louis Schmidt's name appeared on the manifest of the *Columbus* until Greig Hutton discovered that fact in his research.

6. This is probably an overstatement, especially as pertains to guitar production, because there are large gaps, especially for 1835 and again for 1839. Surviving records consist of daybooks, journals, and ledgers covering all types of expenditures, as well as guitar orders, but often one or more of these three types is missing for a given period. Martin would often turn one of these accounts books over years later and start writing another type of records in the back. For a more complete look at what is included in the C. F. Martin & Co. Archives, see Philip Gura, *C. F. Martin & His Guitars, 1796–1873* (Chapel Hill: University of North Carolina Press, 2003), 191.

7. Although daguerreotypes were being made in the 1840s, very few were of guitarists. Ambrotypes and tintypes were popular in the US by the late 1850s, but not many images of guitarists have been discovered and as far as we know, no pre–Civil War photographs of musicians playing Martin guitars have surfaced.

8. Unpublished paper by Darcy Karonen.

9. Laurence Libin, *American Musical Instruments in the Metropolitan Museum of Art* (New York: W. W. Norton & Co., Inc., 1985), 130–133.

10. Edward Fehrman was a German music instructor in New York and frequent Martin customer in the 1830s. See Gura, 2003, 41-42, 55.

11. Martin or Schatz, both of whom were in nearby Nazareth, may have been contracted by the keyboard instrument maker to produce the Harp-Guitars, or perhaps to aid in their construction.

12. See figures 4-7, 7-3, and 7-4.

13. Although Greig Hutton's research tells us the order in which these different labels first appeared, their use might have overlapped. Martin may have reserved certain labels for one account while using another label for a different retailer, for instance, a common practice among instrument manufacturers.

14. This instrument has been the cornerstone of the C. F. Martin & Co. Museum since at least the 1960s. It has appeared in almost every book on Martin guitars and has been pictured in many of the company's advertisements and promotional literature.

15. T. F. Merz, the Markneukirchen supplier of a wide range of musical instruments and supplies, shipped boxes of goods to Schatz in Philadelphia before Martin arrived in New York in 1833, making it likely that Schatz was always based in Pennsylvania, not New York.

16. Gura, 2003, 45.

17. Beginning in 1836, Martin also sold German guitars imported from T. F. Merz in Markneukirchen, but these were priced below the least expensive guitars made in New York. The surviving records in Martin's archives indicate a very close match between the number of guitars recorded as being imported from Merz and the number of guitars sold in the price range below the cost of instruments made by Martin and his employees. These records also do not show any other sources of less expensive guitars.

18. Unlike the Martins, Henry Schatz moved back and forth between the New World and his old homeland. He was listed as a guitar maker in a Boston directory from 1845 to 1850, but letters in the Martin Archives from Mrs. Schatz indicate that the entire

Schatz family sailed back across the Atlantic to Saxony in 1850.

19. Charles Bruno was listed as a bookseller at 212 Fulton Street, which probably meant that he was selling music books and sheet music from that location.

20. Bruno returned to Macon, Georgia, where he had originally established a music store upon arriving there from Saxony in 1834. He reappears in the Martin saga in the late 1850s and was one of Martin's two New York wholesalers for several years until losing that role to C. Zoebisch & Sons. Bruno had several different partners, but the firm C. Bruno and Son survived as a major wholesaler of musical instruments and supplies until modern times, when it was acquired by the Kaman Corporation.

21. Justin Holland (1819–1887) was a free African-American who was based in Ohio and had studied guitar with longtime Martin endorser William Schubert. His devotion to the Spanish guitar had taken him to Mexico in 1844 to learn Spanish, but he settled in Cleveland upon his return and made his living teaching guitar and publishing compositions and arrangements for the instrument. In the late 1860s, C. F. Martin Jr. requested music for one of his daughters, by which time Holland was ordering Martin guitars directly from Nazareth, rather than dealing with Zoebisch, Martin's distributor in New York

22. John Coupa was a native of Spain who apparently first settled in Boston before moving to New York. He played guitar on the concert stage but his primary source of income was teaching, and selling guitars. His name first appears in Martin's ledgers in May of 1837.

CHAPTER 4. THE SPANISH GUITAR IN THE UNITED STATES BEFORE 1850

1. Graham Wade, *A Concise History of the Classic Guitar* (Pacific, Missouri: Mel Bay Publications, 2001), 51.

2. Stanley T. Williams, *The Spanish Background of American Literature* (New Haven: Yale University Press, 1955), Vol. I, 3.

3. Harry Bernstein, *Origins of Inter-American Interest 1700-1812* (Philadelphia: University of Pennsylvania Press, 1945), 56.

4. "A Letter from Aaron Monceca…," *The American Magazine and Historical Chronicle*, September 1743, 25.

5. James Tyler and Paul Sparks, *The Guitar and Its Music from the Renaissance to the Classical Era* (Oxford: Oxford University Press, 2002), 193.

6. Thomas Ashe, *Travels in America Performed in 1806, for the Purpose of Exploring the Rivers Alleghany, Monongahela, Ohio, and Mississippi, and Ascertaining the Produce and Condition of Their Banks and Vicinity* (London: R. Phillips, 1808), V. III, 118. The book was known in America, and was reviewed in the popular press. See, for example, the review in *Select Reviews and Spirit of the Foreign Magazines*, August 1810, 108—itself a reprint from the *Edinburgh Review*—which quotes the pertinent passage mentioning guitars.

7. "Chap. VI," *The New American Magazine*, April 1758, 28.

8. William Walton, *Present State of the Spanish Colonies; Including a Particular Report of Hispañola, or the Spanish Part of Santo Domingo; With a General Survey of the Settlements on the South Continent of America* (London: Longman, Hurst, Rees, Orme, and Brown, 1810). Quoted in "Anecdotes of the Mexicans, Including a Description of Mexico, Its Lakes, &c.," *The Analectic Magazine*, June 1813, 493.

9. Substituting "hippies" for the Mexican women, the description rings as true for the conservative, 1950s American mindset surrounding the incitement to "sex, drugs, and rock & roll" that guitars played in the counterculture 160 years later.

10. "Harp and Spanish Guitar," *The Villager, A Literary Paper*, V. 1, No. 5 (June 1819), 76. "The subjoined remarks are from the *London Literary Gazette*."

11. The guitar excelled in this regard as a conveyor of the romance of nature because of its portability into outdoor settings, whereas the piano, for example, remained homebound.

12. See, for example, Frederic V. Grunfeld, *The Art and Times of the Guitar* (New York: Da Capo, 1974); *La Guitarra Espanola; The Spanish Guitar: Catalogue of the Spanish Guitar Exhibition, The Metropolitan Museum of New York & Museo Municipal de Madrid, 1991-1992* (Madrid: Opera Tres, 1993); Alexander Bellow, *The Illustrated History of the Guitar* (Rockville Centre, New York: Franco Colombo Publications, 1970); Tom Evans and Mary Anne Evans, *Guitars: Music, History, Construction and Players from the Renaissance to Rock* (New York: Paddington Press,1977); James Westbrook, *The Century That Shaped the Guitar* (Hove, E. Sussex: Crisps Litho., 2005); and Nick Freeth and Charles Alexander, *The Acoustic Guitar* (Philadelphia: Courage Books, 1999).

13. Perhaps the singular academic study is by Tamara Elena Livingston, "'Strike the Light Guitar': The Guitar and Domestic Music-Making in America, 1750-1850" (Master's thesis, University of Illinois, 1992). Some general statements hereafter may be attributed to her scholarship.

14. Regarding the vast difference between the "English guitar" and Spanish guitar, one historian notes, "These two

distinct instruments share no characteristics other than the fact that each has plucked or strummed strings stretched across a wooden body and a fretted neck." Jeffrey J. Noonan, *The Guitar in America* (Jackson, Mississippi: University Press of Mississippi, 2008), 10.

15. Doc Rossi, "Citterns and Guitars in Colonial America," in Monika Lustig, ed., *Gitarre und Zister: Bauweise, Spieltechnik un Geschichte bis 1800. 22. Musikinstrumentenbau-Symposium 2001* (Dossel, Germany: Stiftung Kloster Michaelstein and Verlag Janos Stekovics, 2004), 155–168.

16. Barbara Lambert, ed., *Music in Colonial Massachusetts 1630–1820* (Boston: The Colonial Society of Massachusetts, 1985), Vol. II, *Music in Homes and in Churches*, 460.

17. Sébastien de Brossard, *Dictionaire de Musique* (Paris: Ballard, 1703). Quoted in Sean Ferguson, *The Guitar Before 1900: What the Dictionaries Reveal*, Guitar Foundation of America, GFA Refereed Monographs 1, 2011. Kindle Edition.

18. Laurence Libin, "The Spanish Guitar; La Guitarra Española," in *La Guitarra Espanola; The Spanish Guitar: Catalogue of the Spanish Guitar Exhibition, The Metropolitan Museum of New York & Museo Municipal de Madrid, 1991-1992* (Madrid: Opera Tres, 1993), 18. For example, newspaper advertisements mention Spanish guitars made in Naples (*New York Evening Post*, 1825), and "a large assortment of Spanish Guitars…from the best French and German makers" ("James L. Hewitt," *Morning Courier and New-York Enquirer*, New York, May 23, 1830).

19. Rossi, 158.

20. *Commercial Regulations of the Foreign Countries With Which the Unites States Have Commercial Intercourse, Collected, Digested and Printed, Under the Direction of the President of the United States, Conformably to a Resolution of the Senate, of the 3rd of March, 1817* (Washington: Gales & Seaton, 1819), 308, 331.

21. "Signor Pucci," *Salem Gazette*, August 15, 1815.

22. Mateo Aleman, *The Life of Guzman D'Alfarache: Or, The Spanish Rogue* (London: Printed for R. Bonwick, et. al., 1708), Book II, Part I, Chap. IV, 267.

23. *New York Gazette*, November 12, 1764, 3.

24. O. G. Sonneck, *Early Concert-Life in America, 1731-1800* (Leipzig: Breitkopf & Härtel, 1907), 130.

25. *New England Palladium*, October 27, 1815.

26. H. Earle Johnson, *Musical Interludes in Boston 1795-1830* (New York: Columbia University Press, 1943), 295.

27. "Church, Chamber, and Barrel Organ…," (Advertisement), *The Euterpeiad; or, Musical Intelligencer, and Ladies Gazette*, V. 1, No. 3 (April 15, 1820), 12.

28. As early as 1732, the guitar is described as, "…used especially by Spanish ladies (thus the word *Spagnuola* is often used to describe it)." Johann Gottfried Walther, *Musikalisches Lexicon* (Leipzig: Deer, 1732). This gender distinction carries over through English culture into North America where, "The guitar, like the piano, was not an orchestral instrument and therefore was an acceptable instrument for women to play." Deborah L. Nolan, "The Contributions of Nineteenth-Century Women to Guitar Performance, Composition, and Pedagogy" (Master's thesis, California State University, Fullerton, 1983), 10.

29. Robert E. Riegel, *Young America 1830-1840* (Westport, Connecticut: Greenwood Press, 1949), 367. While girls learned to play the piano as parlor accompaniment, "men preferred the violin and the flute." Pianos became more prominent in the parlor when "in 1837 Chickering patented the first practical frame for an upright" (p. 368). "The twenty years between the panics of 1837 and 1857 saw an unparalleled prosperity…Economic conditions…allowed more families to buy pianofortes, if not pianofortes then melodeons, if not melodeons then guitars—and if not guitars, then certainly sheet music for singing; since after all, most popular songs could be bought for twenty-five cents a copy." Carl Bode, *Antebellum Culture* (Carbondale, Illinois: Southern Illinois University Press, 1970 reprint of 1959 edition), 20. In 1830, there was a new piano for every 4,800 persons, while by 1860 there was a new piano for every 1,500. Bode, 20.

30. "The spread of home music making in America belonged to a larger trend in the early 1800s, which saw a growing middle class embrace ideals of refinement and gentility. More and more families set aside a room in their house for activities separate from the workaday world: for reading, conversation, games and music." " In transforming their homes into artistic statements of sorts, women lavished special attention on the parlor." Richard Crawford, *America's Musical Life.* (New York: W. W. Norton, 2001), 221, 236.

31. Tamara Elena Livingston, "Strike the Light Guitar: The Guitar and Domestic Music-Making in America, 1750-1850" (Master's thesis, University of Illinois, 1992), 125.

32. *Ibid.*, 128.

33. "After a modest beginning and a gradual expansion in the eighteenth and early years of the nineteenth centuries, music publishing in America grew steadily and at an accelerating rate. To the 26 publishing houses founded before 1820, 20 new firms were added before the end of the decade, 31 between 1830 and 1839, 37 between 1840 and 1849,

and 66 between 1850 and 1861." James H. Stone, "The Merchant and the Muse: Commercial Influences on American Popular Music before the Civil War," *Business History Review,* V. 30, N. 1 (March 1956), 5. While production of sheet music was "no more than 600 pieces between 1787 and 1800, the trade by the late 1820s was turning out that many titles per year, growing to 1,600 annually in the early 1840s and 5,000 in the early 1850s." Richard Crawford, *America's Musical Life* (New York: W. W. Norton, 2001), 232. "1841 through 1860 saw an immense increase in the parlor-song public." "In the 1840s, accounts of laborers, factory workers and members of farm families who perform parlor songs increase greatly." Nicholas E. Tawa, *Sweet Songs for Gentle Americans; The Parlor Song in America, 1790-1860* (Bowling Green, Ohio: Bowling Green University Press, 1980), 6, 21.

34. John A. Frey, "Irving, Chateaubriand, and the Historical Romance of Granada," in Stanley Brodwin, ed., *The Old and New World Romanticism of Washington Irving* (Westport, Connecticut: Greenwood Press, 1986), 91.

35. Stanley T. Williams, Vol. I, 64.

36. *Ibid.*, 94.

37. Richard L. Kagan, ed., *Spain in America: The Origins of Hispanism in the United States* (Urbana and Chicago: University of Illinois Press, 2002), 56.

38. The word "love" appears on forty-three pages, "romantic" on nineteen pages, "romance" on eleven pages, and "picturesque" on ten pages. One gets the picture.

39. Washington Irving, *The Alhambra* (Boston: Ginn and Company, 1915), 15, 66, 101, and 334, respectively.

40. Henry Wadsworth Longfellow, *Outre-Mer: A Pilgrimage Beyond the Sea* (Boston: Houghton Mifflin, 1882), Revised Edition, 233.

41. James Radomski, "Some Notes Towards the Biography of Trinidad Huerta," *Soundboard,* Vol. XXXI, No. 2/3 (2006), 39–50. See also his earlier article: James Radomski, "Trinidad Huerta y Caturla (1804–1875): First Spanish Virtuoso Guitarist to Concertize in the U.S.," *Inter-American Music Review,* Vol. 15, No. 2 (Summer/Fall 1966), 103-121.

42. Douglas Back, "Guitar on the New York Concert Stage, 1816-1890, as Chronicled by George C. D. Odell and George Templeton Strong," *Soundboard,* Vol. XXV, No. 4 (Spring, 1999), 12.

43. Javier Suárez-Pajares and Robert Coldwell, eds., *A.T. Huerta (1800-1874) Life and Works* (N.p.: DGA Editions, 2006), 5.

44. Of no small cultural significance, the first appearance of the phrase "noble savage" (often misattributed to Jean Jacques Rousseau) was in Dryden's play, *The Conquest of Granada* (1672).

45. *Op. Cit.,* 5

46. *Journal des Débats,* 16 February 1840.

47. Philip J. Bone, *The Guitar and the Mandolin* (London: Schott & Co., 1972), 173.

48. Suárez-Pajares, 20.

49. *Ibid.,* 8.

50. *National Advocate,* May 18, 1824, 2. See also Peter Danner, "Notes on Some Early American Guitar Concerts," *Soundboard,* Vol. 4, No. 1 (Feb. 1977), 8–9, 21.

51. Suárez-Pajares, 8–12.

52. *Ibid.,* 13.

53. *Ibid.,* 14.

54. *Ibid.,* 15.

55. James Westbrook, *The Century That Shaped the Guitar* (Hove, E. Sussex: James Westbrook, 2005), 132–135.

56. Tyler, 239.

57. Paul Wathen Cox, *Classic Guitar Technique and Its Evolution as Reflected in the Method Books Ca. 1770-1850* (Ph. D. dissertation, Indiana University, 1978). See also, Sharpe, 14; Westbrook, 59; and Brian Jeffery, *Fernando Sor: Composer and Guitarist* (London: Tecla Editions, 1977), 71–72.

58. Untitled article in *The Euterpeiad; An Album of Music, Poetry and Prose,* V. 2, No. 4 (June 15, 1831), 43.

59. "History of the House of Wm. A. Pond & Co.," *American Art Journal,* August 15, 1885, 267.

60. Perhaps future genealogical research may either prove or discredit any connection between the Panormo family in London and the presence of a luthier Panormo in North America.

61. "Musical," *The Literary World,* V. 10. N. 275 (May 8, 1852), 329.

62. "The Gatherer," *The Mirror of Literature, Amusement, and Instruction,* Vol. XXI, No. 601 (April 27, 1833), 272.

63. The author wishes to thank Greig Hutton for providing transcribed spreadsheets of the Martin ledgers.

64. Edwin Williams, ed., *New York As It Is, In 1834* (New York: J. Disturnell, 1834), 236. See also Virginia Larkin Redway, *Music Directory of Early New York City* (New York: New York Public Library, 1941), 26.

65. "Atwill's Piano Forte and Music Saloon" (Advertisement), *Spirit of the Times,* Vol. 5, No. 19 (May 9, 1835), 6.

66. "Atwill's Music Saloon" (Advertisement), *Workingman's Advocate,* Vol. 7, No. 10 (October 24, 1835), 4.

67. "New Music, Musical Instruments, and Musical Merchandise," *Spirit of the Times*, Vol. 6, No. 1 (Feb. 20, 1836), 3. The Martin ledger indicates that Atwill's had six Martin guitars in stock as of January 23, 1836.

68. *Baltimore Director, Corrected Up to May 1833*, 28.

69. It is of no small consequence that Geib and Walker published James Ballard's influential *The Elements of Guitar-Playing* in New York that same year.

70. The advent of steamships in the early 1840s accounted for the sharp rise in trans-Atlantic passages for touring musicians, as it cut the three to six week trip of a sailboat down to a predictable two weeks. See R. Allen Lott, *From Paris to Peoria: How European Piano Virtuosos Brought Classical Music to the American Heartland* (Oxford: Oxford University Press, 2003), 5.

71. Clara Eskine Clement, *Charlotte Cushman* (Boston: Osgood, 1882), 3. See also Katharine A. Ware, ed., *The Bower of Taste*, Vol. II (Boston: Dutton & Wentworth, 1829), 735, where Coupa is described as "teacher of the SPANISH GUITAR, and professor of the French and Italian languages" who "instructs a class of young gentlemen, at his rooms."

72. See, for example, J. B. Coupa, *Instruction Book for the Guitar: Extracted from the Latest Editions of the Best French & Italian Authors* (Boston: J. Ashton, n.d.).

73. In addition to teaching and performing, Coupa also published guitar pieces in New York in 1843, prompting a contemporary musicologist to state: "one of the best American guitar composers working before the Civil War." Peter Danner, "Two Waltzes by J. B. Coupa," *Soundboard*, Vol. XII, No. 1 (Spring, 1985), 53. "Coupa was one of the best guitar composers of the 1840s" (Back, 15); "Arguably wrote some of the best American guitar music in the 19th century." John Louis Salsini, "The Guitar and the Ideal of Femininity in Nineteenth Century America" (Master's Thesis, University of Minnesota, 1990), 66.

74. Philip F. Gura, *C. F. Martin and His Guitars 1796-1873* (Chapel Hill: University of North Carolina Press, 2003), 57, 74.

75. George C. D. Odell, *Annals of the New York Stage* (New York: Columbia University Press, 1927), Vol. IV (1834-1843), 424. A *New York Evening Post* advertisement states he is "lately from Havana."

76. *New York Evening Post*, November 6, 1839.

77. Benedid left the New York scene late in 1844 for Venezuela. There, according to newspaper accounts, he gave concerts in April and May of 1845 and taught briefly before departing Caracas and disappearing from the historical record entirely. See Alejandro Bruzal, *The Guitar in Venezuela* (Saint-Nicolas, Quebec, Canada: Doberman-Yppan, 2005), 47–49.

78. Back, 16.

79. Mariano Soriano Fuertes, *Historia de la Musica Espanola Desde la Venida de los Fenicios Hasta el Ano de 1850* (Madrid: Martin y Salazar, 1855). Domingo Prat's authoritative and famous *Diccionario de Guitarristas* (Buenos Aires: Romero y Fernandez, 1930) quotes the entry on Benedid almost verbatim.

80. Luis F. Leal Pinar, *Guitarreros de Andalucía* (Sevilla, Spain: Giralda, 2004), 183-184.

81. José L. Romanillos and Marian Harris Winspear, *The Vihuela de Mano and The Spanish Guitar* (Guijosa: Sanguino Press, 2002), 36.

82. José L. Romanillos, *Antonio de Torres, Guitar Maker: His Life and Work* (Longmead, Shaftesbury, Dorset: Element Books, 1987), 143.

83. "Sig. Benedid's Concert," *The Albion, a Journal of News, Politics and Literature*, Vol. 2, No. 17 (April 29, 1843), 210.

84. Vera Brodsky Lawrence, *Strong on Music: The New York Music Scene in the Days of George Templeton Strong: Volume I: Resonances, 1836-1849* (Chicago: University of Chicago Press, 1988), 223.

85. *Brother Jonathan*, April 29, 1843, 496.

86. Henri Fleury, ed., *La Chronique de Champagne* (Paris: Techener, 1837), Volume II, 449.

87. Lawrence, 96.

88. "Weekly List of New Publications," *Musical World*, June 16, 1837, 16.

89. "Mme. Castelli & Mr. Sedlatzek beg to announce that their Annual Concert …," *Musical World*, June 25, 1840, 408.

90. Stephen C. Massett, *Drifting About* (New York: Carleton, 1863), 27.

91. Andrew R. Hilen, ed., *The Letters of Henry Wadsworth Longfellow: Volume II, 1837-1843* (Cambridge, Massachusetts: Belknap Press, 1966), 378.

92. James Eliott Cabot, *A Memoir of Ralph Waldo Emerson* (Boston: Houghton Mifflin, 1888), Vol. 2, 470-471.

93. "Probably the most outstanding music education to be found in any seminary before 1830 was at the Moravian Seminary in Bethlehem, Pennsylvania, one of the earliest schools for girls in the country." Judith Tick, *American Women Composers Before 1870* (Rochester: University of Rochester Press, 1995), 42.

94. Jewel A. Smith, *Music, Women, and Pianos in Antebellum Bethlehem, Pennsylvania: The Moravian Young Ladies' Seminary* (Bethlehem, Pennsylvania: Lehigh University Press, 2008), 171.

95. Rufus A. Grider, *Historical Notes on Music in*

Bethlehem, Pennsylvania, from 1741 to 1871 (Philadelphia: J. Hill Martin, 1873), 37.

96. James Ballard, *History of the Guitar: From the Earliest Antiquity to the Present Time* (New York: W. B. Tilton, 1855), 21-22. Martin's ledgers indicate that Ballard was purchasing guitars from Martin in the 1830s.

97. Quoted in *Albany Journal,* Vol. 15, No. 4250 (March 22, 1844).

98. One reviewer notes of De Goni that, "She acquired her beautiful art in Andalusia, among whose fragrant groves and enameled fields the guitar is, in a manner, native." (*Daily National Intelligencer*, February 23, 1843). Fan-braced guitars originated in Andalusia, and it is likely that De Goni learned on such instruments and concertized on them when she arrived in New York prior to meeting Martin.

99. All information obtained from George C. D. Odell, *Annals of the New York Stage* (New York: Columbia University Press, 1927), Vol. IV (1834-1843) and Vol. V (1843-1850). Verified or corrected by notices in the *New York Evening Post* and other newspaper sources.

100. *The Albion, a Journal of News, Politics, and Literature*, February 15, 1840, 55.

101. *Ibid.*, May 27, 1843, 266. In 1844 Ernst published sheet music to "Old Dan Tucker: A Celebrated Ethiopian Ballad Arranged for the Spanish Guitar by Philip Ernst" (New York: C. G. Christman, 1844), thus solidifying its reputation as the first 'crossover hit' by adapting the popular minstrel song for Spanish guitar.

102. Nancy Groce, *Musical Instrument Makers of New York: A Directory of Eighteenth- and Nineteenth-Century Urban Craftsmen* (Stuyvesant, New York: Pendragon Press, 1991) 107, 137.

103. Philip F. Gura, *Manufacturing Guitars for the American Parlor: James Ashborn's Wolcottville, Connecticut, Factory, 1851-56* (Worcester, Massachusetts: American Antiquarian Society, 1994), 119.

104. *Ibid.*, 155.

105. Gura, 2003, 113.

106. Gura, 1994, 119.

107. Before 1846, it should be noted that the firm sold only imported guitars. See "History of the House of Wm. A. Pond & Co.," *American Art Journal.* August 15, 1885, 267.

108. "Firth, Hall & Pond's" (Advertisement), *Yankee Doodle.* V. 1, N. 1 (Oct. 10, 1846), 12.

109. James Ashborn, *Account Book, 1851-1856.* Collection of the American Antiquarian Society, Worcester, Massachusetts.

110. Back, 17. See also Jeff Noonan, "A Desirable and Fashionable Instrument," *Nylon Review (The Official Newsletter of the New York City Classical Guitar Society)*, March 1, 2008.

111. Charles H. Haswell, *Reminiscences of an Octogenarian of the City of New York (1816-1860)* (New York: Harper & Brothers, 1897), 446.

112. Peter Danner, "The Guitar in 19th Century America: A Lost Social Tradition," *Soundboard*, Vol. XII, No. 3 (Fall, 1985), 297.

113. Paul Sparks, *The Classical Mandolin* (Oxford: Clarendon Press, 1995), 23–29.

114. See George S. Kanahele, *Hawaiian Music and Musicians: An Illustrated History* (Honolulu: University Press of Hawaii, 1979); Lorene Ruymar, *The Hawaiian Steel Guitar and Its Great Hawaiian Musicians* (Anaheim Hills, California: Centerstream, 1996); Jim Tranquada and John King, "A New History of the Origins and Development of the 'Ukulele, 1838–1915," *The Hawaiian Journal of History*, Volume 37 (2003), 1–32.

115. All percentages are derived from statistics in Richard Johnston, Dick Boak, and Mike Longworth, *Martin Guitars: A Technical Reference* (New York: Hal Leonard, 2009).

116. John Huber, *The Development of the Modern Guitar* (Westport, Connecticut: Bold Strummer, 1994), 2. For additional information regarding the development of the contemporary classical guitar, see also José L. Romanillos, *Antonio de Torres, Guitar Maker: His Life and Work* (Longmead, Shaftesbury, Dorset: Element Books, 1987); José Ramirez, *Things About the Guitar* (Madrid: Soneto, 1993); *The Classical Guitar: A Complete History* (San Francisco: Miller Freeman, 1997); Sheldon Urlik, *A Collection of Fine Spanish Guitars from Torres to the Present* (Commerce, California: Sunny Knoll, 1997); and José L. Romanillos and Marian Harris Winspear, *The Vihuela de Mano and The Spanish Guitar* (Guijosa: Sanguino Press, 2002).

117. Havelock Ellis, *The Soul of Spain* (Boston: Houghton Mifflin, 1937), xv-xvi.

118. This is beautifully exemplified by an order for a guitar received May 23, 1838, which in the Martin ledger specifies, "*Patent screws three on a side* are greatly preferred both to the scroll head where they are all on one side, and the pegs which are sometimes used."

119. See, for example, Evans, 235, and Jim Washburn and Richard Johnston, *Martin Guitars: An Illustrated Celebration of America's Premier Guitarmaker* (Emmaus, Pennsylvania: Rodale Press, 1997), 35.

120. Washburn and Johnston, 38-39.

121. Gura, 2003, plate 3–15.

122. *Ibid.*, plate 3-16.

123. The author is indebted to David LaPlante for suggesting Gerard, Lacote, and Roudhloff.

124. Back, 15.

125. "Spanish Guitar Repository" (Advertisement), *The Anglo American, a Journal of Literature, News, Politics, Drama, Fine Arts, Etc., Vol. 5, No. 21* (September 13, 1845), 501.

126. Additionally, the great American poet Walt Whitman reported having purchased a guitar in Brooklyn in 1850.

127. "The Spanish Guitar," *The Kaleidoscope*, May 4, 1824, 372.

128. *Ibid.*, 293-294.

129. John Louis Salsini, *The Guitar and the Ideal of Femininity in Nineteenth Century America* (Master's thesis, University of Minnesota, 1990), 31.

130. In mid-nineteenth century North American culture, "Female musicians were idealized as 'angels' or as pure and virtuous paragons of womanhood." Judith Tick, *American Women Composers Before 1870* (Rochester: University of Rochester Press, 1995), 22.

131. "Spanish Minstrels," *Ballou's Pictorial*, Vol. XI, No. 17 (October 25, 1856), 1.

132. Hilen, 378. Letter dated January 19, 1842.

133. *Loc. cit.* Letter dated January 21, 1842.

134. *New York Herald,* May 29, 1842.

135. *The Giulianiad*, Vol. 1, 1833.

136. "Much of the anxiety persons felt was more subtle and psychological, stemming from the vague notion that somehow technological progress was antithetical to the romantic values of nature." Douglas T. Miller, *The Birth of Modern America 1820-1850* (New York: Pegasus, 1970), 86.

CHAPTER 5. THE CADIZ GUITAR AND ITS INFLUENCE ON C. F. MARTIN

1. José L Romanillos,, "Descriptiones Téchnicas de la Guitarras," in *La Guitarra Española; The Spanish Guitar: Catalogue of the Spanish Guitar Exhibition, The Metropolitan Museum of New York & Museo Municipal de Madrid, 1991-1992.* (Madrid: Opera Tres, 1993), 184. "Harmonic bar: Reinforcement bar glued on the inside of the soundboard in a transverse direction."

2. *Ibid.*, 184. "Plantilla: The outline shape of the body of the guitar regardless of the dimensions."

3. See Profile 19.

4. Research by Greig Hutton in the C. F. Martin & Co. Archives.

5. José L. Romanillos and Marian Harris Winspear, *The Vihuela de Mano and The Spanish Guitar.* (Guijosa: Sanguino Press, 2002), 283-284. "The surname is also found written as Page, Pagez, Pajé, Pajes, Pajez or Paxes."

6. *La Guitarra Española; The Spanish Guitar: Catalogue of the Spanish Guitar Exhibition, The Metropolitan Museum of New York & Museo Municipal de Madrid, 1991-1992.* (Madrid: Opera Tres, 1993), 114.

7. *Ibid.*, 118.

8. *Ibid.*, 120.

9. See profiles 11, 16, 17, and 18. All have three fan braces and are among the first known Spanish-influenced guitars by C. F. Martin Sr.

10. This arrangement is seen in guitars made by Heinrich Schatz before, during, and after his working association with C. F. Martin Sr., but quickly disappears in Martin's guitars once Martin adopts the Spanish-style "foot."

11. *Ibid.,* 30

12. Tom Evans and Mary Anne Evans, *Guitars: Music, History, Construction and Players from the Renaissance to Rock* (New York: Paddington Press, 1977), 48.

13. *Loc. cit.*

14. See Chapter 4 by David Gansz.

15. Research by Greig Hutton in the C. F. Martin & Co. Archives.

16. *Ibid.,* Guitars with a wholesale cost of $18, $20, and $25.

17. José L. Romanillos and Marian Harris Winspear, *Exposition de Guitarraras Antiguas Españolas* (Provincal De Alicante), 30–36. A quick survey shows virtually all guitars built before 1850 fitted with "clavijas" (pegs).

18. See profiles 25 and 29.

19. Profiles 35 and 26 (the "De Goni" guitar) show this earliest "proto X"–brace configuration.

20. *Op. cit.,* 83. "This practice of making the backs of different species of wood was often used by eighteenth and nineteenth century guitars makers in Andalucía."

21. *Ibid.*, 124.

22. C. F. Martin Sr. also used a Vienna-style adjustable neck on many of his guitars, and the company continued to use the separate heel on their (least-expensive) guitars in styles 16, 17, and 18 until the 1890s. These necks were made of domestic birch or cherry and required a large amount of work to make the complex joints and apply the ebonized finish. This was indicative, perhaps, of the much greater cost of the imported Spanish cedar used exclusively after c.1860 for the necks of the more expensive styles 20–42.

23. Conversation with José L. Romanillos, 2007. In reference to the Spanish style of guitar construction, they are often mistakenly called "tentellones." The correct

term is "dentellones," (which in Spanish literally means "teeth"), or, alternatively, "peones."

24. "Solera" is the Spanish term for the work board on which the guitar is assembled.

25. Romanillos 1993, 185. "Blocks Supporting Bars, En forma Horqueta/Tuning fork shaped".

26. Evans, 51.

27. Research by Greig Hutton in the C. F. Martin & Co. Archives.

CHAPTER 6. C. F. MARTIN IN PENNSYLVANIA, 1838–1850: A PERIOD OF TRANSITION

1. Philip Gura, *C. F. Martin & His Guitars, 1796–1873* (Chapel Hill: University of North Carolina Press, 2003), 216-17 and nn. 74–81.

2. Despite all the surviving records from the 1830s, including details on Martin's other business partnerships and contracts, there is no record of the on-and-off-and-then-on-again Martin & Schatz partnership.

3. See Chapter 3, note 18 above.

4. See Chapter 4, 68–70.

5. See Chapter 5, 78.

6. The Martin Archives include an invoice from the 1830s showing Martin's purchase of bird's-eye maple veneers. The guitars in Profiles 16 and 17 were probably made from veneers cut from the same log, as the figure in the maple on both instruments is very similar. See Profile 6 for another bird's-eye maple Martin guitar that shows very different figure.

7. See Chapter 5.

8. *Ibid.*

9. As far as we can tell, there was never a period when all Martin guitars were constructed with two-piece sides.

10. Some retailers affixed their own labels to the inside lid of the wooden cases Martin supplied with his guitars, but since cases are often swapped this is not a very reliable reference, especially after such a long period of time.

11. See Gura, 2003, plate 3-9, and marquetry samples from C. H. Burdorf shown on pages 242–243 of this volume

12. See Chapter 7.

13. The appointments on this more deluxe Size 1 with a Martin & Schatz label match descriptions of the ivory-bound "large de Goni" models Martin sold to his dealers in the early 1850s for $26 wholesale. This model was continued as the 1-26 on Martin's first price list, which was drawn up in the late 1860s.

14. Clara's mother Emelie was born in 1835 and married a minister, Herman Julius Ruetenik.

15. From the unpublished manuscript, *Ancestral Album Comprising the Martin and Ruetenik Families, arranged by Clara E. Ruetenik-Whittaker, Cleveland, O. March 1899,* in the C. F. Martin & Co. Archives.

16. See Profiles 21and 22.

17. Letters in the C. F. Martin & Co. Archives.

CHAPTER 7. MADAME DE GONI AND THE SPANISH-AMERICAN GUITAR

1. Mike Longworth, *C. F. Martin & Co., Est. 1833: A History* (Minisink Hills, Pennsylvania: 4 Maples Press, 1988), 39 and 41.

2. Louis Paris and Henri Fleury, eds., *La Chronique de Champagne* (Reims and Paris: Techener, 1837), Volume 2, 449.

3. "Weekly List of New Publications," *The Musical World* (London), V. VI, N. LXVI (June 16, 1837), 16.

4. *The Musical World* (London), June 25, 1840, 408.

5. *Ibid.* July 9, 1840, 26.

6. "Musical—The Spanish Guitar," *The New York Herald*, Nov. 7, 1840, 2.

7. *New York Herald*, December 11, 1840.

8. Vera Brodsky Lawrence, *Strong on Music: The New York Music Scene in the Days of George Templeton Strong: Volume I: Resonances, 1836-1849* (Chicago: University of Chicago Press, 1988), 107.

9. George C. D. Odell, *Annals of the New York Stage* (New York: Columbia University Press, 1927), Vol. IV (1834-1843) and Vol. V (1843-1850).

10. "Concert of Madame De Goni," *New-York American*, December 28, 184.

11. In 1842, Atwill's was described as "a musical world in itself…The location of his establishment is one of the best in the city, and on a fine day the street before it is half-filled with carriages, and the saloon is crowded with beauty and fashion. Amateurs and professional musicians are harmoniously intermingled, and many of the visitors are doubtless attracted by the hope of there seeing the new singer or performer. A popular air is occasionally heard from some instrument, or a snatch of song, and altogether the scene is one of the most brilliant in the city." "Music Stores," *Mirror*, October 8, 1842, 327.

12. Stephen C. Massett, *Drifting About* (New York: Carleton, 1863), 27.

13. William L. Mactier, *A Sketch of the Musical Fund Society of Philadelphia* (Philadelphia: Press of Henry B. Ashmead, 1885), 22. See also: W. G. Armstrong, *A Record of the Opera in Philadelphia* (Philadelphia: Porter & Coates, 1884), 255.

14. Eliza Cope Harrison, ed., *Best Companions: Letters of Eliza Middleton Fisher and Her Mother, Mary Hering Middleton, from Charleston, Philadelphia, and*

Newport, 1839-1846 (Columbia, South Carolina: University of South Carolina Press, 2001), 205.

15. Gustave Blessner, "Don Alonzo: Spanish Dance Composed for the Piano Forte and Dedicated to Donna Dolores Navares de Goni" (Philadelphia, John F. Nunns), 1841.

16. Maud Howe Elliott, *Uncle Sam Ward and His Circle* (New York: Macmillan Company, 1938), 331. (Letter from Charles Sumner to Sam Ward, January 19, 1842).

17. Andrew R. Hilen, ed., *The Letters of Henry Wadsworth Longfellow: Volume II, 1837-1843* (Cambridge, Massachusetts: Belknap Press, 1966), 378. (Letter from Henry Wadsworth Longfellow to Sam Ward, January 19, 1842.)

18. *Loc. cit.* (Letter from by Henry Wadsworth Longfellow to Sam Ward, January 21, 1842.)

19. "Mr. Knoop's Concert," *The Musical Cabinet* (Boston), February 1842, 115.

20. Lubov Keefer, *Baltimore's Music* (Baltimore: J. H. Furst Company, 1962), 128.

21. Jewel A. Smith, *Music, Women, and Pianos in Antebellum Bethlehem, Pennsylvania: The Moravian Young Ladies' Seminary* (Bethlehem, Pennsylvania: Lehigh University Press, 2008), 171.

22. *New-York American*, August 5, 1842; *New York Herald*, August 7, 1842; *New York Herald*, October 10, 1842. The only known Canadian concert took place in Montreal. (See *New York Herald*, November 15, 1842.)

23. *Utica Daily Gazette*, August 16, 1842.

24. *Ibid.*, August 23, 1842.

25. *Op. cit.*, Keefer, 102. "The Rainers counted Margaret, Elena, and Louis with Sr. de Goni and Mr. Dounas (Oct., 1842)…"

26. *Utica Daily Gazette*, December 13, 1842.

27. James Eliott Cabot, *A Memoir of Ralph Waldo Emerson* (Boston: Houghton Mifflin, 1888), Vol. 2, 470-471.

28. *Daily National Intelligencer*, February 23, 1843, 3; *Whig*, cited in Albert Stoutamire, *Music of the Old South: Colony to Confederacy* (Rutherford, New Jersey: Fairleigh Dickinson University Press, 1972); *The Charleston Mercury*, April 22, 1843.

29. "Concerts by the Senora Dolores De Goni and Master George Knoop," *The New World*, Vol. 7, No. 20, November 18, 1843, 607. (The reviewer claims to have heard both Sor and Huerta in concert and finds De Goni has surpassed both.)

30. James Ballard, *History of the Guitar: From the Earliest Antiquity to the Present Time* (New York: W. B. Tilton, 1855), 21-22.

31. Clara Ruetenik Whittaker, "Biography of My Grandfather, Christian Frederick Martin" in *The Book of*

the *Ruetenik Family* (N.p., n.d.), 15-16. The entry is dated December 1913. Held in the Martin Archives. Copy supplied to the author by Richard Johnston. Clara was one of C. F. Martin's granddaughters.

32. Rufus A. Grider, *Historical Notes on Music in Bethlehem, Pennsylvania, from 1741 to 1871* (Philadelphia: J. Hill Martin, 1873), 37.

33. "Concert of Signora de Goni and M. Knoop," *The Anglo American*, V. 2, N. 2 (November 4, 1843), 46. (Review of a concert at the Apollo Saloon, New York, on October 27, 1843).

34. *Albany Evening Journal*, December 1843. From an advertisement placed by Albany, New York music dealer Luke Newland.

35. Variant spellings of her name were not uncommon, as she was referred to in print as De Goni, DeGony, etc.

36. Madame de Goni had departed for Cincinnati late in 1844, with no record of her ever having returned to New York. An 1844 portrait of "Senora De Goni" was painted by James Hamilton Shegogue, and exhibited at the National Academy of Design in New York. A description of it at the time states, "A clever picture executed with fidelity to the original. The composition is pleasing, the neck particularly well painted, and the instrument and accessories executed with more than usual care" ("National Academy of Design," *Knickerbocker*, Vol. 24, No. 1 [July 1844], 76). There is no known reproduction of the work, nor is the whereabouts of the original known at the time of this writing. Perhaps a future researcher might uncover it to see what guitar she is holding.

37. *New York Herald*, April 12, 1844.

38. William E. Smith and Ophia D. Smith, *A Buckeye Titan* (Cincinnati: Historical and Philosophical Society of Ohio, 1953), 209.

39. *The Atlas*, October 24, 1844.

40. Vera Brodsky Lawrence, *Strong on Music: The New York Music Scene in the Days of George Templeton Strong: Volume I: Resonances, 1836-1849* (Chicago: University of Chicago Press, 1988), 353.

41. Smith, 210.

42. The famous American songwriter Stephen Foster resided in Cincinnati from 1846-1850, and may well have attended one of her concerts.

43. Charles R. Wyrick, "Concert and Criticism in Cincinnati, 1840-1850" (Master's thesis, University of Cincinnati, 1965), 61.

44. W. G. Armstrong, *A Record of the Opera in Philadelphia* (Philadelphia: Porter & Coates, 1884), 260.

45. "Le Dilettante; Collection of Choir Pieces for the Guitar" (Cincinnati: Schatzman and Brulon).

46. "Flowers of Andalusia; A Selection of Spanish Melodies" (Baltimore: W.C. Peters, August 6, 1850).

47. "Le Troubadour; A Collection of Instrumental Guitar Music" (Boston, Oliver Ditson).

48. Ivor Mairants, *My Fifty Fretting Years* (Gateshead, Tyne and Wear: Ashley Mark Publishing, 1980), 115.

CHAPTER 8. THE SPANISH GUITAR AS ADOPTED BY JAMES ASHBORN

1. According to census figures, the population of New York City alone rose from 123,000 in 1820 to 312,000 in 1840. See Douglas T. Miller, *The Birth of Modern America 1820-1850* (New York: Pegasus, 1970), 39. See also Robert Ernst, *Immigrant Life in New York City 1825-1863* (New York: Octagon, 1979), 20.

2. This method continues into the present time in the workshop of the late José Ramirez III in Madrid, Spain. See "The Guitar and the Traditional Artisan Workshops" in José Ramirez, *Things about the Guitar* (Madrid, Soneto, 1993), 25-40.

3. Philip F. Gura, *C. F. Martin and His Guitars 1796-1873* (Chapel Hill: University of North Carolina Press, 2003), 106, 194.

4. Joseph Wickham Roe, *Connecticut Inventors* (New Haven: Yale University Press, 1934), Publications of the Tercentenary Commission of the State of Connecticut, XXXIII, 4, 7. Eli Terry "converted to his purpose an old waterpower mill and…applied power for the first time in the construction of American clocks. This use of machinery so reduced the cost of production that the selling price was cut nearly in half." Norris Gilpin Osborn, *History of Connecticut in Monographic Form* (New York: States History Company, 1925) Volume 4, 37.

5. Kenneth D. Roberts, *Eli Terry and the Connecticut Shelf Clock* (Bristol, Connecticut: Ken Roberts Publishing Co., 1973), 28.

6. Henry Terry, *American Clock Making: Its Early History* (Waterbury, Connecticut, 1870), 6. Actually, the patent for "Wheels, for wooden clocks" was dated August 22, 1814. See Edmund Burke, *List of Patents for Inventions and Designs, Issued by the United States from 1790 to 1847* (Washington, D.C.: Gideon, 1847), 187.

7. Phillip T. Young, "Asa Hopkins of Fluteville" (Master's thesis, Yale University School of Music, 1962), 34.

8. *Ibid.,* 39, quoting from Brooks Palmer, *The Book of American Clocks* (New York: Macmillan, 1950).

9. *Ibid.,* 15, 46.

10. Brooks Palmer, *The Book of American Clocks* (New York: Macmillan, 1950), 4 (quoting clock historian Penrose Hoopes).

11. Young, 27.

12. Phillip T. Young, *The Look of Music: Rare Musical Instruments 1500-1900* (Vancouver: Vancouver Museums, 1980), 144.

13. Young, 1962, 37, 39, 43.

14. Young, 1962, 57. Water wheels were constructed inside the building to prevent ice buildups during the winter months. See Kenneth T. Howell and Einar W. Carlson, *Empire Over the Dam; The Story of Waterpowered Industry, Long Since Passed from the Scene* (Chester, Connecticut: Pequot Press, 1974), 25.

15. Young, 1962, 60.

16. Harry Scrivenor, *A Comprehensive History of the Iron Trade Throughout the World* (London: Smith, Elder and Co., 1841), 396. The Litchfield land records again describe Fluteville in 1837: "…a dwelling house, barn, shops, and said manufacturing establishment, and its fixtures, machinery, tools, stoves in it and in said dwelling house, and all the furniture therein." (Young, 1962, 60).

17. *Documents Relative to the Manufactures in the United States, Collected and Transmitted to the House of Representatives in Compliance with a Resolution of Jan. 19, 1832 by the Secretary of the Treasury* (New York: Burt Franklin, 1969 reprint of 1833 original), Doc. 9, No. 1, 992-993, and Doc. 9, No. 26, 1021.

18. "Sixth Annual Fair of the American Institute of New-York, Oct. 16th to 19th, 1833," *Mechanics' Magazine and Journal of the Mechanics' Institute,* V. 2, N. 4 (Oct. 1833), 173. Additionally, "Perth (sic), Hall & Pond" are noted as having exhibited "German flutes." See also "American Institute—New York, List of Premiums Awarded by the American Institute at its Sixth Annual Fair, October, 1833," *Niles' Weekly Register,* V. 45, N. 1145, 153.

19. Iveagh Hunt Sterry and William H. Garrigus, *They Found A Way: Connecticut's Restless People* (Brattleboro, Vermont: Stephen Daye Press, 1938). See the chapter on "Yankee Pedlars" 44-45.

20. Robert E. Eliason, "Firth, Hall & Pond," in Stanley Sadie, ed., *The New Grove Dictionary of Music and Musicians* (New York: Macmillan, 1980), V. 6, 604.

21. *The New York Musical Review and Choral Advocate,* March 1, 1855, 76-77.

22. "Seventh Annual Fair of the American Institute, Held at Niblo's Gardens, October, 1834," *Mechanics' Magazine and Journal of the Mechanics' Institute, V.* 4., N. 4 (October 25, 1834), 241. Reprinted under the same title in *New York Farmer,* 1834, 81.

23. Young, 1962, 92.

24. *Loc. cit.*

25. *Ibid.,* 95.

26. Nancy Groce, *Musical Instrument Makers of New*

York: A Directory of Eighteenth- and Nineteenth-Century Urban Craftsmen (Stuyvesant, New York: Pendragon Press, 1991), 70.

27. "A Glance at the Arts in the Fair of the American Institute," *New York State Mechanic, a Journal of the Manual Arts, Trades, and Manufactures,* V. 1, N. 48, 177.

28. "The March of Trade in New-York," *The New-York Musical Review and Choral Advocate,* December 7, 1854, 424-425. Also reported (although incorrectly attributed to 1855) in Russell Sanjek, *American Popular Music and Its Business: The First Four Hundred Years: Volume II; From 1790 to 1909* (Oxford: Oxford University Press, 1988), 72. Gura cites Sanjek rather than the original.

29. It is interesting to note that, despite Asa Hopkins having died some years before guitars were made in Fluteville, Hopkins' reputed teacher, the woodwind instrument maker George Catlin (1778–1852) of Hartford, advertised himself in the year 1800 as making guitars. See William Waterhouse, *The New Langwill Index: A Dictionary of Musical Wind-Instrument Makers and Inventors* (London, Tony Bingham, 1993), 59.

30. Young, 1962, Appendix B, 128.

31. *Ibid.,* 62. The exact wording is restated in the 1837 agreement (see 78).

32. See Virginia Larkin Redway, *Music Directory of Early New York City* (New York, New York Public Library, 1941), 37; *The New York Mercantile Union Business Directory* (New York: French & Pratt, 1850), 286; Groce, 52.

33. Before 1842, it should be noted that the firm sold only imported guitars. See "History of the House of Wm. A. Pond & Co.," *American Art Journal,* August 15, 1885, 267.

34. *Second Annual Report of the American Institute, of the City of New York: Made to the Legislature for the Year 1842* (Albany: E. Mack, 1843), 92.

35. "A Glance at the Arts in the Fair of the American Institute," *The New York State Mechanic,* November 12, 1842 (V. 1, N. 51).

36. *Third Annual Report of the American Institute, of the City of New York: Made to the Legislature for the Year 1843* (Albany: E. Mack, 1844), 72.

37. "Firth & Hall" (Advertisement), *New-York Daily Tribune,* March 28, 1844 (V. III, N. 302), 1.

38. *Sheldon & Co.'s Business or Advertising Directory* (New York: John F. Trow & Company, 1845), 133.

39. "Chickering's Piana Fortes" (Advertisement), *New York Evening Post,* 1845.

40. "Firth, Hall & Pond's" (Advertisement), *Yankee Doodle.* V. 1, N. 1 (Oct. 10, 1846), 12.

41. *Catalogue of Music, Published by Firth, Hall & Pond* (New York, J. A. Fraetas, printer, 1846).

42. "Firth, Hall & Pond, No. 239 Broadway,Corner of Park Place, and Firth & Hall, No. 1 Franklin Square, New York" (Broadside advertisement), (George F. Nesbitt , printer, New York, c. 1846).

43. "Firth, Hall & Pond, No. 239 Broadway, New York" (Broadside advertisement), (New York, c. 1846).

44. *Report of the Committee of Arrangements of the First National Fair for the Exhibition of American Manufactures* (Washington, 1846), 26. Also reported in "Great National Fair," in *Fisher's National Magazine and Industrial Record* (New-York: Redwood Fisher, 1846), V. III, 175.

45. "Musical Instruments," *Niles' National Register,* V. 20, N. 17 (June 27, 1846), 269.

46. Daniel P. Tyler, *Statistics of the Condition and Products of Certain Branches of Industry in Connecticut, for the Year Ending October 1, 1845* (Hartford, Connecticut: John L. Boswell, 1846), 18.

47. "The March of Trade in New-York," *The New-York Musical Review and Choral Advocate,* December 7, 1854, 424-425.

48. Young, 1962, Appendix B, 128.

49. *Ibid.,* 98.

50. James Ashborn, Account *Book, 1851-1856.* Collection of the American Antiquarian Society, Worcester, Massachusetts.

51. Samuel Orcutt, *History of Torrington, Connecticut, from its First Settlement in 1737, with Biographies and Genealogies* (Albany: J. Munsell, 1878), 133.

52. Superior Court of Litchfield, Connecticut, Volume 1, 18.

53. Lorraine Cook White, gen. ed., *The Barbour Collection of Connecticut Town Vital Records* (Baltimore: Genealogical Publishing, 2002), V. 47 (Torrington 1740-1850), 2. See also Orcutt, 288.

54. "DCM 1424: Firth Hall & Pond / Flute in C.," The Dayton C. Miller Flute Collection, Library of Congress, Washington, D.C.

55. Julia Booth is the first known and named female guitar maker in the historical record.

56. See Orcutt, 10–104. Seven years younger than Ashborn, Austin Hungerford is described in the 1850 Torrington Census as a 26 year-old "Manufacturer," living at home with his parents. Little else is known of Hungerford, other than the fact that, in 1837 (at the age of thirteen), he was attending a college-preparatory boarding school in Ohio. See *Catalogue of the Officers and Students of the Western Reserve College January, 1837* (Hudson, Ohio: James Lowry, printer, 1837) 7.

57. Gura, xiv.

58. Daniel Haskel and J. Calvin Smith, *A Complete Descriptive and Statistical Gazetteer of the United States of America* (New York: Sherman and Smith, 1843), 660. The actual census of 1840 in Wolcottville counted 1,707 persons. ("Census of Connecticut," *The Monthly Chronicle of Events, Discoveries, Improvements, and Opinion,* October, 1840).

59. "The eastern branch proceeds from a small pond near Norfolk line, and runs southerly to Wolcottville, and affords good water power." John Boyd, *Annals and Family Records of Winchester, Conn.* (Hartford, Connecticut: Case, Lockwood & Brainard, 1873), 24.

60. John H. Thompson, *A History of Torrington* (Torrington, Connecticut: Torrington Printing Company, 1934), 18.

61. Orcutt, 85, 133, 134.

62. *Ibid.,* 744.

63. *Ibid.,* 85-86.

64. *Ibid.,* 84-85.

65. Arthur H. Hughes, and Morse S. Allen, *Connecticut Place Names* (Hartford: Connecticut Historical Society, 1976), 598.

66. "Piano Fortes" (Advertisement), *The Message Bird: A Literary and Musical Journal.* V. 1, N. 5 (October 1, 1849), 84.

67. "The water wheel constructed almost entirely of wood was the one great motive power which built early American industries." Kenneth T. Howell and Einar W. Carlson, *Empire Over the Dam; The Story of Waterpowered Industry, Long Since Passed from the Scene* (Chester, Connecticut: Pequot Press, 1974), 25. Ashborn's account book shows payments for occasional repairs to the dam and water wheel.

68. Gura, xiv. Ashborn's guitars were of Spanish design (using three fan braces under the top), featuring a body shape very similar to that used by the Panormo family of luthiers in London during the two decades before Ashborn. Firth, Hall & Pond may well have utilized a Panormo instrument on which to model their own, as they were known to have sold a Panormo guitar as early as 1831. See the untitled article in *The Euterpeiad; An Album of Music, Poetry and Prose*, V. 2, No. 4 (June 15, 1831), 43.

69. *Ibid.*, 118.

70. M. E Bruné, "James Ashborn: Innovative Entrepreneur," *Vintage Guitar*, April 2005, 100. The author goes on to note that Ashborn's method of factory production was the precursor to "other companies such as Martin, Gibson, and Taylor" (104).

71. Philip F. Gura, *Manufacturing Guitars for the American Parlor: James Ashborn's Wolcottville, Connecticut, Factory, 1851-56* (Worcester, Massachusetts: American Antiquarian Society, 1994), 71. "In the years from 1830 to 1850 there were, roughly, three classes of labor; the proprietors actively engaged in the management, the English mechanics, and native helpers. By 1850 the supplanting of the English mechanics by American workmen who had either been taught or had by themselves developed skill had been generally accomplished." William Gilbert Lathrop, *The Brass Industry in the United States; A Study of the Origin and the Development of the Brass Industry in the Naugatuck Valley and Its Subsequent Extension Over the Nation* (New York: Arno Press, 1972, reprint of 1926 revised edition), 95.

72. Gura, 2003, 106, 194.

73. Gura, 1994, 125.

74. See Gura, 1994, 133, and Jim Washburn and Richard Johnston, *Martin Guitars: An Illustrated Celebration of America's Premier Guitarmaker* (Emmaus, Pennsylvania: Rodale Press, 1997), 54.

75. Washburn and Johnston, 42.

76. *Charter of the Naugatuck Railroad Company, Together with Statistical Facts Respecting its Prospective Business and Present Situation* (New Haven: J. H. Benham, 1848), 3. The Naugatuck Railroad Company was organized in February of 1848 (see Orcutt, 185).

77. "Railroads on the Eastern Side of the Hudson River, Now Constructing or in Contemplation, and Connecting with the City of New York," *The American Quarterly Register and Magazine,* V. 1, N. 2 (September 1848), 388. "More than twice as much New England mileage was completed in 1848 and 1849 than in all the years from 1843 through 1847." Albert Fishlow, *American Railroads and the Transformation of the Ante-Bellum Economy* (Cambridge, Massachusetts: Harvard University Press, 1965), 248.

78. "Naugatuck Railroad: On Arrival of Trains from New York," *American Railway Times,* V. 1, N. 72 (December 11, 1849), 3.

79. Thompson, 17.

80. Alain C. White, *The History of the Town of Litchfield, Connecticut 1720-1920* (Litchfield, Connecticut: Enquirer Print, 1920), 209; Orcutt, 187; Lathrop, 1972, 83; John Boyd, *Annals and Family Records of Winchester, Conn.* (Hartford, Connecticut: Case, Lockwood & Brainard, 1873), 438.

81. Thompson, 17; Sidney Withington, *The First Twenty Years of Railroads in Connecticut* (New Haven: Published for the Tercentenary Commission by the Yale University Press, 1935), 26; Gura, 2003, 114.

82. "The report of 1832, published by the federal government, estimated that three-quarters of the manufactured product of Connecticut found its market in New York, Philadelphia, Boston, Providence, and Baltimore. From those cities it was distributed to the interior or exported. When commercial connections of this kind were established, the Connecticut manufacturer could divest himself of the responsibility for seeking out the ultimate consumer of his wares." Clive Day, *The Rise of Manufacturing in Connecticut, 1820-1850* (New Haven: Yale University Press, 1935), Publications of the Tercentenary Commission of the State of Connecticut, XLIV, 15.

83. Orcutt, 187.

84. At the northern end of the line, in Winsted, the clockmaker William L. Gilbert (who would later hire the former Fluteville manager—and, by then his son-in-law—Isaac B. Woodruff, to manage his clock factory) heavily supported the railroad. Similarly, in Thomaston (immediately south of Fluteville), the prosperous clock-maker Seth Thomas—after whom the town was named—pledged $15,000 to the railroad, at it would greatly benefit shipment of his wares also (Orcutt, 187).

85. Kenneth T. Howell, and Einar W. Carlson, *Empire Over the Dam; The Story of Waterpowered Industry, Long Since Passed from the Scene* (Chester, Connecticut: Pequot Press, 1974), 18.

86. *New York Post* advertisement.

87. *Morning Courier & Enquirer.*

88. *New-York Daily Tribune*, March 28, 1844.

89. *The Message Bird: A Literary and Musical Journal,* V. 1, No. 5 (October 1, 1849).

90. "Musical," *The Literary World,* V. 10, N. 275 (May 8, 1852), 329.

91. See, for example, "William Hall & Son Guitars" (Advertisement), *The Musical World and Journal of the Fine Arts,* V. III, N. 13 (March 1, 1852), 190. The identical advertisement appears one month later in another journal: "William Hall & Son Guitars" (Advertisement), *The Literary World,* V. 10, N. 271 (April 10, 1852), 257. See also, *New Catalogue of Music at the Reduced Prices, Published by William Hall & Son* (New York, G.F. Nesbitt, printer, 1855), 7. (The sole extant copy resides at Harvard University). Essentially the same text is reproduced as "Hall's Guitars" (Advertisement), *New York Musical Review and Gazette,* June 16, 1855, 202. The ad ran in issues through July 14, 1855. Martin's 1856 wholesale prices for their guitars ranged from $17 to $42, up to double the price of an Ashborn (see Washburn & Johnston, 54). Remarkably, Ashborn was able to keep his wholesale prices the same from 1851–1856.

92. A letter in the Martin Archives reveals that, a year later, on June 18, 1856, Firth, Pond & Co. wrote to C. F. Martin & Co. hoping to make an arrangement with Martin to carry his guitars, because they no longer were carrying Ashborn's instruments.

93. "New Arrangement of Styles and Numbers, Great Improvement in Hall's Guitars" (Advertisement), *New York Musical Review and Gazette,* August 11, 1855, 280. The same advertisement appears as "New Arrangement of Styles and Numbers, Great Improvement in Hall's Guitars" (Advertisement), *New York Musical World*, Vol. 14, No. 249 (January 5, 1856). See also the expanded ad in *New York Musical World*, March 8, 1856, 120.

94. "Hall's Guitars, Already Unsurpassed in Tone and Durability" (Advertisement), *The Musical World*, October 29, 1859, 12.

95. "Musical Novelties To Be Had at the Music Store of William Hall & Son" (Advertisement), *New York Musical World*, March 8, 1856, 120.

96. Washburn and Johnston, 259.

97. See, for example, 1861-1862 advertisements in such obscure newspapers as the *Corrector* (Sag Harbor, New York, located on eastern Long Island), and the *Republican Watchman* (Monticello, New York, in the Catskill mountains).

98. *The Connecticut Register* (Hartford: Brown & Gross, 1865), 27; Orcutt, 267; Gura, 1994, 122.

99. "Accordeons from $3" (Wm. A. Pond & Co. advertisement), *Harper's Weekly*, March 12, 1864, 174.

100. Orcutt, 86; Dave Hunter, *Acoustic Guitars: An Illustrated Encyclopedia* (San Diego: Thunder Bay Press, 2003), 18; Michael Wright, "Ca. 1855 James Ashborn Model 2," *Vintage Guitar*, December, 2002, 100; Gura, 1994, 122. Ashborn's decision to close the guitar factory was, doubtless, aided by the prevailing economic climate in Wolcottville in 1863. "At that time Wolcottville was in a state of almost unbroken sleep, if not approaching decay, property of every description being at its lowest mark. Almost every manufacturing enterprise in and around the village had closed, and several had closed in bankruptcy; the woolen mill and brass mill held on, but the latter held by doing almost nothing" (Orcutt, 602).

101. Gura 2003, 116; see also Gura 1994, 128.

102. Connecticut General Assembly, *Roll of State Officers and Members of General Assembly of Connecticut from 1776 to 1881* (Hartford, Connecticut: Press of the Case, Lockwood & Brainard Co., 1881), 393.

103. Orcutt, 86.

104. *Ibid.,* 107; Thompson, 18; *History of Litchfield County, Connecticut, with Illustrations and Biographical Sketches of its Prominent Men and Pioneers* (Philadelphia: J. W. Lewis & Co., 1881), 636.

105. Edwin M. Lieberthal, *Progress Through Precision: The First 125 Years at the Torrington Company* (Torrington, Connecticut: The Torrington Company, 1992), 13.

106. "Estate of Jas. Ashborn / His Last Will & Testament," Vol. 4, 465-456, Litchfield County, Connecticut.

107. *Wolcottville, Conn.* (Boston: O. H. Bailey, c. 1875).

108. "Ashburn," *Wolcottville Register*, Vol. III, No. 20 (December 16, 1876).

109. "Report of the Tariff Commission, Appointed Under Act of Congress, Approved May 15, 1882," in *Index to the Miscellaneous Documents of the House of Representatives for the Second Session of the Forty-Seventh Congress, 1882-1883* (Washington: Government Printing Office, 1883), 365-366.

110. An engineering innovator, Ashborn received U.S. Patents for a unique *capo de astra* in 1850, and improved traditional friction (i.e. violin-style) tuning pegs of a higher ratio in 1852. Furthermore, he capitalized on the minstrel banjo craze and produced banjos of a very high quality in the 1850s, now much sought after by collectors.

111. See Gura, 1994, 133, and Jim Washburn and Richard Johnston, *Martin Guitars: An Illustrated Celebration of America's Premier Guitarmaker* (Emmaus, Pennsylvania: Rodale Press, 1997), 54.

112. Gura, 2003, 123.

113. Bernard DeVoto, *The Year of Decision, 1846* (Boston: Houghton Mifflin, 1943), 218-219.

114. Norris Galpin Osborn, *History of Connecticut in Monographic Form* (New York: States History Company, 1925), Volume 4, 89.

CHAPTER 9. C. F. MARTIN IN PENNSYLVANIA, 1850–1867: FINE TUNING

1. The last surviving letter from Coupa to Martin is dated February 7,1850, and gives no hint of any illness. (The letter is in the C. F. Martin & Co. Archives.)

2. Martin listed "winders" in a slightly later inventory, so he apparently wound strings at Cherry Hill. This practice of winding strings (gut string sets) that were sold to both wholesale and retail customers was continued into the early twentieth century. Later, Martin had its own brand of steel strings, but these were made for them, as Martin didn't make its own steel strings until it purchased a string company in the 1970s. (C. F. Martin & Co. Archives.)

3. As explained in more detail in Chapter 10, it is difficult to be certain when a particular Martin guitar was constructed, and the models shown in Profiles 33 and 34 may be earlier than 1850. The one with a Martin & Coupa label

was almost certainly constructed before Coupa's death, but as the paper labels are tightly glued in and neatly aligned, it seems likely that those labels were affixed during construction, so at least some guitars with Martin & Coupa labels may have been sold after Coupa's death.

4. Martin Archives. The pricing mentioned in C. F. Jr.'s notes suggests that the guitar sold to John Heath was similar in cost to the "Lula" and "Crystal Palace" guitars described in Martin's ledgers just a few years later.

5. Madame de Goni performed at the first Niblo's Garden, which was destroyed by fire in September 1846. It was enlarged and rebuilt, opening again in the summer of 1849, and C. F. Martin Jr. was apparently attending shows there about a year later, by which time Niblo's was even offering Italian opera. In 1866, it staged *The Black Crook*, which many historians consider to be the first musical comedy, making Niblo's an important venue in the history of what we now call "the Broadway musical."

6. Hope's Express carried many of the shipments to New York City in the early 1850s, but Martin used a number of different shipping companies as his web of retailers expanded. Adams Express Company, for instance, was often chosen for deliveries to dealers in the Ohio and Mississippi River valleys. Most cities were served by more than one shipping company, and dealers were evidently allowed to choose which shipper they preferred. This choice was recorded next to the dealer's name in Martin's ledgers, and the logistical nightmare of making so many-different shipping arrangements probably contributed to Martin's later decision to have most of his sales handled by a New York distributor, such as Zoebisch & Sons.

7. Philip F. Gura, *C. F. Martin and His Guitars 1796-1873* (Chapel Hill: University of North Carolina Press, 2003), 98–101, "Meeting Obligations in the Market Economy."

8. It is curious that during the early 1850s, the lowest Martin models were given the black-stained neck, as were the highest models (those with a wholesale cost of $30 or more), but guitars in the middle price range were always given cedar necks. By later in the decade, black-stained necks with the cone-shaped heel rarely appear on higher models, and once the "Vienna screws" (Stauffer) headstock was abandoned, only Martin's least expensive models would continue to get the black neck. The 10-string guitar shown in Profile 38 is an exception to this rule, but there may have been other exceptions as well.

9. The much smaller size 5 terz was also available, but was rarely ordered at this time, and there were other sizes such as 3½ that are seldom seen in the ledgers

10. In letters from Zoebisch to Martin, he refers to suppliers in Markneukirchen by name in very familiar

terms. Both Zoebisch's sons and Bruno's son, traveled back to Martin's old hometown in Saxony on business, and both the Zoebisch and Bruno firms imported and sold a wide range of musical instruments and accessories from that region.

11. We do not know the inspiration for this early harp-guitar form, but it was only early for a North American example. Since Olaf Ericson was almost certainly Swedish, the similar "Swedish lute" may have been what he was trying to emulate. But there were other guitars with extra bass strings being made in Europe, and Freidrich Schenk, also a disciple of Stauffer, was making larger and more elaborate versions as early as the 1830s. It is possible that Martin was aware of these other guitars with extra bass strings before Olaf Ericson requested one.

CHAPTER 10. MARTIN'S EVOLUTION TO AN AMERICAN GUITAR

1. Even when letters from Martin's primary sales agent have survived, they do not reveal any discussion of changing or modifying anything about the guitars being ordered except string action, which Coupa described as "hard to play"(higher string action) or "easy to play" (lower string action). A few letters from Coupa to Martin dated 1849 and early 1850 suggest that after a decade of doing business together, the two men had developed a kind of code that allowed Coupa to describe what he wanted in few words, often including little more than the price. In several of these letters, Coupa's most common phrase, after stating the price, is "the same as the last," or "the same as before," so he was apparently repeating earlier orders of guitar styles that Martin had already standardized. Differences from his usual requests, however, would be noted, as in February of 1850 when he asks for "1 at $18, one size larger than usual."

2. Philip F. Gura, *C. F. Martin and His Guitars 1796-1873* (Chapel Hill: University of North Carolina Press, 2003), 101

3. Martin's lowest-priced models, which became Style 17 about a decade later, were also made with solid, not individual block "dentellone" and not kerfed, linings (the support glued to the edges of the sides that reinforce the joint with the top and back of the body). Solid linings were another feature left over from the earlier Austro-German styles, and would continue to be used on Style 17 models until the late 1890s. Although these guitars continued to be given top bracing with three fans, this pattern was not quite the same as the 3-fan pattern seen in the Spanish models shown in this volume (the later Style 17 fan bracing had a transverse brace just above the

tail block and small "finger" braces on both the bass and treble sides of the outer fan braces). See page 200 in this chapter where $17 models are described.

4. In 1873, the year of C. F. Martin's death, the company sold 244 guitars, most of them to Zoebisch & Sons, and seventy-seven of that total were 2½-17 and 3-17 models. Zoebisch often ordered 2½-17 models six at a time. From Daybook, 1867–1874, C. F. Martin & Co. Archives.

5. The Spanish guitars from Cadiz that so captivated New York guitar players in the 1840s were constructed in an entirely different manner and sequence than the Austro-German style of guitar making practiced by Martin and his compatriots. Martin built a guitar's neck separately from the body, joining the neck to the body after both had been finished (with varnish or French polish). Spanish style construction, on the contrary, begins with joining the sides to the heel of the neck, as the neck heel and neck block inside the body are one and the same (there is no joint). In Spanish construction gluing the back to the sides is the last step in constructing the guitar, whereas Martin glued the back of the guitar to the sides, and then added the soundboard, to complete the body. And there were other differences in the construction sequence as well, as with Martin gluing the bridge to the soundboard was the last step, as it could only be aligned properly with the neck after the guitar's body and neck had been joined. In Spanish guitar construction, however, the bridge was usually glued to the top before the top was glued to the sides. These differences meant that many details on Spanish guitars, elements that were a natural consequence of how those instruments were constructed, were instead time-consuming obstacles for Martin. The stylistic features of Spanish guitars that could easily be incorporated into the Austro-German construction sequence, such as altering the soundhole rosette and the shapes of the guitar's body and headstock, to name just a few, were the elements that survived in what became the American style of guitar. Martin was willing to change the appearance, and the sound, of his guitars to suit demand, but not how he put them together. See Chapter 5 for more information.

6. Style 17 guitars have undergone more radical, and frequent, changes than any other of Martin's original styles. Style 17 was a mainstay throughout the nineteenth century but was not included in Frank Henry Martin's revisions that resulted in the 1898 price list. The style number was revived in 1906 for models given mahogany back and sides, then was discontinued again in 1917 when Style 18 was switched from rosewood to mahogany. Style 17 returned again in 1921 as a model made with an all-mahogany body, including the top. See Richard Johnston, Dick Boak, and Mike Longworth, *Martin Guitars: A Tech-*

nical Reference (New York: Hal Leonard, 2009), 57.

7. What we now call a "Stauffer headstock" was apparently rarely used after the late 1840s, and with few exceptions it was only used on size 2, or smaller, models. Coupa ordered a few guitars with this headstock in 1849, but once Martin's daybooks have survived, starting in 1852, there were apparently few requests for it. None were ordered in 1852, then four guitars are listed with "one-side screw" headstocks in 1853, all size 2 or 2½, and all with a wholesale cost of $34 or higher. No orders for this old-style headstock appear in following years, but some special orders do not appear in the daybooks so we should not assume that the long curved headstock disappeared completely by 1854.

8. Readers should not make the mistake of thinking that the guitars shown in this volume are representative of Martin's production in the pre–Civil War period. Ivory fingerboards and ivory-wrapped headstocks, not to mention rosettes lit like Christmas trees with pearl inlay, were always features associated with luxurious custom orders placed by wealthy customers. But such guitars have often been cherished because their quality is unmistakable, and thus have survived in good condition and are now preserved by serious collectors who were willing to lend them to this project for photography and study. Most of the plainer examples from this same period, although made in far greater numbers, have not enjoyed the same fate, and have had oversized bridges and modern tuners added because for decades they were just "little Martin parlor guitars" with low value.

9. Unfortunately, we cannot be sure what the word *Spanish* meant in these early ledger entries. In the early 1860s, the $18 models often had "Spanish," or an abbreviation, following the model code, but we can't be certain if that referred to the fan bracing or to a lingering use of the tie-block bridge (or perhaps to something else). Because such guitars are not dated, and the markings and features changed very little, assigning a date of manufacture is difficult. Is a 2-18 with tie-block bridge from the late 1840s or from the early 1860s? Everyone at Martin certainly knew what "Spanish" meant but at least for now, we do not, and we should not assume that the word "Spanish" in an 1837 Martin ledger meant the same thing that it did in a daybook entry over twenty years later.

10. Numbering systems in which a higher number indicates a smaller size apparently originated with wire, where a smaller diameter was achieved by drawing the wire more times through a drawing die. A #3 gauge wire, for example, required more passes through the drawing dies than did a #1 gauge wire.

11. For the period from 1852–1864, where daybooks covering Martin's guitar production are remarkably complete, there are only 21 size 5 terz guitars listed, with all but one of those sold in the 1850s. The sales are highly inconsistent, Martin would not sell any size 5 models for years but would then take orders for two or three from one dealer. During this period Martin also sold a couple of size 4 models which were probably also tuned as terz guitars.

12. Martin also made at least two other sizes, 3½ and 4, but less than ten combined were sold in the 1852–64 period from which daybooks have survived. Dimensions on surviving examples of size 3½ are variable, so they may have been made without specific body molds. Since size 3 is already so small, it is assumed that size 3½ was ordered for young people, probably young ladies of means, as none of the seven sold were inexpensive styles.

13. James Westbrook, *The Century That Shaped the Guitar* (Hove, E. Sussex: Crisps Litho., 2005), 169.

14. Gura, 2003, 76

15. Because Philip Gura so thoroughly covered surviving letters in the Martin Archives regarding the guitar made for the Crystal Palace exhibit (Gura, 2003, pp. 89–94), we have not repeated that information here. We also do not know what the Crystal Palace guitar looked like, and to complicate matters further, Martin entered more than one guitar in the Crystal Palace exhibition. Martin archives show a "Crystal Palace guitar rosewood polished case", with no mention of its size or appointments, being shipped May 4, 1854 to Hilbus & Hitz in Washington, DC, with a price of $160, but there are two more listings with that unique name. A size 2 Crystal Palace guitar was sold for $70 in late December, 1856, and a size 2½ Crystal Palace is shown as having been sold in November of 1859. The first listing mentions a polished rosewood case, like the one associated with the guitar in Profile 39 and shown in this volume on page 197, while there is no mention of special cases with the two later Crystal Palace entries in Martin's daybook. The three entries, with radically different prices, and two different sizes, suggests that "Crystal Palace" may have become a general description for later presentation grade Martin guitars. However because of the polished rosewood case (it is finished with French polish, the same finish Martin used on his guitars), and, because there is no mention of the size of the initial Crystal Palace guitar shipped to Hilbus & Hitz in 1854, the guitar shown as Profile 39 may be the same instrument despite the fact that its interior construction would suggest that it was made at least a few years earlier.

16. Several American guitar manufacturers later made the retail price of a new model that same guitar's model code, for instance Gibson's Super 400, introduced in 1934, at the height of the Great Depression, with a retail price of $400. Many of Gibson's models from this

period had model codes derived from the retail, or "list" price given in the catalog, including the SJ-200, and this practice was continued with several of the ES series electrics that followed. Subsequent price increases, of course, wiped out the obvious connection between price and model code. Martin revived the use of a model code derived from the retail price with its D-50 and then its D-100, but of course the list price included an additional three zeros.

17. In the early 1850s, $17 models in size 3 far outnumber size 2½ models with the same price, but that ratio would be reversed by the end of the decade.

18. Most, but not all, 1850s listings of the $26 size 1, or "large de Goni," for instance, include mention of a "pearl soundhole" (rosette). No 1-26 models with the "& Co." stamp, however, have surfaced with that feature, yet the early 1870s pricelist describes the 1-26 model as "inlaid with pearl, ivory bound." This suggests that the pricelist was describing the 1-26 as it used to be appointed, and not as it was when that list was first printed. Because of Martin's adoption of the style/price shorthand in the late 1850s, we cannot be sure about the appointments on a majority of the many 1-26 models that appear in early 1860s records in Martin's archives.

19. Martin's spruce-lined backs are quite different from the "plywood" construction we associate with inexpensive instruments, which usually have at least three layers of veneer with the middle layer's grain running at 45 or 90 degrees to the inner and outer layers. The grain of the thin inner spruce veneer in Martin's lined backs runs vertically, as does the grain of the outer hardwood veneer. This explains why those backs often display cracks, despite being made with two layers. Spruce-lined backs have been found only on models with a wholesale cost of $22 or above, and in size 2 or smaller, but at least one listing in C. F. Martin Jr.'s notes from 1850 suggest that Martin also sold size 1 models with "double back."

20. See note 6 above for a summary of the evolution of Style 17.

21. Records in the Martin Archives covering the early 1850s list a few plain rosewood models that sold for $16, but often on the same page are listings for guitars with an identical description that were sold to other dealers for the more common wholesale cost of $17. Despite the descriptions of each guitar found in these early records, it's important to remember that they are little more than summaries intended for internal use. Martin had a number of old accounts by this time that he had been supplying with guitars for a dozen years or more, so he was probably intimately familiar with their preferences, and in some cases certain dealers may have made specific requests that resulted in a less expensive instrument, or certain dealers may have facilitated

payments to Martin that resulted in special terms. In the late 1840s, Martin was selling a few small guitars to John Coupa for as little as $14, but we don't know if those instruments were made with rosewood or mahogany.

22. Gura, 2003, 156–158

23. There was a size 0 model sold in 1854 with a wholesale cost of $24, but the description suggests that it had more plain appointments than size 2½ models with the same price.

24. The term "5-9-5" in reference to rosettes is simply a count of the concentric light and dark lines in the three-ring pattern. Its innermost and outer rings both have five lines, black-white-black-white-black, while the wider center ring has a pattern consisting of nine alternating dark and light lines. This is the rosette pattern that has been continued on Martin Style 28 guitars, and many other models, to the present day.

25. In surviving records from after 1850, the first listing of a Martin guitar with "pearl ornament," meaning pearl around the top edge instead of marquetry, is in late 1853. It's difficult to track these early pearl-bordered models because they were often ordered with other deluxe appointments, such as a cedar case, which also increased the price. Aside from Crystal Palace and Presentation models, it appears that about a half-dozen pearl-bordered models were sold before 1859, all of them size 2 or 2½. After those late 1858 "pearl round the hoop" descriptions, we are dependent on the size/price shorthand in Martin's daybooks, and another half-dozen entries of Style 40 models appear until the records go missing in mid-1864. One of the last pages in the 1864 daybook includes the May 28 sale of an 0-40 to Zoebisch and Sons, the first record of a large pearl-bordered Martin guitar. The first listing of Style 42 is a 2-42 sold on November 2, 1858, to Peters & Sons in Cincinnati. Sales of both Style 40 and 42 were slow until the 1890s, when the highly decorated mandolins of that era increased demand for more ornate guitars

26. A total of 86 size 0 models were sold by mid-1864, when Martin's records regarding which models were sold again go on holiday. Although a majority of the 0 size models sold before 1863 had a wholesale cost of $27, the descriptions of those models, before use of the size/price code eliminated such details, suggest that most $27 size 0 models lacked the pearl rosette and ivory fingerboard binding found on the smaller size 2 and 2½ models sold for $27 during the same period.

27. Since there are extended periods with no surviving records, there were possibly other orders for 00 size models. One 00 with the pre-1867 stamp, but in very poor condition, has surfaced in Northern California,

and although it has standard Style 28 appointments its construction is unique among early Martins examined to date. It has a deeper body, over 25-inch string scale, double X top bracing (the second X is between the bridge plate and the end block), and a wider tie-block bridge with the saddle in the middle, above the tie-block. A paper label inside this guitar indicates it was in San Francisco before the 1870s. It was possibly ordered by Edward Pique, a teacher who had been a Martin dealer in the early 1850s in Philadelphia but who was ordering Martin guitars from San Francisco by 1858. Earlier correspondence with Pique indicates he provided Martin with detailed instructions for some of the guitars he ordered. See also Gura, 2003, 82.

28. Books on cabinetry written before 1900 mention the difficulty of obtaining large logs of Brazilian rosewood. Larger Martin models like the size 0 could only be made with wider rosewood boards, and the logs large enough to yield lumber of that size may have been sold at a premium even at this early date. Inflation in the cost of materials would certainly have increased Martin's cost for larger deluxe guitars more than for smaller examples, as they would require more ivory binding as well as more rosewood.

CHAPTER 11. EARLY MARTIN GUITAR DESIGN AND CONSTRUCTION: WHAT SURVIVED

1. Philip F. Gura, *C. F. Martin and His Guitars, 1796–1873* (Chapel Hill: University of North Carolina Press, 2003), 185.

2. For further information about this stylistic transition, see chapters 4 and 5.

3. As discussed in Chapter 10, and in David LaPlante's Chapter 5, this retreat from the more exact Spanish style was probably due to the differences between the production methods and sequence of guitar assembly that Martin was accustomed to, rather than a rejection of Spanish guitar design.

4. Gura, 2003, 134–149.

5. Over a century after the last recorded sale of Martin guitars with the "Stauffer head" and "one-side screw" tuners, boxes of unused tuners identical to the ones found on guitars from the pre–Civil War era were discovered in the attic of Martin's old North Street factory. This suggests that it was a lack of demand that ended their use, not a lack of supply.

6. Jim Washburn and Richard Johnston, *Martin Guitars: An Illustrated Celebration of America's Premier Guitar Maker* (Emmaus, Pennsylvania: Rodale Press, 1997*)*, 152-3.

7. Gura, 2003, 158.

8. C. F. Martin & Co. Archives.

9. Walter Carter, *Gibson, 100 Years of an American Icon* (Los Angeles: General Publishing Group, 1996) 22–25 and 52–55.

10. This was probably inspired by Lyon & Healy's Washburn guitar catalogs, in which, as early as 1889, each style of guitar was offered in three sizes. See Hubert Pleijsier, *Washburn Prewar Instrument Styles* (New York: Hal Leonard Corporation. 2007) 58–62.

11. The rise of "private brands" was, of course, all about gaining a competitive edge. Large music stores, especially those with more than one branch, were under increasing competition from the rising number of small music stores that were served by wholesale music houses, or "jobbers," who gave small retailers access to major brands. Once large stores, or a chain, no longer had a monopoly, they began to develop brands their competitors would not be able to stock. Southern California Music, a chain of five stores in Southern California, and the Oliver Ditson Co. of Boston and its New York branch, were the first to get Martin to build unique instruments that only they could sell. The earliest production runs of these instruments, usually guitars and ukuleles, had no markings indicating where they were made. ★

GLOSSARY

This glossary is highly selective, consisting of terms specifically relevant to the period covered in the book.

back strip. Decorative marquetry or wood purfling inserted or inlaid into the joint between the pieces of a guitar's back.

binding. A strip of wood, ivory, or baleen fitted into the outer edge of a guitar's body where the sides meet the top or back.

book-matched. A single piece of wood cut and laid open like a book, so that the grain of the two sides forms a mirror image.

dentellones. Spanish term meaning "teeth" and referring to small individual glue blocks used to form the lining between top and sides or back and sides (see linings below).

dovetail joint. Joint used to fit the neck into the body and consisting of male and female elements that are both double tapered.

ebonized. Made to look like ebony through the use of shellac and the addition of black pigment. Most often applied to the wood on a guitar's neck.

fan bracing. Struts arranged in a radial pattern to support the top of the guitar.

flitch. A longitudinal section of a log. Sheets or veneers used on a range of guitars but made from the same flitch will have notably similar grain patterns.

friction peg. Tuning mechanism, similar to a violin peg, consisting of a round tapered shaft with a button on the outside end.

flower. C. F. Martin's term for a small decorative element, usually made of ivory and pearl, located below or on either end of the bridge.

German silver. A silver-white alloy developed by early nineteenth-century German metalworkers and used to make frets for guitars and other instruments. Also known as nickel silver, the alloy is typically composed of 60% copper, 20% nickel, and 20% zinc. Many of the guitars C. F. Martin built between 1840 and 1850 also had nuts made of German silver.

harmonic bars. Horizontal braces fitted above and below the soundhole to support the top.

headstock. Portion of the neck above the fretboard on which the tuning devices (pegs or machines) are mounted. Also called peghead.

horqueta. Spanish for "tuning fork–shaped" and describing a long, side-reinforcing bracket, which originally came into use because the sides of early guitars were often made up of two or more pieces. The ends of top and back braces were fitted into the broad, notched ends of the horqueta. Thus, the braces and their horqueta essentially formed an internal frame for the body of the guitar.

key joint. Dovetail joint in which a central piece is fitted between the two elements of the neck and heel in separate heel construction.

linings. Additional wood glued to the edge of the sides to increase the gluing surface between the sides and top or back. These can be individual glue blocks, continuous solid bent strips, or solid strips that are "kerfed" with regularly spaced cuts leaving a thin flexible web of wood allowing it to be formed to the side.

machine tuners. Geared mechanical tuners consisting of either a pair of three tuners mounted on a metal plate on either side of a slotted headstock or a single set of six tuners lined up on the straight side of a scroll headstock.

marquetry. Inlayed decorative wood strip made up of multiple laminations of contrasting colors and patterns.

modified bridle joint. Complex joint with a raised "dart" used on nineteenth-century Martin guitars.

neck block. Wooden block cut with the female portion of the dovetail joint into which the neck is fitted.

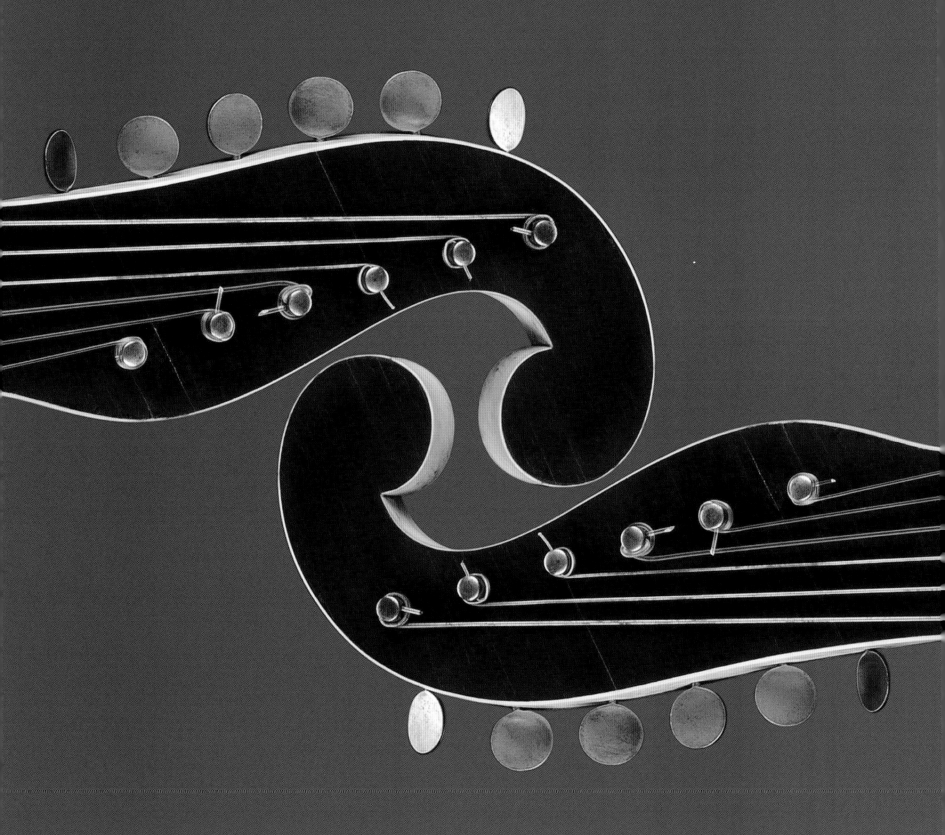

plantilla. Spanish, meaning "footprint" and referring to the overall size and shape of the profile of a guitar's top.

purfling. Decorative wood or ivory strips between the binding and top or back (see marquetry above).

pyramid bridge. Style of rectangular bridge, either tied or with pins, with a raised pyramid-shaped decorative form at each end.

rear block. Analogous to the neck block, the rear block is located at the lower or butt end of the guitar and holds the two side pieces together

Renaissance style. Contemporary term describing a guitar body style in which the front and back profiles of the upper bout meet the neck in a reverse curve similar to bowed instruments in the viol family. No evidence has surfaced to date indicating what term, if any, Martin and his contemporaries used to describe this body shape.

rim. Preliminary assembly consisting of the two sides joined with the neck block and rear block before being attached to the top or back.

rosette. The decorative rings or banding surrounding the sound hole.

scarf joint. Spanish mode of joining the headstock to the neck consisting of planing an angled surface at the upper end of the neck and lower end of the headstock to create a large glue surface for attaching the two components together.

screws. Early term for machine tuners consisting of either a pair of two-side screws used on slotted headstocks or a single in-line set used on scroll headstocks.

scroll headstock. Headstock with front profile similar to the side profile of a violin peghead. Popularly called a "Stauffer headstock," it has six-on-a-side mechanical tuning machines on one side, a reverse ogee curve on the other side, and a scroll volute at the top end.

separate heel. Lower portion of the neck consisting of a rounded cone-shaped piece joined with a key joint to the neck shaft. Popularly referred to as an "ice cream cone" heel by modern collectors and builders.

Spanish foot. Extension of the neck block that forms additional gluing surface between the neck and back of the guitar.

Spanish heel. A curved extension of the neck shaft that joins the neck to the upper portion of the body of the guitar. In contrast to separate heel construction, a Spanish heel is an integral extension of the neck shaft. Spanish heels are found on virtually all modern guitars.

strut. An individual brace used to support the top.

terz guitar. A small-bodied guitar with a shorter scale that is tuned three half tones higher than standard guitar pitch.

tie bridge. A bridge on which the strings are attached by being tied around a raised wood block. Typically found on Spanish guitars.

transverse bar. Top brace fastened across the top in an approximately perpendicular direction to the longitudinal axis of the guitar. Transverse bars, or lateral bracing, were the method of supporting the top of Martin's earliest Austro-German style guitars and were replaced by fan bracing or X bracing.

two-side-screw. Three-on-a-plate mechanical tuning devices mounted on either side of a slotted headstock.

veneered back. Guitar back consisting of two thin layers of wood glued together to make up the thickness of the back.

Vienna style. Referring to the Austro-German guitar style of Martin's earliest guitars. Also popularly known as "Stauffer style" after Johann Georg Stauffer who developed, patented, and popularized the stylistic elements.

Vienna tuners. Six-on-a-side mechanical tuning machines and decorative cover plate fitted to the Vienna scroll style headstock.

v-joint. Referring generally to a headstock joint that forms a visible "V" shape (includes modified bridle joint).

volute. Raised portion ("dart") where the neck meets the peghead and forms a thumb stop at the peghead end of the neck shaft.

X brace. The two largest top struts, which are located on both sides of the soundhole and cross just below the soundhole, forming a strong, x-shaped main support of the top.

BIBLIOGRAPHY

For further information about the history of Martin guitars and C. F. Martin & Co. see:

Gura, Philip F. *C. F. Martin and His Guitars, 1796–1873.* Chapel Hill, North Carolina: The University of North Carolina Press, 2003.

Johnston, Richard, Dick Boak, and Mike Longworth. *Martin Guitars: A History Revised and Updated.* New York: Hal Leonard Books, 2008.

Johnston, Richard, Dick Boak, and Mike Longworth. Martin Guitars: *A Technical Reference Revised and Updated.* New York: Hal Leonard Books, 2009.

Washburn, Jim and Richard Johnston. *Martin Guitars: An Illustrated Celebration of America's Premier Guitar Maker.* Emmaus, Pennsylvania: Rodale Press, 1997.

Despite recent advances in scholarship, the best English language surveys of the entire history of guitars and of the history of American acoustic guitars remain:

Evans, Tom and Mary. *Guitars: Music, History, Construction and Players from the Renaissance to Rock.* New York and London: Paddington Press Ltd., 1977.

Gruhn, George and Walter Carter. *Acoustic Guitars and Other Fretted Instruments.* San Francisco: GPI Books, 1993.

The best broad survey on the history of American musical instruments is:

Libin, Laurence. *American Musical Instruments in the Metropolitan Museum of Art.* New York: W. W. Norton, 1985.

Stauffer and nineteenth-century Viennese guitars are exhaustively covered in the recently published and exemplary book:

Hofmann, Erik Pierre, Pascal Mougin, and Stefan Hackl. Stauffer & Co.: *The Viennese Guitar of the 19th Century.* Germolles-sur-Grosne, France: Editions des Robins, 2011.

Unfortunately there is no comparable history to date of the early guitar trade in Markneukirchen, Germany.

One of the few books in English to authoritatively review the early history of Spanish guitars is:

The Spanish Guitar: La Guitarra Espanola. New York: The Metropolitan Museum of Art and Madrid, Spain: Museo Municipal, 1991.

CONTRIBUTORS

DAVID GANSZ

David Gansz lives in Yellow Springs, Ohio, with his wife and two children, and works as Vice President of Information Technology at Edison State Community College. The son of a music professor, he has played guitar since childhood. Educated at Westtown School, Oxford and Canterbury Universities, Bard College, and the University of Michigan, he holds degrees in Theology, Art History, Writing, and Library & Information Science. An accomplished poet, his literary archives and books reside at the University of California, San Diego. He has authored and edited publications regarding education, and his biographical overview of James Ashborn appears in the *Grove Dictionary of American Music, 2nd Edition* (Oxford University Press). His areas of scholarly research include the history of the guitar in Granada, Spain; the guitar in Hawaii and its impact on the development of the steel-string guitar in twentieth century America; and the Schoenberg/Bourgeois/Martin collaboration of the 1980s.

RICHARD JOHNSTON

Richard Johnston co-founded Gryphon Stringed Instruments in Palo Alto, California, in 1969 with Frank Ford. A former guitar maker and repairman, he has been a contributing editor of *Acoustic Guitar* magazine since its inception in 1991, and has written many articles on vintage guitars and the guitar industry for that publication and for *The Fretboard Journal*. He joined *Antiques Roadshow* as a fretted instrument appraiser in 2007.

In 2008, Richard completed an updated two-volume rewrite, with Martin's Dick Boak, of Mike Longworth's *Martin Guitars: A History*. He also wrote *Martin Guitars, An Illustrated Celebration* with co-author Jim Washburn (1997) and has contributed chapters to a number of other books on guitars, including *Acoustic Guitars: The Illustrated Encyclopedia; Vintage Guitars: The Instruments, The Players, The Music; Acoustic Guitar: The Composition, Construction, and Evolution of One of World's Most Beloved Instruments;* and *Custom Guitars: A Guide to Contemporary Handcrafted Guitars.*

DAVID LAPLANTE

David LaPlante built his first guitar in 1966 at the age of sixteen and is a lifelong guitar player, singer, and performer. David spent thirty-four years creating exhibits at the New York State Museum in Albany New York, retiring in 2008, and has devoted four decades to the study of the early Martin guitar and the Spanish guitar. He has built over 100 guitars and has restored many others of significance (some included in this volume). His clients have included many amateur and professional musicians, including Noel Paul Stookey, the "Paul" of Peter, Paul and Mary. David has now concentrated his efforts on the building of the Spanish classical guitar. In 2007, he traveled to Siguenza, Spain, to study with the world-renowned guitar maker Jose Romanillos. David combines a traditional approach and a broad knowledge of guitar history and aesthetics to produce one-of-a-kind signature instruments.

ROBERT SHAW

Robert Shaw, who copyedited this book and assisted co-editor Peter Szego with its content and design, is an independent curator, scholar, and editor who has written more than a dozen books on guitars, quilts, bird decoys, and other handmade objects. His most recent book, *Electrified: The Art of the Contemporary Guitar,* was published in 2011.

Bob was curator at the Shelburne (VT) Museum from 1981–1994, where he worked with that institution's world-renowned collections of American folk art. He has curated exhibitions at such major American museums as the National Gallery of Art, the University of Michigan Art Museum, and the Dallas Museum of Natural History; lectured at dozens of institutions; contributed to numerous books and exhibition catalogs; written articles for *The Magazine Antiques* and many other periodicals; and served as a consultant to publishers, museums, private collectors, and Sotheby's.

PETER SZEGO

Peter Szego is a scholar and collector of pre–Civil War banjos and guitars and related art and ephemera. He is also an old-time musician who plays guitar, banjo, and fiddle, and an occasional tap dancer. Professionally, Peter practiced architecture and was founding partner of several firms that provided marketing communications, consulting, and research services to building products manufacturers.

Peter and *Antiques Roadshow* appraiser Fred Oster of Vintage Instruments in Philadelphia co-chaired the Early Martin Guitar Conferences that led to the creation of this book, and he has headed the team of scholars who contributed essays for the project. Peter also conceived the book's content and design, with input from co-editor Robert Shaw, and graphic designer Steve J. Hill. Previously, Peter co-curated the catalogued exhibition "Birth of the Banjo" at the Katonah Museum of Art with Robert Shaw and George Wunderlich, and he co-chairs the annual Nineteenth Century Banjo Gathering with scholar, author, and collector Jim Bollman.

ARIAN SHEETS

Arian Sheets has been Curator of Stringed Instruments at the National Music Museum, University of South Dakota, since 2001. She has an academic background in music performance and art history as well as experience in musical instrument conservation. Her research interests are diverse and include mass production in the music industry, American guitars, early electric instruments, experimentation in instrument design, and the historical development of the violin.

JAMES WESTBROOK

James Westbrook is a British-based organologist whose particular interest is in guitar construction. He is the author of two popular books: *Guitars through the Ages* (2002) and *The Century that Shaped the Guitar* (2006) and co-author of *The Complete Illustrated Book of the Acoustic Guitar* (2012). He has given papers for The Classical Guitar Festival of Great Britain, European Guitar Teachers Association, The American Musical Instrument Society, San Francisco Conservatory of Music, and Guild of American Luthiers.

In 2013, James was awarded a PhD from the University of Cambridge for his research into guitar making in nineteenth-century London. He has given numerous interviews to guitar magazines, newspapers, radio, and television, and has been program consultant to the BBC. James is also a part-time luthier and restorer whose greatest claim to fame is that he once sold a guitar to C. F. Martin & Co.—albeit an original terz guitar by Stauffer for their museum.

INDEX

moustache bridge, *37*
  of Stauffer, Johann Georg, *4*
Mozart, Wolfgang Amadeus, 2
multi-colored marquetry, *212*, 221
musical instructors, 68, 230, 234
  Coupa as, 88, 90, 103–4
musical instruments. *See also specific*
    instruments
  catalogs, *25*
  distributors of, 18–19
  market changes, 24–27
musicians. *See specific musicians*
Musikinstrumenten-Museum Markneukirchen,
    289
Muslims, 60

N
Naples, 2, 4
Napoleon, XVI
Nashville, TN, 108
National Music Museum, XIV, 289
Naugatuck Railroad, *146*
  Ashborn's production and, 147–48
Naugatuck River, *146*
  industrialization along, 138–40
Nazareth, PA, *34*, 42, 44, 90, 155, 236
  Martin, Christian Frederick, Jr., in, 173–74,
    229, 230
  Martin, Christian Friedrich, in, 45
  Schatz in, 55
Neuhauser, Leopold, 2
Neukirchen, *19*
New Jersey, 233
New Orleans, LA, 108, 135, 230
New York, NY, 230
  Benedid, Francisco, in, *70*
  Coupa, John, in, *70*
  de Goni in, *70*, *132*
  Figaro Spanish Students in, 231
  Great Fire, XI
  immigrants in, IX, XI
  libraries in, 60
  Martin, Christian Frederick, Jr. in, 168, 199
  Martin, Christian Friedrich, in, 28, 88, 170,
    174, 234

population of, 257*n*1
  Spanish guitars used in, 102–3
New York Herald, 88
New York Philharmonic, IX
New York Tribune, 135
Niblo's Garden, 30, *68*, 69, 261*n*5
nickel silver
  nuts, *117*, 223, *224*
  tuners, *217*
North, Simeon, 138
North Main Street, *173*
Nuremberg, 2
nylon strings, 72–73

O
Oakes, David R., 289
OM models, 237
organ, 145, *146*
Origin of Species (Darwin), XVII
Oster, Fred, XIII, 289
Otis, Allyne, 132
Outre-Mer: A Pilgrimage Beyond the Sea
    (Longfellow), 64

P
Paganini, Niccolo, 2, 5, 134
Pagés, Francisco, 69
Pagés, Josef, 10, 66, 80
Pagés, Juan, XVI, 77, 80
Panic of 1837, XVII, *42*, 43, 44, *53*, 108
Panormo, Angiolina, *66*
Panormo, Joseph, XVI, 66
Panormo, Louis, 10, 71, 74, 77, 149
Panormo guitar, 71
Pan-Pacific Exposition, 72
Parson, H., 203
patents
  of Ashborn, *158*
  of Ertl, 5, *15*
  heads, 227, 230
  Legnani model, 5
  of Stauffer, Johann Georg, 5
Patio Leones, *63*
Paul, Les, 227
"Paul Revere's Ride" (Longfellow), 64

Paulus, August, 21
Paulus, Eva Regina, 248*n*2
Paulus family, 19
peaked headstock, *196*
pearl, 10, *103*, *118*, 196, 199, *216*, *220*, 227,
    263*n*8, 264*n*25
  bordering, 203, *208*, 221
  flowers, *192*
  handles, *217*
  rosettes, *202*, 225
  round the hoop, *220*
peddlers, 140
Peden, John, 289
pegheads, *82*, 97, 230
pegs
  Ashborn patented, *158*
  friction tuning, *153*, *180*, *188*, *214*
  ivory, 196
  Martin, Christian Friedrich, designs, 73
  side mounted, 24
Pennsylvania, 88–108, 173
Perfumo, Enrique, 76
Perfumo, Juan, 76
Peter, Paul & Mary, 133
Peters, W. C., *170*
Peters, Webb & Company, 172
Petersburg, VA, 230
Peters & Son, *104*, 195
Pfretzschner, Elias, 19
Philadelphia, PA, 30, 32, 35, 45, 104
  de Goni in, 132
  libraries in, 60
  Scherr in, 35
Phillip, John, *75*, *83*
piano, 132
  factory-made, *24*
  makers of, 20
  women playing, 249*n*29
piano-forte, 30, 62, 141, 250*n*29
pickguard, *234*
pin bridges, 128
  scooped back edge, 227
  two-piece, *159*
Pique, Edward, 265*n*27
pitch pipes, *6*

ILLUSTRATION CREDITS

Unless otherwise credited below, all photographs of guitars were taken by John Sterling Ruth, and the images are copyright by C. F. Martin & Co., Inc.

We gratefully acknowledge the following collectors and museums for permitting us to include their guitars:

Chris Andrada: Profile 15; figures 6-4, 6-5
Tony Creamer: Profile 18; figures 6-5
Gryphon Stringed Instruments: Profile 38
David LaPlante: Profiles 13, 21; figures 5-1, 5-3, 5-4, 5-5, 5-7, 5-8, 5-11 (left), 6-6
C. F. Martin Guitar Museum, Nazareth, PA: Profiles 5, 8, 19, 26, 40; figures 3-2, 3-11, 3-15, 6-5, 9-12, 10-13, 10-15, 10-17, 10-18, 10-19, 10-20, 10-22
Metropolitan Museum of Art, New York: Profiles 3, 10. Photographs in these two profiles were provided by the Museum, which owns copyright to the images.
Fred Oster: Profiles 16, 23, 25, 44; figures 5-3, 5-7, 6-1, 6-5, 6-7, 9-9, 11-6
John Peden: Profile 34; figures 5-10, 5-11 (right), 11-9
Peter Szego: Profiles 4, 6, 14, 28, 30; figures 3-3, 3-4, 5-1, 5-9, 5-11 (center), 6-11, 6-12, 8-16, 8-25, 8-26, 8-28, 8-30, 11-1, 11-4
Matt Umanov: Profiles 41, 42; figures 10-1
The guitars in Profiles 1, 2, 7, 9, 11, 12, 17, 20, 22, 24, 27, 29, 30, 31, 32, 33, 35, 36, 37, 39, 43, and 45 are in private collections.

All uncredited photos of guitars shown in figures are also courtesy of private collectors, who wish to remain anonymous.

The following illustrations were provided by the listed sources, who own copyright to the images. All uncredited illustrations of archival material are in the public domain.

Christie's, Inc., Musical Instrument Department, New York: 11-29
Giovanni Accornero Collection, courtesy of Edizioni Il Salabue, Turin: 1-2, 1-3
Gruhn Guitars: 10-12
Gryphon Stringed Instruments, photograph by Frank Ford: 11-10 both. Photograph by Grant Groberg: 5-6 bottom, 10-7, 10-9, 10-10, 10-11, 10-16, 11-5, 11-15, 11-19, 11-20, 11-30, 11-31
Erik Pierre Hofmann: 1-11
Kunsthistorisches Museum, Vienna, Austria: 1-12
Bernard & S. Dean Levy, Inc., New York: 3-1
C. F. Martin & Co., Inc.: 2-1, 2-3, 6-9, 6-10, 9-1, 9-2, 9-3, 9-6. 9-7, 9-10, 9-11, 9-13, 9-14, 10-8, 10-23, 10-24, 10-25, 10-26, 10-27, 11-11, 11-12, 11-13, 11-21, 11-23, 11-25, 11-26, 11-27, 11-28
Malcolm Maxwell: 1-5, 1-6, 1-8
Musikinstrumenten-Museum Markneukirchen: 2-5 (left), 2-9
Milwaukee Mandolin Orchestra: 11-24
The National Music Museum, The University of South Dakota, photo by Jonathan Santa Maria Bouquet: 1-10, 2-4 (center), 2-5 (right), 2-8, 2-10, 2-11. Photo by Bill Willroth Sr.: 2-4 (left and right)
David R. Oakes: 8-7, 8-17
University of South Dakota Archives and Special Collections, Mahoney Collection: 2-6
Stan Werbin: 11-22
James Westbrook: 1-1, 1-4, 1-9, 5-7
Wien Museum Karlsplatz, Vienna, Austria: 1-13

Left: This carte-de-visite of the "comic Bell and Mr. Heywood" (as this dapper duo is identified in a pencil inscription below the image) probably dates to around the time of C. F. Martin's death in 1873. The Martin guitar held by the seated Mr. Heywood is, however, significantly earlier. It does not conform to the list of appointments found on any standard models described in the first Martin price list of 1868, making it the earliest Martin guitar known in a period photograph. Although the "comic Bell" is almost certainly Digby Valentine Bell (1849–1917), who went on to gain fame as a comic actor in Gilbert & Sullivan operas, vaudeville, and on Broadway, we do not know what happened to Mr. Heywood or his Martin. Digby Bell stood only 5'5" inches tall, which gives a sense of the scale of his partner's guitar.